DUMBARTON OAKS
MEDIEVAL LIBRARY

Jan M. Ziolkowski, General Editor

OLD ENGLISH LEGAL WRITINGS

WULFSTAN

DOML 66

Old English Legal Writings

WULFSTAN

Edited and Translated by

ANDREW RABIN

DUMBARTON OAKS
MEDIEVAL LIBRARY

HARVARD UNIVERSITY PRESS
CAMBRIDGE, MASSACHUSETTS
LONDON, ENGLAND
2020

First Printing

Library of Congress Cataloging-in-Publication Data
Names: Wulfstan, Archbishop of York, –1023, author. | Wulfstan,
    Archbishop of York, –1023. Works. Selections (2020) | Wulfstan,
    Archbishop of York, –1023. Works. Selections (2020). English. | Rabin,
    Andrew, editor, translator.
Title: Old English legal writings / Wulfstan ; edited and translated by
    Andrew Rabin.
Other titles: Dumbarton Oaks medieval library ; 66.
Description: Cambridge, Massachusetts : Harvard University Press, 2020. |
    Series: Dumbarton Oaks medieval library; DOML 66 | Includes
    bibliographical references and index. | Texts in the original Old English
    with English translations on facing pages; introduction and notes in
    English.
Identifiers: LCCN 2020008166 | ISBN 9780674247482 (cloth)
Subjects: LCSH: Wulfstan, Archbishop of York, –1023—Political and
    social views. | Catholic Church—Great Britain—Government—Early
    works to 1800. | Church and state—Great Britain—Early works to
    1800. | Great Britain—Politics and government—To 1485—Early works
    to 1800.
Classification: LCC PR1796 .R329 2020 | DDC 274.2/03—dc23
LC record available at https://lccn.loc.gov/2020008166

Contents

CONTENTS

ROYAL LEGISLATION

CONTENTS

.

vii

Introduction

It is one of history's ironies that someone of such promi-
nence to his contemporaries as Archbishop Wulfstan of York
(d. 1023) should be so little known today. During his lifetime
Wulfstan served in three of England's most powerful ecclesiastical offices (bishop of London, bishop of Worcester,
and archbishop of York), authored a series of homilies now
considered landmarks of early English prose, drafted legislation on behalf of Kings Æthelred and Cnut, and composed
tracts on civil and Church governance that outlined an ex-
pansive vision of an ideal Christian kingdom. Yet despite
the profound influence he exercised on the political and religious life of early eleventh-century England, much of his
own life is shrouded in mystery. Little is known of his career
beyond its most general contours, and even the boundar-
ies of his corpus remain subject to dispute. Indeed, it has
been only within the last ninety years that most of Wulfstan's nonhomiletic works have come to be recognized as
his. As a result, many of the texts in this volume are edited
here for the first time in English and likewise for the first
time within the context of Wulfstan's thought and career. In
bringing together editions of his most significant works on
law, politics, and ecclesiastical governance, this anthology is
thus intended to shed light on the range of Wulfstan's legal

writings while also demonstrating the vibrancy of English political thought in the decades before the Norman Conquest.

WULFSTAN'S LIFE AND CAREER

No reliable evidence for Wulfstan's life survives prior to the *Anglo-Saxon Chronicle* entry for 996 that records his appointment as bishop of London. The age at which Wulfstan's contemporaries were elevated to their first bishoprics varied widely, but a 996 appointment indicates that he was most likely born sometime between 946 and 966, with a date closer to the latter being the more plausible. His later association with Worcester, patronage of Peterborough, and burial at Ely have led to suggestions that his family originated in either the west midlands or southeastern Danelaw, though this is little more than speculation. Similarly subject to guesswork are the nature of Wulfstan's education and the circumstances surrounding his entry into the Church. He almost certainly spent his early years attached to a monastery, though, as his later advocacy for monastic regularity and his opposition to lay involvement in Church governance make a secular background unlikely.

Wulfstan's career begins to come into focus with his elevation to the bishopric of London, in which he served from 996 to 1002. The see of London at the turn of the millennium occupied a distinctive place in the English Church: London's proximity to the court and the thriving mercantile economy meant that those elected to the see were chosen as much to preserve the diocese's sometimes delicate relationship with the king and ensure the continued support of

London's financial sector as for their religious attainments. The uniquely political nature of this position brought Wulfstan his first formal role at court, where he associated himself with a faction of reformist ecclesiastics led by Archbishop Ælfric of Canterbury (d. 1005). Ælfric appears to have viewed Wulfstan as a friend and ally, eventually naming him both the executor of his will and one of its leading beneficiaries. Perhaps the most revealing indication of Wulfstan's reformist activities, however, is the occurrence of his name alongside that of Ælfric and other reformers, such as Bishop Wulfsige of Sherborne (d. 1002), on the witness lists of the six so-called "penitential charters" issued after 996 by Æthelred to atone for his youthful misdeeds. Wulfstan's close affiliation with the reformist party shaped his approach to his other episcopal duties as well. In homilies composed during this period, he urged clerics of his diocese to observe orthodox religious practices strictly while also emphasizing the moral obligations of the episcopacy and the close relationship between civil and ecclesiastical law— all themes that would recur frequently in his later writings.

In 1002, Wulfstan left London to become bishop of Worcester and archbishop of York. Although joint appointments of this sort were often frowned upon, it was not uncommon for the limited resources of the York archdiocese to be supplemented by simultaneous election to a wealthier see. Moreover, from a political standpoint, questions regarding the Danelaw's loyalty meant that the king preferred those with northern appointments to have ties to the south as well. It was during these first years at York and Worcester that the earliest of Wulfstan's surviving tracts on civil and ecclesiastical governance were composed, perhaps in response to the administrative needs of his new positions. The move north did not diminish Wulfstan's growing influence at court: by the Council of Enham in 1008 he had become chiefly responsible for drafting the legislation issued in Æthelred's name. It was during this period also that Wulfstan refined his distinctive homiletic style, culminating with the earliest versions of his most famous homily, the *Sermo Lupi ad Anglos,* likely composed in approximately 1009.

Wulfstan maintained his position at court following the 1016 collapse of Æthelred's government and the accession of the conqueror Cnut. Under the new administration, he continued to serve as one of the king's chief counselors and as the primary author of royal legislation. He reached his greatest influence in the years between 1018 and 1023, which witnessed the composition of his most ambitious works, the law codes *1* and *2 Cnut* and the final version of *The Institutes of Polity,* the most comprehensive statement of his political philosophy. Wulfstan also remained active in ecclesiastical matters following the conquest. Although he retired from the bishopric of Worcester in 1016, he retained vicarious authority over the see through his successor, Leofsige, who likely acted primarily as a suffragan. At York, Wulfstan worked to consolidate the archdiocese's landholdings and recover alienated property. The preservation of several of his homilies in the York Gospels likewise points to his continued involvement in the see's spiritual affairs. Wulfstan died at York on May 28, 1023, following which he was buried at Ely in accordance with his wishes. His remains were reinterred several times before reaching their current resting place, the chantry chapel of Bishop Nicholas West, in 1771.

Political Tracts

Over the course of his career, Wulfstan composed a variety
of tracts on such topics as the proper exercise of royal authority, the inviolability of ecclesiastical sanctuary, and the
structure of the ideal society. Although the extent to which
these tracts reflected actual practice remains unclear, they
nonetheless provided Wulfstan with the opportunity to promote his views on how best to govern a Christian kingdom.
It is in these texts that we see Wulfstan honing his distinctive "homiletic style," combining the moral admonitions and
rhetorical flourishes of a sermon with the legalistic vocabulary and causal syntax of a law code. Wulfstan draws these
two seemingly incompatible genres together through the use
of a vigorous prose idiom that borrows the rhythm, allitera-
tion, and occasionally even something resembling the me-
ter of Old English poetry. This mingling of genres is the result of neither accident nor carelessness on Wulfstan's part:
rather, it reflects the archbishop's view of his ecclesiastical
and legislative roles as two halves of a single enterprise. For
Wulfstan, the minister and the lawgiver share the same obligation to safeguard the political stability and the moral integrity of the community.

Wulfstan's political tracts pose a number of problems
for the modern reader. Their intended audience is often unknown, as is the extent of their circulation. His habit of
revising his texts repeatedly, frequently over a number of
years, means that many of his works survive in multiple versions and, indeed, may never have been understood to be
"finished," at least not in a modern sense. Even more thorny
is the question of the texts' reliability. Wulfstan took a deep

interest in English legal history, yet he did so as a propagandist seeking historical precedent for current policy. And in the absence of such precedent, he appears to have felt little compunction about creating it. As a result, his tendency to manufacture documents (such as *The Laws of Edward and Guthrum*) or claim precedent where none may exist (as in *On the Ranks of People and Law* in *The Compilation on Status*) can blur the line between historical fact and fiction. Yet for all of their difficulties, the political tracts offer a vivid illustration of the way in which Wulfstan developed his views of social order and Christian governance.

Of Wulfstan's surviving political tracts, arguably the earliest is *The Laws of Edward and Guthrum,* which likely dates to between 1002 and 1004, just after his appointment to the archbishopric of York, though a later date has recently been suggested. The text professes to be a treaty between Edward the Elder (ca. 874–924) and the Viking king Guthrum (d. ca. 890) in terms similar to those of the treaty Guthrum sealed with Edward's father, Alfred. Although it is manifestly a forgery, Wulfstan almost certainly did not intend this—or any of his other "forgeries," such as *The Canons of Edgar*—to be taken at face value. Beyond the mention of Alfred, Edward, and Guthrum in the opening clauses, there is little in the text that reflects the concerns of early Viking Age England. Rather, the pseudo-historical preface provides Wulfstan with an authoritative precedent for a series of clauses on such topics as the payment of Church dues and the proper observance of religious festivals that reflect the priorities of the Monastic Reform movement. It is unclear why Wulfstan chose to assign this text to Edward and Guthrum, though it has been suggested that evoking the Viking king under whom the Danelaw was founded may have been a way of appealing to the Anglo-Danish population of his new archdiocese, York.

A similar approach to legal history can be found in Wulfstan's *Compilation on Status,* the most ambitious of his early attempts to articulate a vision of an ordered Christian society. Taken together, the texts collected here describe an idealized version of England's legal past in which social hierarchies were strictly observed and the ranks of the Church were properly respected. The *Compilation* consists of a core of ninth-century texts—the first half of *On Wergild, On the Law of the Mercians,* and *On the Mercian Oath*—to which Wulfstan added an introductory text *(On the Ranks of People and Law),* the second half of *On Wergild,* and a concluding text *(On Priests' Oaths).* Perhaps the most discussed passages in the *Compilation* are the clauses in *On Ranks* setting forth the criteria for social mobility. There is considerable disagreement, however, over whether these clauses—and indeed many of the other practices Wulfstan describes as having previously been observed—describe a real state of affairs or whether they are instead yet another product of the archbishop's fertile legal imagination.

The roughly contemporary text *On Sanctuary* offers Wulfstan's most extended argument for the inviolability of ecclesiastical protection, a topic he returns to frequently in his other writings as well. Although it occurs alongside *8 Æthelred* in London, British Library, Cotton MS Nero A.i, its sole manuscript witness, internal evidence suggests that the text was likely composed in tandem with *The Compilation on Status,* perhaps between 1006 and 1008. The text consists of three parts: an initial statement of principles (clauses

1–2), an extended catalog of past and present sanctuary laws (clauses 3–19), and a homiletic conclusion (clauses 20–31). The text is striking both for the extensive research Wulfstan apparently undertook in collecting the various sanctuary practices cataloged here—among other things, *On Sanctuary* contains his most detailed discussion of the Kentish and West Saxon laws of the seventh and eighth centuries —and for the way in which it consistently emphasizes the superiority of ecclesiastical protection over secular power. Moreover, in keeping with his practice in *Edward-Guthrum* and *The Compilation on Status,* Wulfstan also presents a revised version of the legal past, in this case by introducing changes into earlier laws that elevate the standing of Church officers over that of their secular counterparts. Given that this text and the *Compilation* were likely both composed just as Wulfstan was making his first forays into the drafting of royal legislation, they provide valuable insight into his views of civil and ecclesiastical governance just at the time he was first in a position to translate those views into legal policy.

More puzzling is Wulfstan's other treatise on ecclesiastical protection, *Northumbrian Church Sanctuary.* This short text also survives only in London, British Library, Cotton MS Nero A.i, where it has been interposed immediately after *8 Æthelred* 5.2, a clause setting out penalties for the violation of sanctuary. The text's date is unknown, though its manuscript context suggests that it was likely composed at roughly the same time as *8 Æthelred,* around 1012–1014. Unfortunately, further study of the text has been significantly hindered by an ill-advised attempt by the editor Felix Liebermann to treat the manuscript with sulfuric acid, leaving large portions of the folio on which it occurs all but unreadable. The original text now survives only as a fragment, making Liebermann's transcription the only complete witness.

One of Wulfstan's most explicit discussions of the extent (and limits) of royal authority occurs in *The Oath of the King (Promissio regis)*, an Old English rendering of the promises made by the king at his coronation along with a brief discussion in the form of a homily on the obligations of a ruler to his people. Initially dated to the reign of Edgar, the text was recently shown to be the work of Wulfstan, possibly composed for use at a royal assembly toward the end of Æthelred's reign, possibly between 1014 and 1016. The vision of kingship expressed in *Oath* is one strongly influenced by the political theology of the Monastic Reform: the king is portrayed as a sacral figure invested with the duty both to rule his kingdom justly and to act in a pastoral capacity toward his people. At the same time, the text bears many of the hallmarks of Wulfstan's style, including rhythmic prose, the catalog of sinners ("ban wizards entirely, eliminate witchcraft, banish the slayers of kin") and the reuse of themes and phrases from his other writings, particularly in this case the earlier version of *The Institutes of Polity*. More than just an encapsulation of the archbishop's views on Christian kingship, however, *Oath* also provides a useful illustration of how Wulfstan chose to express his views when directly addressing Æthelred and his court.

The most substantial of Wulfstan's political tracts is *The Institutes of Polity* (the title is a modern editorial convention), a collection of short, quasi-independent chapters outlining his vision of the ideal Christian kingdom. Organized hierarchically, the chapters of *Polity* expand *The Compilation on Status*'s discussion of social rank into an elaborate account of the obligations expected of each of society's members. The text is perhaps best known for its division of the kingdom into *oratores* (those who pray), *bellatores* (those who fight), and *laboratores* (those who work), placing it among the earliest examples of medieval "estates literature." Yet Wulfstan's vision encompasses more than just a catalog of social obligations: for Wulfstan, the exterior social world and the interior moral world are inextricably linked. As he points out in *Polity*'s final chapter (pointedly using the first-person plural to include himself in the injunction), fulfilling our social obligations also requires us to "order our words and deeds rightly, fervently cleanse our inmost thoughts, truly keep our oath and pledge, and frequently reflect on the great judgment to which we all must go." In essence, Wulfstan argues that a virtuous society and a virtuous soul are interdependent: the ideal Christian kingdom can be realized only when both inner self and outer community are ordered according to God's divine plan.

Polity presents its editors with several significant problems. As with many of Wulfstan's other political tracts, little is known of the intended audience or the extent of its circulation. Moreover, given the many variations between its manuscript witnesses, it is far from clear whether the latest versions represent what Wulfstan might have considered a finished text or, indeed, an entirely unified one. Even the order and number of chapters can vary between manuscripts, meaning that *Polity* must be understood, at least in part, as a modern editorial construct. Although the loosely hierarchical ordering of the chapters suggests they were meant to be read together, none of the various manuscripts of *Polity* combines them under a single rubric or otherwise explicitly identifies them as components of a single text. It was only in 1840 that the chapters were first edited as a distinct work and given the title they now carry. Not until 1918 was Wulfstan identified as their author.

What can be said with more confidence is that Wulfstan appears to have worked on the text in two primary phases: the first between 1008 and 1010 *(1 Polity)*, perhaps in response to the increasing chaos that marked the closing years of Æthelred's reign, and then a later revision *(2 Polity)* between 1018 and 1023, reflecting the changed circumstances of Cnut's rule. Both versions of *Polity* are included in this volume. Though *Polity* raises many questions for its readers, taken as a whole it represents the most ambitious exercise in political theory to survive from pre-Conquest England.

Tracts on Ecclesiastical Governance

Central to Wulfstan's model of the ideal Christian society is a vision of the Church restored to theological orthodoxy and governed by a politically engaged, monastically trained episcopate. Unlike his contemporary Ælfric of Eynsham, who wished to see the Church remain largely separate from politics and the attendant risk of moral taint, Wulfstan viewed bishops' duties as encompassing participation in secular governance no less than ecclesiastical leadership. As he writes in *Polity,*

> Bishops are the messengers and teachers of God's law, and they must proclaim justice and forbid injustice. And anyone who disdains to listen to them may take issue about that with God himself. And if bishops fail

by not curbing sin or forbidding injustice or making known God's law, but by mumbling with their mouths when they should shout, woe to them for that silence!

Wulfstan explores this theme in more detail in a series of tracts outlining the proper management of Church affairs. Although, like his political tracts, Wulfstan's tracts on ecclesiastical governance are bedeviled by unresolved questions of readership, circulation, and textual completeness, they nonetheless provide valuable insight into his views on the political obligations of the Church as well as a glimpse of his approach to his episcopal duties.

Yet this is not the ecclesiastical tracts' only significance: as the most densely sourced of his works, these texts shed considerable light on Wulfstan's intellectual influences and writing practices. Relatively few of the prescriptions in the ecclesiastical tracts originate with Wulfstan himself. Rather, they represent an assemblage of materials taken from a range of primarily contemporary and near-contemporary sources, particularly Carolingian and post-Carolingian canonists of the ninth and tenth centuries and English writers affiliated with the Monastic Reform movement. Of the former, Wulfstan draws most frequently on the works of Hincmar of Reims, Theodulf of Orléans, Atto of Vercelli, Adso of Montier-en-Der, Ghaerbald of Liège, Abbo of Saint-Germain-des-Prés, Sedulius Scottus, Jesse of Amiens, and Amalarius of Metz. Of the latter, Wulfstan borrows from such foundational Reformist texts as the *Regularis concordia* and, perhaps most notably, the writings of his sometime correspondent Ælfric of Eynsham. The impression conveyed by the texts used by Wulfstan is of a writer less interested in problems of abstract theology than in more immediate issues of Church governance and the just exercise of authority. No less revealing is the manner in which Wulfstan incorporates such influences into his writing: unlike his contemporaries, he only very rarely identifies his sources. In part, this may reflect the fact that many of his works were likely composed as he traveled between York, Worcester, and the itinerant royal court, thus forcing the archbishop to rely on his notes or memory rather than on the kind of full monastic library enjoyed by his more sedentary contemporaries. More than this, however, the freedom with which Wulfstan both borrowed from previous writers and, just as frequently, reworked his sources for his own ends allowed him to develop a distinct authorial and authoritative voice with which to articulate his social vision. For Wulfstan, the sources upon which he drew were not objects of reverence, but rather tools for the construction of his ideal Christian society.

Among Wulfstan's earliest tracts on ecclesiastical governance is the short text *On Episcopal Duties* (also known as *Episcopus*). The sole surviving text of *Episcopal Duties* occurs in Oxford, Bodleian Library, MS Junius 121. Likely composed sometime after *Edward-Guthrum,* perhaps between 1002 and 1008, the text provides one of the clearest examples of Wulfstan's views concerning the role the Church ought to play in matters of law and politics. Wulfstan begins with the assertion that "it is proper for a bishop to offer guidance in all things, both in religious and secular matters," and then proceeds to offer an account of the bishop's role in resolving legal disputes, standardizing weights and measures, ensuring the proper treatment of slaves, and overseeing the spiritual life of his diocese. Many of the ideas, and even some of the phrasing, will recur in the law codes 5 and 6 *Æthelred,* making this an important precursor to Wulfstan's activities as a legislator. Moreover, even beyond its significance for Wulfstan's own career, *Episcopal Duties* also provides some of the earliest surviving evidence for the use of the parish as a unit of jurisdiction and for the distinction between the legal rights of urban and rural communities. Accordingly, although primarily concerned with bishops' privileges and responsibilities, *Episcopal Duties* sheds light as well on the early development of Wulfstan's political thought and, more broadly, the legal practices of eleventh-century England.

Wulfstan takes a somewhat more limited view of episcopal obligations in the Latin text *On the Remedy of Souls (De medicamento animarum).* The text survives in London, British Library, Cotton MS Nero A.i, where it is interpolated into a series of excerpts from canon law collected by Wulfstan over the course of his career. The manuscript was originally owned by Wulfstan, and *Remedy,* along with several of the other texts it contains, is corrected and annotated in the archbishop's own hand. Although its date is unknown, the similarity of certain passages of *Remedy* to sections of *1 Polity* and *On Sanctuary* suggests that it may have been composed in approximately 1008–1010. Significant portions of Wulfstan's argument in this text are based on passages found in the *Collectio canonum Hibernensis,* an eighth-century anthology of Carolingian canon law assembled by Irish monks that served as one of his most frequently used reference works. As in *On Sanctuary,* Wulfstan here emphasizes the superiority of ecclesiastical over lay authority, though he also cautions bishops against overmuch involvement in secular affairs, especially legal or political matters. Within the context of his other works, however, Wulfstan's admonition seems more directed at those bishops who engage in secular dealings to the neglect of their episcopal duties, rather than at those who use their political influence to advance the Church's moral agenda.

Proper episcopal demeanor is the focus of the text edited here as *Instructions for Bishops,* also known by its Latin rubric *Incipit de synodo.* Its date is unknown, as is that of the episcopal synod from which it supposedly originates, although 1008, 1011, 1013, and 1022 have all been suggested as possibilities. However, whether the injunctions collected here originated with Wulfstan or if he was merely the drafter, they provide a window into the professional life of an eleventh-century bishop. Less taken up with matters spiritual or legal, the text concerns itself instead with the relationship of bishops to their peers, the makeup of the episcopal household, appropriate pastimes for a bishop, and proper behavior when participating in religious ritual. If this text is somewhat less ideologically ambitious than his other writings, it nonetheless illustrates Wulfstan's firm belief that the moral integrity of a Christian community depends on the example set by its leaders.

Wulfstan summarizes his views on episcopal obligations in homiletic form in *An Admonition to Bishops.* Structured as a series of reprimands directed as much at himself as at his audience, the text highlights what Wulfstan saw as the principal threats to episcopal integrity: greed, idleness, corruption, decadence, and ambition for worldly advancement. Although previous editors have divided the *Admonition* into clauses much like a law code, the markers of orality ("Yet nonetheless it is an evil truth which I speak," "But what I say is true"), frequent use of the first-person plural, and sermonic conclusion all suggest that Wulfstan composed it, if not for use as a homily, then at least as an address to his fellow bishops. The text survives only in London, British Library, Cotton MS Nero A.i, where it follows *Instructions for Bishops,* perhaps indicating that the two texts were written for the same occasion. The title is a modern editorial convention, as the text lacks a rubric in the manuscript. *Admonition*'s date is unknown; however, the parallels with the later versions of *Polity* and *The Canons of Edgar* as well as with the homilies edited by Dorothy Bethurum as numbers 16, 17, and 20 indicate that it was probably composed later in the archbishop's career, perhaps between 1018 and 1023.

Wulfstan's most elaborate tract on ecclesiastical governance is *The Canons of Edgar,* an extended set of decrees synthesizing his views on the vocation and obligations of the priesthood. The text survives in two slightly different recensions, one slightly longer than the other. Although Wulfstan appears to have revisited *Canons* at several points throughout his career, it likely reached what modern readers take to be its final version in around 1017–1018. The text's title is taken from the rubric to the earlier version, which attributes the text to the tenth-century king of that name. Edgar was a leading patron of the Monastic Reform, and Wulfstan praises him frequently elsewhere in his writings. *Canons*'s attribution to Edgar indicates that it may initially have been intended to be another of Wulfstan's "forgeries," though the more innocuous rubric to *2 Canons*—titled merely *Synodalia decreta* (Synodal Decrees)—suggests that by this point he no longer felt the need to manufacture historical precedent as he had earlier in his career. The text draws on a wide range of sources, which share an interest in the duties and behavior of the secular clergy. This raises the possibility that Wulfstan may have composed *Canons* to serve as a handbook for diocesan priests serving a lay congregation. The fact that *Canons* later came to serve as the primary source for *The Northumbrian Priests' Law,* however, suggests that the text did at least come to play a role in the pastoral life of Wulfstan's home diocese of York.

ROYAL LEGISLATION

Wulfstan came closest to realizing his political vision in the legislation he composed on behalf of Æthelred and Cnut. The legislation he produced between 1008 and his death in 1023 represents the most wide-ranging program of legal reform since the ninth-century *domboc* (law code) of King Alfred the Great. Although many of the more specific decrees reflect the priorities of king and council, the laws' phrasing and, no less importantly, their ideological framework come from the pen of the archbishop of York. It is in these texts that Wulfstan's characteristic merging of the legal and the homiletic reaches its apex: the conditional if-then syntax common to Old English law here mingles with the admonitory rhetoric and pious exhortations of a sermon to create hybrid texts designed to remake England into Wulfstan's vision of the ideal Christian society. In effect, royal decree is never distinct from moral imperative, while the spiritual truths of the Church find their earthly manifestation in the laws of the king.

As ambitious as these texts are, however, they present

many of the same interpretive difficulties as other examples of Old English royal law. Although more vernacular legislation survives from pre-Conquest England than from any other early medieval kingdom, there is little indication that any of these laws were ever actually used to settle a legal dispute. Although they were almost certainly observed more frequently than the available evidence suggests, it is striking that no surviving charter or dispute record ever cites a piece of legislation to justify its conclusions. In some cases, the finding even appears to run counter to what the king's laws would prescribe. It seems likely, then, that many of Wulfstan's laws may have been promulgated more as statements of royal ideology than as effective instruments of governance. Indeed, it is difficult to see how many of the individual clauses in Wulfstan's legislation could be translated into real practice. Yet if the legal prescriptions in these texts can often appear more aspirational than actual, they nonetheless provided Wulfstan with a means of promoting his vision of a Christian social order to a kingdom-wide audience.

The meeting of the king's council at Enham (Hampshire) on May 16, 1008, marks Wulfstan's first known foray into the composition of royal law. Two texts resulted from this meeting, though it is far from clear that both were intended to function as fully enforceable legislation. The more likely candidate for the meeting's "official" decree is the text now referred to as 5 *Æthelred*. The pastoral content of these manuscripts reflects the largely religious orientation of the law code itself. Although 5 *Æthelred*'s decrees do touch on secular matters (the regulation of currency, the provisioning of the army and navy, certain crimes specific to individual regions, and the penalties for conspiring against the king), the

majority of the text is taken up with homiletic exhortations
and legal prescriptions concerning the application of religious principles to the civil life of the kingdom. This inter-
mingling of the secular and the spiritual both imbues royal
legislation with the authority of divine commandment and
characterizes it as a natural extension of Christian doctrine.
The drafting of royal law thus serves Wulfstan as a means of
advancing his program to restore not just political stability
but religious orthodoxy to the kingdom.

The other law code associated with the Enham meeting,
6 Æthelred, occupies a more ambiguous place in Wulfstan's
canon. The text survives in Old English and Latin versions,
the latter likely produced slightly later than the former. Particularly striking in the Latin version is the addition of a
final clause that explicitly attributes the text to Wulfstan.
Both Old English and Latin survive as additions to London,
Cotton MS Claudius A.iii, a pontifical used by Wulfstan early
in his career. Many of the clauses resemble those of *5 Æthelred,* though they occur in a different order. The text of *6
Æthelred* also elaborates on its predecessor's prescriptions
in ways suggestive of Wulfstan's later works, particularly in
its foregrounding of clauses related to ecclesiastical law and
its more detailed list of dues owed the Church. It seems
likely, then, that *6 Æthelred* represents not an official enact-
ment but instead a draft of *5 Æthelred* that Wulfstan used to
experiment with policies that would later become regular
features of his legislative writings.

The next set of laws authored by Wulfstan resulted from
a meeting of the royal council at Bath in 1009 to devise a response to the most recent Viking invasion. Like *6 Æthelred,*
these decrees survive in both a Latin and an Old English

version—designated 7 and *7a Æthelred* by modern editors—
though here the differences between the two texts are much
more pronounced. The original Old English text of 1009 has
been lost, but the Latin version, included in the twelfth-
century legal compilation *Quadripartitus,* is likely a reason-
ably close approximation. The surviving Old English version,
preserved in Cambridge, Corpus Christi College MS 201, is
a draft prepared by Wulfstan, probably as an intermediate
text between the original law code and his later revision of
the code into a homily. In both versions, the emphasis is on
the use of penitential rituals to purge the kingdom of sin
collectively so that it might thereby escape God's punishment and expel the invaders. The Old English version, however, replaces the legal prescriptions and circumstantial specificity of *7 Æthelred* with sermonic exhortations and moral
admonition. The effect of this alteration is to translate the
latter's response to an individual invasion into a broader
statement of religious principle. Taken together, the two
versions of *7 Æthelred* thus offer both an impression of the
archbishop at work and an illustration of the penitential
steps he viewed as necessary for the moral regeneration of
the English kingdom.

Little is known about the circumstances surrounding the
issuance of *8 Æthelred,* though its rubric dates it to 1014. It
survives in two witnesses, the latter of which breaks off immediately after the sanctuary clauses, to which are then appended the related short tract *Northumbrian Church Sanctuary* (see above). The law code begins with the curious statement that it is merely "one of the decrees" promulgated by
the king, though it is unclear whether this phrase indicates
that multiple pieces of legislation were issued on the same

occasion or whether it instead simply refers to the many laws promulgated by Æthelred over the course of his reign. In either case, this legislation stands out from the other laws Wulfstan composed for the king: not only is it even more explicitly focused on ecclesiastical matters than its predecessors, but it also adopts a much broader historical perspective. Borrowing entire clauses from *The Compilation on Status*, Wulfstan uses that collection's retrospective tone as a way to evoke the golden era of Monastic Reform under Kings Æthelstan, Edmund, and Edgar. Under the circumstances, it is difficult to take the mention of these earlier kings as anything other than a thinly veiled rebuke of England's current ruler. Furthermore, if the 1014 dating is correct, then the promulgation of this code coincides with the collapse of Æthelred's government. The references to an earlier age of political stability and moral virtue thus offer yet another example of Wulfstan using a privileged past to respond to present crises.

Both 9 and 10 *Æthelred* survive only as fragments. Of these, 9 *Æthelred* occurs in London, British Library, Cotton MS Otho A.x, which was nearly destroyed in the Ashburnam House fire of 1731. Although little about the text is certain, the prologue indicates that it was promulgated following a meeting of the royal council at Woodstock (Oxfordshire), which suggests a probable date between 1009 and 1016. In the case of 10 *Æthelred,* the sole copy of the text has been bound into Vatican, Codex Reginensis Latina 946, a fourteenth-century French miscellany. The date of its original promulgation is unknown, although it may have been another version of the 1008 Enham codes (5 and 6 *Æthelred*).

Following Æthelred's death in 1016, Wulfstan continued

to serve as the primary drafter of royal legislation under the Danish conqueror, Cnut. The earliest set of laws authored by Wulfstan on behalf of the new king is the text now referred to as *Cnut's Oxford Legislation of 1018,* or more briefly as *Cnut 1018,* which survives only in Cambridge, Corpus Christi College MS 201. Although initially viewed as a sort of pastiche made up of "spare parts" from *6 Æthelred* and *1–2 Cnut,* more recent scholarship has shown it to be a carefully ordered compilation that likely represents the enactments of the meeting between the Danes and the English at Oxford mentioned in the entry for 1018 in the *Anglo-Saxon Chronicle.* It seems probable, though, that the surviving text is less an accurate transcription of these enactments than a rendering of them revised by Wulfstan for his own use.

Evidence of the respect that the new king held for Wulfstan can be found in *Cnut's Proclamation of 1020.* This text, which survives only in the York Gospels (York, Minster Library, Additional MS 1), was initially composed during Cnut's return to Denmark in 1019–1020. Internal evidence indicates, however, that Wulfstan subsequently revised a large portion of it (particularly its final paragraph) for further circulation or oral delivery. That Wulfstan should have been involved in the drafting and promulgation of such a document in the king's absence indicates the confidence the Danes had in the English archbishop. At the same time, Wulfstan's intervention recasts the document in significant ways. The opening clauses are very much in the voice of a conqueror addressing his new subjects, promising justice in exchange for obedience. The passages more explicitly by Wulfstan, however, circumscribe the king's authority by emphasizing that his rule is nonetheless subordinate to the law of God. In effect, much as he does with the revisions incorporated into the later version of *Polity,* Wulfstan here positions the king within a Christian hierarchy that grants him power, but also threatens to withdraw it should he act unjustly.

Wulfstan's greatest achievement as a legislator came with the promulgation of the law codes referred to as *1* and *2 Cnut.* The balance between the ecclesiastical prescriptions in *1 Cnut* and the secular ones in the contemporaneous *2 Cnut* have led some scholars to suggest that the two texts might once have comprised a single law code similar to *2–3 Edgar,* although this claim has been the subject of considerable debate. Whichever is the case, their scope, elevated rhetoric, and sweeping vision of moral renewal make them both a fitting summation of Wulfstan's career and the most sophisticated legal texts to be produced in England since the ninth century.

1 Cnut was likely promulgated sometime between 1020 and Wulfstan's death in 1023. One copy of the text survives in a manuscript owned and annotated by Wulfstan himself, which is the basis for the text and translation here. It provides a comprehensive account of the moral obligations of both the Church and its English flock, thereby serving as a summation of Wulfstan's views on the relationship between ecclesiastical governance and royal authority. Drawing not just on legal precedent but also on the works of Carolingian canonists, *The Institutes of Polity,* and *The Canons of Edgar, 1 Cnut* conceives of England as subject to the law of God and held to moral standards which, if obeyed, would enable the kingdom to fulfill its destiny as a holy society.

Wulfstan's longest—and possibly last—major piece of legislation, *2 Cnut,* is arguably Anglo-Saxon England's most innovative and wide-ranging set of laws. Once again, Wulfstan draws heavily on his previous legal writings, particularly the Enham codes, *8 Æthelred, Cnut 1018,* and *The Institutes of Polity.* Yet these borrowings make up only just over half of the text: more than a third of *2 Cnut* has no known source, raising the likelihood that these clauses represent innovations of Wulfstan's own. Moreover, even in clauses that have an identifiable precursor, the borrowed passages are frequently revised, expanded, or significantly rewritten in order to subordinate them to Wulfstan's purposes rather than those of his source. Indeed, Wulfstan takes more liberties with his source material in *2 Cnut* than he does in any of his prior law codes. The effect is a text that fully expresses Wulfstan's political vision. He adopts in *2 Cnut* a comprehensive approach to English society under which the ordinances of the Church are fully integrated into the laws of the kingdom, the legal rights and religious obligations of each subject are clearly articulated, and the integrity of the community depends on its obedience to a divinely ordained moral order. As in *The Institutes of Polity,* the redemption of society from both worldly dangers and the threat of eternal damnation here relies on the Christian virtue of the individual soul no less than that of the political collective. When both are ordered as God intended, then the salvation of the kingdom will finally be within reach.

APPENDIX I: QUESTIONABLE ATTRIBUTIONS

Relatively few of Wulfstan's works explicitly identify him as their author. Instead, to reconstruct his corpus scholars have had to rely on his unique writing style, contextual clues, manuscript provenance, and his inveterate habit of self-quotation. While his authorship of most texts in this volume has been securely established, there are also works that exhibit enough Wulfstanian features to be associated with the archbishop, but not enough to allow for a firm attribution. Yet even if such texts may not have been composed by Wulfstan himself, they still testify to his influence on the writing of law in the early eleventh century.

Among the most debated works associated with Wulfstan is *The Northumbrian Priests' Law,* preserved alongside other Wulfstanian texts in Cambridge, Corpus Christ College MS 201. The text is divided into two parts, with the first (clauses 1–45) directed primarily at clergy and the second (clauses 46–67) addressing the whole of the York diocese. Although the text was attributed to the archbishop for much of the twentieth century, more recently scholars have argued that it may instead be the work of either Ælfric Puttoc or Cynesige, Wulfstan's successors to the see of York. The text draws heavily on Wulfstan's *Canons of Edgar,* but beyond these passages the prose shows little sign of the archbishop's customary vigor. Moreover, several passages—most notably those on clerical marriage—seem to depart from the more orthodox positions adopted in other of Wulfstan's works. If *The Northumbrian Priests' Law* is not by Wulfstan, then Liebermann's suggestion that it ought to be dated to sometime between 1028 and 1060 seems most plausible.

Equally controversial is the attribution to Wulfstan of the early eleventh-century text *The Obligations of Individuals (Rectitudines singularum personarum)* and its companion piece *On Reeves (Gerefa*—the Old English title is singular, though the convention is to render it in the plural). Though originally distinct, the two are treated as a single text in their sole manuscript witness, and Latin versions are also found in the twelfth-century compilation *Quadripartitus*. The focus of both *Obligations* and *On Reeves* is on the proper administration of a farm and its workers, suggesting that the motive in joining them together was to create a comprehensive manual of estate management. The texts show evidence of multiple authors, and it has been speculated, largely on stylistic grounds, that Wulfstan may have adapted the two pieces and linked them together. More recent scholarship, however, has argued that the stylistic similarities to Wulfstan's other works are not sufficient to justify such a conclusion. Any resemblance may simply be coincidental, or it may well be the case, as with *The Northumbrian Priests' Law,* that the similarities to Wulfstan's writings reflect the efforts of one of his associates familiar with the archbishop's tone and style.

APPENDIX 2: REVISIONS AND REWORKINGS

Wulfstan's habit of repeated revision was not limited to his own writings. He also reworked the legislation of previous kings, possibly as a way of trying out some of the ideas he would later incorporate into the laws of Æthelred and Cnut. There is no evidence that he ever intended these revised texts to circulate as actual legislation; rather, they appear to have been drafts primarily composed for personal use. As such, they provide valuable insight into the archbishop's legal mind at work.

It is unknown when or in what order Wulfstan carried out his revisions, but the earliest of the law codes to have attracted his interest is *1 Æthelstan,* likely the earliest of Æthelstan's laws, though its date of promulgation remains uncertain. Its initial composition took place under the direction of Archbishop Wulfhelm of Canterbury, whose influence may have been what attracted Wulfstan's interest. Two versions of the text survive: a Latin version in the twelfth-century compilation *Quadripartitus* and an Old English version in two manuscripts associated with Wulfstan. Differences between the Latin and the Old English versions suggest that in transcribing the earlier text, Wulfstan introduced his own perspective and phrasings, particularly concerning the payment of Church dues, to recast the material for his own use.

One of the first pieces of legislation to reflect the priorities of the Monastic Reform, *1 Edmund* was likely promulgated in either 942 or between 944 and 946. The text survives in three post-Conquest anthologies of Old English laws as well as in two pre-Conquest manuscripts associated with Wulfstan. As was the case with *1 Æthelstan,* the versions of the text in manuscripts linked to Wulfstan exhibit differences of both style and content, suggesting that he once again reworked earlier legislation to reflect current preoccupations.

The joint law code designated *2 Edgar* and *3 Edgar* by modern editors shows even more evidence of Wulfstanian intervention than do *1 Æthelstan* and *1 Edmund,* including several clauses that repeat nearly word for word passages found in the legislation Wulfstan composed for Æthelred and Cnut. The text's initial date of promulgation is unknown, though it must have occurred prior to that of the clearly later *4 Edgar* sometime in either 962 or 963. The split between ecclesiastical *(2 Edgar)* and secular *(3 Edgar)* ordinances, along with the extensive interest Wulfstan appears to have taken in its prescriptions, have led to the suggestion that this text served as a model for *1–2 Cnut,* though this claim remains subject to debate.

EDITING WULFSTAN

In the century following the Norman Conquest, Wulfstan's legal writings remained influential, although the archbishop's association with them was gradually forgotten. Passages from *Polity* and several of his other tracts were incorporated into so-called "composite homilies" of the later eleventh century, while the legislation of Æthelred and Cnut came to be included in the great twelfth-century compilations *Instituta Cnuti, Consilatio Cnuti, Leges Edwardi Confessoris, Leges Henrici Primi,* and *Quadripartitus.* Wulfstan's legal writings also feature prominently in the twelfth-century legal anthologies *Textus Roffensis* and Cambridge, Corpus Christ College MS 383. In none of these cases, however, is Wulfstan named as either author or drafter. Instead, when his name was mentioned at all (as it was by William of Malmesbury), it was as an example of the perceived corruption of the Anglo-Saxon Church, though such accusations reflected the perspectives of England's new Norman overlords rather than an accurate representation of Wulfstan's integrity or that of his contemporaries.

With the rise of the common law in the late twelfth and early thirteenth centuries, Wulfstan's name and works gradually faded into oblivion. However, the revival of interest in pre-Conquest England that accompanied the English Reformation brought with it a renewed fascination with Wulfstan's legal writings, though the archbishop himself was not yet recognized as their author. William Lambarde's 1568 *Archaionomia* provided the *editio princeps* for several of Wulfstan's works, including *Edward-Guthrum* (treated as an actual tenth-century law code rather than an eleventh-century forgery), the three central texts of *The Compilation on Status,* and *1–2 Cnut.* Lambarde's edition, though, suffered from a number of shortcomings, the most notable of which was his use of reconstructed texts that had been translated into Latin and then retranslated into Old English as a linguistic experiment by his friend Lawrence Nowell. This use of early modern pastiches rather than authentic Old English law codes was not realized until 1923. Yet Lambarde's was not the only contribution to the recovery of Wulfstan's reputation during this period: equally significant was Archbishop Matthew Parker's recognition of the historical and artistic importance of Wulfstan's homiletic masterpiece, the *Sermo Lupi ad Anglos,* and Humphrey Wanley's 1705 attribution of the text to the archbishop of York. In naming Wulfstan as the author, Wanley developed a set of stylistic criteria that allowed him to identify fifty-three homilies and several shorter tracts as the work of the archbishop.

Over the course of the next two centuries, Wulfstan's reputation as a homilist grew, though his work as a legislator and political theorist remained largely unrecognized. In 1723, David Wilkins became the first to print the chapters that make up *The Institutes of Polity,* though he did not treat them as components of a single text, nor did he attribute their composition to Wulfstan. A broader range of Wulfstan's legislation—again, unattributed—was included in the two great nineteenth-century editions of Old English law,

Reinhold Schmid's *Die Gesetze der Angelsachsen* (1832, rev. ed. 1858) and Benjamin Thorpe's *Ancient Laws and Institutes of England* (1840), the latter of which also included *Polity* (giving the text its modern title), *The Canons of Edgar,* and a number of the shorter political and ecclesiastical tracts. The whole of Wulfstan's legislation and the remaining unedited political tracts finally made it into print with the publication of Felix Liebermann's magisterial, three-volume *Die Gesetze der Angelsachsen* (1903–1916). Far more comprehensive and reliable than any of its predecessors, Liebermann's *Gesetze* remains the authoritative edition of most of the texts included within it. Nonetheless, in the case of the texts associated with Wulfstan, Liebermann's edition is woefully out of date. Although he suspected that Wulfstan may have had something to do with several of the laws of Æthelred, he was too conservative an editor to go so far as to acknowledge the extent of the archbishop's influence. Moreover, he continued to place *Edward-Guthrum* wrongly in the tenth century, treated the texts from Lambarde as a lost manuscript rather than an early modern pastiche, mistakenly edited *Cnut 1018* as a draft of *1–2 Cnut,* and incorrectly dated *1–2 Cnut* to the decade following Wulfstan's death in 1023. As brilliant an accomplishment as Liebermann's *Gesetze* surely is, its treatment of early eleventh-century English legislation has been largely overturned by more recent scholarship.

The editions of Anglo-Saxon legislation by Frederick Attenborough and Agnes Robertson (1922 and 1925, respectively) provided up-to-date English translations of the Old English laws, yet they also reiterated many of the errors of their predecessors. It was only through the work of the scholars Dorothy Whitelock, Dorothy Bethurum, and Karl

Jost that the full scope of Wulfstan's activities began to become clear, and their collective efforts have formed the basis of all subsequent work on Wulfstan. Despite their efforts, however, Liebermann's editions have yet to be replaced even as the extent of Wulfstan's corpus continues to expand. Indeed, while recent scholarship has done much to settle some of the questions surrounding the archbishop's life, thought, and career, major gaps persist. It is hoped that the present volume will be of use in resolving some of these gaps.

Despite the name on the cover, a book is never the work of one individual, and I am deeply grateful to the many people who have had a hand in producing this one. Thanks are owed first to Dan Donoghue, both for inviting me to take up this project and for his unstinting good humor, support, and editorial guidance along the way. Only those who have published in this series can truly appreciate the time, labor, and spectacular eye for detail that Managing Editor Nicole Eddy contributes to these editions. This volume would be immeasurably diminished in both quality and substance without her efforts. Finally, I have been very fortunate to have Rob Fulk and Susan Irvine as reviewers. Their knowledge and generosity can be found on nearly every page.

This book is dedicated to my wife, Shira, and my sons, Ari and Eli.

POLITICAL TRACTS

The Laws of Edward and Guthrum

Þis syndon þa domas ðe Ælfred cyncg and Guþrum cyncg gecuron.

Pr   And þis is seo gerædnis eac þe Ælfred cyng and Guðrum cyng, and eft Eadward cyng and Guðrum cyng, gecuran and gecwædon þa þa Engle and Dene to friþe and to freondscipe fullice fengon. And þa witan eac, þe syððan wæron, oft and unseldan þæt seolfe geniwodon and mid gode gehihtan.

Pr.1 Ðæt is ærest þæt hig gecwædon: þæt hi ænne God lufian woldon and ælcne hæþendom georne aweorpen.

Pr.2 And hig gesetton woruldlice steora eac, for ðam þingum þe hig wistan þæt hig elles ne mihton manegum gesteoran, ne fela manna nolde to godcundre bote elles gebugan swa hy sceolden; and þa woruldbote hig gesetton gemæne Criste and cynge swa hwar swa man nolde godcunde bote gebugan mid rihte to bisceopa dihte.

1   And þæt is þonon ærest þæt hig gecwædon, þæt cyricgrið binnan wagum and cyninges handgrið stande efne unwemme.

2   And gif hwa Cristendom wyrde oððe hæþendom weorþige wordes oððe weorces, gylde swa wer swa wite swa lahslitte, be þam þe syo dæd sy.

The Laws of Edward and Guthrum

These are the measures agreed upon by King Alfred and King Guthrum.

Pr   And this also is the decree which King Alfred and King Guthrum, and later King Edward and King Guthrum, agreed upon and proclaimed when the English and the Danes fully resolved on peace and friendship. And also the councilors, those who came after, often and frequently renewed it and strengthened it with improvements.

Pr.1 This is foremost among those things which they agreed upon: that they would love the one God and wholeheartedly reject every heathen practice.

Pr.2 And they also established secular penalties, for they knew that otherwise they could not govern many people, nor would many men otherwise comply with Church discipline as they should; and they decreed that secular compensation will be shared by Christ and king wherever anyone refused to submit properly to Church penance at the order of the bishops.

1   Next, they also agreed that sanctuary within church walls and sanctuary received from the king's hand shall remain equally inviolable.

2   And if anyone violates Christian practice or shows reverence for heathenism by word or deed, he must pay either his wergild or a penalty or *lahslit,* according to the nature of the deed.

3   And gyf gehadod man gestalie oððe gefeohte oððe for-
swerige oððe forlicge, gebete þæt be þam þe seo dæde sy
swa be were swa be wite swa be lahslitte; and for Gode huru
bete swa canon tæce and þæs borh finde oððe carcern gebuge.

3.1   And gif mæssepreost folc miswyssige æt freolse oððe
æt fæstene, gylde xxx scillinga mid Englum and mid Denum
þreo healfmarc.

3.2   Gif preost to rihtandagan crisman ne fecce oððe fulluhtes forwyrne þam þe þæs þearf sy, gylde wite mid Englum
and mid Denum lahslit, þæt is twelf oran.

4   And æt syblegerum þa witan geræddan þæt cyng ah
þone uferan and bisceop þone nyþeran, butan hit man gebete for Gode and for worulde be þam þe seo dæd sy, swa
bisceop getæce.

4.1   Gif twegen gebroðra oððe twegen genydmagas wið an
wif forlicgan, beten swyþe georne, swa swa man geþafige,
swa be wite swa be lahslitte, be þam þe seo dæde sy.

4.2   Gif gehadod man hine forwyrce mid deaþscylde,
gewilde hine man and healde to bisceopes dome.

5   And gif deaþscyldig man scriftspræce gyrne, ne him
man næfre ne wyrne.

5.1   And ealle Godes gerihto forðige man georne be Godes
mildse and be þam witan þe witan toledan.

6   Gif hwa teoþunge forhealde, gylde lahslit mid Denum,
wite mid Englum.

3   And if a man in orders steals or fights or commits perjury or adultery, he shall atone according to the nature of the
deed, either with his wergild or with a penalty or with *lahslit;*
and indeed, he must do penance before God as the canon
decrees and either find a surety or submit to imprisonment.

3.1   And if a priest misleads the people concerning a holy
day or a fast, he must pay thirty shillings among the English
or three half-marks among the Danes.

3.2   If a priest does not fetch the holy oil on the proper day
or denies baptism to one who needs it, he must pay a penalty
among the English and *lahslit* of twelve oras among the
Danes.

4   And in cases of incest the councilors ruled that the
king shall have jurisdiction over the upper and the bishop
the lower, unless penance is performed before God and the
world, as the bishop decrees according to the nature of the
deed.

4.1   If two brothers or two close relatives lie with the same
woman, they must atone most fervently, just as it may be allowed, with a penalty or with *lahslit,* according to the nature
of the deed.

4.2   If a man in orders compromises himself with a capital
crime, he is to be arrested and held for the bishop's judgment.

5   And if someone sentenced to death desires confession,
it shall never be denied to him.

5.1   And all God's dues shall be rendered assiduously for
God's mercy and because of the penalties which the councilors assigned.

6   If anyone withholds his tithe, he shall pay *lahslit* among
the Danes or a penalty among the English.

6.1   Gif hwa Romfeoh forhealde, gylde lahslit mid Denum, wite mid Englum.

6.2   Gif hwa leohtgesceot ne gelæste, gylde lahslit mid Denum, wite mid Englum.

6.3   Gif hwa sulhælmyssan ne sylle, gylde lahslit mid Denum, wite mid Englum.

6.4   Gif hwa ænigra godcundra gerihto forwyrne, gylde lahslit mid Denum, wite mid Englum.

6.5   And gif he wigie and man gewundie, beo his weres scyldig.

6.6   Gif he man to deaþe gefylle, beo he þonne utlah, and his hente mid hearme ælc þara þe riht wille.

6.7   And gif he gewyrce þæt hine man afylle þurh þæt he ongean Godes ryht oððe þæs cynges geonbyrde, gif man þæt gesoðige, licge ægylde.

7   Sunnandæges cypinge gif hwa agynne, þolie þæs ceapes and twelf orena mid Denum and xxx scillinga mid Englum.

7.1   Gif frigman freolsdæge wyrce, þolie his freotes oððe gylde wite oððe lahslite. Ðeowman þolie his hyde oððe hydgyldes.

7.2   Gif hlaford his þeowan freolsdæge nyde to weorce, gylde lahslitte se hlaford inne on Deone lage and wite mid Englum.

8   Gif frigman rihtfæsten abrece, gylde wite oððe lahslite. Gif hit þeowman gedo, ðolie his hyde oððe hydgyldes.

6.1 If anyone withholds the dues owed to Rome, he shall pay *lahslit* among the Danes or a penalty among the English.

6.2 If anyone does not pay the dues for the lighting of the church, he shall pay *lahslit* among the Danes or a penalty among the English.

6.3 If anyone does not pay his plow dues, he shall pay *lahslit* among the Danes or a penalty among the English.

6.4 If anyone withholds his Church dues, he shall pay *lahslit* among the Danes or a penalty among the English.

6.5 And if he fights and wounds anyone, he will be liable for his wergild.

6.6 If he causes anyone's death, then he will become an outlaw and be hunted with enmity by all those who wish for justice.

6.7 And if he acts in such a way as to cause his own death through resistance to God's justice or the king's, and if that is shown to be true, no compensation need be paid for him.

7 If anyone does business on a Sunday, he shall forfeit his purchases and twelve oras among the Danes and thirty shillings among the English.

7.1 If a freeman works on a holy day, he shall forfeit his freedom, or pay a penalty or *lahslit*. A slave will receive a whipping or pay to redeem himself.

7.2 If a master compels his slave to work on a holy day, he must pay *lahslit* within the Danelaw and a penalty among the English.

8 If a freeman breaks a legally mandated fast, he must pay a penalty or *lahslit*. If a slave does so, he shall receive a whipping or pay to redeem himself.

9   Ordel and aðas syndan tocwedene freolsdagum and rihtfæstendagum; and se ðe þæt abrece, gylde lahslit mid Denum, wite mid Englum.

9.1 Gif man wealdan mage, ne dyde man næfre on Sunnandæges freolse ænigne forwyrhtne, ac wylde and healde þæt se freolsdæg agan sy.

10   Gif limlæwed lama þe forworht wære weorþe forlæten and he æfter þam ðreo niht alibbe, siððan man mot hylpan be bisceopes leafe, se ðe wylle beorgan sare and saule.

11   Gif wiccan oððe wigleras, mansworan oððe morðwyrhtan oððe fule, afylede, æbære horcwenan ahwar on lande wurðan agytene, ðonne fyse hi man of earde and clænsie þa ðeode, oððe on earde forfare hy mid ealle buton hig geswican and þe deoppor gebetan.

12   Gif man gehadodne oððe ælðeodigne, þurh enig ðing, forræde æt feo oððe æt feore, þonne sceal him cyng beon— oððan eorl ðær on lande—and bisceop ðere þeode for mæg and for mundboran, buton he elles oðerne hæbbe; and bete man georne be ðam þe seo dæd sy Christe and cyninge, swa hit gebyrige; oððe þa dæde wrece swiðe deope þe cyning sy on ðeode.

9   Ordeals and oaths are prohibited on holy days and legally mandated fast days; and one who violates that shall pay *lahslit* among the Danes or a penalty among the English.

9.1   If it can be managed, no one sentenced to death should ever be executed on a Sunday festival, but he is to be confined and held until the holy day has ended.

10   If a mutilated man who might have been executed comes to be abandoned and he survives for three nights, afterward, with the bishop's permission, anyone who wishes to heal his injuries and his soul might help him.

11   If magicians or wizards, perjurers or murderers, or foul, corrupted, notorious prostitutes come to be discovered anywhere in the land, then they must be expelled from the country and the realm cleansed, or from the country they must be utterly wiped out unless they desist and repent most deeply.

12   If a man in orders or a foreigner is, by any means, cheated of his goods or his life, then the king—or the lord of that land—and bishop of that people shall act as kinsman and protector, unless he has another; and compensation must readily be paid to Christ and the king according to the nature of the deed; or he who is king of that people must punish the crime most harshly.

The Compilation on Status

Be leode geþincðum and lage

1   Hit wæs hwilum on Engla lagum þæt leod and lagu for be geþincðum, and þa wæron leodwitan weorðscipes wyrðe, ælc be his mæðe, eorl and ceorl, þegen and þeoden.

2   And gif ceorl geþeah þæt he hæfde fullice fif hida agenes landes, cirican and kycenan, bellhus and burhgeat, setl and sundernote on cynges healle, þonne wæs he þanon forð þegenrihtes weorðe.

3   And gif þegen geþeah þæt he þenode cynge and his rad-stefne rad on his hirede; gif se þonne hæfde þegen þe him filigde, þe to cinges utware fif hida hæfde, and on cinges sele his hlaforde þenode, and þriwa mid his ærende gefore to cinge, se moste syððan mid his foraðe his hlaford aspelian æt mistlicon neodan and his onspæce geræcan mid rihte, swa hwær swa he sceolde.

4   And se þe swa geþogenne forwyrhtan næfde swore for sylfne æfter his rihte oððe his þolode.

5   And gif þegen geþeah þæt he wearð to eorle, þonne wæs he syððan eorlrihtes weorðe.

6   And gif massere geþeah þæt he ferde þrige ofer widsæ be his agenum cræfte, se wæs þonne syððan þegenrihtes weorðe.

The Compilation on Status

On the Ranks of People and Law

1   In the laws of the English, it once was that people and law were ordered by status, and the people's councilors were treated with dignity, each according to his rank, noble and commoner, thane and lord.

2   And if a commoner prospered so that he had fully five hides of his own property with a church and kitchen, a bell house and fortified gate, a seat and an appointed role in the king's hall, then he was worthy of a thane's rights ever after.

3   And if a thane prospered so that he waited upon the king and rode on his business among his retinue, then, if he had a thane who followed him, who had five hides for the king's service and had waited upon his lord in the king's hall and had gone three times on his business to the king, then his thane afterward might represent his lord in various obligations with his initial oath and handle his litigation, wherever he must.

4   And he who did not have such a worthy representative swore for himself to his rights or forfeited his case.

5   And if a thane prospered so that he became a noble, he was afterward worthy of a noble's rights.

6   And if a merchant prospered so that he fared three times over the open sea by his own means, he was afterward worthy of a thane's rights.

7   And gif leornere geþeh þurh lare þæt he had hæfde and þenode Christe, se wæs þonne syððan mæðe and munde swa micelre wyrðe swa ðærto gebyrede, buton he forworhte þæt he þære hadnote notian ne moste.

8   And gif hit gewurde þæt man gehadedum oððe ælþeodigum ahwar gederode wordes oððe weorces, þonne gebyrede cinge and bisceope þæt hig þæt bettan swa hig raþost mihton.

Be wergylde

1   Cynges wergild is inne mid Englum on folcriht xxx þusend þrymsa: xv þusend ðrymsa byð þæs weres and xv þusend þæs cynedomes; se wer gebyreð þam magum and seo cynebot þam leodum.

2   Æþelinges wergyld is xv þusend þrymsa.

3   Bisceopes and ealdermannes, viii þusend þrymsa.

4   Holdes and hehgerefan, iiii þusend þrymsa.

5   Mæsseþegenes and woruldþegenes, ii þusend þrymsa.

6   Ceorles wergild is cc and vi and lx þrymsa, þæt bið twahund scyllinga be Myrcna lage.

7   And gif Wilise man geþeo þæt he hæbbe hywisc landes and mage cynges gafel forðbringan, þonne byð his wergild ccxx scillinga.

7.1   And gif he ne geþeo butan to healfre hide, þonne sy his wergild lxxx scillinga.

7   And if a student prospered by his learning so that he took orders and served Christ, he was afterward worthy of such respect and protection as was fitting thereto, unless he should sin so that he could not practice his ministry.

8   And if it so happened anywhere that someone injured one in orders or a stranger by word or deed, then it was the responsibility of the king and the bishop to remedy it as swiftly as they could.

On Wergild

1   According to the folk law of the English people, a king's wergild is thirty thousand thrymsas: fifteen thousand thrymsas are for the man and fifteen thousand thrymsas are for the kingship. The personal wergild belongs to his kinsmen and the royal compensation belongs to the people.

2   A nobleman's wergild is fifteen thousand thrymsas.

3   For a bishop and an ealdorman, eight thousand thrymsas.

4   For a Danish nobleman and a high reeve, four thousand thrymsas.

5   For a priest and a secular thane, two thousand thrymsas.

6   A commoner's wergild is two hundred and sixty-six thrymsas, that is, two hundred shillings according to the law of the Mercians.

7   And if a Welshman prospers so that he possesses a hide of land and can pay the king's tribute, then his wergild shall be two hundred and twenty shillings.

7.1   And if he does not prosper to more than half of a hide, then his wergild will be eighty shillings.

8   And gif he ænig land næbbe and þeh freo sy, forgylde man hine mid LXX scillinga.

9   And gif ceorlisc man geþeo, þæt he hæbbe v hida landes to cynges utware and man hine ofslea, forgylde man hine mid II þusend þrymsa.

10   And þeh he geþeo þæt he hæbbe helm and byrnan and gold fæted sweord, gif he þæt land nafaþ, he byþ ceorl swa þeah.

11   And gif his sunu and his suna sunu þæt geþeoð þæt hy swa micel landes habbað, syððan byþ se offspring gesið-cundes cynnes be twam þusendum þrymsa.

12   And gif hig þæt nabbað, ne to þam geþeon ne magan, gylde man cyrlisce.

Be Mircna laga

1   Ceorles wergyld is on Myrcna lage CC scillinga.

1.1   Ðegenes wergyld is syx swa micel, þæt byð XII hund scillinga.

2   Ðonne byð cyninges anfeald wergild syx þegena wer-gyld be Myrcna laga, þæt is XXX þusend sceatta, þæt bið ealles CXX punda.

3   Swa micel is þæs wergyldes on folces folcriht be Myrcna laga.

3.1   And for ðam cynedome gebyrað oðer swilc to bote on cynegylde.

4   Se wer gebyreð magum and seo cynebot þam leodum.

8 And if he does not have any land but is still free, then compensation for him shall be seventy shillings.

9 And if a commoner prospers so that he possesses five hides of land for his obligations to the king and anyone kills him, compensation for him shall be two thousand thrymsas.

10 Yet even if he prospers so that he possesses a helmet and a coat of mail and a gold-plated sword, if he does not possess the land he will still be a commoner.

11 And if his son and his son's son prosper so that they have sufficient land, then the offspring will be of the rank of *gesith* at two thousand thrymsas.

12 And if they do not have it and cannot acquire enough, their compensation will be that of a commoner.

On the Law of the Mercians

1 According to the law of the Mercians, a commoner's wergild is two hundred shillings.

1.1 The wergild of a thane is six times as much, that is, twelve hundred shillings.

2 According to the law of the Mercians, then, the king's individual wergild is the wergild of six thanes, that is, thirty thousand sceattas, which is one hundred and twenty pounds in all.

3 So much is wergild in the folk law of the people, according to the law of the Mercians.

3.1 And for the kingship there is a second compensation owed equal to that for the king.

4 The wergild belongs to his kinsmen and the royal compensation to the people.

Be Mirciscan aðe

1   Twelfhyndes mannes að forstent vi ceorla að; forðam, gif man þone twelfhyndan man wrecan sceolde, he við full-wrecen on syx ceorlan, and his wergyld við six ceorla wer-gyld.

Be gehadodra manna aðe

1   Mæssepreostes að and worldþegenes is on Engla lage geteald efen dyre; and for ðam seofon cirichadan, þe se mæssepreost þurh Godes gife geþeah, þæt he hæfde, he við þegenrihtes wyrþe. Seofonfealde gyfa syndan Haliges Gastes; and vii stæpas syndan cyriclicra grada and haligra hada; and vii syðan Godes þeowas sceolon God herian dæghwamlice on cyrcan and for eall Cristen folc þingian georne.

1.1   And eallum Godes freondum gebyreð swyðe rihte þæt hi Godes cyrcan lufian and wurðian, and Godes þeowas friðian and griþian.

1.2   And se þe heom gederie mid worde oððe mid weorce viifealdre bote gebete hit georne be þam þe seo dæd sy and be þam þe se had sy gif he Godes mildse geearnian wylle.

1.3   Forðam haligdom and hadas and gehalgode Godes hus a man sceal for Godes ege wurðian georne.

2   And to hadbote, gif liflyre wurðe, toeacan þam riht-were, þene forman stæpe bete man mid ane punde and mid godre bote þingie georne.

On the Mercian Oath

1   The oath of a man with a wergild of twelve hundred shillings equals the oath of six commoners; therefore, if a man with a wergild of twelve hundred shillings must be avenged, he will be fully avenged to the value of six commoners; furthermore, his wergild will be the wergilds of six commoners.

On Priests' Oaths

1   A priest's oath and a secular thane's are considered equal in English law; and because of the seven Church degrees that the priest has acquired through the grace of God, he is worthy of a thane's rights. Sevenfold are the gifts of the Holy Spirit; and seven are the steps of ecclesiastical ranks and holy orders; and seven times daily should God's servants praise God in church and diligently advocate for all Christian people.

1.1   And it is most rightly proper for all friends of God that they love God's Church and venerate it, and preserve and protect God's servants.

1.2   And he who injures them by word or deed must diligently remedy it with sevenfold compensation according to the deed and according to the order if he wishes to earn God's favor.

1.3   For out of fear of God, one must always diligently honor the sanctity, orders, and house of God.

2   And as compensation for one in orders if loss of life occurs, the perpetrator must make amends for the first rank by paying one pound in addition to the standard wergild, and he must diligently make peace by sincere atonement.

3   And to hadbote, gif feorhlyra wurðe, toeacan þam riht-
were æt þam oðran stæpe ii pund to bote mid godcundan
scrifte.

4   And to hadbote, gif fullbryce wurðe, toeacan þam riht-
were æt þam þryddan stæpe iii pund to bote mid godcundan scrifte.

5   And to hadbote, gif fullbryce wurðe, toeacan þam riht-
were æt þam feorðan stæpe iiii pund to bote, mid godcundan scrifte.

6   And to hadbote, gif fullbryce wurðe, toeacan þam riht-
were æt þam fiftan stæpe v pund to bote, mid godcundan
scrifte.

7   And to hadbote, gif fullbryce wurðe, toeacan þam riht-
were æt þam syxtan stæpe vi pund to bote, mid godcundan
scrifte.

8   And to hadbote, gif fullbryce wurðe, toeacan þam riht-
were æt þam seofoðam stæpe vii pund to bote, mid godcundan scrifte.

9   And to hadbote, þær sambryce wurðe, bete man georne
be ðam þe seo dæd sy.

9.1   And hadbot mid rihte an dæl þam biscope, oðer þam
wigbede and þridde þam gefærscipe.

3   And as compensation for one in orders if loss of life occurs, the perpetrator must make amends for the second rank by paying two pounds in addition to the standard wergild and by doing spiritual penance.

4   And as compensation for one in orders if a full breach of the peace occurs, the perpetrator must make amends for the third rank by paying three pounds as a penalty in addition to the standard wergild and by doing spiritual penance.

5   And as compensation for one in orders if a full breach of the peace occurs, the perpetrator must make amends for the fourth rank by paying four pounds as a penalty in addition to the standard wergild and by doing spiritual penance.

6   And as compensation for one in orders if a full breach of the peace occurs, the perpetrator must make amends for the fifth rank by paying five pounds as a penalty in addition to the standard wergild and by doing spiritual penance.

7   And as compensation for one in orders if a full breach of the peace occurs, the perpetrator must make amends for the sixth rank by paying six pounds as a penalty in addition to the standard wergild and by doing spiritual penance.

8   And as compensation for one in orders if a full breach of the peace occurs, the perpetrator must make amends for the seventh rank by paying seven pounds as a penalty in addition to the standard wergild and by doing spiritual penance.

9   And as compensation for one in orders if a partial violation occurs, the perpetrator must diligently make amends according to the deed.

9.1 And one part of the compensation for one in orders rightly shall go to the bishop, a second part to the altar, and a third part to the community.

10   A man sceal mid rihte dom æfter dæde and medemung be mæþe for Gode and for worulde.

11   And wise wæran worldwitan þe to godcundan rihtlagan þas laga setton folce for steore, and halidom and hadas for Godes lufan wurðodon and Godes hus and Godes þeowas deoplice griðedon.

10   One must always pass a judgment appropriate for the deed and set a penalty appropriate for the rank in both divine and secular affairs.

11   And wise were the councilors who added these laws to the ecclesiastical canons for the guidance of the people, and who venerated the sacraments and holy orders for the love of God, and greatly honored God's house and God's servants.

On Sanctuary

Be griðe and be munde

1   Godes grið is ealra griða selast to geearnianne and geor-nost to healdanne, and þær nehst, þæs cynges.

2   Ðonne is rihtlic þæt Godes cyricgrið binnan wagum and Cristenes cyninges handgrið stande efen unwemme.

3   And hwilum wæran heafodstedas and healice hadas micelre mæðe and munde wyrðe and griðian mihton þa þe þæs beðorfton and þærto sohtan, aa be ðære mæðe þe þærto gebyrede.

4   And þus hit stod on ðam dagum inne mid Englum ðæt gyf feorhscyldig man cyning gesohte, arcebiscop, oððon æþeling, þonne ahte he nigon nihta grið feore to gebeorge, butan him se cyng rumran fyrstes geunnan wolde.

5   And gyf he gesohte leodbiscop oððe ealdorman oððon healicne heafodstede, þonne ahte he vii nihta grið, butan man leng geunnan wolde.

6   And on Cantwara lage, cyning and arcebiscop agan ge-licne and efen dyrne mundbryce.

7   And on þam lagum is arcebiscopes feoh endlyfangylde and cynges is nigongylde.

On Sanctuary

Concerning Sanctuary and Protection

1   Of all forms of sanctuary, the sanctuary of God is the best to deserve and the most diligently to be held, and next to that, the king's.

2   Therefore, it is right that the sanctuary within the walls of God's church and the sanctuary received from the hand of a Christian king remain equally inviolable.

3   And it once was that capital cities and those of high rank were entitled to great privileges and could offer protection and sanctuary to those who needed it and sought it there, always in keeping with the privileges that belonged thereto.

4   And it so stood in those days among the English that if a condemned man sought the king, the archbishop, or a nobleman, then he had nine nights' sanctuary in which to save his life, unless the king wished to grant him more time.

5   And if he appealed to a suffragan bishop or an ealdorman or an important capital city, then he had sanctuary for seven nights, unless he was granted more.

6   And in the laws of the Kentish people, the king and archbishop are owed an equal and likewise costly penalty for the violation of their protection.

7   And according to those laws, elevenfold compensation is due for the archbishop's property and ninefold for the king's.

8   And Christes cyrican mundbyrd is efne swa cynges.

9   And on Suðengla lage, griðlagu þus stent: ðæt, gif hwa gefeohteð on cyrican oððon on cynges huse, þonne sy forworht eal þæt he age, and sy on cynges dome, hwæðer he lif age þe nage.

10   And gif hwa gefeohteð on mynstre butan cyrcean, gebete eall mid fulre bote þæt þærto gebyrige be mynstres mæðe.

11   And gyf hwa cynges mundbrice elles gewyrce, gebete þæt mid v pundum on Engla lage, arcebiscopes and æþelinges mundbrice mid þrim pundum; oðres biscpæs and ealdormannes mid ii pundum.

12   And gyf man beforan æðelinge oððe arcebiscpe gefeoht agynneð, mid CL scillinga gebete; gyf beforan oðran biscpe oððe ealdormen þis gelimpe, mid C scillingum gebete.

13   And on Norðengla lage stent þæt se ðe ofslehð man binnan cyricwagum, he bið feorhscyldig.

13.1   And se ðe gewundað, se bið handscyldig.

13.2   And se þe man ofslehð binnan cyricderum, sylle þære cyrican CXX scillinga be Norðengla lage.

14   And frigman se ðe cwicne on þære mundbyrde geyfelige, sylle xxx scillinga.

15   And se þe in cynges byrig oððon on his neaweste feohteð oððe steleð, he bið feorhscyldig, nimþe se cyng alyfan wille þæt man wergylde alysan mote.

8   And the penalty for violating the protection of Christ's church is that same as that for violating the protection of the king.

9   And according to southern English law, the law of sanctuary stands thus: if anyone fights in church or in the king's house, then he is to forfeit all that he owns, and it is the king's judgment whether he lives or dies.

10   And if anyone fights within the minster close outside a church, he is to compensate for all with the full penalty to which the church is entitled according to its status.

11   And if anyone otherwise violates the king's protection, he is to compensate for that with five pounds according to English law; violation of an archbishop's and nobleman's protection with three pounds; another bishop's and ealdorman's with two pounds.

12   And if anyone starts a fight in the presence of a nobleman or archbishop, he is to compensate with one hundred and fifty shillings; if this occurs in the presence of another bishop or ealdorman, he is to compensate with one hundred shillings.

13   And it stands in northern English law that anyone who slays a man within church walls is to be condemned to death.

13.1 And anyone who wounds shall lose his hand.

13.2 And anyone who slays a man within the church doors is to give to that church one hundred and twenty shillings according to northern English law.

14   And a freeman who injures a living person under protection is to give thirty shillings.

15   And anyone who fights or steals in the king's compound or in his vicinity is to be condemned to death, unless the king permits that he may be redeemed with his wergild.

16 And gyf forworht man friðstol gesece and þurh þæt
feorh geyrne, þonne sy þreora an for his feore, bute man bet
gearian wylle: wergyld, ece þeowet, hengenwitnuncg.

17 And beo þæra þreora swylc hit beo—gylde he, þeowige
he and þolige he—finde borh, gyf he mæge; and gyf he ne
mæge, þonne swerie he þæt he æfre ne stele ne feoh ne æt-
bere ne witnunge ne wrece.

18 And gyf he þyssa ænig aleoge, nahwar he eft his feorh
gefare ne geyrne.

19 Hælnesgrið and hadgrið healde man mid rihte æfre
swyþe georne, and Godes lagum fylge and lareowum hlyste,
swa þærto gebyrige.

19.1 Biscpas syndan bydelas and Godes lage lareowas and hy
scylan georne oft and gelome clypian to Christe, and for eal
Christen folc þingian geornlice, and hy scylan bodian and
bysnian georne godcunde ðearfe Christenre þeode.

20 Se þe oferhogie þæt he heom hlyste, hæbbe him
gemæne þæt wið God sylfne.

21 Ac sume men syndan, þe for heora prytan and eac for
gebyrdan, forhogiað þæt hy hyran godcundan ealdran, swa
swa hy sceoldan, gif hy riht woldan; and agynnað oft hyrwan
þæt hy scoldan herian, and taliað þe wyrsan for heanan gebyrdan þa ðe heora yldran on worolde ne wurdan welige ne
wlance þurh woroldglenge, ne on lænan liffæce rance ne
rice.

16 And if a condemned man seeks sanctuary and thereby saves his life, then unless greater mercy is shown, he is to receive one of three penalties in exchange for his life: wergild, perpetual enslavement, or punishment by hanging in bonds.

17 And whichever of these three it is—whether he pays, serves, or suffers—he is to arrange for security if he can; and if he cannot, then he is to swear that he will never commit robbery nor steal livestock nor avenge his punishment.

18 And if he breaks any of these oaths, he may not go anywhere in his life or take flight.

19 The security and ecclesiastical privileges of the sanctuary are always to be observed most assiduously according to the law, and God's laws are to be followed and teachers are to be heeded, as is appropriate to them.

19.1 Bishops are the messengers and teachers of God's law and they must fervently call to Christ often and frequently, and readily intervene on behalf of all Christian people, and they must preach and diligently set an example for the spiritual benefit of the Christian people.

20 Anyone who rejects what he hears from them must settle his dispute with God himself.

21 But there are some who, because of their pride and also their birth, refuse to heed their spiritual betters, just as they ought to do if they desired virtue; and they often begin to blame what they should praise, and judge those to be inferior because of their humble birth whose ancestors were not in this world either wealthy or made proud through their worldly finery, or in this transitory life prosperous or powerful.

21.1 Ac þa ne beoð na wise ne fullice gescade, þe Gode nel-laÞ hyran ne bet understandan hu oft he of lytlan aræerde to miclan þa þe him hyrdan and mid rihte gecwemdon.

21.2 We witan þæt, þurh Godes gyfe, þræl wearð to ðegene and ceorl wearð to eorle, sangere to sacerde and bocere to biscpe.

22 And hwilum wearð geworden, swa swa God wolde, sceaphyrde to cynge and se wearð swyþe mære; eac wearð geworden, swa swa God wolde, fiscere to bioscope, and se wæs swyþe dyre and Christe gecweme.

23 Swilce syndan Godes gyfa, þe eaþe mæg of lytlan aræran to miclan eall þæt he sylf wile, eal swa se sealmscop soðlice sæde þa ða he þus sang: *Quis sicut dominus Deus noster et reliqua, suscitans a terra inopem et de stercore erigens pauperem ut collocet eum cum principibus, cum principibus populi sui.*

23.1 Swylc understandað þa ðe Godes ege habbað and wis-domes gymað.

24 And wise eac wæron on geardagum woroldwitan þe ærest gesettan to godcundan rihtlagan woroldlaga biscpan and gehalgedan heapan, and haligdom and hadas for Godes lufan weorðedan, and Godes hus and Godes þeowas deop-lice griðedan.

25 And on hwam mæg huru æfre ænig man on worolde swyðor God wurðian þonne on cyrcan and on hælnessan, and eft on gehalgedan healican hadan?

26 And la, hwilcan geþance mæg ænig man æfre huruþinga þæt don, þæt he hine on cyrican georne gebiddæ and to Godes weofedan geornlice gebuge, and ær oððon æfter, inne

21.1 Indeed, they are neither wise nor entirely perceptive who will not obey God nor better understand how often he has raised from insignificance to greatness those who obeyed him and pleased him rightly.

21.2 We know that, through God's grace, a slave has become a thane and a commoner become a nobleman, a choir singer become a priest, and a scholar become a bishop.

22 And it once came to pass, just as God decreed, that a shepherd became a king and he was exceedingly great; it also came to pass, just as God decreed, a fisherman became a bishop, and he was greatly beloved and pleasing to Christ.

23 Such are the gifts of God, who can easily raise from insignificance to greatness all that he himself wishes, just as the psalmist truly said when he sang thus: *Who is as the Lord, etc., raising up the needy from the earth, and lifting up the poor out of the dunghill that he may place him with princes, with the princes of his people.*

23.1 This is understood by those who have a fear of God and heed wisdom.

24 And wise also were the councilors in former days who first added secular laws to the just ecclesiastical canons for bishops and holy assemblies, and venerated sanctity and the holy orders for the love of God, and steadfastly protected God's house and God's servants.

25 And indeed, where in the world can anyone ever worship God better than in churches and in sanctuaries, and in the high holy orders also?

26 And after all, how can anyone ever think that he may pray especially fervently in church and bow willingly to God's altars, but before or after, within or without, pillage

oððe ute, cyrican berype and wyrde oððe wanige þæt to cyrcan gebyrige?

27 Oððon hwilcan geþance mæg ænig man æfre geþencan on his mode þæt he to sacerdan heafod ahylde, and bletsunge gyrne, and heora mæssan on cyrcan gestande, and æt hlafgange heora hand cysse, and sona þær æfter hy hrædlice syððan scyrde oððe scynde mid worde oððe weorce?

28 Ac haligdom and hadas and gehalgode Godes hus a man sceal for Godes ege weorðian georne, and inwerdre heortan æfre God lufian.

29 And eac is mycel nydþearf manna gehwylcum, þæt he oðrum beode þæt riht, þæt he wille þæt man him beode, be þam þe his mæð sy.

30 Ealle we habbað ænne heofonlicne fæder and ane gastlice modor. Seo is *Ecclesia* genamod, þæt is Godes cyrice, and þy we syn gebroðra.

31 And þonne is rihtlic eac þæt ure ælce oðerne healde mid rihte, and þæt ælc cyrice sy æfre on Godes ealmihtiges griðe and on ealles Cristenes folces.

31.1 Forðam ælc cyricgrið is Cristes agen grið, and ælc Cristen man ah micle þearfe þæt he on ðam griðe mycle mæþe wite.

the church and destroy or damage that which belongs to the church?

27 Or by what stretch of the imagination can anyone ever think in his mind that he may bow his head to the priests, desire their blessings, attend their Masses in church, and kiss their hand during the procession with the host, yet then immediately thereafter injure or abuse them by word or deed?

28 But holiness and the holy orders and the hallowed house of God shall always be fervently venerated for fear of God, and God always be loved with one's innermost heart.

29 And it is also a great necessity for every person to offer others the justice he wishes to be given to him, just as is his due.

30 We all have one heavenly father and one spiritual mother. She is named *Ecclesia,* that is, God's Church; and therefore we are brothers.

31 And then it is also right that each of us treat one another with justice, and that every church be ever in the protection of God almighty and of all Christian people.

31.1 Therefore, every church sanctuary is Christ's own sanctuary, and every Christian has a fundamental responsibility to hold that sanctuary in great reverence.

Northumbrian Church Sanctuary

1   And on Norðhymbra lage is sanctus Petrus cyricfrið and sanctus Wilfriðus and sanctus Iohannes binnan cyric-wagum þreo hundred æt cwicum men, and æt deadum bot-leas.

2   And oðera stowa grið is læsse mærþe, aa be stowe mæþe.

3   And preoste cyricgangas syndan forbodene wifum and wæpnum.

4   And cyricgrið dyre æghwar be mæðe ofer ealle ðam rice.

Northumbrian Church Sanctuary

1   And according to the law of the Northumbrians, the compensation owed for a violation of Church sanctuary at Saint Peter's, Saint Wilfrid's, and within the walls of Saint John's is three hundred if the victim is alive, but it cannot be compensated for if he is dead.

2   And the sanctuary protection of other locations is less in scale, always according to the status of the site.

3   And a priest is forbidden from attending church with women or weapons.

4   And Church sanctuary is to be respected everywhere according to its degree over the entire kingdom.

The Oath of the King

1 *Promissio regis*

Ðis gewrit is gewriten stæf be stæfe be þam gewrite þe Dunstan arcebisceop sealde urum hlaforde æt Cingestune þa on dæg þa hine man halgode to cinge, and forbead him ælc wedd to syllanne butan þysan wedde, þe he up on Cristes weofod lede, swa se bisceop him dihte: "On þære Halgan Þrynnesse naman, ic þreo þing behate Cristenum folce and me underðeoddum: an ærest, þæt Godes cyrice and eall Cristen folc minra gewealda soðe sibbe healde; oðer is þæt ic reaflac and ealle unrihte þing eallum hadum forbeode; þridde, þæt ic behate and bebeode on eallum domum riht and mildheortnesse, þæt us eallum arfæst and mildheort God þurh þæt his ecean miltse forgyfe, se lifað and rixað." *FINIT.*

2 Se Cristena cyng þe þas þing gehealdeð he geearnað him sylfum woroldlicne weorðmynt, and him ece God ægðer gemiltsað ge on andwerdum life ge eac on þam ecean þe æfre ne ateorað. Gif he þonne þæt awægð þæt Gode wæs behaten, þonne sceal hit syððan wyrsian swyðe sona on his þeode, and eall hit on ende gehwyrfð on þæt wyrste, butan he on his liffæce ær hit gebete. Eala leof hlaford, beorh huruþinga georne þe sylfum! Geþenc þæt gelome þæt þu scealt þa heorde forð æt Godes dome ywan and lædan þe þu

34

The Oath of the King

This text is transcribed letter by letter from that which Archbishop Dunstan presented to our lord at Kingston on the day when he was consecrated as king, and he forbade him from making any promise except this promise, which he placed upon Christ's altar just as the bishop instructed him: "In the name of the Holy Trinity, I pledge three things to the Christian people and those subject to me: first, that God's Church and all the Christian people in my realm shall enjoy true peace; second, that I forbid theft and all unjust things to all classes of people; third, that I pledge and command there to be justice and mercy in all judgments, so that the good and merciful God who lives and rules may thereby grant all of us his eternal grace." *THE END*.

The Christian king who adheres to these things will win honor for himself in this world, and the eternal God will show mercy to him both in this present life and in that eternal life which will never end. Yet if he betrays that which was promised to God, then straightaway things will grow worse among his people, and in the end it will all come to the worst, unless he previously repents for it during his lifetime. Indeed, dear lord, at the very least, zealously protect yourself! Constantly bear in mind that at God's judgment you must bring forth and lead that flock to which you are chosen

eart to hyrde gescyft on þysum life, and þonne gecennan hu þu geheolde þæt Crist ær gebohte sylf mid his blode.

3   Gehalgodes cynges riht is þæt he nænigne man ne fordeme, and þæt he wuduwan and steopcild and ælþeodige werige, and amundige; and stala forebeode, and unrihthæmedu gebete, and siblegeru totwæme, and grundlunga forebeode wiccan and galdra adilige, mægmyrðran and manswaran of earde adrife; þearfan mid ælmyssan fede, and ealde and wise and syfre him to geþeahterum hæbbe, and rihtwise mæn him to wicnerum sette, for þan swa hwæt swa hig to unrihte gedoð þurh his aful, he his sceal ealles gescead agyldan on Domesdæg.

shepherd in this life, and then you will have to render an account of how you oversaw that which Christ himself previously purchased with his blood.

The duty of a consecrated king is to condemn no one unjustly, and to preserve and protect widows, orphans, and strangers; and to prohibit theft, curb illicit intercourse, separate those engaged in incest, ban wizards entirely, eliminate witchcraft, banish the slayers of kin and perjurers from this land; and to feed the poor with alms, take the old and wise and prudent as his advisors, and appoint virtuous men as his deputies, for whatsoever they do that is unjust at his instigation, he must render an account of all of it on Judgment Day. 3

The Institutes of Polity (1)

Be cinincge

Cristenum cyninge gebyrað swiðe rihte þæt he sy on fæder stæle Cristenra þeode and on ware and on wearde Cristes gespeliga, ealswa he geteald is. And him gebirað eac þæt he eallum his afole Cristendom lufige and hæðendom ascunige, and þæt he Godes cyrcan æghwar georne weorðige and werige, and eal Cristen folc sibbige and sehte mid rihtere lage, swa he geornost mæge. And þurh þæt he sceal geþeon Gode, þe he riht lufige and unriht ascunige.

2   And him gebyreð þæt he geornlice fylste þam, þe riht willan and a hetelice styre þam þe þwyres wyllan. He sceal mandæde men þreagean þearle mid woroldlicre steore, and he sceal ryperas and reaferas and woroldstruderas hatian and hynan, and eallum Godes feondum styrnlice wiðstandan. And ægðer he sceal beon mid rihte, ge milde ge reðe: milde þam godum and styrne þam yfelum. Ðæt bið cyninges riht and cynelic gewuna, and þæt sceal on þeode swyþost gefremian. La, þurh hwæt sceal Godes þeowum and Godes þearfum frið and fultum cuman butan þurh Crist and þurh Cristenne cyning? Ðurh cyninges wisdom folc wyrð gesælig, gesundful, and sigefæst. And þy sceal wis cyning Christendom and cynedom miclian and mærsian, and a he sceal

38

The Institutes of Polity (1)

Concerning the King

It most properly befits a Christian king to act as a father to a Christian people and to be Christ's representative in their protection and defense, just as he is required to be. And it befits him also to love the Christian faith with all his might and reject heathen practices, and to zealously honor and protect God's Church everywhere, and reconcile and bring peace to all Christian folk with just law, as readily as he can. And in that way he shall thrive before God if he embraces justice and rejects injustice.

And it is fitting for him to zealously aid those who seek justice and always fiercely restrain those who pursue wickedness. He must punish the evil severely with worldly discipline, and he must detest and destroy thieves, robbers, and desecrators of property, and harshly repel all of the enemies of God. And in the pursuit of justice he must be both merciful and severe: merciful to the good and strict with the evil. This is the king's duty and a royal practice, and it will achieve the most among the people. After all, how shall relief and comfort come to God's servants and God's poor except through Christ and a Christian king? Through a king's wisdom, the people will become happy, prosperous, and glorious. Accordingly, the wise king must extend and enlarge Christendom and his kingdom, and he must always resist

hæþendom hindrian and hyrwan. He sceal boclarum hlystan swyþe georne, and Godes beboda geornlice healdan, and ge-lome wið witan wisdom smeagan, gyf he Gode wile rihtlice hyran. And gif hwa to þam stræc sy ahwar on þeode þæt riht nelle healdan, swa swa he scolde, ac Godes lage wyrde oððe folclage myrre, þonne cyþe hit man þam cynge, gif man þæt nyde scyle; and he þonne sona ræde ymbe þa bote and gewylde hine georne to þam, þe his þearf sy, huru unþances, gif he elles ne mæge. And do, swa him þearf is: clænsige his þeode for Gode and for worolde gif he Godes miltse geearnian wylle.

3 *Be cinedome*

Eahta sweras syndon þe rihtlicne cynedom trumlice upwe-gað: soðfæstnes *(veritas)* and modþwærnes *(patientia)* and rumheortnes *(largitas)* and rædfæstnes *(persuasibilitas)* and egesfulnes *(correctio malorum)* and firðrungnes *(exultatio bono-rum)* and lihtengnes *(levitas tributi)* and rihtwisnes *(equitas iudicii)*. And seofon þing gedafeniað rihtwisum cyninge: An ærest, þæt he swiþe micelne Godes ege hæbbe *(deum timere);* and oðer, þæt he æfre rihtwisnesse lufige *(veritatem diligere);* and þridde, þæt he eadmod sy wið gode *(humilem in bonos);* and feorðe, þæt he stiðmod sy wið ifele *(superbum in malos);* and fifte, þæt he a symle þearfena helpe *(pauperes pascere);* and sixte, þæt he Godes circan forðige and friðige *(ecclesiam dei adiuvare et defendere);* and seofoðe, þæt he be freondum and fremdan fadige gelice on rihtlican dome *(inter propinquos et alienos similem esse in iusto iudicio)*.

4 Ælc cynestol stent on þrim stapelum, þe fullice ariht stent: an is *oratores;* and oðer is *laboratores;* and þridde is

and repress heathenism. He must study the learning found in books most attentively, and diligently heed God's commandments, and pursue wisdom with his council, if he wishes to obey God faithfully. And if anyone is so rebellious anywhere among the people that he will not obey the law as he should, but flouts the law of God or resists the law of the people, then it must be made known to the king if necessary; and then at once he will confer concerning the remedy and, as is his responsibility, zealously subdue him, indeed by force if he cannot do otherwise. And he must do what is necessary for him: purify his people before God and the world if he wishes to earn God's favor.

Concerning Kingship   3

There are eight columns that firmly uphold just kingship: honesty *(truth)*, patience *(patience)*, generosity *(largesse)*, reasonableness *(openness to counsel)*, fearsomeness *(correction of sins)*, virtuousness *(promotion of virtue)*, restraint *(reasonableness in taxation)*, and righteousness *(fairness in judgment)*. And there are seven things that are appropriate for a righteous king: first, that he have a very great fear of God *(fear God)*; second, that he love righteousness always *(value truth)*; third, that he be humble before the virtuous *(humble toward the good)*; fourth, that he be stalwart against evil *(severe against the wicked)*; fifth, that he always aid the needy *(help the poor)*; sixth, that he promote and protect God's *Church (support and defend God's Church)*; and seventh, that he rule in righteous judgment for both friend and stranger *(pass equal judgment for friend and stranger)*.

Each throne that stands fully as it should rests upon three   4
pillars: first, *those who pray;* second, *those who labor;* and third,

bellatores. Oratores syndon gebedmen þe Gode sculon þeowian and dæges and nihtes for ealne þeodscipe þingian
georne. *Laboratores* sindon weorcmen þe tilian sculon þæs þe
eal þeodscipe big sceal libban. *Bellatores* syndon wigmen þe
eard sculon werian wiglice mid wæpnum. On þisum þrim
stapelum sceal ælc cynestol standan mid rihte. And awacige
heora ænig, sona se stol scilfð; and forberste heora ænig
þonne rist se stol nyðer, and þæt wurð þare þeode eal to unþearfe. Ac staðelige man and strangige and trimme hi georne
mid wislicre Godes lage; þæt wurð þam þeodscipe to langsuman ræde. Forðam soð is þæt ic secge: awacige se Cristendom, sona scylfð se cynedom; and aræge man unlaga ahwar
on lande oððe unsida ahwar to swiðe, þæt cymð þare þeode
eal to unþearfe. Ac do man swa hit þearf is: alecge man unriht and aræge up Godes riht; þæt mæg to þearfe for Gode
and for worlde. Amen.

5   *De episcopis*

*Paulus dicit: "Oportet enim episcopum inreprehensibilem esse," et
reliqua.* Biscopum gebiriað ealdlice wisan, and wisdom and
wærscipe on wordum and on weorcum, and geþincða on
ðeawum, buton ofermettum. Ne gerisað heom prita, ne
idela rænca, ne micele ofermetta, ne ræde weametta, ne
ænige higeliste wordes ne weorces. Ac þæt him bið weorðlic,
þæt hi a habban arwurðe wisan on eallum heora þeawum,
and beþencan heora dæda wislice and wærlice, þæt hi aðor
ne beon ne wordes ne weorces ne ealles to ræde ne to
swiðlæte, ac swa hit gerise. Forðam soð is þæt ic secge,
gelife, se þe wille: heardlic eornost and wislic wærscipe and

those who fight. Those who pray are the clergy who must serve God and fervently plead for all the people day and night. *Those who labor* are the workers who must toil for that by which the entire community may live. *Those who fight* are the warriors who must protect the land by waging war with weapons. On these three pillars must each throne rightly stand. If any of them weaken, immediately the throne will tremble; and if any of them fail, then the throne will crumble to pieces, and that will bring the people entirely to ruin. Therefore, they are to be diligently steadied, strengthened, and reinforced with God's wise law; in that way they will bring lasting guidance to the people. For what I say is true: if the Christian faith weakens, the kingdom will soon fall; and if injustice is exalted anywhere in the land or evil customs anywhere too eagerly, then the people will be brought entirely to ruin. Instead, one must do what is needed: suppress injustice and exalt the law of God; that may be to our benefit before God and the world. Amen.

Concerning Bishops   5

Paul says, "It behoveth therefore a bishop to be blameless," etc. It befits bishops to have a venerable bearing, and wisdom and prudence in words and deeds, and nobility in their conduct, without arrogance. Nor is pride appropriate for them, nor idle vanity, nor great conceit, nor a quick temper, nor any heedlessness in word or deed. But they are to be honorable, and always have a respectable bearing in all their doings, and reflect upon their deeds wisely and prudently, so that they never be all too quick nor too careless in word or deed, but act as is appropriate. For what I say is true, believe it who will: it is much more worthy for each wise man to have bold

stedefæst modstaðol mid micclum geþilde and anfeald wise
on fullan gerade bið witena gehwilcum weorðlicre micele,
þonne he his wisan for ænigum þingum fagige to swiðe. And
huru ne geriseð biscopum æfre, ne æt ham ne on siðe, to
higeleas wise, ac wisdom and weorðscipe gedafenað heora
hade, and gedrihða gerisað þam þe heom filiað.

6 *Item*

Byscopas sculon bocum and gebedum filigan, and dæges and
nihtes, oft and gelome, clipian to Criste and for eal Cristen
folc þingian georne. And hi sculon leornian and rihtlice
læran, and ymbe folces dæda geornlice smeagan. And hig
sculon bodian and bisnian georne godcunde þearfe Cristenre þeode. And ne sculon hi ænig unriht willes geþafian, ac
to ælcan rihte geornlice filstan. Hi sculon Godes ege habban
on gemynde and ne eargian for worldege ealles to swiðe. Ac
bodian hi symle Godes riht georne and unriht forbeodan,
gime se þe wille; forðam wace bið se hirda funden to heorde
þe nele þa heorde þe he healdan sceal—mid clipunge be-
werigan buton he elles mæge—gif þar hwilc þeodscaða
scaðian onginneð. Nis nan swa yfel scaða swa is deofol silf.
He bið aa ymbe þæt an: hu he on manna sawlum mæst ge-
scaðian mæge. Þonne motan þa hyrdas beon swiðe wacole
and geornlice clipigende, þe wið þone þeodscaðan folce sculon scyldan. Ðæt sindon biscopas and mæssepreostas þe
godcunde heorde gewarian and bewerian sculon mid wislican laran, þæt se wodfræca wulf to swiðe ne slite ne to fela

zeal, wise prudence, steadfast firmness of mind with great patience, and a resolute disposition in full reason than to alter his manner all too frequently for any cause. And indeed it is never appropriate for bishops, either at home or abroad, to behave immaturely, but wisdom and honor are proper for their rank, and sober conduct befits those who accompany them.

Furthermore   6

Bishops must keep to their books and prayers, and day and night, often and frequently, call upon Christ and fervently intercede for all Christian people. And they must learn and teach rightly, and conscientiously watch over the deeds of the people. And they must preach and sincerely exemplify the spiritual commission to a Christian people. And they must not knowingly permit any injustice, but readily promote all that is just. They must hold the fear of God in their mind and not grow all too timid for fear of the world. But let him who will take heed always be sure to zealously proclaim the law of God and forbid injustice; for the shepherd will be judged weak for the flock who will not defend the flock that he must protect—by calling out if he can do nothing else—if any corruptor of the people begins to pillage there. There is no corruptor so evil as the devil himself. He is always concerned with one thing: how he might most defile the souls of men. Therefore, those shepherds who would protect the people against the corruptor must be most watchful and vigorous in their warnings. Those are the bishops and the priests who must protect and oversee their spiritual flock with wise teaching, so that the ravenous wolf does not

ne abite of godcundre heorde. And se ðe oferhogige, þæt he
heom hliste, habbe him gemæne þæt wiþ God silfne.

7   Eala, fela is swaþeah þara þe hwonlice gimað and lithwon
reccað ymbe boca beboda oððe biscpa lare; and eac ymbe
bletsunga oððe unbletsunga leohtlice lætað, and na ne understandað, swa swa hi scoldon hwæt Crist on his godspelle
swutollice sæde, þa þa he þus cwæð: *Qui nos audit et reliqua.
Et iterum: Quodcumque ligaveritis. Alibi etiam scriptum est:
Quodcumque benedixeritis. Et psalmista terribiliter loquitur dicens: Qui noluit benedictionem, prolongabitur ab eo.*

8 *Be eorlum*

Eorlas and heretogan and þas worlddeman and eac swa gerefan agan neodþearfe þæt hi riht lufian for Gode and for
worlde; and nahwar þurh undom for feo, ne for freondscipe,
forgiman heora wisdom, swa þæt hi wændan unriht to rihte
oððe undom deman earmon to hynðe. Ac a hi sculon circan
ofer ealle oðre þingc weorðian and werian, and wuduwan
and steopcild hi sculon retan and þearfena helpan and þeowetlingan beorgan, gif hi Godes willan rihte willað wyrcan.
And þeofas and þeodscaðan hi sculon hatigan, and riperas
and reaferas hi sculon hynan, buton hi geswican. And symle
hi sculon a unriht swiðe ascunian. Forþam soð is þæt ic
secge, gelife se ðe wille: wa ðam þe woh dryfð, buton he geswice! Witod he sceal drefan dymne and deopne hellewites
grund, helpes bedæled. Ac to lyt is þara nu ða, þe þæt understand swa swa man scolde. Ac do freonda gehwilc ealswa hit
þearf is: warnige hine silfne and beorge him georne þæt he

wound too greatly nor devour too many of their spiritual flock. And let anyone who disdains to listen to them settle that with God himself.

Sadly, nonetheless there are many of those who lightly re- 7 gard and little heed the precepts of the books or the teachings of the bishops; and also frivolously ignore blessings or curses, and do not understand as they should what Christ in his Gospel clearly said when he spoke thus: *He that heareth, etc. And likewise: Whatsoever thou shalt bind, etc. Elsewhere too it is written:* Whatever *you have blessed. And the psalmist, speaking chillingly, says: he would not have blessing, and it shall be far from him.*

Concerning Nobles 8

Nobles, generals, secular judges, and also reeves are obliged to embrace justice before God and the world; and never through foolishness arising from bribery nor out of friendship, neglect their wisdom so that they twist injustice into justice or pronounce unjust rulings harmful to the poor. But they must always venerate and protect the Church over all other things, and they must console widows and orphans, aid the poor, and defend helpless slaves, if they wish to fulfill God's will rightly. They must abhor thieves and villains, and they must suppress robbers and criminals, unless they cease their crimes. And they must always greatly detest injustice. For it is the truth that I speak, believe it who will: woe unto that person who pursues injustice, unless he turn aside! He will certainly sink, bereft of help, into hell's dark and deep abyss. Too few, however, are those now who understand that as one should. But each friend shall do as is most necessary: warn and protect himself thoroughly so as not to anger God

Gode ne abelge ealles to swiðe, ac cweme his Drihtene mid rihtlicre dæde.

9 *Be sacerdum*

Riht is þæt sacerdas on heora scriftscirum willice and wærlice læran and lædan þa godcundan heorda þe hig healdan sculon. And ægðer hi sculon, ge wel bodian ge wel bisnian, and Godes circan geornlice lufian and for eal Cristen folc geornlice gebiddan.

10 *Be gehadedum mannum*

Eallum Cristenum mannum is micel þearf þæt hi riht lufian and unriht ascunian. And huru gehadedum is þæs mæst þearf þe ægðer sculon ge wel bodian ge wel bisnian oðrum mannum. Mannum gebireð ælc clænnes, forðam þe hi sculon eallum oðrum mannum ælce unclænnesse forbeodan, gif hi riht doð. And ælce clænnesse hi sculan be heom silfum gebisnian. Þonne is hit swiðe egeslic þæt þa þe scoldan eallum Cristenum mannum riht bodian and eac wel bisnian, þæt hi syn sume wordene bysen to forwirde swiðor þonne to ðearfe. Þæt sindon þa æwbrycan þe þurh healicne had ciricæwe underfengon and þæt siððan abræcan. Nis nanum weofodþegne alifed þæt he wifian mote; ac is ælcum forboden. Nu is þeah þara ealles to fela, þe þone æwbryce wyrcað and geworht habbað, ac ic bidde for Godes lufan and eac eornostlice beode, þæt man ðæs geswice. Læwedum men is ælc wif forboden, buton his rihtæwe; and gehadode syndon sume swa þurh deofol beswicene þæt hi wifiað on unriht and forwyrcað hi silfe þurh þone æwbrece, þe hig on wuniað. Ac ic bidde georne þæt man þæs geswice. Cirice is sacerdos

all too greatly, but instead please his Lord with righteous deeds.

Concerning Priests 9

It is right that priests in their parishes willingly and sensibly lead and instruct the spiritual flock which they are to protect. They must both preach well and set a good example, and zealously exalt God's Church and diligently pray for all Christian people.

Concerning Those in Orders 10

There is a great need for all Christians to embrace justice and reject injustice. And indeed, for those in orders it is the greatest necessity that they both preach well and set a good example for others. All forms of purity are appropriate for people in orders, for they must forbid all forms of impurity to others, if they are to do what is right. And they must themselves become an example of every form of purity. Accordingly, it is exceedingly dreadful that of those who must preach righteousness to all Christians and also set a good example, some have become an example of damnation rather than duty: that is, those adulterers who accepted marriage to the Church through their holy orders and later violated it. No clergyman who serves at the altar is permitted to have a wife; rather, it is forbidden to all. Now, however, there are all too many who commit adultery or have committed it, yet for the love of God, I command and solemnly decree that this is to cease. To a layman is every woman forbidden save his lawful spouse; and there are some in orders so deceived by the devil that they take a wife unlawfully and destroy themselves through the adultery in which they abide. But I urgently command that they cease. The priest's wife is the

æwe. Nah he mid rihte ænige oðre; forðam ne gebirað sacerdan nan ðingc, naðor ne to wife ne to worldwige, gif hi Gode
willað rihtlice hiran and Godes laga healdan, swa swa heora
hade gedafenað mid rihte.

11 *Be abbodum*

Riht is þæt abbodas and huru abbatissan fæste on mynstrum
singallice wunigan and georne heora heorde simle begiman,
and aa heom wel bisnian and rihtlice bodian; and næfre
ymbe woroldcara ne idele wlænca ne prita ne carian to
swiðe, ac oftost hi abisgian mid godcundan neodan. Swa gebireð abbodan and munuchades mannum.

12 *Be munecum*

Riht is þæt munecas dæges and nihtes inweardre heortan a
to Gode þencan and geornlice clypian and mid eallum eadmedum regollice libban. Filigan heora bocum and gebedum
georne and æghwilce wlænce and idele rænce and sindrige
æhta and unnytte dæda and untidspræca forhogian mid
ealle. Swa gebyreð munecan.

13 *Be minecenan*

Riht is þæt mynicena mynsterlice macian, efne swa we cwædon æror be munecum, and næfre wið worldmen ænigne gemanan worldlicre cyððe habban to swiðe.

14 *Be preostum and be nunnan*

Ryht is þæt preostas and efen wel nunnan regollice libban
and clænnesse healdan be þam þe hi willan on mynstran

Church. By right he has no other; for neither a wife nor the warfare of this world are fitting for a priest in any way, if he wishes to obey God properly and heed God's law in a manner appropriate to his status.

Concerning Abbots 11

It is right that abbots and, in particular, abbesses remain perpetually secure in their monasteries and always conscientiously oversee their flocks, and ever set a good example for them and preach rightly; and they are never to be concerned too greatly with worldly cares or idle vanity or pride, but they are to occupy themselves most often with spiritual needs. This is fitting for abbots and monastics.

Concerning Monks 12

It is right that monks always reflect upon God in their innermost heart by day and night and sincerely pray and live according to their rule with all humility. They are to adhere diligently to their books and prayers and to entirely reject all arrogance, idle vanity, private property, frivolous deeds, and foolish speech. Thus it is fitting for monks.

Concerning Women Monastics 13

It is right that women in orders act in a monastic fashion, even as we have said before about monks, and never too greatly have any interaction of a secular nature with people of the world.

Concerning Priests and Nuns 14

It is right that priests and likewise nuns also live according to their rule and preserve their chastity if they desire to live

gewunian oððe for worlde weorðscipes wealdan. Gehado-
dum mannum gebireð ælc clænnes, forðam þe hy sculon eallum oðrum mannum ælce unclænnesse forbeodan, and ælce
clænnesse, gif hi riht doð, hi sculon be heom silfum geornost
gebisnian.

15 Be læwedum mannum

Riht is þæt gehadode men þam læwedum wissian hu hi
heora æwe rihtost sculon healdan. Ðæt bið rihtlic lif þæt
cniht þurhwunige on hys cnihthade oððæt he on rihtre
mædenæwe gewifige and habbe þa siððan and nænige oðre
þa hwile seo libbe. Gif hire þonne forðsið getimige, þonne is
rihtast, þæt he þanonforð wuduwa þurhwunige. Þeah be
þæs apostoles leafe, læwede man mot for neode oðre siðe
wifian. And þeah læwedum mannum wif sy alifed, þeah hi
agon þearfe þæt hi understandan hu hit is alifed. Nagan
læwede men freolstidum ne fæstentidum þurh hæmedþingc
wifes gemanan, þe ma þe heahhades menn þæt þing agon
ænigum timan.

16 Be wudewan

Riht is þæt wuduwan Annan bysene georne filigan: seo wæs
on temple dæges and nihtes þeowigende georne. Heo fæste
swiðe þearle and gebedum filigde and geomrigendum mode
cliopode to Criste and ælmessan dælde oft and gelome; and
aa Gode cwemde þæs þe heo mihte wordes and dæda; and
hæfð nu to leane heofonlice mirhðe. Swa sceal god wuduwe
hiran hyre Drihtene.

in a monastery or earn respect in the world. All forms of purity are appropriate for those in orders, for they must forbid all forms of impurity to others, and if they are to do what is right, they must themselves most zealously become an example of every form of purity.

Concerning Laymen   15

It is right that men in orders instruct the laity how they should best keep their marital vows. That life is virtuous in which a young man remains chaste until he weds a maiden properly, and afterward has her and no other for as long as she lives. Then, if her death occurs, it is most appropriate, that he remain a widower thenceforth. By the Apostle's consent, though, a layman can marry a second time if necessary. And though a wife is permitted to laymen, it is still necessary that they understand how it is permitted. On feasts and in fasting times, laymen may not consort with their wives in sexual activity, any more than those in orders may do that thing at any time.

Concerning the Widow   16

It is right that widows readily abide by the example of Anna: she remained in the temple day and night in heartfelt service. She fasted very rigorously, kept to her prayers, called on Christ with a sorrowful spirit, and handed out alms very frequently; and she always pleased God as much as she could with words and deeds; and now as a reward, she has heavenly bliss. In this way shall a good widow heed her Lord.

17 *Be circan*

Riht is þæt Cristene men Cristendom georne healdan mid rihte and Cristes cirican æghwar geornlice wurðian and werian. Ealle we habbað ænne heofonlicne fæder and ane gastlice modor. Seo is *Ecclesia* genamod, þæt is Godes cirice, and þa we sculon æfre lufian and wurðian. And riht is, þæt ælc cirice sy on Godes griðe and on ealles Cristenes folces; and þæt ciricgrið stande æghwar binnon wagum and gehalgodes cyninges handgrið efenunwæmme. Forðam ælc ciricgrið is Cristes agen grið, and ælc Cristen man ah micele þearfe þæt he on ðam griðe micele mæðe wite. Forðam ælces Cristenes mannes nydþearf is, þæt he Godes cirican lufige and wurðige and hi gelomlice and geornlice sece him silfum to þearfe. And huru gehadode þar sculon oftost þeowian and þenian and for eal Cristen folc þingian georne. Ðonne agan weofodþegnas to smeagenne symle, þæt hi huruþinga heora lif fadian swa swa to circan gebirige mid rihte.

18   Cirice is mid rihte sacerdes æwe, and se þe to circan wurðe gehadod, nage hine ænig man, þe Godes lage recce, þanan to donne, buton he hi mid heafodgilte fullice forwyrce. And þonne sceal Cristes scirgerefa þæt witan and ymbe þæt dihtan and deman, swa swa bec tæcan. Ne scolde man æfre circan derian ne ænig woh beodan on ænige wisan. Ac nu sindon þeah circan wide and side wace gegriðode and ifele geþeowode, clæne beripte ealra gerihta and innan bestrypte ælcera gerisena. And ciricþenas sindon mæðe and munde wel gehwar bedælede. And wa ðam þe þæs wealt,

Concerning the Church   17

It is right that Christians fervently adhere rightly to the Christian faith and readily honor and uphold the Christian Church everywhere. We all have one heavenly father and one spiritual mother. She is named *Ecclesia,* that is, God's Church, which we must always love and respect. And it is right that each church be under the protection of God and of all Christian people; and that Church sanctuary is to prevail within the walls and is to be honored no differently from protection from the king's own hand. Thus, every Church sanctuary is Christ's own sanctuary, and every Christian has a great obligation to treat that sanctuary with great respect. Further, it is the responsibility of every Christian to love and honor God's Church, and he is to seek it out often and willingly for his own benefit. Those in orders also must serve and minister there most often and intercede readily for all Christian people. Accordingly, clergy who serve at the altar must always ensure that they especially set their lives in order in a manner rightly fitting to the Church.

The Church is properly the spouse of the priest, and no 18 person who heeds God's law ought to remove from the Church someone who has taken orders in it, lest he utterly perish in mortal sin. And then must Christ's representative take notice of that and resolve and judge it just as the books instruct. No one must ever damage a church or threaten it with wrongdoing in any way. Yet nonetheless, churches far and wide are now weakly protected and oppressed by evil and entirely deprived of ancient rights and stripped inside of everything proper. Moreover, the Church's servants are everywhere deprived of honor and protection. And woe

þeah he swa ne wene, forðam ælc þara bið witodlice Godes
silfes feond, þe bið Godes ciricena feond and þe Godes ciricena rihta gewanað oððe wyrdeð; ealswa hit awriten is:
Inimicus enim Christi efficitur omnis, qui ecclesiasticas res usur-
pare iniuste conatur, et reliqua. And egeslice spræc sanctus
Gregorius be þam eac, þa ða he þus cwæð: *Si quis ecclesiam*
Christi denudauerit uel sanctimonia uiolauerit, anathema sit. Ad
quod respondentes omnes dixerunt: Amen. Micel is neodþearf
manna gehwilcum, þæt he wið ðas þingc beorge hym georne;
and æghwilc Godes freond warnige hine simle, þæt he
Cristes bride to swiðe ne misbeode. Ealle we sculon ænne
God lufian and wurðian and ænne Cristendom georne healdan and ælcne hæðendom mid ealle awurpan.

19   *Be eallum Cristenum mannum*

Riht is þæt ealle Cristene men heora Cristendom rihtlice
healdan and þam life libban þe heom to gebyreð æfter
Godes rihte and æfter woroldgerisenum; and ealle heora
wisan be þam þingan geornlice fadian þe ða hi wisian þe hi
wislice and wærlice wisian cunnan. And þæt is þonne ærest
ræda firmest: þæt manna gehwilc ofer ealle oðre þingc ænne
God lufige and ænne geleafan anrædlice habbe on þone þe
us ealle ærest geworhte and mid deorwurðan ceape eft us gebohte. And eac we agan þearfe þæt we geornlice smeagan hu
we symle magon Godes agene beboda rihtlicost healdan and
eal þæt gelæstan þæt þæt we behetan þa we fulluht underfengon oððe þa ðe æt fulluhte ure foresprecan wæron. Þæt
is þonne ærest: þæt þæt man behateð þonne man fulluhtes
girneð þæt man aa wille deofol ascunian and his unlara
georne forbugan and ealle his unlaga symle awurpan and

unto him who causes this, even if he does not realize it, for each of those who is the enemy of God's churches and who weakens or violates the rights of God's churches is assuredly the enemy of God himself; as it is written: *For anyone becomes the enemy of Christ who attempts to wrongly make use of the goods of the Church, etc.* And Saint Gregory spoke fearsomely about this also, when he said thus: *Whoever plunders the Church of Christ or violates its sanctity is to be anathema. Responding to which, all said: Amen.* Everyone has a great duty to defend himself vigorously against these things; and each friend of God is to always watch over himself, so that he not mistreat the bride of Christ too greatly. We all must love and praise one God and diligently adhere to one Christian faith and reject every heathen practice with all our might.

Concerning All Christian People

It is right that all Christian people properly uphold their Christian faith and live the life appropriate to them according to the law of God and the customs of the world; and diligently arrange all manner of things according to the guidance of those who can advise them wisely and truly. And this, then, is the most important of precepts: that each person love the one God over all other things and resolutely have one faith in him who first created us all and purchased us again at a dear price. And we also have need to reflect sincerely how we can always keep God's own commandments most rightly and perform all that we—or those who were our sponsors—promised when we received baptism. This, then, is first: that one promises when one seeks baptism to always spurn the devil and zealously avoid his evil teachings and always reject his injustice and eternally resist all of his

ecelice wiðsacan ealles his gemanan; and manysiþes sona
þaræfter mid rihtan geleafan soðlice swutelað þæt man
þanonforð aa wile on ende God æfre lufian and ofer ealle
oðre ðingc hine a lufian and æfre his larum geornlice filigan
and his agene beboda rihtlice healdan. And ðonne bið ðæt
fulluht, swilce hit wed sy ealra þara worda and ealles þæs behates, gehealde se ðe wille. And englas beweardiað þanonforð æfre manna gehwilcne, hu he gelæste æfter his fulluhte,
þæt þæt man behet ær, þa man fulluhtes girnde.

20   Uton þæt geþencan oft and gelome, and georne gelæstan
þæt þæt we beheton þa we fulluht underfengon, ealswa us
þearf is. And uton word and weorc rihtlice fadian and ure
ingeþanc clænsian georne and að and wed wærlice healdan
and gelome understandan þone micclan dom, þe we ealle to
sculon; and beorgan us georne wið ðone weallendan bryne
hellewites, and geearnian us þa mærða and þa mirhða, þe
God hæfð gegearwod þam ðe his willan on worlde gewurcað.

company; and swiftly thereafter sincerely proclaim many times with true faith that one thenceforth will always love one God forever, always love him over all other things, zealously heed his teachings forever, and keep his own commandments properly. And then that baptism will become like a covenant of all those words and all those promises, fulfill it who will. Thenceforth, angels will oversee every man forever after his baptism, how he fulfills what he earlier promised when he sought baptism.

Let us reflect upon that repeatedly and sincerely abide by that which we promised when we received baptism, just as is our obligation. And let us order our words and deeds rightly, fervently cleanse our inmost thoughts, truly keep our oath and pledge, and frequently reflect on the great judgment to which we all must go; and zealously shield ourselves against the swelling flame of hellish torments, and earn for ourselves the glories and happiness which God has prepared for those who work his will in the world.

The Institutes of Polity (2)

1 *Be heofonlicum cyninge*

In nomine domini. An is ece cyning, wealdend, and wyrhta ealra gesceafta. He is on riht cyning and cyninga wuldor, and ealra cyninga betst þe æfre gewurde oððe geweorðe. Him symble sy lof and wuldor and ece wyrðmynt a to worulde. Amen.

2 *Be eorðlicum cyninge*

Cristenum cyninge gebyreð on Cristenre þeode þæt he sy, ealswa hit riht is, folces frofer and rihtwis hyrde ofer Cristene heorde. And him gebyreþ þæt he eallum mægne Cristendom rære and Godes cyrican æghwær georne fyrðrie and friðie. And eall Cristen folc sibbie and sehte mid rihtre lage, swa he geornost mæge; and ðurh ælc þing rihtwisnesse lufie for Gode and for worulde. Forðam þurh þæt he sceall sylf fyrmest geþeon and his þeodscipe eac swa þe he riht lufie for Gode and for worulde. And him gebyreð þæt he geornlice fylste þam ðe riht willan and a hetelice styre þam ðe þwyres willan. He sceal mandæde menn þreagan þearle mid woruldlicre steore, and he sceal ryperas and reaferas and ðas woruldstruderas hatian and hynan, and eallum Godes feondum styrnlice wiðstandan. And ægðer he sceal beon mid rihte, ge milde ge reþe: milde þam godum and

The Institutes of Polity (2)

Concerning the Heavenly King

In the name of the Lord. One is the eternal king, ruler, and maker of all creation. By right, he is the king and the glory of kings, and the greatest of all kings who ever were or will be. For him let there always be praise and glory and eternal veneration forever and ever. Amen.

Concerning the Earthly King

It befits the Christian king of a Christian people to be, as is proper, a comfort to his people and a just shepherd over a Christian flock. And it is fitting for him to promote Christianity with all his might and everywhere zealously honor and protect God's Church. He shall reconcile and bring peace to all Christian folk with just law, as readily as he can; and in every way he shall embrace righteousness before God and the world. For in this way, he shall himself thrive first and his people likewise if he embraces justice before God and the world. And it is fitting for him to zealously aid those who seek justice and always fiercely restrain those who pursue wickedness. He must punish evil men severely with worldly discipline, and he must detest and destroy thieves, robbers, and desecrators of property, and harshly repel all of the enemies of God. And in the pursuit of justice he must be both merciful and severe: merciful to the good and strict

styrne þam yfelum. Ðæt bið cynincges riht and cynelic gewuna, and þæt sceal on þeode swyðost gefremian.

3   La, þurh hwæt sceal Godes þeowum and Godes þearfum frið and fultum cuman butan þurh Crist and þurh Cristenne cyning? Þurh unwisne cyning, folc wyrð geyrmed for oft, næs æne, for his misræde. Þurh cynincges wisdom folc wyrð gesælig and gesundful and sigefæst. And ðy sceal wis cyning Cristendom and cynedom miclian and mærsian, and a he sceal hæþendom hindrian and hyrwan.

4   He sceal boclarum hlystan swyðe georne, and Godes be-boda geornlice healdan, and gelome wið witan wisdom smeagan, gif he Gode wile rihtlice hyran. And gif hwa to þam strec sy ahwær on þeode þæt riht nelle healdan swa swa he sceolde, ac Godes lage wyrde oððe folclage myrre, þonne cyðe hit man þam cyninge, gif man þæt nyde scyle; and he þonne sona ræde embe þa bote and gewylde hine geornlice to ðam, þe his þearf sy, huru unþances, gif he elles ne mæge. And do, swa him þearf is: clænsige his þeode for Gode and for worulde gif he Godes mildse geearnian wille, and smeage gelome hwæt him sy to donne and hwæt to forganne after Godes rihte. And þanan him sceal swyðost æfre arisan word and weorðscipe, ægðer ge on life ge æfter life, þæt he Godes riht lufie and unriht ascunie and godcunde lare georne gehyre oft and gelome him sylfum to þearfe. Forþam sona unstrangað se þe lytel hafað lichamlices fostres, and se ðe seldan hafað gastlicne foster sona hit his sawle derað swiðe þearle; ac se byð gesælig þe godcunde lare oftost gehyreð and geornlicast healdeþ.

with the evil. This is the king's justice and a royal practice, and it will achieve the most among the people.

Indeed, how shall relief and comfort come to God's servants and God's poor except through Christ and a Christian king? Through an unwise king, the people will become miserable—not once, but very often!—because of his foolish counsel. Through a king's wisdom, the people will become happy, prosperous, and glorious. Accordingly, the wise king must extend and enlarge Christendom and his kingdom, and he must always resist and repress heathenism.

He must study the learning found in books most attentively, and diligently heed God's commandments, and pursue wisdom with his council, if he wishes to obey God faithfully. And if anyone is so rebellious anywhere among the people that he will not obey the law as he should, but flouts the law of God or resists the law of the people, then it must be made known to the king if necessary; and then at once he will confer concerning the remedy and, as is his responsibility, zealously subdue him, indeed by force if he cannot do otherwise. And he must do what is necessary for him: purify his people before God and the world if he wishes to earn God's favor, and frequently reflect on what he must do and what avoid according to God's law. And his name and reputation will ever increase both in this life and in the afterlife, just as long as he embraces God's justice, rejects injustice, and diligently heeds divine teaching often and frequently, as he himself requires. For he who takes too little bodily nourishment swiftly becomes feeble, and he who seldom takes spiritual nourishment will soon do great injury to his soul; but he is happy who most often heeds and most zealously obeys divine teachings.

5 *Be cynedome*

Eahta sweras syndon þe rihtlicne cynedom trumlice upwe-
gað: soðfæstnys, modþwærnes, rumheortnes, rædfæstnes,
(veritas, patientia, largitas, persuasibilitas), egesfulnes, fyrð-
ringnes, lihtingnes, rihtwisnes, *(correctio malorum, exultatio
bonorum, levitas tributi, equitas iudicii)*. And seofon þing gedafeniað rihtwisum cyninge: an ærest, þæt he swyðe micelne
Godes ege hæbbe; and oðer, þæt he æfre rihtwisnesse lufige;
and ðridde, þæt he eadmod sy wið gode; and feorðe, þæt he
stiðmod sy wið yfele; and fifte, þæt he Godes þearfum fre-
frige and fede; and syxte, þæt he Godes cyrcan fyrðrige and
friðige; and seofoðe, þæt he be freondan and be fremdan
fadige gelice on rihtlican dome.

6 *Be cynestole*

Ælc riht cynestol stent on þrym stapelum, þe fullice ariht
stent. An is *oratores;* and oðer is *laboratores;* and ðridde is *bellatores. Oratores* sindon gebedmen þe Gode sculan þeowian
and dæges and nihtes for ealne þeodscipe þingian georne.
Laboratores sindon weorcmen þe tilian sculon þæs ðe eall
þeodscype big sceall libban. *Bellatores* syndon wigmen þe
eard sculon werian wiglice mid wæpnum. On þyssum ðrym
stapelum sceall ælc cynestol standan mid rihte on Cristenre
þeode. And awacie heora ænig, sona se stol scylfð; and ful-
berste heora ænig, þonne hrysð se stol nyðer, and þæt wyrð
þære þeode eall to unþearfe. Ac staþelige man and strangie
and trumme hi georne mid wislicre Godes lare and mid rihtlicre woruldlage; þæt wyrð þam þeodscype to langsuman

Concerning Kingship 5

There are eight columns that firmly uphold just kingship: honesty, patience, generosity, reasonableness *(truth, patience, largesse, openness to counsel)*, fearsomeness, virtuousness, restraint, righteousness *(correction of sins, promotion of virtue, reasonableness in taxation, fairness in judgment)*. And seven things are appropriate for a righteous king: first, that he have a very great fear of God; second, that he love righteousness always; third, that he be humble before the virtuous; fourth, that he be stalwart against evil; fifth, that he comfort and feed God's poor; sixth, that he promote and protect God's Church; and seventh, that he rule in righteous judgment for both friend and stranger.

Concerning the Throne 6

Each just throne that stands fully as it should rests upon three pillars: first, *those who pray;* second, *those who labor;* and third, *those who fight. Those who pray* are the clergy, who must serve God and fervently plead for all the people day and night. *Those who labor* are the workers who must toil for that by which the entire community may live. *Those who fight* are the warriors who must protect the land by waging war with weapons. On these three pillars must each throne rightly stand in a Christian polity. If any of them weaken, immediately the throne will tremble; and if any of them fail, then the throne will crumble to pieces, and that will bring the people entirely to ruin. Therefore, they are to be diligently steadied, strengthened, and reinforced with God's wise teachings and with just worldly law; in that way they will bring lasting guidance to the people. And what I say is true:

ræde. And soð is þæt ic secge: awacie se Cristendom, sona
scylfð se cynedom; and arære man unlaga ahwar on lande
oððe unsida lufige ahwar to swiðe, þæt cymð þære þeode
eall to unþearfe. Ac do man swa hit þearf is: alecge man unriht and rære up Godes riht, þæt mæg to þearfe for Gode
and for worulde. Amen.

7   *Be ðeodwitan*

Cyningan and bisceopan, eorlan and heretogan, gerefan and
deman, larwitan and lahwitan gedafenað mid rihte for Gode
and for worulde, þæt hi anræde weorðan and Godes riht
lufian. And bisceopas syndon bydelas and Godes lage lareowas, and hi sculan riht bodian and unriht forbeodan. And
se þe oferhogige þæt he heom hlyste hæbbe him gemæne
þæt wið God sylfne. And gif bisceopas forgymað, þæt hi
synna ne styrað ne unriht forbeodaþ ne Godes riht ne cyþað,
ac clumiað mid ceaflum, þær hi sceoldan clypian, wa heom
þære swigean! Be þam spræc se witega and grimlice þus
cwæð: *Haec dicit dominus: Si non adnuntiaveris iniquo iniquita-
tem suam, sanguinem eius de manu tua requiram.* "Gif þu þam
synfullan nelt," cwæð ure Drihten, "synna gestyran and unriht forbeoden and ðam manfullan mandæda cyðan, þu
scealt þa sawle bitere forgyldan!" Ðis mæg to heorthoge
æghwylcum bisceope; beþence hine georne be þam, þe he
wylle.

8   And se þe nele Godes bodan hyran mid rihte, ne godcundre lare gyman swa he sceolde, he sceall hyran feondan, gyf
he nele freondan; forþam se bið Godes oferhoga, þe Godes
bodan oferhogað, ealswa Crist sylf on his godspelle swyto-
lice sæde, þa þa he þus cwæð: *Qui vos audit, me audit et qui vos*

if Christian faith weakens, the kingdom will soon fall; and if injustice is exalted anywhere in the land or evil customs are anywhere too eagerly embraced, then the people will be brought entirely to ruin. Instead, one must do what is needed: suppress injustice and exalt the law of God; that may be to our benefit before God and the world. Amen.

Concerning the Counselors of the People   7

It rightly behooves kings and bishops, nobles and generals, reeves and judges, the learned and the legal counselors to be of one mind and embrace God's justice before God and the world. And bishops are the messengers and teachers of God's law, and they must proclaim justice and forbid injustice. And anyone who disdains to listen to them may take issue about that with God himself. And if bishops fail by not curbing sin or forbidding injustice or making known God's law, but by mumbling with their mouths when they should shout, woe to them for that silence! The prophet spoke of them and thus said harshly: *Thus sayeth the Lord: If thou declare not his wickedness to the wicked, I will require his blood at thy hand.* "If you will not curb the sins of the sinful," said our Lord, "and forbid injustice and proclaim the wickedness of the wicked, for that soul you shall pay bitterly!" This can be taken to heart by every bishop; let him sincerely reflect upon it, he who will.

And he who will not rightly heed God's messengers, nor   8 attend to divine teaching as he should, must listen to his enemies if not to his friends; for he rejects God who rejects God's messenger, as Christ himself in his Gospel clearly said when he spoke thus: *He that heareth you, heareth me; and he*

spernit, me spernit. He cwæð, "se ðe eow hyreð me gehyreð, and se þe forhogað eow, me he forhogað."

9   Eala, swær is seo byrðen þe Godes bydel beran sceall gif he nele georne unriht forbeoden; forðam þeh he sylf tela do and oðer man misdo, þæt him sceall gederian, and gif he nele styran. And þeh Godes bydel misdo, ne beseo man na þærto, ac gyme his lare, gif he tela lære. Swa swa Crist lærde, þæt man don sceolde, þa þa he on his godspelle swutolice þus cwæð: *Que hi dicunt, facite, que autem faciunt, facere nolite.* He cwæð, "fyliað heora larum and na heora synnum." Ne sceal ænig man æfre for bisceopes synnum hine sylfne forgyman, ac fylige his lare, gif he wel lære. And la, leofan men, doð, swa ic bidde, butan gebelge, hlystað, hwæt ic secge: Ic wat swyðe georne me sylfne forworhtne wordes and dæde ealles to swyðe, ne dear þeah for Godes ege forswygian mid ealle fela þara þinga, þe dereð þisse þeode.

10   *Item de episcopis*

Bisceopas sculan bocum and gebedum fyligean, and dæges and nihtes, oft and gelome, clypian to Criste and for eall Cristen folc þingian georne. And hi sceolan leornian and rihtlice læran, and ymb folces dæda geornlice smeagan. And hi scylan bodian and bysnian georne godcunde þearfe Cristenre þeode. And ne scylan hyg ænig unriht willes geþafian ac to ælcan rihte geornlice fylstan. Hy sculan Godes ege habban on gemynde and ne eargian for woruldege ealles to swyðe. Ac bodian hy symle Godes riht georne and unriht forbeodan, gyme, se þe wille; forðam wace bið se hyrde

that despiseth you, despiseth me. He said: "he who hears you, hears me and he who rejects you, rejects me."

Sadly, onerous is the burden which God's messenger must 9 bear if he will not zealously combat injustice; for although he acts virtuously himself and another person acts wickedly, he himself shall suffer if he does not correct it. And if God's messenger acts wickedly, one should overlook that, but rather heed his teaching if what he teaches is good. Christ taught just what people should do when he clearly spoke thus in his Gospel: *Whatsoever they shall say to you, do: but according to their works do ye not.* He said, "Follow their teachings, and not their sins." One must not ever neglect oneself because of a bishop's sins, but follow his teaching if he teaches well. And indeed, dear people, do as I ask and listen to what I say without taking offense: very well do I know myself to be entirely too sinful in word and deed, but for fear of God I dare not stay wholly silent about many of the things which wound this people.

Likewise, Concerning Bishops 10

Bishops must keep to their books and prayers, and day and night, often and frequently, call upon Christ and fervently intercede for all Christian people. And they must learn and teach rightly, and conscientiously watch over the deeds of the people. And they must preach and sincerely exemplify the spiritual commission to a Christian people. And they must not knowingly permit any injustice but readily promote all that is just. They must hold the fear of God in their mind and not grow all too timid for fear of the world. But let him who is willing always be sure to zealously proclaim the law of God and forbid injustice; for the shepherd will be

funden to heorde, þe nele þa heorde, þe he healdan sceal—
huru mid clypunge bewerian, butan he elles mæge—gif þær
hwylc þeodsceaþa sceaþian onginneþ. Nis nan swa yfel
sceaþa swa is deofol sylf. He bið aa ymbe þæt an hu he on
manna sawlum mæst gesceaþian mæge. Þonne motan þa
hyrdas beon swiþe wacore and geornlice clypiende, þe wið
þone þeodsceaðan folce scylan scyldan. Þæt syndon bisceopas and mæssepreostas þe godcunde heorde gewarian and
bewerian scylan mid wislican laran, þæt se wodfreca werewulf to swiðe ne toslite ne to fela ne abite of godcundre
heorde. And se þe oferhogie, þæt he heom lyste, hæbbe him
gemæne þæt wið God sylfne.

11   Eala, fela is swaþeah þæra þe hwonlice gymað and lyt-
hwon reccað embe boca beboda oððe bisceopa lara; and eac
embæ bletsunga oððe unbletsunga leohtlice lætað, and na
understandaþ swa swa hy sceoldan, hwæt Crist on his godspelle swutollice sæde, þa þa he þus cwæþ: *Qui vos audit, et
reliqua. Et item: Quodcumque ligaveritis et cetera. Et item: Quorum remiseritis peccata, remittuntur eis, et cetera. Alibi etiam
scriptum est: Quodcumque benedixeritis, et cetera. Et psalmista terribiliter loquitur dicens: Qui noluit benedictionem, prolongabitur
ab eo.* Swylc is to beþencenne and wið Godes yrre to war-
nienne symle. Nu lære we eac georne manna gehwylcne, þæt
he Godes larum and his lagum fylgie, þonne geearnað he
him ece myrhðe.

12 *Item*

Bisceopes dægweorc, ðæt bið mid rihte his gebedu ærest
and ðonne his bocweorc, ræding oððon rihting, lar oððon
leornung; and his cyrictida on rihtlicne timan a be þam

judged weak for the flock who will not defend the flock that he must protect—even by calling out if he can do nothing else—if any corruptor of the people begins to pillage there. There is no corruptor so evil as the devil himself. He is always concerned with one thing: how he can most defile the souls of men. Therefore, those shepherds who would protect the people against the corruptor must be most watchful and vigorous in their warnings. Those are the bishops and the priests who must protect and oversee their spiritual flock with wise teaching, so that the ravenous werewolf does not wound too greatly nor devour too many of their spiritual flock. And let anyone who disdains to listen to them settle that with God himself.

Sadly, there are nonetheless many of those who lightly regard and little heed the precepts of the books and the teachings of the bishops; and also frivolously ignore blessings or curses, and do not understand as they should what Christ in his Gospel clearly said when he spoke thus: *He that heareth, etc. And likewise: Whatsoever thou shalt bind, etc, etc. And likewise: Whose sins you shall forgive, they are forgiven them, etc. Elsewhere too it is written: Whatever you have blessed, etc. And the psalmist, speaking chillingly, says: he would not have blessing, and it shall be far from him.* This is to be reflected upon and the wrath of God always to be shielded against. Now we also strongly enjoin everyone to heed God's teachings and his laws; then they will secure for themselves eternal joy.

Furthermore

The proper daily work of a bishop is: first his prayers and then his studies, reading or acting rightly, teaching or learning; and his canonical hours at the proper times, always

þingum, þe þærto gebyrige; and þearfena fotþweal and his
ælmesgedal and weorcwisung, be ðam þe hit neod sy. Eac
him gerisað handcræftas gode, and þæt man on his hirede
cræftas begange, huru þæt ðær ænig to idel ne wunige. And
eac him gerisð wel, þæt he on gemote oft and gelome godcunde lare dæle þam folce, þe he þonne mid sy.

13 *Item*

A gerist bisceopum wisdom and wærscype and þæt þa habban weorðlice wisan, þa þa heom fylian, and þæt hy sundor-
cræfta sumne eac cunnen. Ne geriseð ænig unnytt æfre mid
bisceopum, ne doll ne dysig ne to oferdruncen ne cildsung
on spæce ne idel gegaf on ænig wisan, ne æt ham ne on siðe
ne on ænigre stowe. Ac wisdom and wærscipe gedafeniað
heora hade, and gedrihþa gerisaþ þam, ðe heom fyliað.

14 *Be eorlum*

Eorlas and heretogan and ðas worulddeman and eac swa gerefan agan nydþearfe þæt hi riht lufian for Gode and for
worulde; and nahwar þurh undom, for feo ne for freondscype, forgyman heora wisdom swa þæt hi wendan unriht to
rihte oðþon undom deman earmum to hynþe. Ac a hy sculan
cyrican ofer ealle oðre þing wyrðian and werian, and wudewan and steopcild hy sculon retan, þearfena helpan, and þeowetlingan beorgan, gif hi Godes willan rihte willað wyrcan.
And þeofas and ðeodsceaðan hy scylan hatian, and ryperas
and reaferas hy sculan hynan, butan hy geswican. And symle

along with those things which are relevant thereto; and cleansing the feet of the needy and the distribution of alms and the supervision of works where it is necessary. Good handicrafts are also suitable for him, and it is proper that those in his service practice crafts, so that indeed no one remain too idle there. And it also fully appropriate for him, when he is at a meeting, to relate the divine teachings often and frequently to those people with whom he then is.

Furthermore 13

For bishops, wisdom and discretion are always appropriate, and those who practice them—and also who learn a special craft—have praiseworthy ways. Nothing useless is ever appropriate for bishops, neither thoughtlessness nor foolishness nor drunkenness nor childishness in speech nor idle frivolousness of any kind, neither at home nor on a journey nor in any place. But wisdom and discretion suit their status, and dignity befits those who follow them.

Concerning Nobles 14

Nobles, generals, secular judges, and also reeves are obliged to embrace justice before God and the world; and never through foolishness, whether out of bribery or friendship, neglect their wisdom so that they twist injustice into justice or pronounce unjust rulings harmful to the poor. But they must always venerate and protect the Church over all other things, and they must console widows and orphans, aid the poor, and defend helpless slaves, if they wish to fulfill God's will rightly. They must abhor thieves and villains, and they must suppress robbers and criminals, unless they cease their crimes. And they must always greatly detest injustice. For it

hy sculon unriht swyðe ascunian. Forþam soð is þæt ic secge, gelyfe se þe wille: wa þam, þe woh drifð ealles to lange, butan he geswice! Witodlice he sceall drefan dimne and deopne hellewites grund, helpes bedæled. Ac to lyt is þara þe þæt understande swa swa man sceolde; ac God hit gebete! Ac do freonda gehwylc, eallswa hit þearf is: warnige hine georne and beorge him sylfum, þæt he God ne abelge ealles to swyðe, ac cweme his Drihtne mid rihtlicre dæde.

15 *Be gerefan*

Riht is ðæt gerefan geornlice tylian and symle heora hlafordan strynan mid rihte. Ac nu hit is geworden ealles to swyðe, syððan Eadgar geendode, swa swa God wolde, þæt ma is þæra rypera þonne rihtwisra, and is earmlic ðing þæt ða syndon ryperas þe sceoldan beon hyrdas Cristenes folces. Hy rypað þa earman butan ælcere scylde oðre hwile and hynað þa heorde, þe hi sceoldan healdan, and mid yfelan holan earme men beswicað, and unlaga rærað on æghwylce wisan earmum to hynþe and wydewan bestrypað oft and gelome. Ac hwilum, man ceas wislice þa men on þeode folce to hyrdum, þe noldan for woruldsceame ne ne dorstan for Godes ege ænig ðing swician ne strynan on unriht; ac stryndan mid rihte. And syððan hit man sohte be þam ealra geornast, þe nearwlicast cuðan swician and befician, and mid leasbregdum earmum mannum derian, and of unbealafullum raþost feoh geræcan. Syððan man gremede God swyðe þearle oft and gelome. And wa þæs gestreones þam þe his mæst hafaþ on unriht gestryned, butan he geswice and ðe deoppor gebete for Gode and for worulde.

is the truth that I speak, believe it who will: woe unto that person who pursues injustice all too long, unless he turn aside! He will certainly sink, bereft of help, into hell's dark and deep abyss. Too few, however, are those who understand that as one should; but may God correct that! But each friend shall do as is most necessary: warn and protect himself so as not to anger God all too greatly, but instead please his Lord with righteous deeds.

Concerning Reeves 15

It is right that reeves toil assiduously and always provide for their lord properly. But now since Edgar died, just as God willed, it has come to pass all too much that there are more thieves than righteous people, and it is a terrible thing that they are thieves who should be the shepherds of the Christian people. At times they steal from those who are poor through no fault of their own and torment the flock which they should protect, and abuse the unfortunate with evil slander, and promote unjust laws in every way to exploit the needy and rob widows again and again. But formerly these men were chosen wisely as shepherds for the people and they dared not behave dishonestly nor obtain anything unjustly because of worldly shame and the fear of God; instead, they acquired things properly. Yet afterward, this has been pursued most eagerly of all by those who understood how to cheat and swindle most cruelly, and to harm the unfortunate with deceit, and to extract money from the innocent most swiftly. Since then, God has been greatly provoked again and again. And woe unto that man who has acquired most of his wealth through injustice, unless he turn aside and repent all the more deeply before God and the world.

16 *Be sacerdum*

Sacerdas sculan on heora scriftscirum wislice and wærlice
lædan and læran þa godcundan heorda þe hi healdan sculan.
Ægðer hi sculan, ge wel bodian ge wel bysnian oðrum mannum; and ægðer hi scylon æt Godes dome gescead agyldan,
ge heora sylfra dæda ge ealles þæs folces, þe hi to Godes
handa healdan sceolan. And gyf hi aht gedon scylon, ne magon hi wandian, naþer ne for ege ne for lufe æniges mannes,
þæt hi riht ne bodian and unriht forbeodan. Wace byð se
hyrde æt falde nyt þe nele þa heorde, þe he healden sceal
mid hreame bewerian butan he elles mæge, gif þær hwylc
þeodsceaða sceaðian onginneð. Nys nan swa yfel sceaða swa
is deofol sylf. He bið aa embe þæt an: hu he on manna
sawlum mæst gesceaþian mæge. Þonne motan þa hyrdas
beon swyðe wacore and georne clypiende, þe wið þone
þeodsceaþan folce gescyldan sculan. Þæt syndon bisceopas
and mæssepreostas þe godcunde heorde gewarian and bewerian sculon mid wislicre lare. Ðy he ne mæg wandian, gyf
he him sylfum gebeorgan sceall, naþor ne for lufe ne for ege,
þæt he mannum þæt rihtteste ne secge. Ne mæg he wandian
naðor ne for heanum ne for ricum, forðam ne deþ he naht
eargie he oðþon hine forsceamige riht to spreconne. Earme
gefæreð he, gif þurh his hnescnysse, seo heord forwurð, þe
he healdan sceall, and he sylf forð mid. Ðeah ure heorda
hwylc an sceap forgyme, we willað þæt he hit forgylde. And
hwæt gefarað þonne æt Godes egeslican dome þa hyrdas, þe
ne cunnon gehealdon þa godcundan heorde þe Crist mid his
agenum life gebohte, and þe hi healdon sceoldan, gif hi
cuðan? Ac naþor þurh larleaste hi ne cunnon ne lædan, ne

Concerning Priests

Priests in their parishes must wisely and sensibly lead and instruct the spiritual flock which they are to protect. They must both preach well and set a good example for others; and at God's judgment, they must render into God's hand an account both of their own deeds and of those people they are to oversee. And if something must be done, they may not hesitate, neither out of fear nor love of any person, to proclaim justice and forbid injustice. The shepherd will be of little use to the fold who will not protect the flock, which he must defend with an outcry if he can do nothing else, if some corruptor of the people begins to raid. There is no corruptor as evil as the devil himself. He is concerned with one thing always: how he may defile to the utmost the souls of men. Therefore must those shepherds who would protect the people against the corruptor be most watchful and vigorous in their warnings. Those are the bishops and the priests who must protect and oversee their spiritual flock with wise teaching. Thus if he would protect himself he must not hesitate either out of love or fear to say to men that which is most just. Nor may he hesitate before either the humble or the mighty, for he does not do as he ought if he grows timid or ashamed to proclaim what is right. He will fare miserably if, through his weakness, the flock which he must protect perishes, and he himself with it. Should any of our shepherds overlook even one sheep, we will require that he pay for it. And then how will those shepherds fare at God's fearful judgment, who cannot protect the spiritual flocks which Christ purchased with his own life, and which they must protect if they can? Because of their lack of learn-

læran, ne lacnian hi rihtlice. Mid hwam wene we, forgyldað hi hi þonne? Wa heom þonne, þæt hi æfre underfengon þæt hi gehealdon ne cuðon! La, hu mæg blind man oðerne lædan? Hu mæg unlæred dema oðerne læran? Wa þam witodlice, þe godcunde heorde underfehð and naþer gehealdan ne can, ne hine sylfne ne þa heorde, þe he healdan sceolde, and wyrs þam þe can and nele.

17   Eala, eala, fela is þæra þe sacerdhades on unriht gyrnað, swa hit þincan mæg, swyðost for idelum gylpe and for gitsunge woruldgestreona, and ne cunnon na, þæt hy cunnon sceoldan. Be þam cwæð se witega and ðus cwæð, *Ve sacerdotibus qui comedunt peccata populi, et reliqua.* "Wa þam sacerdum," he cwæð, "þe fretað and forswelgað folces synna." Þæt syndon þa ðe nellað oððe ne cunnon oððon ne durron folc wið synna gewarnian and synna gestyran, ac gyrnað þeah heora sceatta on teoþungum and on eallum cyricgerihtum; and naðor ne hi mid bysnungum wel ne lædað, ne mid bodungum wel ne lærað, ne mid dædbotum wel ne lacniað, ne mid gebedrædenne fore ne þingiað. Ac læccað of manna begeatum loc hwæt hi gefon magan, eallswa gyfre hremnas of holde doð þær þær hi to magon. Hit is ealles þe wyrse, syððan hy hit ealles habbað: þonne ne ateoð hi hit na swa swa hi sceoldan, ac glencgað heora wif mid þam þe hi weofoda sceoldan; and maciað eall heom sylfum to woruldwlence and to idelre rence, þæt hi Gode sceoldan don to weorðunge on cyriclicum þingum oððon on earmra manna hyððum oððon on hernumenra bygenum oððon on sumum þingum þe mihte to langsumere ðearfe ægðer ge heom sylfum ge eac þam, þe heom on Godes est heora þing syllað.

ing, they cannot lead nor teach nor tend them properly. With what do we expect them to pay for them then? Therefore, woe unto them that they ever accepted that which they could not protect! Indeed, how can a blind man lead another? How can an ignorant judge instruct another? Truly, woe unto them who receive a spiritual flock and can neither tend to themselves nor to the flock which they must protect, and worse than those who can and will not.

Alas, alas, there are many of those who, as it may seem, 17 seek the priesthood wrongfully, especially for idle glory and worldly wealth, and they do not know that which they should know. About them the prophet spoke and said thus: *Woe unto the priests who eat the sins of the people, etc.* "Woe to the priests," he said, "who devour and consume the people's sins." Those are the ones who will not, know not how, or dare not warn the people against sins and punish sins, but nonetheless desire their money in the form of tithes and all Church dues; yet they neither lead them well with examples, nor teach them well with preaching, nor heal them well with penances, nor intercede for them with prayer. Instead, they scavenge people's possessions for whatever they can grab, just as gluttonous ravens do from a carcass wherever they can. It is all the worse, once they have it all: then they do not treat it in any way as they should, but they decorate their women with that which should be on the altars; and they exploit for their own worldly pride and idle vanity that which they should put toward the worship of God in Church affairs or toward assistance to the needy or toward the ransoming of captives or toward some matters which might be of enduring benefit both to themselves and to those who give them their goods for the love of God. There is great

Þonne is mycel þearf, þæt se þe ær ðissum misdyde, þæt he heononforð hit georne gebete.

18   Forðam understande, se þe cunne: mycel is and mære þæt sacerd ah to donne folce to þearfe, gif he his Drihtne gecwemð mid rihte. Mycel is seo halsung and mære is seo halgung þe deofla afyrsað and on fleame gebringað, swa oft swa man fullað oðþon husel halgað. And englas þær hwearfiað and ða dæda beweardiað and, ðurh Godes mihta, þam sacerdum fylstað swa oft swa hi Criste þeniað mid rihte. And swa hi doð symle, swa oft swa hi geornlice inneweardre heortan clypiað to Criste and for folces neode þingiað georne. And þi man sceall, for Godes ege, mæþe on hade gecnawan mid gesceade.

19   La leof, deope us is beboden þæt we geornlice mynegian and læran scylan, þæt manna gehwylc to Gode buge and fram synnum gecyrre. Se cwyde is swyðe egeslic, þe God þurh þone witegan be þam cwæð þe Godes folce riht bodian sculon, þæt syndon bisceopas and mæssepreostas. He cwæð be þam, *Clama, ne cesses, quasi tuba et reliqua,* "Clypa hlude and ahefe up ðine stemne swa hlude swa byme and gecyð minum folce, þæt hit fram synnum gecyrre." Gif ðu þonne þæt ne dest, ac forswugast hit, and nelt folce his þearfe gecyðan, þonne scealt ðu ealra þæra sawla on Domesdæg gescead agyldan, þe þurh þæt losiað, þe hi nabbað þa lare and ða mynegunge, þe hi beþorftan. Þes cwyde mæg beon swyðe gemyndelic eallum þam, þe to ðam gesette syn, þæt hi Godes folce riht bodian sculan. And folc ah eac mycele þearfe, þæt hi wære beon þæs cwydes þe þæræfter gecweden is. He cwæð, se witega, æfter þam: "Gif ðu folce riht bodast

need, then, that he who erred beforehand readily repent for it henceforth.

Therefore, let him understand who can: great and won- 18 drous is that which a priest must do for the benefit of the people, if he wishes to please his Lord properly. Great is the exorcism and wondrous is the blessing which expels devils and puts them to flight, just as often as a person is baptized or the host is consecrated. And angels hover there and oversee those deeds and, through God's might, aid those priests just as long as they serve Christ properly. Thus they do always, as often as they fervently call upon Christ with their innermost heart and readily intercede for the needs of the people. Accordingly, for fear of God, the reverence of holy orders must be understood with discernment.

Indeed, dear friends, it is solemnly commanded to us that 19 we must fervently admonish and teach that every person is to submit to God and refrain from sins. That decree is most fearsome, which God spoke through his prophet concerning those who must preach righteousness to God's people, namely the bishops and the priests. Concerning them, he said, *Cry, cease not; like a trumpet, etc.* "Cry loudly, and raise up your voice as loudly as a trumpet, and preach to my people so that they refrain from sins." Yet if you do not do that, but pass over it in silence, and will not make known to the people their obligation, then you must render an account at Judgment Day for all those souls which are lost because they lack the teaching and the admonition that they required. Let this decree be most remembered by all those who are entrusted to preach righteousness to God's people. And the people also have a great need to be mindful of the decree delivered after this one. The prophet said after that: "If you

and ðu hit gebigean ne miht to rihte, þonne gebyrhst ðu þeh
þinre agenre sawle"; and se þe woh drifð and geswican nele,
he sceal habban þæs ece wite. Þæt is, þæt hi þonne sceolan
to helle faran mid sawle and mid lichoman and mit deofle
wunian on hellewitum. Wa þam, þe þær sceall wunian on wi-
tum; him wære betere, þæt he næfre on weorulde man ne
gewurde þonne he gewurde. Nis se man on life þe areccan
mæge ealle þa yrmða þe se gebidan sceall se ðe on þa witu
ealles behreoseð; and hit is ealles þe wyrse, þe his ænig ende
ne cymð næfre to worulde.

20 *Be gehadedum mannum*

Gehadedum mannum gebyreð ælc clænnes, forðam þe hi
sculon eallum oðrum mannum ælce unclænnesse forbeodan.
And ælce clænnesse, gif hi riht doð, hi sculon be heom sylfum
geornost gebysnian. Þonne is hit swyþe egeslic þæt ða þe
sceoldan eallum Cristenum mannum riht bodian and eac
wel bysnian, þæt hi syn sume gewordene bysen to forwyrde
swyðor þonne to þearfe. Þæt syndon þa æwbrecan þe þurh
healicne had ciricæwe underfengan and syððan þæt abræcan. Nis nanum weofodþene alyfed þæt he wifian mote; ac
is ælcum forboden. Nu is þeah þæra ealles to fela þe þone
æwbryce wyrcað and geworht habbað. Ac ic bidde for Godes
lufan and eac eornostlice beode þæt man þæs geswice.
Læwedum men is ælc wif forboden butan his rihtæwe; gehadode syndon sume swa þurh deofol beswicene þæt hi
wifiað on unriht and forwyrcað hi sylfe þurh ðone æwbryce

82

proclaim righteousness to the people yet you cannot bend them to righteousness, then you will save your own soul nonetheless"; and he who pursues wickedness and will not cease, he shall have eternal punishment. That is, they must then travel to hell in soul and body and dwell with the devil in infernal suffering. Woe to anyone who must dwell there in suffering: better it would have been for such a person to have never become a human being in this world than to have become one. There is no one alive who can recount all of the sorrows which must be endured by one who falls entirely into that suffering; and it is all the worse, in that an end never will come to it for all eternity.

Concerning Those in Orders 20

All forms of purity are appropriate for those in orders, for they must forbid all forms of impurity to others. And if they do what is right, they must themselves most assiduously become an example of every form of purity. Accordingly, it is exceedingly dreadful that of those who must preach righteousness to all Christians and also set a good example, some have become an example of damnation rather than duty. Those are adulterers who accepted marriage to the Church through their holy orders and later violated it. No clergyman who serves at the altar is permitted to have a wife; rather, it is forbidden to all. Now, however, there are all too many who commit adultery or have committed it. Yet for the love of God, I command and solemnly decree that this is to cease. To a layman is every woman forbidden save his lawful spouse; and there are some in orders so deceived by the devil that they take a wife unlawfully and destroy themselves through the adultery in which they abide. But I

þe hi on wuniað. Ac ic bidde georne þæt man þæs morðes heononforð georne geswice. Cyrice is sacerdes æwe, and nah he mid rihte ænige oðre; forðam ne gebirað sacerdan nan ðingc ne to wif ne to worldwige, gif hi Gode willað rihtlice hiran and Godes lage healdan swa swa heora hade gedafenað mid rihte.

21   Constantinus, se mæra casere, gesamnode swyðe my-celne sinoð on þære ceastre Nicea for trymmincge rihtes ge-leafan. On ðam sinoðe wæron CCC and XVIII biscopa of manegum leodscipum gegaderode, and hi þær geswutelodon rihtne geleafan. And gesettan þa þæs to swutelunge þone mæssancredan þe man wide singð, and cyricþenunga heo fægere gedihtan, and mænige oðre þing ægþer ge be Godes þeowum ge be Gode sylfum. Hy cwædon þær, ealle an-rædlice, þæt hit riht wære, gif weofodþen—þæt is biscop oððe mæssepreost oððe diacon—gewifode, þæt he þolode æfre his hades and amansumod wurde, butan he geswice and ðe deoppor gebete. Feower synoðas wæron gesamnode for rihtan geleafan ymbe þa halgan Þrynnysse and ymbe Cristes menniscnesse. Se forma wæs on Nicea and se oðer wæs syððan on Constantinopolim, þær wæron CL biscopa. Se ðridda wæs on Effesum, CC biscopa, and se feorða wæs on Calcedonea, fela biscopa ætgædere. And ealle hi wæron an-ræde æt eallum þam ðingum þe man on fruman on Nicea ge-sette, and ealle hi forbudon æfre ælc wiflac weofodþenum.

22   Ðencan ða nu, þe to þam ðryste syn þæt hi God oferseoð and swa maniges haliges mannes dom, swa on þissum sinoðum gesamnode wæron and gehwær syððon, hwylces leanes hy hym wenan magon and eac wenan ne þurfon. Ac

urgently command that they cease henceforth from this mortal sin. The priest's wife is the Church, and by right he has no other; for neither a wife nor the warfare of this world are fitting for a priest in any way, if he wishes to obey God properly and heed God's law in a manner appropriate to his status.

Constantine, the great emperor, convened a very impor- 21 tant synod in the city of Nicea for the affirmation of the true faith. Gathered at that synod were three hundred and eighteen bishops from many peoples, and there they proclaimed the true faith. And then, as an affirmation of this, they established the Mass Creed which is sung widely, and they arranged the church services appropriately, and many other matters concerning both God's servants and God himself. They decreed there, entirely unanimously, that if a clergyman who serves at the altar—that is, a bishop or priest or deacon—took a wife, he must forfeit forever his order and be excommunicated, unless he desist and repent the more sincerely. Four synods were convened concerning the true faith in the holy Trinity and concerning Christ's humanity. The first was in Nicea and the second was later in Constantinople, where there were one hundred and fifty bishops; the third was in Ephesus of two hundred bishops and the fourth was in Chalcedon, of many bishops together. And they were all of one mind about all of those matters which were first decided at Nicea, and they forbade entirely and forever all sexual activity by those who serve at the altar.

Let them now reflect, those who are so arrogant that they 22 neglect God and the judgment of so many holy people such as were gathered at these synods and everywhere afterward, what reward they can expect for themselves and also need

gewitod witan þæt hi yfel lean habban sculon and grimlice
Godes graman þurh þæt, þe hy swa God gremiað, þæt hi eall
heora lif libbað on fylðe. Weofodþenas ic bidde þæt hi
beðencan hi sylfe and geswican ælcere fylðe. And þa, þe ær
þyssan þone ungewunan hæfdon þæt hi heora wif glengdan
swa hi weofoda sceoldan, geswican þæs ungewunon and
glencgan heora cyrican be þam þe hi betst magon, þonne
wealdað hy heom sylfum ægðer ge godcundes rædes ge
woruldcundes weorðscypes. Nis preostes cwene ænig oðer
þing butan deofles grin, and se ðe mid þam gegrinod byð
forð oþ his ende, he byð þurh deofol fæste gefangen, and he
eac syðþon mot faran on feonda hand and forfaran mid ealle.
Ac helpe gehwa georne hys sylfes þa hwile þe he mage and
mote, and gebuge ælc man fram unrihte to rihte; þonne ge-
byrhð man wið ece wite. And eac, se þe þurhwunað on godum dædum forð oð his ende, he þæs habban sceal ece
edlean. Nu eow is soð asæd: understandaþ eow sylfe be ðam,
þe ge willan. God eow getrymme to eowre agenre þearfe and
us ealle gehealde, swa his wylla sy. Amen.

23 *Be abbodum*

Riht is þæt abbodas and huru abbadissan fæste on mynstrum singallice wunian and georne heora heorda symle be-
gyman, and aa heom wel bysenian and rihtlice bodian. And
næfre ymbe woruldcara ne idele pryda ne carian to swyþe ne
ealles to gelome, ac oftost hi abysgian mid godcundan neodan. Swa gebyreð abbodan and munuchades mannum.

not expect. Yet they may know with certainty that they must receive an evil reward and the wrath of God fearsomely because they so enrage God in that they live all of their lives in filth. I entreat those clergymen who serve at the altar that they examine themselves and refrain from all corruption. Moreover, may those who beforehand engaged in the sinful practice of decorating their women with that which should be on the altars, end that sinful practice and decorate their churches as best they can, so that they command for themselves both spiritual wisdom and earthly honor. Nor is a woman for a priest anything other than a snare of the devil, and he who is thus trapped will be caught fast by the devil from then on until his end and, furthermore, he must fall then into the hand of fiends and perish entirely. But let everyone eagerly help themselves while they may and can, and let each person turn away from sin to righteousness; then will he be redeemed from eternal torment. And indeed, he who persists in good deeds from then on until his end shall receive eternal reward as recompense. To you, now, has the truth been spoken: understand it yourself, you who will. May God strengthen you to your own advantage, and protect us all as his will may be. Amen.

Concerning Abbots   23

It is right that abbots and, in particular, abbesses remain perpetually secure in their monasteries and always conscientiously oversee their flocks, and ever set a good example for them and preach rightly. And they are never to be concerned too greatly nor all too frequently with worldly cares or idle vanity, but they are to occupy themselves most often with spiritual needs. Thus is fitting for abbots and monastics.

87

24 *Be munecum*

Riht is þæt munecas beon dæges and nihtes inweardre heortan a to Gode þencan and geornlice clypian and mid eallum eadmedum regollice libban. And hy symle asyndrian fram woruldbysegan swa hi geornost magan, and don swa heom ðearf is: carian æfre hu hi swyðost magan Gode gecweman and eall þæt gelæstan, þæt þæt hi behetan, þa hi had underfengon; fylian heora bocum and gebedum georne; leornian and læran swa hi geornost magon; and æghwylce wlence and idele rence and syndrige æhte and unnytte dæde and untidspæce forhogian mid ealle. Swa gebyreð munecum. Ac hit is yfel soð, swa hit þincan mæg, þæt sume synd to wlance and ealles to rance and to widscriþole and to unnytte and ealles to idele ælcere goddæde and to mandæde on dyrnlican galscype, inne aidlode and ute awildode. And sume syn apostatan þe sceoldan, gyf hi woldan, wesan Godes cempan innan heora mynstran, þæt synd þa þe hadas awurpan and on woruldþingan wuniað mid synnan.

25 Eall hit færeð yfele ealles to wide. Swa swyðe hit wyrsað wide mid mannum, þæt þæs hades men, þe þurh Godes ege, hwylum wæron nyttoste and geswincfulleste on godcundan þeowdome and on boccræfte, þa syndon nu wel forð unnyttaste gewelhwær and ne swincaþ a swiðe ymbe ænige þearfe for Gode ne for worulde. Ac maciað eall be luste and be eþnesse, and lufiað oferwiste and idele blisse, woriað and wandriað and ealne dæg fleardiað, spelliað and spiliað and nænige note dreogað. Þæt is laðlic lif þæt hi swa maciað; eac hit is þe wyrse þe ealdras hit ne betað, ne sylfe swa wel farað

Concerning Monks 24

It is right that monks always reflect upon God in their innermost hearts by day and night and sincerely pray and live according to their rule with all humility. And they always are to sever themselves from secular occupations as diligently as they can, and they are to fulfill that which is their obligation: to consider always how they can best please God and perform all that they promised when they took orders; to adhere diligently to their books and prayers; to learn and teach as best they can; and to entirely reject all arrogance, idle vanity, private property, frivolous deeds, and foolish speech. Thus it is fitting for monks. But it is an evil truth, as one might suspect, that some are too arrogant and altogether too proud, too susceptible to straying, too worthless, altogether too lazy for any good deed, and too corrupted by hidden lusts, inwardly slack and outwardly strict. Some even are apostates who could, if they wished, be God's champions in their monasteries, especially those who have rejected their orders and dwell sinfully amid worldly things.

All too commonly do all things fare badly. So much does 25 it worsen widely among men that those in orders who, through fear of God, once were the most useful and industrious in divine service and scholarship, are now indeed everywhere the most useless and never work seriously to any benefit for God or the world. Instead, they act wholly for pleasure and ease, and they love gluttony and idle pleasure, they meander and stray and waste the entire day, they gossip and play and accomplish nothing of any significance. It is a loathsome life that they lead; and it is the worse in that their elders do not correct it, but to some degree they themselves

sumes swa hi sceoldan. Ac we agan neode þæt we hit gebetan, swa we geornost magan, and weorðan anmode to
gemænelicre þearfe for Gode and for worulde.

26 *Be mynecenan*

Riht is þæt mynecena mynsterlice macian, efne swa we cwædon æror be munecan, and ne towettan woruldmannum ne
ænige sundorcyððe to heom habban ealles to swyðe, ac a
regolice libban and hi symle asyndrian fram woruldbysegan
swa hi geornost magan.

27 *Be preostan and be nunnan*

Riht is ðæt preostas and efen wel nunnan regollice libban
and clænnysse healdan be þam, þe hi willan on mynstran
gewunian oððon for worulde weorðscypes wealdan.

28 *Be læwedum mannum*

Riht is ðæt gehadode men læwede wissian hu hi heora æwe
rihtlicost sculon healdan. Þæt bið rihtlic lif þæt cniht þurhwunige on his cnihthade oðþæt he on rihtre mædenæwe gewifige, and hæbbe þa syððan and nænige oðre þa hwile þe
seo libbe. Gif hire þonne forðsið gebyrige, þonne is rihtost
þæt he þananforð wydewa þurhwunige. Ðeah be ðæs apostoles leafe læwede man mot for neode oðre siðe wifian; ac þa
canones forbeodaþ þa bletsunge þærto þe to frumwifunge
gesette syn and eac is geset dædbot swylcum mannum to
donne. And preoste is forboden, þæt he beon ne mot, on
ðam wisan, þe he ær wæs æt þam brydlacum þær man eft
wifað, ne þa bletsunge don þe to frumwifunge gebyrað. Be

do not behave as well as they should. Yet we have need to correct it as urgently as we can, and become dedicated to the common good before God and the world.

Concerning Women Monastics 26

It is right that women in orders act in a monastic fashion, even as we have said before about monks, and not consort with men of the world nor have all too much familiarity with them, but they are to live always according to their rule and to sever themselves from worldly occupations as best they can.

Concerning Priests and Nuns 27

It is right that priests and likewise nuns also live according to their rule and preserve their chastity if they desire to live in a monastery or earn respect in the world.

Concerning the Laity 28

It is right that men in orders instruct the laity how they should best keep their marital vows. That life is virtuous in which a young man remains chaste until he weds a maiden properly, and afterward has her and no other for as long as she lives. Then, if her death occurs, it is most fitting that he remain a widower thenceforth. By the Apostle's consent, though, a layman can marry a second time if necessary; however, the canons forbid the blessings thereto which are reserved for a first marriage and a penance is fixed for such men to perform. Moreover, a priest is forbidden from presiding in the way that he did previously at a marriage at which a man weds a second time, nor may he perform the blessing specified for a first wedding. By that one may know

þam man mæg witan þæt hit eallunga riht nis þæt wer wifige
oðþon wif ceorlige oftor þonne æne. And huru hit byð to
mænigfeald gewyrðe hit þriddan siðe, and mid ealle misdon,
gewyrðe hit oftor. And þeah læwedum mannum wif sy alyfed, þeah hi agon þearfe þæt hi understandan hu hit is alyfed. Nagon læwede men freolstidum ne fæstentidum þurh
hæmedðing wifes gemanan, þe ma þe heahhades men þæt
ðing agan ænigum timan.

29 Be wudewan

Riht is ðæt wydewan Annan bysenan geornlice fylian. Seo
wæs on temple dæges and nihtes þeowiende georne. Heo
fæste swyðe þearle and gebedum fyligde and geomeriendum
mode clypode to Criste and ælmessan dælde oft and gelome. And aa Gode gecwemde þæs ðe heo mihte wordes and
dæde and hæfð nu to edleane heofonlice myrhðe. Swa sceall
god wydewe hyran hyre Drihtne.

30 Be cyrican

Riht is ðæt Cristene men Cristendom georne healdan mid
rihte and Cristes cyrican æghwær geornlice weorþian and
werian. Ealle we habbað ænne heofonlicne fæder and ane
gastlice modor: seo is *Ecclesia* genamod, þæt is, Godes cyrce,
and þa we sculon æfre lufian and weorðian. And riht is þæt
ælc cyrice sy on Godes griðe and on ealles Cristenes folces;
and þæt cyricgrið stande æghwær binnan wagum and gehalgodes cynincges handgrið efenunwemme. Forðam ælc cyricgrið is Cristes agen grið, and ælc Cristen man ah mycle
þearfe þæt he on þam griðe mycle mæþe wite. Forðam ælces

that it is not entirely proper that a man take a wife or a woman take a husband after the first time. And indeed it is too many if it should happen a third time, and wholly wrong if it happens more often. And though a wife is permitted to laymen, it is still necessary that they understand how it is permitted. On feasts and in fasting times, laymen may not consort with their wives in sexual congress, any more than those in orders may do that thing at any time.

Concerning Widows 29

It is right that widows readily abide by the example of Anna. She remained in the temple day and night in heartfelt service. She fasted very rigorously and kept to her prayers and called on Christ with a sorrowful spirit and handed out alms very frequently. She always pleased God as much as she could with words and deeds, and now as a reward she has heavenly bliss. In this way shall a good widow heed her Lord.

Concerning the Church 30

It is right that Christians fervently adhere rightly to the Christian faith and readily honor and uphold the Christian Church everywhere. We all have one heavenly father and one spiritual mother: she is named *Ecclesia,* that is, God's Church, which we must always love and respect. And it is right that each church be under the protection of God and of all Christian people; and that Church sanctuary is to prevail within the walls and is to be honored no differently from protection from the king's own hand. Thus, every Church sanctuary is Christ's own sanctuary, and every Christian has a great obligation to treat that sanctuary with great respect. Further, it is the responsibility of every

Cristenes mannes nydþearf is þæt he Godes cyrican georne lufige and weorðige, and hi gelomlice and geornlice sece him sylfum to ðearfe. And huru gehadode þær sculon oftost ðeowian and ðenian and for eall Cristen folc ðingian georne. Þonne agan weofodðenas to smeagenne symble þæt hi huruðinga heora lif fadian, swa swa to cyrcan gebyrige mid rihte.

31   Cyrice is mid rihte sacerdes æwe, and se ðe to cyrican weorðe gehadod, nage hine ænig man, ðe Godes lage recce, þanon to donne, butan he hi mid heafodgylte fullice for-wyrce. And ðonne sceall Cristes scirgerefa þæt witan and ymbe þæt dihtan and deman swa swa bec tæcan. And ne sceolde man æfre cyrican derian ne ænig woh beodan on ænige wisan. Ac nu syndon þeah cyrcan wide and side wace gegriðode and yfele geðeowode and clæne berypte ealdra gerihta and innan bestrypte ælcera gerisena. And cyricþenas syndon mæðe and munde gewelhwær bedælde. And wa þam þe ðæs wealt, þeh he swa ne wene, forðam ælc ðara byð witodlice Godes sylfes feond, þe byð Godes cyricena feond and ðe Godes cyricena riht wanað oðþon wyrdeþ, ealswa hit awriten is: *Inimicus enim Christi efficitur omnis, qui ecclesiasticas res usurpare iniuste conatur, et reliqua.* And egeslice spræc sanc-tus Gregorius be ðam eac, þa ða he þus cwæð: *Si quis eccle-siam Christi denudaverit vel sanctimonia violaverit, anathema sit. Ad quod respondentes omnes dixerunt: Amen.* Mycel is neod-þearf manna gehwilcon þæt he wið þas ðinc beorge him georne, and æghwylc Godes freond warnige hine symble þæt he Cristes bryde to swyðe ne misbeode. Ealle we sculon ænne God lufian and weorðian and ænne Cristendom

Christian to sincerely love and honor God's Church, and he is to seek it out often and willingly for his own benefit. Those in orders also must serve and minister there most often and intercede readily for all Christian people. Accordingly, clergy who serve at the altar must always ensure that they especially set their lives in order in a manner rightly fitting to the Church.

The Church is properly the spouse of the priest, and no person who heeds God's law ought to remove from the Church someone who has taken orders in it, lest he utterly perish in mortal sin. And then must Christ's representative take notice of that and resolve and judge it just as the books instruct. And no one must ever damage a church or threaten it with wrongdoing in any way. Yet nonetheless, churches far and wide are now weakly protected and oppressed by evil and entirely deprived of ancient rights and stripped inside of everything proper. Moreover, the Church's servants are everywhere deprived of honor and protection. And woe unto him who causes this, even if he does not realize it, for each of those who is the enemy of God's churches and who weakens or violates the rights of God's churches is assuredly the enemy of God himself; as it is written: *For anyone becomes the enemy of Christ who attempts to wrongly make use of the goods of the Church, etc.* And Saint Gregory spoke fearsomely about this also, when he said thus: *Whoever plunders the Church of Christ or violates its sanctity is to be anathema. Responding to which, all said: Amen.* Everyone has a great duty to defend himself vigorously against these things; and each friend of God is to always watch over himself, so that he not mistreat the bride of Christ too greatly. We all must love and praise one God and diligently adhere to one Christian faith and

georne healdan and ælcne hæþendom mid ealre mihte awyrpan. And utan ænne cynehlaford holdlice healdan, and
freonda gehwylc oðerne healde mid rihtan getrywðan.

32 *Be eallum Cristenum mannum*

Riht is ðæt ealle Cristene men heora Cristendom rihtlice
healdan, and ðam life libban þe heom to gebyrað æfter
Godes rihte and æfter woruldgerysenum; and heora wisan
ealle be þam ðingan geornlice fadian, þe ða wisian, ðe hy wislice and wærlice wisian cunnon. And þæt is þonne ærest
ræda firmest: þæt manna gehwylc ofer ealle oðre þinc ænne
God lufige and ænne geleafan anrædlice hæbbe on ðæne, þe
us ealle ærest geworhte and mid deorwyrðum ceape eft us
gebohte. And eac we agan þearfe þæt we geornlice smeagan
hu we symble magan Godes agene beboda rihtlicost healdan
and eall þæt gelæstan þæt þæt we behetan þa we fulluht underfengon oðþon þa þe æt fulluhte ure forespræcon wæron.
Ðæt is ðonne ærest: þæt þæt man behateþ þonne man fulluhtes gyrnð þæt man a wile deofol ascunian and his unlare
georne forbugan and ealle his unlaga symble awyrpan and
ecelice wiðsacan ealles his gemanan; and manisiðes sona
þærafter mid rihtan geleafan soðlice swytelað þæt man
þananforð aa wile on ænne God æfre gelyfan and ofer ealle
oðre þing hine a lufian and æfre his larum geornlice fylgean
and his agene beboda rihtlice healdan. And þonne bið þæt
fulluht swylce hit wedd sy ealra þæra worda and ealles ðæs
behates, gehealde se ðe wille. And soð is þæt ic secge: englas
beweardiað þananforð æfre manna gehwylcne, hu he gelæste
æfter his fulluhte, þæt man behet ær, þa man fulluhtes
gyrnde.

reject every heathen practice with all our might. And let us faithfully uphold one royal lord, and let each friend support the other with true devotion.

Concerning All Christian People

It is right that all Christian people properly uphold their Christian faith, and live the life appropriate to them according to the law of God and the customs of the world; and diligently arrange all manner of things according to the guidance of those who can advise them wisely and truly. And this, then, is the most important of precepts: that each person love the one God over all other things and resolutely have one faith in him who first created us all and purchased us again at a dear price. And we also have need to reflect sincerely how we can always keep God's own commandments most rightly and perform all that we—or those who were our sponsors—promised when we received baptism. This, then, is first: that one promises when one seeks baptism to always spurn the devil and zealously avoid his evil teachings and always reject his injustice and eternally resist all of his company; and swiftly thereafter one sincerely proclaims many times with true faith that one thenceforth will always believe in one God forever, always love him over all other things, zealously heed his teachings forever, and keep his own commandments properly. And then that baptism will become like a covenant of all those words and all those promises, fulfill it who will. And what I say is true: thenceforth, angels oversee every man forever after his baptism, how he fulfills what he earlier promised when he sought baptism.

33 Utan þæt geðencan oft and gelome and georne gelæstan
þæt þæt we behetan þa we fulluht underfengan, ealswa us
þearf is. And utan word and weorc rihtlice fadian, and ure
ingeðanc clænsian georne and að and wedd werlice healdan
and gelome understandan þone mycclan dom, þe we ealle to
scylon; and beorgan us georne wið þone weallendan bryne
hellewites, and geearnian us ða mærða and ða myrhða, ðe
God hæfð gegearwod þam ðe his willan on worulde gewyr-
cað. Amen.

Let us reflect upon this repeatedly and sincerely abide by 33
that which we promised when we received baptism, just as is
our obligation. And let us order our words and deeds rightly,
fervently cleanse our inmost thoughts, truly keep our oath
and pledge, and frequently reflect on the great judgment to
which we all must go; and zealously shield ourselves against
the surging flame of hellish torments, and earn for ourselves
the glories and happiness which God has prepared for those
who work his will in the world. Amen.

TRACTS ON ECCLESIASTICAL GOVERNANCE

On Episcopal Duties

Item

1   Bisceope gebyreð ælc rihting, ge on godcundan þingan ge on woruldcundan.

2   He sceall gehadode men ærest gewissian, þæt heora ælc wite hwæt him mid rihte gebyrige to donne and eac hwæt hy woruldmannum agan to beodanne.

3   He sceal beon symle ymbe some and ymbe sibbe swa he geornost mæg.

4   He sceall georne saca sehtan and frið wyrcan mid þam worulddeman þe riht lufian.

5   He sceall æt tihtlan ladunge gedihtan, þæt ænig man oðrum ænig woh beodan ne mæge aðor oððe on aþe oððe on ordale.

6   Ne sceall he geþafian ænig unriht, ne woh gemet ne fals gewiht; ac hit gebyreð þæt be his ræde fare and be his gewitnesse æghwylc lahriht, ge burhriht ge landriht. And ælc burhgemet and ælc wægpundern beo be his dihte gescift swiðe rihte, þe læs ænig man oðrum misbeode and ðurh þæt syngige ealles to swyþe.

7   A he sceal scyldan Cristenum mannum wið ælc þæra þinga þe synlic bið; and þy he sceal on æghwæt hine þe swyðor teon, þæt he þe geornor wite hu seo heord fare þe he

On Episcopal Duties

1 It is proper for a bishop to offer guidance in all things, both in religious and secular matters.

2 First, he must oversee men in orders so that each of them may know what is properly fitting for him to do and also what they should preach to the laity.

3 He must always be concerned with reconciliation and peace as fervently as he can.

4 He must readily resolve disputes and make peace along with those secular judges who love justice.

5 He must oversee the defense in response to an accusation, so that no one can inflict harm on another through an oath or an ordeal.

6 He must not permit any injustice, neither an incorrect measurement nor a false weight; but it is proper that every law—both law in the town and law in the country—undergo his review and consent. And every town measurement and every weigh scale is to be properly adjusted under his supervision, lest any man defraud another and thereby sin all too greatly.

7 He must always shield Christians against each of those things which are sinful; and thus he must devote himself the more deeply in all matters so that he might know the more truly how the flock fares which he must tend on God's

to Godes handa gehealdan sceall, þæt deofol to swyðe þæron na sceaþige, ne his falses to fela ongemang ne gesawe.

8   Ne wyrð næfre folces wise wel geræde ne wið God well geborgen on þam earde, þe man wohgestreon and mæst falses lufað. Þy sculan Godes freond ælc unriht alecgan and riht aræran and na geþafian, þæt ðurh fals and ðurh wohgestreon men to swyðe forwyrcean hi sylfe wið þæne rihtwisan God, þe ælc unriht ascunaþ.

9   Eallum Cristenum mannum gebyreð þæt hi riht lufian and unriht ascunian; and huru gehadode men scylon a riht reran and unriht alecgan; þy sculon bisceopas mid woruld-deman domas dihtan, þæt hi ne geþafian, gyf his waldan magan, þæt ðær ænig unriht up aspringe.

10   And sacerdum gebyreþ eac on heora scriftscirum þæt hi georne to rihte æthwam fylstan and na geþafian, gif hi hit gebetan magan, þæt ænig Cristen man oðrum derige ealles to swyðe, ne se maga þam unmagan, ne se hearra þam hean-ran, ne se scirman his gingran, ne se hlaford his mannum, ne furðum his nydþeowan.

11   Be þæs scriftes dihte and be his sylfes gemete gebyreþ mid rihte, þæt ða nydþeowan hlaferdum wyrcan ofer ealle þa scire, þe he on scrife.

12   And riht is, þæt ne beo ænig metegyrd lengre þonne oðer, ac beon be þæs scriftes gemete ealle gescyfte; and ælc gemet on his scriftscire and æghwylc gewihte beo be his dihte gescyft swiðe rihte; and gif ðær hwæt bisæces sy, seme se biscop.

behalf, so that the devil may not inflict harm too greatly on them nor sow too much of his falseness among them.

8   The people's ways will never be well reasoned or well protected by God in that land where ill-gotten gains and the greatest falsehoods are held dear. Thus, God's friends must quell each injustice and encourage what is right and never permit men to ruin themselves too greatly through false-hood and ill-gotten gains before the righteous God who despises all injustice.

9   It is proper for all Christians to love righteousness and hate injustice; and indeed, men in orders must always support what is right and reject what is wrong; thus, bishops must pronounce sentences with secular judges so that they do not permit, if it is in their power, any injustice to spring up there.

10   And likewise it is proper for priests in their parishes to readily assist each person to obtain justice and never permit, if they can correct it, any Christian to inflict injury on another all too greatly, neither the strong on the weak, nor the higher on the lower, nor the shire official on his inferior, nor the lord on his men, nor even his slaves.

11   It is rightly proper that slaves work for their lords according to the guidance of the confessor and under his own supervision throughout the entire shire in which he hears confession.

12   And it is right that there not be any measuring stick longer than another, but all are to be standardized according to the confessor's measure; and each measure in his parish and each weight is to be standardized very precisely according to his direction; and if anything there is disputed, the bishop will judge.

13   Hit bið ælces hlafordes agen þearf þæt he his nydþeo-
wum byrge swa he betst mæge, for ðam þe hy syn Gode efen
leofe and þa ðe syndon freolse, and us ealle he gebohte mid
gelican weorðe.

14   Ealle we syndon Godes agene nydþeowan; and swa he
gedemð us, swa we her demað þam þe we on eorðan dom
ofer agan.

15   Þy we agan þearfe þæt we ðam beorgan þe us scylan hyran; þonne gebide we þe mare gebeorh æt Godes agenum
dome.

13   It is the responsibility of every master to protect his slaves as best he can, for they are loved by God as much as those who are free, and he bought us all for the same price.

14   We are all God's own slaves, and he judges us just as we judge those over whom we hold power here on earth.

15   Accordingly, we have an obligation to protect those compelled to serve us; then we may experience a greater protection at God's own judgment.

On the Remedy of Souls

De medicamento animarum

1   Episcopi igitur et presbyteri prae omnibus sint semper sol-
liciti de cura ecclesiarum et de medicamento animarum non
solum suarum verum etiam et omnium. Confitentibus quoque ac paenitentibus omnimodo succurrant et indifferenter
paenitentiae leges paenitentibus iniungant, divinis eos in-
struentes dogmatibus et consolatoriis verbis ortantes, ut in
vigiliis et ieiuniis et fletibus et diversis corporum castigatio-
nibus, sed et orationibus assiduis et elemosinis multis virili-
ter paeniteant. Episcoporum enim est omnia iudicia aeclae-
siastica rite disponere. Et ut non solum verbis sed etiam
exemplis omnes homines instruant, quia status Christianae
religionis et aeclaesiasticae dignitatis ad eorum curam max-
ime pertinent.

2   Laicorum autem non est sed sacerdotum dei de aeclae-
siasticis disputare iudiciis. Isidorus enim dicit: *Omnis mundi-
alis sapiens, si sapiens sit, non iudicet iudicia aeclesiae.* Quondam
igitur fuit vir quidam Oza nomine, qui extendebat manum
ad arcam domini quam calcitrabant boves, et pro illa temeritate percussit eum dominus, et mortuus est. Saul quoque,
quia sacerdotis usurpare ausus est ministerium, merito a
propheta audivit: *Nequaquam regnum tuum ultra consurget.*

On the Remedy of Souls

On the Remedy of Souls

Thus, let bishops and priests always be attentive above all to   1
the care of churches and the remedy of souls, not just their
own but everyone's. Let them provide treatment by all
means to all those confessing and doing penance, and impose the laws of penance fairly upon the penitent, instruct-
ing them in divine teachings and exhorting them with con-
soling words, so that with vigils and fasting and weeping and
various forms of physical punishment, and also with constant prayers and much almsgiving, they may fervently repent. Indeed, it is the responsibility of all bishops to properly oversee ecclesiastical judgments. And they are to instruct all people not just by words but also by examples, because the state of the Christian faith and the dignity of the
Church depend wholly on their care.

Moreover, it is not for the laity but for God's priests to   2
question the judgments of the Church. For Isidore said: *No
wise man of the world, even if he is wise, may pass judgment on the
judgments of the Church.* Thus, there once was a certain man
named Uzza who reached out to touch the ark of the Lord
when the oxen upset it, and for his temerity the Lord smote
him and he died. Likewise, Saul, because he dared to usurp
the role of the priest, deservedly heard from the prophet:
But thy kingdom shall not continue. Also King Ozias, who had

Ozias etiam rex, cum feliciter regnasset in populo, nefanda tandem praesumptione sacerdotium contra ius arripuit. Pro qua temeritate lepra percussus regnum simul et salutem ammisit.

3   His exemplis declaratur valde perniciosum esse regi vel principi vel alicui ex laico ordine disputare aut tractare de ecclesiasticis iudiciis sive canonicis causis. Paulus enim apostolus dicit: *Divitibus huius saeculi praecipe non sublime sapere.* Alexander quoque ad Demetrium regem ait: *Numquam auditum vel ab aliquo factum sit ut praesentibus episcopis laici disputent de canonicis vel aliis ecclesiasticis causis; sed omnium ecclesiasticarum rerum episcopi curam habeant et ea velut deo contemplante dispensent.*

4   Episcopi quoque nullatenus saecularibus iudiciis aut negotiis, curis vel causis se importune occupent sed ecclesiasticis. Lectioni itaque et orationi et verbi dei praedicationi instanter vacent. Apostolus enim dicit: *Nemo militans deo implicet se negotiis saecularibus.* Sicut enim distantia est ordinum, sic et distantia esse debet inter sacerdotale et saeculare iudicium, et nullus sibi usurpare praesumat quod suo ordini non convenit. Bonus enim pastor super gregem Christi semper sollicitus esse debet. Quapropter episcopi curam animarum indesinenter habeant et nequaquam saeculares curas assumant; sed habeant sub se advocatos et praepositos, qui populares causas exerceant et sint semper parati ad resistendum rebellium pertinacium. Et quoniam sunt nonnulli qui parvipendunt divinam doctrinam, ideo oportet eos per saecularis potentiae disciplinam a tam prava

reigned happily over his people, out of contemptible presumption finally seized the office of the priest, contrary to the law. For this effrontery, he was struck with leprosy, and lost his throne and his health at the same time.

By these examples, it is proven to be entirely sinful for a 3 king or prince or anyone from the laity to question or challenge the judgments of the Church or cases of canon law. Indeed, the apostle Paul said: *Charge the rich of this world not to be high-minded.* Alexander likewise said to King Demetrius: *Let it never be heard of or done by anyone that the laity should dispute canonical or other ecclesiastical proceedings in the presence of bishops, but let bishops have responsibility for all church matters and let them oversee them as if they were under the watchful eye of God.*

Also, by no means are bishops to concern themselves in- 4 appropriately with business dealings or cases in secular judgments or legal proceedings rather than ecclesiastical matters. In this way, let them be free for reading and prayer and for the zealous preaching of God's word. For the Apostle said: *No man, being a soldier to God, entangleth himself with secular businesses.* Indeed, just as there is a difference between orders, so there should also be a difference between priestly and secular judgments, and let no one be so bold as to usurp for himself what is not fitting for his order. Indeed, the good pastor of the flock of Christ should always be watchful. For that reason, let bishops always have the care of souls and no concern at all with secular matters; but let them have representatives and managers below them who can oversee the people's affairs and always be ready for the opposition of obdurate rebels. And since there are some who neglect holy doctrine, it is thereby fitting that they be corrected and

consuetudine coercere et corrigere. Sunt quoque multi qui fingunt et dicunt se habere humilitatem in Christo, sed despiciunt obedientiam mandatorum eius, spernuntque praedicatores salutis. Et propterea mentiuntur, quia non sunt humiles sed superbi. Dominus enim dicit: *Qui vos audit, me audit et qui vos spernit, me spernit.* Et item dicit: *Quodcumque ligaveritis super terram,* et reliqua. Alibi etiam scriptum est: Quodcumque *benedixeritis sit benedictum,* et cetera. Et psalmista de maligno terribiliter loquitur, dicens: Qui *noluit benedictionem prolongabitur ab eo.*

5   Quapropter ammonemus et obsecramus omnes vere fidei cultores ut suimet curam exibeant et ut timorem domini semper habeant, praedicatoribusque salutis ut humiliter obedient, quia ipsi rationem reddituri sunt in die tremendi iudicii quomodo subiectos erudiant, et subditi quomodo doctoribus obtemperent. Est itaque opus cotidianum hoc episcoporum regulariter viventium, ut in lege domini sint meditantes die ac nocte, deumque iugiter laudantes, discipulos docentes, populo praedicantes et assiduis precibus exorantes divine maiestatis clementiam pro salute omnium.

turned away from such perverse practices by the force of secular punishment. Likewise, there are many who deceive and proclaim themselves to be humble before Christ, but they scorn obedience to his commands and despise the call of his preachers. And therefore they lie, for they are not humble but proud. Indeed, the Lord says: *He that heareth you, heareth me; and he that despiseth you, despiseth me.* And he also says: *Whatsoever thou shalt bind upon earth,* etc. Elsewhere it is written: And whatsoever *He that blesseth thee shall also be blessed,* etc. And the psalmist speaking with terrible anger, says: He who *would not have blessing, and it shall be far from him.*

Thus we admonish and entreat all true believers to show 5 care for themselves, and always have fear of God, and humbly heed the calls of his preachers, for they themselves must render an account at the dreaded Day of Judgment as to how they instructed his subjects and how his subjects followed their teachers. It is therefore the daily work of those bishops living rightly that they be meditating day and night upon the law of God, praising him always, teaching students, preaching to the people, and pleading for the mercy of the divine majesty with constant prayer for the salvation of all.

Instructions for Bishops

Incipit de synodo:

1   *"Deus in adiutorium meum intende,"* ter; *"Gloria patri";* *"Kyrie eleison"; "Pater noster"* et *"Ne nos inducas"; "Adiuva nos, Deus"; "Adiutorium nostrum"; "Benedicamus Domino"; "Benedicite"; benedictio:*

2   *Omnipotens Deus sua vos clementia benedicat et sensum in vobis sapientiae salutaris infundat. Catholicae vos fidei documentis enutriat et in sanctis operibus perseverabiles reddat. Gressus vestros ab errore convertat et viam vobis pacis et caritatis ostendat. Quod ipse praestare dignetur.*

3   Bisceopum gebyreð on sinoþe ærost þinga, þæt hi smeagan ymbe anrædnesse and soðe gesibsumnesse heom betweonan, and hu hi Cristendom magan fyrmest aræran and hæþendom swyðost afyllan; and hæbbe ælc bisceop canonboc to sinoðe.

4   Bisceopum is mycel þearf for Gode and for worulde, þæt hi rihtlice anræde weorðan and ealla an lufian; and gif man anum woh beode, betan hit ealle.

5   Bisceopum gebyreð, þæt ælc oþerne warnige gyf he hwæt be oðrum gehyre oððe sylf agyte, and ælc oþerne bæftan werige and nan oðrum his þearfe ne hele, ac weorðþige

Instructions for Bishops

From the synod:

1   *"O God, come to my aid," to be recited three times; "Glory be to the Father"; "Lord, have mercy"; "Our Father" and "Lead us not"; "Help us, O God"; "Our help"; "Let us bless the Lord"; "Glorify the Lord"; a benediction:*

2   *May almighty God bless you with mercy and impart to you a sense of redemptive wisdom. May he support you with the doctrines of the Catholic faith and render you constant in holy works. May he turn your steps from error and show to you the way of peace and charity. May he grant that it be so.*

3   Above all things, it is appropriate for bishops in a synod to seek out unanimity and true harmony between themselves, and how they might best uphold the Christian faith and most firmly reject heathen practices; and each bishop is to have a book of canon law at the synod.

4   There is a great need for bishops to be truly unanimous and all value the same thing in spiritual and secular matters; and if a wrong is done to one of them, they all are to remedy it.

5   It is appropriate for bishops that each one warn his colleague if he hears or himself discovers anything about him, and each is to defend his colleague behind his back, and no one is to withhold from his colleague that which he needs, but each is to show respect to his colleague in word and

ælc oþerne wordes and dæde, and beon, swa heom to gebyreð: *Quasi cor unum et anima una.*

6   Bisceopum gebyreð þæt symle mid heom faran and mid
heom wunian wel geþungene witan, huru sacerdhades, þæt
hi wið rædan magan for Gode and for worulde and þæt
heora gewitan beon on æghwylcne timan, weald hwæt heom
tide.

7   Bisceopum gebyreð þæt æfre sy god lar on heora hire-
dum, and beon, þær hi beon, beon a ymbe wisdom and
æghwylc gefleard heom unwyrð lætan.

8   Bisceopum gebyreþ þæt hi ne beon to gliggeorne, ne
hunda ne hafeca hedan to swyðe, ne woruldwlence ne idelre
rence.

9   Bisceopum gebyreð þæt hi ne beon to feohgeorne æt
hadunge, ne æt halgunge ne æt synbote, ne on ænige wisan
on unriht ne strynan.

10   Bisceopum gebyreð, gif ænig oðrum abelge, þæt man
geþyldige oð geferena some, butan heom sylfe geweorðan
mæge, and na sceotan na to læwedum mannum ne ne scen-
dan na hy sylfe.

11   Bisceopum gebyreð gyf hwylcum hwæt eglige swyðe, þe
he ne betan ne mæge, cyðe hit his geferum and beon syððan
ealle georne ymbe þa bote and na ne geswican, ær hi hit gebetan.

12   Bisceopum gebyreþ þæt hi æfre on ænine man curs ne
settan butan hy nyde scylan. Gyf hit þonne ænig for micclum gewyrhtum nyde gedo, and man gebugan nelle þonne

deed, and to be, as is proper for them, *as if of one heart and one soul.*

6   It is appropriate for bishops that experienced counselors, particularly in holy orders, travel with them always and dwell with them so that they can confer with them concerning spiritual and secular issues and so that they can act as witnesses for them at any time, should anything befall them.

7   It is appropriate for bishops that there always be proper doctrine in their households and that, wherever they are, they always concern themselves with wisdom and deem all folly unworthy of them.

8   It is appropriate that bishops not be overly concerned with trifling amusements, nor care too much for hounds or hawks, nor worldly pomp or empty pride.

9   It is appropriate that bishops not be too greedy at their ordination, nor at their consecration, nor when accepting penance for sins, and they are not to acquire anything wrongly in any way.

10   It is appropriate for bishops that, if one of them angers another, the latter await patiently the mediation of their fellows, unless they can come to an agreement between themselves, but they are never to refer it to laymen nor to demean themselves.

11   It is appropriate for bishops that if something troubles any one of them too greatly, and he cannot resolve it, he is to make it known to his colleagues and they are to offer assistance readily, and not cease until it is resolved.

12   It is appropriate for bishops never to sentence anyone to excommunication unless they must out of necessity. If anyone must do so out of necessity for a great offense, and the miscreant still refuses to submit to justice, then he is to

gyt to rihte, þonne cyðe hit man eallum geferum, and hi ealle þonne settan on þæt ylce and him þæt cyðan. Gebuge þonne syððan and gebete þe deoppor, gif he Godes miltse and blet-sunge recce.

13 Bisceopum gebyreð þæt hi ægðer ge heora agene wisan rihtlice fadian ge ælces hades men to rihte gemyngian.

14 Bisceopum gebyreð þæt hi mid geþylde geþolian þæt hi sylfe gebetan ne magan oð þæt hit þam cyncge gecyþed weorðe, and bete he syððan Godes æbylhþe þær bisceop ne mæge, gif he Godes willan rihte wylle wyrcean and his agene cynescype rihtlice aræran.

announce it to all of his fellows, and they are to sentence him in the same way and make that known to him. Then afterward he is to submit and repent all the more deeply, if he seeks the mercy and blessing of God.

13   It is appropriate for bishops both to conduct their own lives virtuously and to remind those of every rank of what is right.

14   It is appropriate for bishops to suffer patiently that which they themselves cannot resolve until it is made known to the king, and he then must rectify the offense against God when the bishop cannot, if he desires to do God's will properly and rightly uphold his own royal dignity.

An Admonition to Bishops

Biscpas scoldan symle Godes riht bodian and unriht forbeodan. And witodlice, sona swa biscpas rihtes adumbiað, and
sona swa hy eargiaþ and hy rihtes forscamiað and clumiað
mid ceaflum þonne hy scoldan clypian, sona heora wyrðmynt bið waniende swiðe. Ðonne is hit yfel soð þeh þæt ic
secge: sume we synt gewunode þæt we syn to liðie and to lofgeorne; and we willwyrdað mannum æfter freondscipe and
þurh þæt olæcað oftost on unnyt, and soþes geswygiað ealles
to swyþe. And hit is egeslic gewuna þæt we eac habbað: sylfe
we bysniað oft and gelome þæt we geornost scoldan æghwær forbeodan, þæt is woroldwlence and idele rence; and
we oferdruncen lufiað to georne, and mid þam huru þencað
þæt we us sylfe weorðian wide, þe we oðre men drencan to
swyþe. Ac us eallum gebyrede, gyf we riht woldan, þæt we
mid wisdome ægþer drænctan ge ure agen andgyt ge ælces
þera þe us to come, and na mid oðrum drince to oferlice
swyðe, ac be mannes mæðe mid fullan gescade.

2   La, yfele gebyrede biscopum æfre þæt hy woroldmannum
for idelum gylpe cwemdon on unriht ahwar to swyðe; eac hit
is þe wyrse, þe hy unmannum olæcað georne æfter here-
worde. Wið gligmen we ficiað and þam ure feoh gifað, and

An Admonition to Bishops

Bishops must always proclaim God's justice and forbid injustice. And indeed, just as soon as bishops fall silent about what is right and as soon as they grow fearful and come to be ashamed of what is right, and mumble with their mouths when they should cry out, immediately their integrity greatly diminishes. Yet nonetheless it is an evil truth which I speak: some of us are inclined to be too accommodating and too eager for praise; and we offer sweet words to men for their friendship and thereby most often flatter needlessly, and all too often do we remain silent about the truth. Moreover, we also have a terrible habit: over and over again we exemplify in ourselves what we should forbid most zealously everywhere, that is, worldly pride and idle vanity; and we embrace drunkenness too eagerly, and indeed, we believe that our acclaim grows far and wide when we intoxicate others too greatly. Yet it would be appropriate for us all, if we desired what is right, that we intoxicate with wisdom both our own intellect and that of each of those who come to us, and not with other drink in great excess, but with proper distinction according to one's capacity.

Sadly, it has always poorly suited bishops that, for the purpose of idle boasting, they wrongfully curried favor with secular people everywhere too greatly; and it is worse that they willingly flatter the wicked in search of praise. We delude ourselves with entertainers, and give them our money, 2

wið scandwyrde we olæcað georne, willað habban hereword
and scyldan wið unword. Eal þæt is idel and Gode unge-
cweme. Ne gebyrað us æfre þæt we on unriht awiht gestrynan, ne hit eac ræd ne bið þæt we rihte begytan myrran
on unnyt; ac us symle gebyreð þæt swyðe rihte þæt we Godes
þearfan geornlice gladian mid feo and mid fodan, þæs þe we
don magan.

3   Eac us bið gerisenlic þæt we urum freondum luffeorme
dælan, swa swa hit gerise. And huru ne geriseð biscopum
æfre on ænigum ealasele þæt hy to lange clyfian on bænce,
ne æt ham ne on siðe, ac ægðer gemedmigan. Ac we syn
gewunode, swa we na ne scoldan, þæt we taliað to rihte, loc
hwæt us gelicigie, and fylgað urum luste ealles to swyðe. And
we hogiað eac swyþost a ymbe þa þing þe we læst scoldan:
smeagað ymbe woroldcara and idele bisga, and þringað æfter
þrymme and æfter woroldwlence. And we unriht gestreon
eac lufiað to swyþe: syllað wið weorðe oðre hwile, þæt we
orcepe scoldan mid rihte.

4   Ac soð is þæt ic secge, gecnawe se ðe wille: a syððan
biscpas awendan heora wisan of regollicre wisan eall to
woroldwisan, syððan heora weorðscipe wæs waniende
swyþe. Ðonne is þære bote timlice micel þearf. La, utan þæt
geþencan oft and gelome and georne ure wisan gelogian mid
geþincþan, and understandan þæt soð is: þæt næfre ne
geriseð geþungenre ylde to geonclic wise ealles to swyðe; ne
ealdan esne ne bið buton tale þæt he hine sylfne wyrce to
wencle on dollican dædan oþþon on gebæran.

and we willingly offer flattery in exchange for shameful words; we desire praise and to shield ourselves from insult. All of these are vain and displease God. It is never appropriate for us to obtain anything unlawfully, nor indeed is it sensible that we squander what has been rightly obtained on foolishness; but it is always most truly appropriate for us to comfort God's needy willingly with money and food, insofar as we can.

Moreover, it is suitable for us to give our friends loving hospitality, as is appropriate. And indeed, it is never suitable for bishops to linger too long on the bench at a drinking hall, either at home or on a journey, but they are to be moderate in both. But we are accustomed, as we never should be, to consider whatever pleases us to be right and to pursue our desires all too greatly. And we also always reflect the most upon those things which we should the least: we contemplate worldly cares and idle pursuits, and we seek after glory and worldly vanity. And we also love unlawful gain too greatly: we sell sometimes for a price that which we properly should give for free. 3

But what I say is true, recognize it who will: ever since bishops have turned wholly away from canonical practices to worldly practices, their honor has been diminishing greatly. Therefore, there is much need for repentance immediately. Indeed, let us think on that often and frequently, and diligently order our practices with integrity, and understand what is true: that immature behavior is never appropriate for one of mature age in any way; nor is an old man without fault when he makes himself like a child through foolish actions or behavior. 4

The Canons of Edgar

Synodalia decreta

1   Riht is þæt preostas beon geornlice Gode þeowiende
and ðeniende and for eall Cristen folc ðingiende; and þæt
hig ealle beon a heora ealdre holde and gehyrsume, and ealle
anræde to gemænre þearfe; and þæt ælc sy oðrum on fultume and on helpe ge for Gode ge for worulde; and þæt heo
beon heora woruldhlafordum eac holde and getrywe æfter
Godes rihte.

2   And riht is þæt ælc wurðie oðerne; and hyran þa gingran georne heora yldrum, and lufian and læran þa yldran
georne heora gingran.

3   And we lærað þæt hi to ælcon sinoðe habban ælce geare
becc and reaf to godcundre þenunge, and blæc and bocfel to
heora gerædnessum, and þreora daga biwiste.

4   And we lærað þæt preosta gehwilc to sinoðe hæbbe his
cleric and gefædne man to cnihte, and nænigne unwitan þe
disig lufige; ac faran ealle mid gefæde and mid Godes ælmihtiges ege.

5   And riht is þæt preostas on sinoðe gif heom hwæt derige and gif heom ænig man healice misboden hæbbe. Fon hi
þonne ealle on swylce hit hym eallum gedon beo and ge-
fylstan to þæt man hit gebete swa bisceop getæce.

124

The Canons of Edgar

1 It is right that priests are to be obeying and serving God willingly and praying for all Christian people; and that they all be faithful and obedient to their lord always, and wholly single-minded for the common good; and that each be supportive and helpful to others in both spiritual and secular matters; and that they also be faithful and true to their secular lords, in keeping with God's law.

2 And it is right that each respect the other; and the younger willingly obey their elders, and the elders willingly love and instruct the younger.

3 And we instruct that at each yearly synod they are to have books and robes for the holy service, and ink and parchment for their decrees, and provisions for three days.

4 And we instruct that each priest at the synod is to have his clerk and a well-mannered man as an attendant, and no one ignorant who loves foolishness; but all are to proceed with decorum and with fear of almighty God.

5 And it is right that priests make it known at a synod if anyone injures them and if anyone has seriously abused them. Let them receive it just as if it had been done to them all and assist so that it can be rectified just as the bishop directs.

6   And riht is þæt preosta gehwylc on sinode gecyðe gyf he on his scriftscyre ænine man wite Gode oferhyre oþðon on heafodleahtrum yfele befallen, þe he to bote gebigean ne mæge oððe ne durre for woruldafole.

7   And riht is þæt nan sacu þe betweox preostum sy ne beo gescoten to woruldmanna some, ac seman and sibbian heora agene geferan oððe sceoton to ðam bisceope gyf man nyde sceole.

8   And riht is þæt ænig preost sylfwilles ne forlæte þa cyrican þe he to gebletsod wæs, ac hæbbe þa him to rihtæwe.

9   And riht is þæt nan preost oðrum ne ætdo ænig þæra þinga þe him to gebyrige, ne on his mynstre, ne on his scrift-scire, ne on his gyldscipe, ne on ænigum þæra ðinga þe him to gebyrige.

10   And riht is þæt ænig preost ne underfo oðres scolere butan þæs leafe þe he ær folgade.

11   And riht is þæt preosta gehwylc toeacan lare leornige handcræft georne.

12   And riht is þæt ænig gelæred preost ne scende þone samlæredan, ac gebete hine gif he bet cunne.

13   And riht is þæt ænig forðboren preost ne forseo þone læsborenan, forðam gif hit man ariht asmeaþ, þonne syn ealle men anra gebyrda.

14   And riht is þæt preosta gehwylc tylige him rihtlice and ne beo ænig mangeara mid unrihte ne gytsiende massere.

15   And riht is þæt preosta gehwylc fulluhtes and scriftes tyðige sona swa man gyrne; and æghwær on his scriftscyre

6   And it is right that every priest make it known at the synod if he knows of anyone in his parish disobedient to God or plunged by evil into mortal sin whom he cannot sway to repentance or dares not because of their power in the world.

7   And it is right that no dispute between priests is to be submitted to the adjudication of laymen, but their own colleagues are to settle it and make peace or submit it to the bishop if one must.

8   And it is right that no priest out of his own self-will abandon the church into which he was ordained, but he is to keep it as his lawful wife.

9   And it is right that no priest deprive another of any of those things which belong to him, neither in his church, nor in his parish, nor in his guild, nor in any of those things which belong to him.

10   And it is right that a priest not receive another's student without the consent of him he followed previously.

11   And it is right that every priest study a handcraft as well as his scholarship.

12   And it is right that a learned priest not insult someone poorly taught, but correct him if he knows better.

13   And it is right that a highborn priest not disparage one of lower birth, for if one understands it properly, then all are of equal birth.

14   And it is right that every priest support himself properly and not be any sort of corrupt dealer or grasping merchant.

15   And it is right that every priest consent to baptism and confession as soon as anyone requests it; and he is to instruct that each child throughout his parish is to be

beode þæt ælc cild sy gefullod binnon VII nihtum and þæt
ænig man to lange unbiscopad ne wyrðe.

16   And riht is þæt preosta gehwylc Cristendom geornlice
lære and ælcne hæþendom mid ealle adwæsce; and forbeode
wyllweorðunga and licwigelunga, and hwata, and galdra, and
treowwurðunga and stanwurðunga, and ðone deofles cræft
þe man dryhð þær man þa cild þurh þa eorðan tihð, and ða
gemearr þe man drihð on geares niht on mislicum wigelun-
gum and on friðsplottum, and on ellenum and on manegum
mislicum gedwimerum þe men on dreogað fela þæs þe hi ne
sceoldan.

17   And riht is þæt ælc Cristen man his bearn to Cristendome geornlice wenige and him pater noster and credan
getæce.

18   And riht is þæt man geswice freolsdagum hæðenra
leoða and deofles gamena.

19   And riht is þæt man geswice sunnandæges cypincge.

20   And riht is þæt man geswice higleasra gewæda and
dyslicra geræda and bysmorlicra efesunge.

21   And we lærað þæt man geswice cifesgemanan and lufige rihtæwe.

22   And riht is þæt ælc man leornige þæt he cunne pater
noster and credan be ðam þe he wille on gehalgodum licgan
oþðon husles wyrðe beon; forðam he ne bið wel Cristen þe
þæt geleornian nele, ne he nah mid rihte oðres mannes to
onfonne æt fulluhte ne æt bisceopes handa, se ðe þæt ne
can, ær he hit geleornige.

23   And riht is þæt freolsdagum and rihtfæstendagum ænig
geflit ne beo betweox mannum.

baptized within seven nights and that one is not to remain unconfirmed for too long.

16   And it is right that every priest ardently preach the Christian faith and wholly eradicate every heathen practice; and forbid the worship of wells and the raising of the dead, and divination and sorcery, and the worship of trees and stones, and that devil's trick which is performed when children are drawn through the earth, and the deception performed on New Year's night in various magical practices, and in heathen refuges, and in elder trees, and in the many diverse superstitions in which people do much that they should not.

17   And it is right that every Christian readily tutor his children in Christianity and teach them the Paternoster and the Creed.

18   And it is right that on holy days one refrain from heathenish songs and devil's games.

19   And it is right that one refrain from trade on a Sunday.

20   And it is right that one refrain from frivolous clothing and thoughtless elegance and shameful hairstyles.

21   And we instruct that one is to refrain from fornication with a concubine and love one's lawful wife.

22   And it is right that every man study so that he learns his Paternoster and Creed if he wishes to lie in a consecrated grave or be worthy to receive the sacrament; for he is not truly a Christian who will not learn it, nor may he who does not know it legitimately sponsor another at baptism or confirmation until he learns it.

23   And it is right that on holy days and legally designated fast days there be no conflict between people.

24   And riht is þæt man freolsdagum and rihtfæstendagum forga aþas and ordela.

25   And riht is þæt ælc wer forga his wif freolstidum and rihtfæstentidum.

26   And riht is þæt preostas cyrican healdan mid ealre arwyrðnysse to godcundre þenunge and to clænan þeowdome, and to nanum oðrum þingum; ne hy þær ænig unnyt inne ne on neaweste ne geþafian; ne idele spæce, ne idele dæde, ne unnyt gedryh, ne æfre ænig idel; ne binnan cyrictune ænig hund ne hors ne cume, ne swyn þe ma, þæs þe man wealdan mæge.

27   And riht is þæt man into cyrican ænig þing ne logie þæs þe þærto ungedafenlic sy.

28   And riht is þæt man æt cyricwæccan swyðe dreoh sy, and georne gebidde, and ænig gedrync ne ænig unnytt ðær ne dreoge.

29   And riht is þæt man innan cyrican ænine man ne byrige butan man wite þæt he on life Gode to ðam wel gecwemde þæt man þurh þæt læte þæt he sy þæs legeres wyrðe.

30   And riht is þæt ænig preost on ænigum huse ne mæssige butan on gehalgodre cyrican, butan hyt sy for hwilces mannes oferseocnesse.

31   And riht is þæt preost æfre ne mæssige butan onufan gehalgodum weofode.

32   And riht is þæt preost æfre ne mæssige butan bec; ac beo se canon him ætforan eagum. Beseo to gyf he wylle, þæ læs þe him misse.

33   And riht is þæt ælc preost hæbbe corporale þonne he mæssige and subumbrale under his alban, and eall mæssereaf wurðlice behworfen.

24   And it is right that one forgo oaths and ordeals on holy days and legally designated fast days.

25   And it is right that every man forgo his wife during holy times and legally designated fast times.

26   And it is right that priests, with all reverence, preserve churches for holy observances and pure service, and for no other use; nor are they to permit any foolishness inside nor in the vicinity; neither idle speech, nor idle deeds, nor thoughtless actions, nor any idleness ever; nor that any dog nor horse come within the church precincts, much less a pig, if it can be avoided.

27   And it is right that nothing be brought into a church that is unbecoming of it.

28   And it is right that one be very sober at church vigils, and pray fervently, and not engage in any drinking nor foolishness there.

29   And it is right that no one be buried inside the church unless it is known that he pleased God so well in his life that he is therefore believed to be worthy of that burial place.

30   And it is right that a priest not celebrate Mass in any building except a consecrated church, except in the case of someone's extreme sickness.

31   And it is right that a priest never celebrate Mass except on a consecrated altar.

32   And it is right that a priest never celebrate Mass without the book; but the canon is to be before his eyes. He may consult it if he wishes, so as not to make a mistake.

33   And it is right that every priest have a corporal when he celebrates Mass and an amice under his alb, and all the Mass vestments in a worthy state.

34 And riht is þæt ælc preost tylige georne þæt he gode and huru rihte bec hæbbe.

35 And riht is þæt ænig mæssepreost ana ne mæssige þæt he næbbe þone þe him acweðe.

36 And riht is þæt ænig unfæstende man husles ne abyrige, butan hit for oferseocnysse sy.

37 And riht is þæt ænig preost anes dæges oftor ne mæssige þonne þriwa mæstra ðinga.

38 And riht is þæt preost a geara husel hæbbe þam þe þearf sy, and þæt georne on clænnysse healde, and warnige þæt hit ne forealdige. Gyf ðonne hit forhealden sy, þæt his man brucan ne mæge, þonne forbærne hit man on clænum fyre and ða axan under weofode gebringe, and bete wið God georne se ðe hit forgyme.

39 And riht is þæt preost æfre ne geþristlæce þæt he mæssige butan he eall hæbbe þæt to husle gebyrige: þæt is clæne oflete and clæne win and clæne wæter. Wa þam þe mæssan onginð butan he ælc þara hæbbe, and wa þam þe þær ful to deð; forðam he deð þonne gelice þam ðe Iudeas dydon þa hi mengdon eced and geallan togædere and hit syððan on bysmor Criste gebudon.

40 And riht is þæt æfre ne geweorðe þæt preost mæssige and sylf þæt husel ne þicge, ne man gehalgod husel æfre eft halgige.

41 And riht is þæt ælc calic gegoten beo þe man husel on halgige, and on treowenum ne halgige man ænig; ne nænne man fullige oftor þonne æne.

42 And riht is þæt ealle þa ðing þe weofode neah beon and to cyrcan gebyrian beon swyðe clænlice and wurðlice behworfene, and ðær ænig þing fules neah ne cume; ac

34   And it is right that every priest strive conscientiously to have good and, likewise, correct books.

35   And it is right that a priest not celebrate Mass alone so that he has no one to answer him.

36   And it is right that no one receive the sacrament without fasting, except in the case of extreme sickness.

37   And it is right that a priest not celebrate Mass more often than three times in one day at most.

38   And it is right that a priest always have the host prepared for those who need it, and that he carefully keep it in a pure condition, and be sure that it does not decay. Then, if it is not cared for, so that one cannot use it, it is to be burned in a clean fire and the ashes placed under the altar, and he who neglects it is to atone sincerely to God.

39   And it is right that a priest not presume to celebrate Mass unless he has all that is necessary for the sacrament: that is, a pure wafer, pure wine, and pure water. Woe to him who commences the Mass unless he has each of these, and woe to him who puts anything foul in there; for he does then just as the Jews did when they mixed vinegar and gall together and afterward gave it in mockery to Christ.

40   And it is right that it never transpire that a priest celebrate Mass and not himself receive the host, nor should he ever consecrate the Eucharist after it has been consecrated.

41   And it is right that every chalice in which the host is consecrated be cast of metal, and that it not be consecrated in one made of wood; nor should anyone be baptized more than once.

42   And it is right that all those things which are near the altar and belong to the church be kept most cleanly and worthily, and that nothing foul come near there; but the

gelogige man þone haligdom swyðe arwurðlice. And a sy byrnende leoht on cyrican þonne man mæssan singe.

43   And riht is þæt man ne forgyme ænig gehalgod þing: ne halig wæter, ne sealt, ne stor, ne hlaf, ne gehalgode axan, ne gehalgod oflete, ne ænig þing haliges. Ac forbærne hit man on clænum fyre, butan his man elles notian mæge, and ða axan under weofode gebringe.

44   And riht is þæt ænig wifman neah weofode ne cume þa hwile þe man mæssige.

45   And riht is þæt man on rihtne timan tida hrincge, and preosta gehwylc þonne his tidsang on cyrcan gesece and ðær, mid Godes ege, hi georne gebiddan and for eall folc þingian.

46   And riht is þæt mæssapreosta nan ne cume gewæpned binnan cyrican dura, ne binnan weofodstealle butan his oferslope, ne huru æt ðam weofode þæt he þær þenige butan þære wæde.

47   And riht is þæt ænig gehadod mann his sceare ne helige, ne hine misefesian ne læte, ne his beard ænige hwile hæbbe, be þam þe he wille Godes bletsunga habban and sancte Petres and ure.

48   And riht is þæt ealle preostas æt freolsan and æt fæstenan anræde beon, and ealle on ane wisan beodan þæt hi folc ne dwelian.

49   And riht is þæt ælc fæsten beo mid ælmessan gewurðod, þæt is þæt gehwa on Godes est ælmessan georne sylle; þonne bið his fæsten Gode gecweme.

50   And riht is þæt preostas on cyricþenungum ealle an dreogan, and beon efenforðe ofer geares fæc on eallum cyricþenungum.

hallowed objects are to be arranged most reverently. And a light is always to be burning in church when one sings the Mass.

43   And it is right that nothing consecrated be overlooked: not the holy water, nor the salt, nor the incense, nor the bread, nor the consecrated ashes, nor the consecrated host, nor anything holy. But it is to be burned in a pure fire, unless it can still be used, and the ashes placed under the altar.

44   And it is right that no woman approach the altar while Mass is being celebrated.

45   And it is right that one ring the hours at the proper time, and then every priest is to attend his service in the church and there, for fear of God, fervently pray and intercede for all people.

46   And it is right that no priest come within the church doors while armed or within the sanctuary without his stole, or especially that he serve at the altar without that garment.

47   And it is right that a man in orders not hide his tonsure, nor permit his hair to be cut improperly, nor keep his beard for any length of time, insofar as he desires to have God's blessing and Saint Peter's and ours.

48   And it is right that all priests be of one mind about holy days and fasts, and all proclaim them in the same way so that they do not mislead the people.

49   And it is right that every fast be observed with almsgiving, that is, that one should give alms willingly for the grace of God; then his fast will be pleasing to God.

50   And it is right that priests conduct church services all in the same way, and be equally far along over the course of the year in all church services.

51   And riht is þæt preostas geogoðe geornlice læran and
to cræftum teon, þæt hy cyricfultum habban.

52   And riht is þæt preostas ælce sunnandæge folce bodian
and a wel bysnian.

53   And riht is þæt ænig Cristen man blod ne þycge.

54   And riht is þæt preostas folc mynegian þæs þe hi Gode
don sculon to gerihtum on teoþungum and on oðrum
þingum. And riht is þæt man þisses mynegige to Eastrum,
oðre siðe to gangdagum, þriddan siðe to middan sumera
þonne bið mæst folces gegaderod. Ærest sulhælmessan XV
niht ofer Eastran, geogoðe teoðunge be Pentecosten, Romfeoh be Petres mæssan, eorðwæstma be Ealra Halgena mæssan, cyricsceat to Martinus mæssan, and leohtgesceotu
þriwa on geare: ærest on Easter æfen, and oðre siðe on Candelmæsse æfen, þriddan siðe on Ealra Halgena mæsse æfen.

55   And riht is þæt preostas swa dælan folces ælmessan
þæt hi ægðer don ge God gegladian ge folc to ælmessan we-
nian.

56   And riht is þæt man betæce ænne dæl preostum,
oþerne dæl to cyricneode, þriddan dæl þam þearfum.

57   And riht is þæt preostas sealmas singan þonne hy ða
ælmessan dælan, and ða þearfan georne biddan þæt hi for
þæt folc þingian.

58   And riht is þæt preostas beorgen wið oferdruncen and
hit georne belean oðrum mannum.

51 And it is right that priests willingly teach the young and instruct them in handiwork, so that they may have assistance in church.

52 And it is right that priests preach to the people each Sunday and always set a good example.

53 And it is right that Christians not consume blood.

54 And it is right that priests remind the people of that which they must give to God as dues in the form of tithes and in other ways. And it is right that one remind them of this at Easter, again at Rogation, and a third time at midsummer, when the most people are gathered. First plow dues are fifteen nights after Easter, the tithing of the young animals by Pentecost, the dues to Rome by the Feast of Saint Peter, the tithe on the fruits of the earth by the Feast of All Saints, Church dues by the Feast of Saint Martin, and dues for the lighting of the church three times a year: first on Easter eve, a second time on Candlemas eve, and a third time on the eve of the Feast of All Saints.

55 And it is right that priests distribute the people's alms in a manner that both pleases God and accustoms the people to almsgiving.

56 And it is right that one portion be set aside for the priests, a second portion for the church's needs, a third portion for the poor.

57 And it is right that priests sing psalms when they give out alms, and that the poor ardently beg that they intercede for the people.

58 And it is right that priests preserve themselves against drunkenness and zealously forbid it in others.

59   And riht is þæt ænig preost ne beo ealusceop, ne on ænige wisan gliwige mid him sylfum oðrum mannum, ac beo swa his hade gebyrað, wis and woerðfull.

60   And riht is þæt preostas wið aþas beorgan heom georne and hi eac swyþe forbeodan.

62   And riht is þæt ænig preost ne stande on leasre gewitnesse, ne þeofa gewita beo.

63   And riht is þæt preost bisæce ordol æfre ne geæþe.

64   And riht is þæt preost wið þegen ne ladige butan þegenes foraþe.

65   And riht is þæt preost ne beo hunta ne hafecere ne tæflere, ac plege on his bocum swa his hade gebyrað. Se canon segð: *Gyf hwylc gehadod man on huntaþ fare, gyf hit bið clerec forga* XII *monað flæsc, diacon twa gear, mæssepreost þreo, bisceop* VII.

66   And gyf hwylc bisceop oððe mæssepreost oððe ænig gehadod man hine sylfne rædlice oferdrince, oððe he þæs geswice, oððe his hades þolige.

67   And riht is þæt preostas aa gearuwe beon to folces gerihtum.

68   And riht is þæt ælc preost scrife and dædbote tæce þam þe him andette, and eac to bote fylste, and seoce men huslige þonne heom þearf sy, and eac hy smyrige gif hi þæs gyrnan, and æfter forðsiðe georne behweorfe, and ne geþafige ænig unnytt æt þam lice, ac hit mid Godes ege wislice bebyrge.

68a   And riht is þæt ænig preost ne lufige wifmanna neawiste ealles to swiþe, ac lufige his rihtæwe, þæt is his cyrice.

59   And it is right that a priest not be a singer among drunkards, nor himself entertain other men in any way, but he is to act in keeping with his status, wise and respectable.

60   And it is right that priests fervently guard themselves against oaths and also zealously forbid them.

62   And it is right that a priest not stand in false witness or be an accessory of thieves.

63   And it is right that a priest never use his oath to validate a questionable ordeal.

64   And it is right that a priest not defend himself against a thane unless that thane has sworn an initial oath.

65   And it is right that a priest not be a hunter or a hawker or a gambler, but entertain himself with his books in keeping with his status. The canon says: *If anyone in orders goes hunting, if he is a cleric he is to abstain from meat for twelve months, a deacon for two years, a priest for three, a bishop for seven.*

66   And if any bishop or priest or any man in orders knowingly makes himself drunk, either he must cease doing so or lose his status.

67   And it is right that priests always be ready to perform the rites to which the people are entitled.

68   And it is right that every priest absolve and assign penance to anyone who confesses to him, and also guide him to atonement, and administer the sacrament to the sick when they need it, and also anoint them if they desire it, and willingly see to the arrangements after death, and not permit any carelessness around the body, but bury it wisely with fear of God.

68a   And it is right that a priest not love the company of women all too greatly, but love his lawful wife, that is, his church.

68b And riht is gif weofodþen his agen lif be boca tæcincge rihtlice fadige, þonne sy he fulles þegnscipes wyrþe ge on life ge on legere. Gyf he his lif misfadige, wanige his wyrðscipe be ðam þe seo dæd sy. Wite, gif he wylle, ne gebyrað him naðor ne to wife ne to woruldwige, gif he Gode wile rihtlice hyran and Godes lage rihtlice healdan.

68c Dunstan gedemde þæt se mæssepreost nære, gif he wif hæfde, ænige oðre lade wyrþe butan eallswa læwede sceolde þe efenboren wære, gif man mid tihtlan þæne belede.

68d And riht is gyf weofodþen hine hrihtlice healde, þonne sy he fulles weres and wurðscipes wyrðe.

68e And gyf hit gewurðe þæt man mid tihtlan and mid uncræftum sacerd belecge þe regollice libbe, and he hine sylfne wite þas clæne, mæssige gyf he durre, and ladige on þam husle, hine sylfne æt anfealdre spræce. Æt ðryfealdre spræce ladige gif he durre, eac on þam husle, mid twam his gehadan.

68f Gif man diacon tihtlige þe regollice libbe anfealdre spræce, nime twegen his gehadan and ladige hine mid þam. And gif man hine tihtlige ðryfealdre spræce, nime six his gehadan and ladige mid þam, and beo he sylf seofeða.

68g And gif man folciscne mæssepreost mid tihtlan belecge þe regollif næbbe, ladige hine swa diacon þe regollife libbe.

68b And it is right that if a clergyman who serves at the altar orders his own life properly according to the precepts of the books, then he is worthy of the full status of a thane, both in life and in death. If he does not order his life properly, his status is to diminish according to his deeds. May he know, if he will, that he is not to involve himself with a wife or with the warfare of this world, if he desires to heed God properly and properly keep God's laws.

68c Dunstan ruled that a priest, if he had a wife, was not entitled to clear himself by any means other than that of a layman who was born his equal, if one accused him.

68d And it is right that if a clergyman who serves at the altar conducts himself properly, then he is to be entitled to full wergild and honor.

68e And if it so happens that a priest who lives according to a rule is charged with an allegation and a claim of wrongful behavior, and he knows himself to be innocent of that, he may celebrate Mass if he dares, and clear himself through the Eucharist against a simple accusation. Against a three-fold accusation, he may also, if he dares, clear himself through the Eucharist with two of his rank.

68f If a deacon who lives according to a rule is charged with a simple accusation, he may select two of his rank and clear himself with them. And if he is charged with a threefold accusation, he may select six of his rank and clear himself with them, and he himself shall be the seventh.

68g And if a charge is brought against a secular priest who does not live according to a rule, he may clear himself in the manner of a deacon who lives according to a rule.

68h And gyf man freondleasne weofodþen mid tihtlan belecge þe aðfultum næbbe, ga to corsnæde, and ðær þonne æt gefare þæt þæt God wylle, butan he on husle ladian mote.

68i And gif man gehadodne mid fæhðe belecge and secge þæt he wære dædbana, ladige mid his magum þe fæhða motan mid beran oððe fore betan. And gyf he sy mægleas, ladige mid geferan oððe on fæstan fo, gif he þæt þurfe, and ga to corsnæde, and þæræt gefare swa swa God ræde.

69 And riht is þæt preosta gehwylc ægþer hæbbe ge fulluhtele ge seocum smerels, and a gearu sy to folces gerihtum, and Cristendom fyrðrige georne on æghwylce wisan, and ægðer do ge wel bodige ge wel bysnige. Þonne geleanað him þæt God ælmihtig swa him leofost bið. Amen.

68h And if a charge is brought against a clergyman who serves at the altar and who lacks friends and supporters for his oath, he is to undergo the ordeal of the consecrated bread, and thereby experience that which God wills, unless he is allowed to clear himself with the Eucharist.

68i And if a man in orders is charged with feud and it is alleged that he is a murderer, he is to clear himself with his kin, who may either extend the feud or compensate for it. And if he has no kin, he may exonerate himself with the support of his colleagues or fast to prepare for the ordeal of consecrated bread, and there endure whatever God decides.

69   And it is right that every priest have both baptismal oil and oil for anointing the sick, and always be prepared to perform the rites to which the people are entitled, and zealously promote Christianity in every way, and both preach well and set a good example. Then almighty God will reward him for that, in the manner most pleasing to him. Amen.

ROYAL LEGISLATION

5 Æthelred

In nomine Domini, anno Dominicae incarnationis MVIII:

Pr   Ðis is seo gerædnes þe Engla cyng and ægðer ge gehadode ge læwede witan gecuran and geræddan.

1   Ðæt is þonne ærest: þæt we ealle ænne God lufian and
weorðian, and ænne Cristendom georne healdan, and ælcne
hæðendom mid ealle aweorpan; and þæt we habbað ealle
ægþer ge mid worde ge mid wedde gefæstnod, þæt we under
anum cynedome ænne Cristendom healdan willað.

1.1   And ures hlafordes gerædnes and his witena is þæt man
rihte laga up arære and ælce unlaga georne afylle, and þæt
man læte beon æghwylcne man rihtes wyrþe.

1.2   And þæt man frið and freondscype rihtlice healde innan þysan earde for Gode and for worolde.

2   And ures hlafordes gerædnes and his witena is þæt man
Cristene menn and unforworhte of earde ne sylle, ne huru
on hæþene leode; ac beorge man georne, þæt man þa sawla
ne forfare þe Crist mid his agenum life gebohte.

3   And ures hlafordes gerædnes and his witena is þæt man
Cristene men for ealles to lytlum to deaðe ne fordeme.

5 Æthelred

In the name of the Lord, 1008 years since the incarnation of the Lord:

Pr   This is the decree which the king of the English and both his ecclesiastical and secular councilors have approved and proclaimed.

1   Therefore this is foremost: that we all love and praise the one God, and fervently uphold one Christian faith, and entirely reject all heathen practices; and that we have all committed, both by word and by pledge, that we will adhere to one Christian faith under one royal authority.

1.1   And the decree of our lord and his councilors is that just laws be upheld and each injustice zealously eradicated, and that each person be afforded their legal rights.

1.2   And that peace and friendship be justly preserved in this land before God and the world.

2   And the decree of our lord and his councilors is that those who are Christian and free of guilt shall not be sold out of this land, and especially not to heathen people; but we must zealously ensure that the souls not be destroyed which Christ purchased with his own life.

3   And the decree of our lord and his councilors is that Christians are not to be sentenced to death for entirely too little.

3.1   Ac elles geræde man friðlice steora folce to þearfe, and ne forspille for lytlum Godes handgeweorc and his agenne ceap, þe he deore gebohte.

4   And ures hlafordes gerædnes and his witena is þæt ælces hades menn georne gebugan for Gode and for worolde, ælc to þam rihte, þe him to gebyrige.

4.1   And huruþinga Godes þeowas—biscopas and abbudas, munecas and mynecena, preostas and nunnan—to rihte gebugan and regollice libban, and for eall Cristen folc þingian georne.

5   And ures hlafordes gerædnes and his witena is þæt muneca gehwylc þe ute sy of mynstre and regoles ne gyme, do swa him þearf is: gebuge georne into mynstre mid eallum eadmettum and misdæda geswice and bete swyþe georne þæt he abrocen hæbbe. Geðence word and wedd, þe he Gode betæhte.

6   And se munuc þe mynster næbbe cume to scirebiscope and trywsie hine sylfne wið God and wið men, þæt he huru þreo þing þanan forð healdan wille: þæt is his clænnese and munuclice scrudware and þeowian his Drihtne, swa wel swa he betst mæge.

6.1   And gyf he þæt gelæste, þonne bið he wyrðe, þæt hine man þe bet healde, wunige þær he wunige.

7   And canonicas, þær seo ar sy þæt hy beoddern and slæpern habban magan, healdan heora mynster mid rihte and mid clænnesse, swa heora regol tæce; oððon riht is, þæt þolige þære are se ðe þæt nelle.

8   And ealle mæssepreostas we biddað and lærað þæt hy beorgan heom sylfum wið Godes yrre.

3.1 Instead, merciful penalties are to be established for the good of the people, and so that God's handiwork, which he paid for himself at a high cost, not be destroyed.

4 And the decree of our lord and his councilors is that those of every rank shall faithfully submit before God and the world to the duty most appropriate for them.

4.1 And indeed, God's servants—bishops and abbots, male and female monastics, priests and nuns—are to submit to their duty and live according to their rule, and fervently intercede for all Christian people.

5 And the decree of our lord and his councilors is that each monk who is out of a monastery and not in compliance with his rule shall do what is necessary for him: readily surrender himself to a monastery with all humility, renounce his misdeeds, and sincerely repent for the rules he has broken. Let him reflect upon the word and pledge that he devoted to God.

6 And the monk who does not have a monastery shall come to the bishop of the diocese and commit himself before God and men to especially observe three things thenceforth: that is, his celibacy, his monastic habit, and his service to God as best he can.

6.1 And if he fulfills that, then he will be worthy of higher esteem wherever he resides.

7 And canons, when their holding is such that they possess a refectory and a dormitory, shall hold their monastery with propriety and celibacy, just as their rule instructs; or else he who will not do that must forfeit his holding.

8 And we require and instruct all priests to protect themselves against the wrath of God.

9   Fulgeorne hy witan þæt hy nagon mid rihte þurh hæmedþing wifes gemanan.

9.1   And se ðe þæs geswican wille and clænnesse healdan hæbbe he Godes miltse, and þærtoeacan to woroldweorð-scype, þæt he sy þegenweres and þegenrihtes wyrðe, ge on life ge on legere.

9.2   And se þe þæt nelle þæt his hade gebyrige wanige his weorðscype ge for Gode ge for worolde.

10   And æghwylc Cristen man eac unrihthæmed georne forbuge and godcunde laga rihtlice healde.

10.1   And sy ælc cyrice on Godes griðe and on ðæs cynges and on ealles Cristenes folces.

10.2   And ænig man heonan forð cyrican ne ðeowige, ne cyricmangunge mid unriht ne macie, ne cyricþen ne utige butan biscopes geþehte.

11   And gelæste man Godes gerihta georne æghwylce geare.

11.1   Ðæt is sulhælmessan xv niht onufan Eastran and geogoðe teoðunge be Pentecosten and eorðwæstma be Ealra Halgena mæssan and Romfeoh be Petres mæssan and leoht-gescot þriwa on geare.

12   And saulsceat is rihtast þæt man symle gelæste æt openum græfe.

12.1   And gyf man ænig lic of rihtscriftscire elles hwar lecge, gelæste man saulsceat swa þeh into þam mynstre þe hit to hyrde.

12.2   And ealle Godes gerihta fyrðrige man georne, ealswa hit þearf is.

12.3   And freolsa and fæstena healde man rihtlice.

13   Sunnandæges freols healde man georne, swa þærto ge-byrige.

9   They know full well that they may not rightfully engage in sexual relations with a woman.

9.1   But he who will renounce marriage and practice celibacy will have God's favor, and also, as a privilege in this world, he shall be deemed worthy of a thane's wergild and a thane's rights, both in life and after death.

9.2   But he who will not act in a manner fitting for his order shall diminish his honor before God and the world.

10   And every Christian must diligently avoid unlawful intercourse and rightly uphold the divine law.

10.1 And each church shall be under the protection of God and of the king and of all Christian people.

10.2 And henceforth no one shall persecute the church, nor wrongfully make it an object of exchange, nor expel a cleric without the bishop's permission.

11   And God's dues are to be paid readily every year:

11.1 that is, plow dues fifteen nights after Easter, the tithe of the young animals by Pentecost, the tithe on the fruits of the earth by the Feast of All Saints, the dues to Rome by the Feast of Saint Peter, and the dues for the lighting of the church three times a year.

12   And it is most appropriate that dues for the souls of the dead always be paid while the grave is yet open.

12.1 And if any person's body is buried other than in its proper parish, the dues should still be paid to the church to which he belonged.

12.2 And all God's dues are to be given willingly, just as is required.

12.3 And feasts and fasts are to be properly observed.

13   The Sunday holy day shall be held properly, as is fitting thereto.

13.1 And cypinga and folcgemota on ðam halgan dæge geswice man georne.

14 And sancte Marian freolstida ealle weorðie man georne,
ærest mid fæstene and syððan mid freolse.

14.1 And to æghwylces apostoles heahtide fæste man and
freolsige; buton to Philippus and Iacobus freolse ne beode
we nan fæsten for þam Eastorlican freolse.

15 Elles oðre freolsa and fæstena healde man georne, swa
swa þa heoldan þa ðe betst heoldan.

16 And sancte Eadwerdes mæssedæg witan habbað
gecoren, þæt man freolsian sceal ofer eal Englaland on xv
kalendas Aprilis.

17 And fæstan ælce Frigedæg butan hit freols sy.

18 And ordal and aðas syndan tocweðen freolsdagum and
rihtymbrendagum and fram Adventum Domini oð octabas
Epiphanie and fram Septuagessiman oð xv niht ofer Eastran.

19 And beo ðam halgum tidan, ealswa hit riht is, eallum
Cristenum mannum sib and som gemæne, and ælc sacu ge-
twæmed.

20 And gyf hwa oðrum scyle borh oððon bote æt worold-
lican þingan, gelæste hit georne ær oððon æfter.

21 And sy ælc wydewe, þe hy sylfe mid rihte gehealde, on
Godes griðe and on þæs cynges.

21.1 And sitte ælc XII monað werleas; ceose syððan þæt heo
sylf wille.

22 And æghwylc Cristen man do, swa him þearf is: gyme
his Cristendomes georne and gewunige gelomlice to scrifte
and unforwandodlice his synna gecyðe and geornlice bete,
swa swa him man tæce.

13.1 And one must assiduously avoid markets and meetings on that holy day.

14 And each of the Feasts of Saint Mary is to be celebrated faithfully, first with fasting and then with a holiday.

14.1 And for the feast of each apostle there is to be fasting and a holiday, but we order no fast for the Feasts of Philip and James because of Easter.

15 Otherwise, feasts and fasts are to be kept assiduously, just as they were kept when they were kept best.

16 And the council has determined that the Feast of Saint Edward shall be celebrated throughout England on the fifteenth day before the kalends of April.

17 And there shall be a fast each Friday unless it is a feast.

18 And ordeals and oaths are prohibited during feasts and Ember Days and from Advent until the fourteenth night after midwinter and from the Septuagesima until the fifteenth night after Easter.

19 And at holy times, just as is proper, there is to be peace and friendship among all Christians, and each dispute is to be resolved.

20 And if anyone must pay a debt or compensation to another because of a worldly matter, he is to do so promptly before or after the feast.

21 And all widows who comport themselves properly shall be under the protection of God and the king.

21.1 And each of them is to remain husbandless for twelve months; then she may choose as she pleases.

22 And every Christian shall do what is required: attend diligently to his Christian faith, go frequently to confession, confess his sins without hesitation, and sincerely repent just as he is instructed.

22.1 And gearwige eac to huslgange oft and gelome gehwa hine sylfne.

22.2 And word and weorc fadige mid rihte and að and wedd wærlice healde.

23 And æghwylc unriht aweorpe man georne of þysan earde, þæs þe man gedon mæge.

24 And swicollice dæda and laðlice unlaga ascunige man swyðe, þæt is: false gewihta and woge gemeta and lease ge- witnessa and fracodlice ficunga;

25 and egeslice manswara and deoflice dæda on morð- weorcan and on manslihtan, on stalan and on strudungan, on gitsungan and on gifernessan, on ofermettan and on ofer- fyllan, on swiccræftan and on mistlican lahbrycan, on had- brycan and on æwbrican and on mæniges cynnes misdædan.

26 Ac lufige man Godes riht heonan forð georne wordes and dæde; þonne wyrð þysse þeode sona God milde.

26.1 And beo man georne ymbe friðes bote and ymbe feos bote æghwar on earde, and ymbe burhbota on æghwylcan ende and ymbe fyrdunga eac, be ðam þe man geræde, aa þonne neod sy;

27 and ymbe scipfyrðrunga, swa man geornost mæge, þæt æghwylc geset sy sona ofer Eastran æghwylce geare.

28 And gyf hwa butan leafe of fyrde gewende þe se cyning sylf on sy, plihte him sylfum and ealre his are.

28.1 And se þe elles of fyrde gewende, beo se cxx scillinga scyldig.

29 And gyf ænig amansumad man, butan hit friðbena sy, on þæs cynges neaweste ahwar gewunige, ær ðam þe he hæbbe godcunde bote georne gebogene, þonne plihte he him sylfum and eallan his æhtan.

154

22.1 And everyone is also to prepare themselves often and frequently to receive the sacrament.

22.2 And words and deeds are to be ordered properly, and oath and pledge carefully upheld.

23 And all injustice is to be banished from this land as much as possible.

24 And fraudulent deeds and hateful injustices are to be entirely rejected, that is: false weights and counterfeit measures and perjured testimony and shameful deceptions;

25 and dreadful falsehoods and devilish deeds, such as murder and manslaughter, theft and robbery, avarice and cupidity, gluttony and overindulgence, treachery and countless violations of the law, of holy orders, of marriage vows, and misdeeds of many kinds.

26 But God's law is to be willingly embraced henceforth in word and deed; then will God immediately show mercy to this people.

26.1 And the improvement of public safety, the improvement of the currency throughout the land, the improvement of fortifications everywhere, and military service are to be carefully overseen in the manner decreed as the need arises;

27 and the provisioning of ships as fully as possible so that they will be prepared just after Easter each year.

28 And if anyone deserts an army led by the king himself, he shall risk forfeiture of his life and all his property.

28.1 And he who deserts any other army is to be penalized 120 shillings.

29 And if anyone who has been excommunicated, unless he is seeking protection, remains anywhere in the king's proximity before he has fully submitted to spiritual penance, he shall risk forfeiture of his life and all his possessions.

30   And gyf hwa ymb cyninges feorh syrwe, sy he his feores scyldig; and gif he ladian wille, do þæt be ðæs cynges wergylde oððe mid þryfealdan ordale on Engla lage.

31   And gyf hwa forsteal oððon openne wiþercwyde ongean lahriht Christes oððe cyninges ahwar gewyrce, gylde swa wer swa wite swa lahslite, aa be ðam þe seo dæd sy.

31.1 And gyf he ongean riht þurh æhlyp geonbyrde and swa gewyrce, þæt hine man afylle, licge ægylde eallan his freondan.

32   And æfre alicgan heonan forð þa unlaga þe ær þysan wæran to gewunelice wide.

32.1 Ðæt is þonne an ærest æt ðam ætfengan, þe swicigen manswican lufedan be westan, þe mænigne man geswænctan and on unriht gedrehtan.

32.2 And oðer is, þæt gewitnessa ne moston standan, þeah hi fulgetreowe wæron and hi swa sædan swa hi to woldon swerian.

32.3 Ðridde is æt swigean, þæt man wolde sweogian and on æftergængan eft siððan sprecan, þæt man on forgængan næfre becliopode.

32.4 And be norðan stod seo unlagu þæt man moste banweorc on unsacne secgan, and þæt scolde standan gif hit wurde swa gecyðed ydæges sona.

32.5 Ac þæt unriht alegde ure hlaford. Þæt he ma mote!

33   And æghwylce unlaga alecge man georne.

33.1 Forþam þurh þæt hit sceal on earde godian to ahte, þe man unriht alecge and rihtwisnesse lufie for Gode and for worolde.

30   And if anyone conspires against the king's life, his life will be forfeit; and if he wishes to be exonerated, he can do so by paying the king's wergild or with the threefold ordeal under English law.

31   And if anyone anywhere acts to obstruct or openly oppose the legal prerogatives of Christ or the king, he shall pay either wergild, a fine, or *lahslit,* according to the nature of the crime.

31.1 And if he resists the law with violence and, so doing, causes his own death, no wergild shall be paid to his friends.

32   And forever henceforth the unlawful practices are to cease which beforehand were too often found widely:

32.1 First of all, concerning the property seizures loved by lying swindlers in the west, which have distressed and wrongfully afflicted many people.

32.2 And the second is that witnesses were not deemed legitimate, though they were fully trustworthy and willing to swear to that which they testified.

32.3 Thirdly, concerning the bringing of lawsuits against an heir after remaining silent that were never brought against his predecessor.

32.4 And in the north there has been the unlawful practice that one can level an accusation of murder against an innocent person and it shall be permitted to stand if it was made immediately on the same day.

32.5 But our lord has brought an end to this wrongful practice. May he do so to others!

33   And all injustice is to be utterly eradicated.

33.1 Because it is by purging injustice and embracing righteousness before God and the world that improvement shall be brought to the land.

34   Ealle we scylan ænne God lufian and weorðian and ælcne hæðendom mid ealle aweorpan.

35   And utan ænne cynehlaford holdlice healdan and lif and land samod ealle werian swa wel swa we betst magan, and God ealmihtigne inwerdre heortan fultumes biddan.

34 We must all love and praise the one God and entirely reject all heathen practices.

35 And let us faithfully support one royal lord and all together defend our lives and our land as best as we can, and pray for help to God almighty with our innermost hearts.

6 Æthelred

Be witena gerædnessan:

Pr   Þis syndan þa gerædnessa þe Engla rædgifan gecuran and gecwædan and geornlice lærdan, þæt man scolde healdan.

1   And þæt is þonne ærest þæra biscpa frumræd: þæt we ealle fram synnum georne gecyrran þæs þe we don magan, and ure misdæda andettan georne, and geornlice betan, and ænne God rihtlice lufian and weorðian, and ænne Christendom anrædlice healdan, and ælcne hæþendom georne forbugan, and gebedrædene aræran georne us betweonan, and sibbe and some lufian georne, and anum cynehlaforde holdlice hyran and georne hine healdan mid rihtan getrywðan.

2   And witena gerædnes is, þæt abbodas and abbodissan heora agen lif rihtlice fadian and eac heora heorda wislice healdan.

2.1   And þæt ælces hades men georne gebugan for Gode and for worolde, ælc to þam rihte þe him to gebyrige.

2.2   And huruþinga Godes þeowas—biscpas and abbodas, munecas and mynecena, canonicas and nunnan—to rihte gecyrran and regollice libban and for eall Christen folc þingian georne.

3   And witena gerædnes is, þæt muneca gehwilc, þe ute of mynstre sy, and regoles ne gyme, do swa him þearf is: gebuge

6 Æthelred

Concerning the decrees of the councilors:

Pr   These are the decrees which the councilors of the English determined upon, pronounced, and solemnly ordered to be obeyed.

1   And this is the principal decree of the bishops: that we all readily turn from sins as much as we can, and sincerely confess our misdeeds, and earnestly repent, and rightly love and praise the one God, and unanimously hold to the one Christian faith, and zealously reject all heathen customs, and truly revere among ourselves the practice of prayer, and genuinely cherish peace and reconciliation, and loyally obey one royal lord, and willingly follow him with proper devotion.

2   And the decree of the councilors is that abbots and abbesses are to order their own lives rightly and also oversee their flocks wisely.

2.1   And people of every rank shall faithfully submit before God and the world to the duty appropriate for them.

2.2   And indeed, God's servants—bishops and abbots, male and female monastics, canons and nuns—are to submit to their duty and live according to their rule, and fervently intercede for all Christian people.

3   And the decree of the councilors is that each monk who is out of a monastery and not in compliance with his rule shall do what is necessary for him: readily surrender

georne into mynstre mid eallum eaðmettum and misdæda geswice and bete swyþe georne þæt he abrocen hæbbe. Geþence word and wedd, þe he Gode betæhte.

3.1 And se munuc þe mynster næbbe, cume to scirebiscop and trywsige hine sylfne wið God and wið men þæt he huru þreo þing þanon forð healdan wille, þæt is: his clænnesse and munuclice scrudware and þeowian his Drihtne, swa wel swa he betst mæge.

3.2 And gif he þæt gelæste, þonne bið he weorðe, þæt hine man þe bet healde, wunige þær he wunige.

4 And canonicas, þær seo ar sy, þæt hy beodern and slæpern habban magan, healdan heora mynster mid clænnesse, swa heora regol tæce; oþþon riht is, þæt þolige þære are se þe þæt nelle.

5 And ealle Godes þeowas, and huruþinga sacerdas, we biddað and lærað þæt hy Gode hyran and clænnesse lufian and beorhgan him sylfum wið Godes yrre.

5.1 Fulgeorne hi witan þæt hy nagon mid rihte þurh ænig hæmedþing wifes gemanan.

5.2 Ac hit is þe wyrse þe sume habbað twa oððe ma, and sum—þeh he forlæte þa he ær hæfde—he be lifiendre þære eft oþere nimð, swa ænigan Cristenan mæn ne gedafenað to donne.

5.3 And se ðe þæs geswican wille and clænnesse healdan hæbbe he Godes miltse, and þærtoeacan to woroldweorð-scipe, þæt he sy þegenweres and þegenrihtes wyrþe, ge on life ge on legere.

5.4 And se þe þæt nelle þæt his hade gebyrige, wanige his weorðscipe ægðer ge for Gode ge for worolde.

himself to a monastery with all humility, and renounce his misdeeds, and sincerely repent for the rules he has broken. Let him reflect upon the word and pledge that he devoted to God.

3.1 And the monk who does not have a monastery shall come to the bishop of the diocese and commit himself before God and men to especially observe three things thenceforth: that is, his celibacy, his monastic habit, and his service to God as best he can.

3.2 And if he fulfills that, then he will be worthy of higher esteem, wherever he resides.

4 And canons, when their holding is such that they possess a refectory and a dormitory, shall hold their monastery with propriety and celibacy, just as their rule instructs; or else he who will not do that must forfeit his holding.

5 And we require and instruct that all servants of God, especially priests, obey God, embrace celibacy, and protect themselves against God's wrath.

5.1 They know full well that they may not rightfully engage in sexual relations with a woman.

5.2 But it is the worse in that some have two or more, and some—though they abandon those they had before—then take others while these are yet living, which it does not behoove any Christian man to do.

5.3 And he who will renounce it and practice celibacy will have God's favor, and also, as a privilege in this world, he shall be deemed worthy of a thane's wergild and a thane's rights, both in life and after death.

5.4 And he who will not act in a manner fitting for his order shall diminish his honor before God and the world.

6 And la, gyt we willað biddan freonda gehwylcne and eal folc eac læran georne þæt hy inwerdre heortan ænne God lufian and ælcne hæþendom georne ascunian.

7 And gif wiccan oððe wigeleras, scincræftcan oððe horcwenan, morðwyrhtan oððe mansworan ahwar on earde wurðan agytene, fyse hy man georne ut of þysan earde and clænsige þas þeode, oþþe on earde forfare hy mid ealle, butan hy geswican and þe deoppor gebetan.

8 And witena gerædnes is þæt man rihte laga up arære for Gode and for worolde and æghwilce unlaga georne afylle.

8.1 And þæt man heonan forð læte manna gehwylcne, ge earmne ge eadigne, folcrihtes wyrðe.

8.2 And þæt man frið and freondscipe rihtlice healde innan þysan earde for Gode and for worolde.

9 And witena gerædnes is þæt man Christene men and unforworhte of earde ne sylle, ne huru on hæþene þeode; ac beorge man georne, þæt man þa sawla ne forfare þe Crist mid his agenum life gebohte.

10 And witena gerædnes is þæt man Christene men for ealles to lytlan to deaðe ne forræde.

10.1 Ac elles geræde man friðlice steora folce to þearfe, and ne forspille for lytlum Godes agen handgeweorc and his agenne ceap, þe he deore gebohte.

10.2 Ac æghwilce dæde toscade man wærlice and dom æfter dæde medemige be mæþe, swa for Gode sy gebeorhlic and for worolde aberendlic.

6 And indeed, we entreat all our friends and likewise zealously instruct all the people that they love the one God with their innermost hearts and vehemently renounce all heathen practices.

7 And if wizards or magicians, conjurors or prostitutes, murderers or perjurers be found anywhere in this land, they are to be zealously expelled from the realm and the people cleansed, or they shall be entirely abolished from the earth, unless they cease and most sincerely repent.

8 And the decree of the councilors is that just laws shall be upheld before God and the world, and all that is unlawful zealously renounced.

8.1 And that henceforth all people, rich and poor, shall be granted their legal rights.

8.2 And that peace and friendship shall be properly preserved throughout this land before God and the world.

9 And the decree of the councilors is that those who are Christian and free of guilt shall not be sold out of this land, especially not to heathen people; but we must zealously ensure that the souls not be destroyed which Christ purchased with his own life.

10 And the decree of the councilors is that Christians are not to be sentenced to death for entirely too little.

10.1 Instead, merciful penalties are to be established for the good of the people, and so that God's handiwork, which he paid for himself at a high cost, not be destroyed.

10.2 But each deed is to be carefully weighed and judgment appropriate to the deed handed down in such a way as shall be justifiable before God and acceptable to the community.

10.3 And geþence swyþe georne se þe oþrum deme, hwæs he sylf gyrne, þonne he þus cweðe: *Et dimitte nobis debita nostra, et reliqua.*

11 And we lærað swyþe geornlice, þæt æghwilc Christen man unrihthæmed georne forbuge and Christene lage rihtlice healde.

12 And æfre ne geweorðe, þæt Christen man gewifige in VI manna sibfæce on his agenum cynne, þæt is binnan þam feorþan cneowe, ne on þæs lafe þe swa neah wære on woroldcundre sibbe, ne on þæs wifes nydmagan, þe he ær hæfde.

12.1 Ne on gehalgodre ænigre nunnan, ne on his gefæderan, ne on ælætan ænig Cristen man ne gewifige æfre.

12.2 Ne na ma wifa þonne an hæbbe; ac beo be þære anre, þa hwile þe heo libbe, se þe wille Godes lage gyman mid rihte and wiþ hellebryne beorgan his sawle.

13 And sy ælc cyrice on Godes griþe and on þæs cynges and on ealles Cristenes folces.

14 And sy ælc cyricgrið binnan wagum and cyninges handgrið efenunwemme.

15 And ænig man heonan forð cyrican ne þeowige, ne cyricmangunge mid unrihte ne macige.

15.1 Ne cyricþen ne utige butan biscopes geþehte.

16 And gelæste man Godes gerihta æghwilce geare rihtlice georne, þæt is sulhælmessan huru xv niht ofer Eastron,

17 and geogoðe teoþunge be Pentecosten and eorðwæstma be Ealra Halgena mæssan,

18 and Romfeoh be Petres mæssan,

18.1 and cyricsceat to Martinus mæssan,

10.3 And the person who judges another shall reflect sincerely upon his own motivations when he recites: *Forgive us our debts, etc.*

11 And we very fervently charge each Christian to diligently avoid unlawful intercourse and rightly uphold the divine law.

12 And it must never so happen that a Christian man take a wife within six degrees of kinship in his own family, that is, his fourth cousin or closer, nor the widow of one so closely related within his earthly family, nor a close relative of his first wife.

12.1 Nor may a Christian man ever marry a professed nun, nor his godmother, nor a divorced woman.

12.2 He may not have more than one wife; but he who desires to obey the law of God rightly and guard his soul from hellfire must stay with one wife as long as she lives.

13 And each church shall be under the protection of God and of the king and of all Christian people.

14 And all sanctuary within church walls and the sanctuary received from the hand of a Christian king are to remain equally inviolable.

15 And henceforth no one shall persecute the Church, nor wrongfully make it an object of exchange.

15.1 Nor may a cleric be expelled without the bishop's permission.

16 And God's dues are to be paid readily every year, that is, plow dues fifteen nights after Easter,

17 and the tithe of the young animals by Pentecost, and the tithe on the fruits of the earth by the Feast of All Saints,

18 the dues to Rome by the Feast of Saint Peter,

18.1 and church dues by the Feast of Saint Martin,

19 and leohtgescot þriwa on geare.

20 And saulsceat is rihtast, þæt man symble gelæste aa æt openum græfe.

21 And gif man ænig lic of rihtscire elles hwar lecge, gelæste man þone saulsceat swa þeh into þam mynstre, þe hit to hyrde.

21.1 And ealle Godes gerihta fyrþrige man georne, ealswa hit þearf is.

22 And freolsa and fæstena healde man rihtlice.

22.1 Sunnandæges freols healde man georne swa þærto gebyrige; and cypinga and folcgemota and huntaðfara and woroldlicra weorca on þam halgan dæge geswice man georne.

22.2 And sancta Marian heahfreolstida ealle weorðige man georne, ærest mid fæstene and syþþan mid freolse.

22.3 And to æghwilces apostoles heahtide fæste man georne, butan to Philippus and Iacobus freolse ne beode we nan fæsten for þam Easterlican freolse, butan hwa wille.

22.4 Elles oþre freolsa and fæstena healde man georne, swa swa þa heoldan þa þe betst heoldan.

23 And ymbrenfæstena, swa swa sanctus Gregorius Angelcynne sylf hit gedihte.

24 And fæste man ælce Frigedæge butan hit freols sy.

25 And ordal and aþas and wifunga æfre syndan tocwedene heahfreolsdagum and rihtymbrenum and fram Aduentum Domini oð octabas Epiphanige and fram Septuagessima oð xv niht ofer Eastran.

25.1 And beo þam halgan tidan, ealswa hit riht is, eallum Cristenum mannum sibb and som gemæne, and ælc sacu totwæmed.

19   and the dues for the lighting of the church three times a year.

20   And it is most appropriate that dues for the souls of the dead always be paid while the grave is yet open.

21   And if any person's body is buried other than in its proper parish, the dues should still be paid to the church to which he belonged.

21.1   And all God's dues are to be given willingly, just as is required.

22   And feasts and fasts are to be properly observed.

22.1   The Sunday holy day shall be kept appropriately as is fitting for it, and markets, meetings, hunts, and worldly business are to be assiduously avoided on that holy day.

22.2   And each of the Feasts of Saint Mary is to be celebrated faithfully, first with fasting and then with a holiday.

22.3   And one must fast readily for the feast of each apostle, but we order no fast for the Feasts of Philip and James because of Easter, unless one wishes to do so.

22.4   Otherwise, feasts and fasts are to be kept assiduously, just as they were kept when they were kept best.

23   And the Ember Fasts are to be kept, just as Saint Gregory himself ordained for the English.

24   And there shall be a fast each Friday unless it is a feast.

25   And ordeals and oaths and marriages are always prohibited during feasts and authorized Ember Days and from Advent until the eighth day of Epiphany and from Septuagesima until the fifteenth night after Easter.

25.1   And at holy times, just as is proper, there is to be peace and friendship among all Christians, and each dispute is to be resolved.

25.2 And gif hwa oðrum scyle borh oððe bote æt worold-lican þingan, gelæste hit him georne ær oððon æfter.

26 And sy ælc wydewe, þe hy sylfe mid rihte gehealde on Godes griðe and on þæs cynges.

26.1 And sitte ælc xii monað werleas; ceose syþþan þæt heo sylf wille.

27 And æghwilc Christen man do, swa him þearf is: gyme his Christendomes georne and gewunige gelomlice to scrifte and unforwandodlice his synna gecyðe and geornlice bete, swa swa him man tæce.

27.1 And gearwige eac to huslgange huru þriwa on geare gehwa hine sylfne, þe his agene þearfe wille understandan, swa swa him þearf is.

28 And word and weorc freonda gehwilc fadige mid rihte, and að and wedd wærlice healde.

28.1 And æghwilc unriht aweorpe man georne of þysan earde, þæs þe man don mæge.

28.2 And swicollice dæda and laðlice unlaga ascunige man swyðe: þæt is false gewihta and woge gemeta and lease ge-witnessa and fracodlice ficunga and fule forligra and egeslice manswara;

28.3 and deoflice dæda on morðweorcum and on man-slihtan, on stalan and on strudungan, on gitsungan and on gifernessan, on ofermettan and on oferfyllan, on swiccræf-tan and on mistlican lahbrican, on æwbrican and on hadbri-can, on freolsbricon and on fæstenbricon, on cyricrenan and on mæniges cynnes misdædan.

29 And la, understande man georne þæt ealswylc is to leanne and næfre to lufianne.

25.2 And if anyone must pay a debt or compensation to another because of a worldly matter, he is to do so promptly before or after the feast.

26 And all widows who comport themselves properly shall be under the protection of God and the king.

26.1 And each of them is to remain husbandless for twelve months; then she may choose as she pleases.

27 And each Christian shall do what is required of him: attend diligently to his Christian faith, go frequently to confession, confess his sins without hesitation, and sincerely repent just as he is instructed.

27.1 And anyone who wishes to understand his own obligations must prepare himself to receive the sacrament at least three times during the year, just as is required of him.

28 And all of our friends must order their words and deeds properly, and carefully uphold their oath and pledge.

28.1 And all injustice is to be banished from this land as much as possible.

28.2 And fraudulent deeds and hateful injustices are to be entirely rejected, that is: false weights and counterfeit measures and perjured testimony and shameful deceptions and foul adulteries and dreadful falsehoods;

28.3 likewise, devilish deeds, such as murder and manslaughter, theft and robbery, avarice and cupidity, gluttony and overindulgence, treachery and countless violations of the law, of marriage vows, of holy orders, of feasts and fasts, of church property, and misdeeds of many kinds.

29 And indeed it is to be wholly understood that all such sins are to be condemned and never to be admired.

30 Ac lufige man Godes riht heonan forþ georne wordes and weorces; þonne wyrð þysse þeode sona God milde.

31 Wutan eac ealle ymbe friþes bote and ymbe feos bote smeagean swyðe georne.

32 Swa ymbe friþes bote, swa þam bondan sy selost and þam þeofan sy laþost.

32.1 And swa ymbe feos bote, þæt an mynet gange ofer ealle þas þeode butan ælcon false.

32.2 And gemeta and gewihta rihte man georne, and ælces unrihtes heonan forð geswice.

32.3 And burhbota and bricbota aginne man georne on æghwilcon ende, and fyrdunga eac and scipfyrdunga ealswa, a þonne neod sy, swa swa man geræde for gemænelicre neode.

33 And wærlic bið þæt man æghwilce geare sona æfter Eastron fyrdscipa gearwige.

34 And gyf hwa folces fyrdscip awyrde, gebete þæt georne and cyninge þa munde; and gif hit man amyrre þæt hit ænote weorðe, forgylde hit fullice, and cyninge þone mundbrice.

35 And gif hwa of fyrde butan leafe gewende þe cyning sylf on sy, plihte his are.

36 And gif morðwyrhtan oððe mansworan oððe æbære manslagan to þam geþristian, þæt hy on þæs cyninges neaweste gewunian ær þam þe hy habban bote agunnen for Gode and for worolde, þonne plihton hy heora are and eallon heora æhtan, butan hit friðbenan syndan.

30   But God's law is to be willingly embraced henceforth in word and deed; then will God immediately show mercy to this people.

31   Let us all also consider very carefully the enhancement of public safety and the improvement of the currency.

32   Public safety is to be improved such that it is best for the citizen and worst for the thief.

32.1 The currency is to be improved so that there is one standard coinage throughout the realm without any adulteration.

32.2 And weights and measures are to be assiduously made right, and all unlawful practices abolished henceforth.

32.3 And improvements to fortifications and bridges are to be undertaken with care on all sides, and also the provisioning of the army and navy as the need arises, just as has been ordained for the common good.

33   And it is prudent to have the warships prepared each year just after Easter.

34   And if anyone damages one of the realm's warships, he is to atone sincerely for that and compensate the king for violating his protection; and if it is destroyed so that it is no longer of any use, he is to make restitution in full and pay the king for the breach of his peace.

35   And if anyone deserts an army led by the king himself, he shall risk forfeiture of his property.

36   And if murderers or perjurers or convicted killers are so bold as to remain in the king's proximity before they have undertaken to do penance before God and the world, then they will be at risk of losing their property and all their possessions, unless they are seeking protection.

37 And gyf hwa ymbe cyninges feorh syrwe, sy he his feores scyldig and ealles þæs þe he age gif hit him ongesoþod weorðe; and gif he hine ladian wille and mage, do þæt be þam deopestan aðe oþþe mid þryfealdan ordale on Ængla lage, and on Dena lage be þam þe heora lagu sy.

38 And gif hwa forsteal ongean lahriht Cristes oþþe cyninges ahwar gewyrce, gylde wer oþþe wite be þam þe seo dæd sy; and gif he geonbyrde and sylf gewyrce, þæt hine man afylle, licge ægylde.

39 And gif hwa nunnan gewemme oþþe wydewan nydnæme, gebete þæt deope for Gode and for worolde.

40 And smeage man symle on æghwilce wisan hu man fyrmest mæge ræd aredian þeode to þearfe, and rihtne Christendom swyþost aræran and æghwilce unlaga geornost afyllan.

40.1 Forþam þurh þæt hit sceal on earde godian to ahte, þe man unriht alecge and rihtwisnesse lufige for Gode and for worolde.

41 Nu wille we eac læran Godes þeowas georne þæt hy huru hy sylfe wærlice beþencan and þurh Godes fultum clænnesse lufian, and georne heora bocum and gebedum fylgean, and dæges and nihtes oft and gelome clypian to Christe and for eal Christen folc þingian georne.

42 Eac we gyt willað myngian georne freonda gehwilcne, ealswa us neod is gelome to donne, þæt gehwa hine sylfne georne beþence.

42.1 And þæt he fram synnan georne gecyrre and oþrum mannum unrihtes styre.

37 And if anyone conspires against the king's life, his life and all that he owns will be forfeit if he is shown to be guilty; and if he wishes to exonerate himself and is granted permission, he can do so with the most serious oath or with the threefold ordeal under English law, and in the Danelaw according to their legal customs.

38 And if anyone anywhere acts to obstruct the legal prerogatives of Christ or the king, he shall pay either wergild or a fine, according to the nature of the crime; and if he resists the law with violence and, so doing, causes his own death, no wergild is to be paid for him.

39 And if anyone defiles a nun or assaults a widow, he must solemnly repent before God and the world.

40 And consideration must always be given in every way to how first to establish policy to meet the needs of the people and to best uphold the true Christian faith and to most zealously eradicate all injustice.

40.1 For it is in this way that improvement in this land can be achieved: by rejecting injustice and embracing righteousness before God and the world.

41 Now we likewise wish to earnestly instruct God's servants to give thought to themselves with special care and with God's help embrace celibacy, and attend diligently to their books and prayers, and call upon Christ often and frequently both day and night, and zealously intercede for all Christian people.

42 Moreover, we also earnestly desire to admonish each of our friends, just as there is often need for us to do, to sincerely give thought to themselves.

42.1 And they are to readily turn from sin, and to curb the injustice caused by others.

42.2 And þæt he oft and gelome hæbbe on gemynde, þæt mannum is mæst þearf oftost to gemunene, þæt is þæt hy rihtne geleafan anrædlice habban on þone soþan God þe is wealdend and wyrhta ealra gesceafta, and þæt hy rihtne Christendom rihtlice healdan, and þæt hy godcundan larea-wan geornlice hyran, and Godes larum and lagum geornlice fylgean.

42.3 And þæt hy Godes cyrican æghwar georne griðian and friþian, and mid leohte and lacum hi gelome gegretan, and hy sylfe þær georne to Christe gebiddan.

43 And þæt hy Godes gerihta æghwylce geare mid rihte gelæstan

43.1 and freolsa and fæstena rihtlice healdan.

44 And þæt hy Sunnandaga cypinga and folciscra gemota georne geswican.

45 And þæt hy Godes þeowas symle werian and weorðian.

46 And þæt hy Godes þearfan frefrian and fedan.

47 And þæt hy wydewan and steopcild to oft ne ahwænan, ac georne hy gladian.

48 And þæt hy ælþeodige men and feorrancumene ne tyr-ian ne ne tynan.

49 And þæt hy oþrum mannum unriht ne beodan ealles to swyþe; ac manna gehwylc oþrum beode þæt riht, þæt he wille, þæt man him beode, be þam þe hit mæð sy; and þæt is swyþe riht lagu.

50 And se þe ahwar heonan forð rihte laga wyrde, Godes oþþon manna, gebete hit georne, swa hwæþer swa hit geby-rige, swa mid godcundre bote swa mid woroldcundre steore.

51 And gif for godbotan feohbot ariseð, swa swa wise wor-oldwitan to steore gesettan, þæt gebyreð rihtlice, be biscpa

42.2 And they are to bear in mind often and frequently that which there is the greatest need to remember, that is, to wholeheartedly maintain proper faith in the true God, who is the lord and maker of all creation, and to properly adhere to the true Christian faith, and to willingly heed their spiritual teachers, and sincerely follow God's laws and teachings.

42.3 And they are to everywhere diligently preserve and protect God's churches, and to visit them frequently with candles and offerings, and there themselves pray fervently to Christ.

43 And that each year God's dues are to be paid promptly

43.1 and feasts and fasts properly kept.

44 And that on Sundays markets and public meetings are to be assiduously avoided.

45 And that God's servants are to be protected and honored.

46 And that God's poor are to be comforted and fed.

47 And that widows and orphans are not to be continually persecuted, but instead uplifted.

48 And that strangers and those who have come from afar are not to be harassed or mistreated.

49 And that they are not to offer injustice to others all too greatly; but that to the best of their ability, everyone is to show that justice to others that they desire to be shown to themselves; and that is a very just law.

50 And henceforth, those who anywhere violate the just laws of God or of men are to diligently make compensation in whichever manner is appropriate, either by spiritual penance or secular punishment.

51 And if money is paid as ecclesiastical compensation, as determined by wise secular judges, according to the decrees

dihte, to gebedbigene and to þearfena hyþþe and to cyricbote and to lardome and to wæde and to wiste þam þe Gode
þeowian and to bocan and to bellan and to cyricwædan, and
næfre to woroldlican idelan glengan; ac for woroldsteoran to
godcundan neodan, hwilum be wite, hwilum be wergylde,
hwilum be halsfange, hwilum be lahslite, hwilum be are,
hwilum be æhte, and hwilum be maran, hwilum be læssan.

52   And a swa man bið mihtigra her nu for worulde oþþon
þurh geþingða hearra on hade, swa sceal he deoppor synna
gebetan and ælce misdæda deoror agyldan, for þam þe se
maga and se unmaga ne beoð na gelice, ne ne magon na gelice byrþene ahebban, ne se unhala þe ma þam halum gelice.
And þy man sceal medmian and gescadlice toscadan, ge on
godcunda scriftan ge on woroldcundan steoran, ylde and
geogoþe, welan and wædle, hæle and unhæle, and hada gehwilcne.

52.1 And gif hit geweorþeð þæt man unwilles oþþe ungewealdes ænig þing misdeð, na bið þæt na gelic þam þe willes
and gewealdes sylfwilles misdeð: and eac se þe nydwyrhta
bið þæs þe he misdeð, se bið gebeorhges and þy beteran
domes symle wyrðe, þe he nydwyrhta wæs þæs þe he worhte.

53   Ælce dæde toscade man wærlice and a dom be dæde
fadige mid rihte and medemige be mæþe for Gode and for
worolde; and miltsige man for Godes ege and liþige man
georne and beorge be dæle þam, þe þæs þearf sy; forþam
ealle we beþurfan, þæt us ure Drihten oft and gelome his
miltse geunne. Amen.

of the bishops it is to be used for prayer and for the benefit of the needy and for church upkeep and for teaching and for clothing and feeding God's servants and for books and for bells and for church vestments, but never for idle worldly vanities; instead, secular penalties are to go toward ecclesiastical needs, whether from fines or from wergild, from *healsfang* or from *lahslit,* from property or from personal possessions, and whether great or small.

52 And the mightier a person is now in this world or the greater the prerogatives of his station, so shall he repent his sins all the more deeply and compensate for his misdeeds the more dearly, for the great and the meek are not alike any more than the sick are like the healthy, nor can they bear a similar burden. And thus age and youth, wealth and poverty, health and sickness, and each social status is to be weighed and appropriately assessed in both spiritual penances and secular punishments.

52.1 And if it befalls that someone commits a crime in any way unwillingly or unknowingly, that shall not be treated as if he intentionally committed a crime, willingly and knowingly; and accordingly, the person who is compelled so that he commits a crime is always to be deemed worthy of mercy and lighter judgments, because he acted out of compulsion.

53 Each deed is to be carefully assessed and the judgment always measured with justice in accordance with the deed and administered fairly before God and the world; and mercy and kindness and a degree of forgiveness are to be extended to those who have need of them; for we all need God to grant us his mercy often and frequently. Amen.

7 Æthelred

Pr   Hoc instituerunt Æþelredus rex et sapientes eius apud Badam.

1   Inprimis ut unus Deus super omnia diligatur et honoretur, et ut omnes regi suo pareant, sicut antecessores sui melius fecerunt, et cum eo pariter defendant regnum suum.

1.1   Et constituerunt inprimis Dei misericordiam et auxilium invocare ieiuniis, elemosinis, confessione et abstinentia a malefactis et iniustitia.

1.2   Hoc est ut detur de omni carruca denarius vel denarii valens.

1.3   Et omnis qui familiam habet efficiat, ut omnis hyremannus suus det unum denarium. Qui si non habeat, det dominus eius pro eo; et omnis tainus decimet totum quicquid habeat.

2   Et instituimus, ut omnis Christianus, qui aetatem habet, ieiunet tribus diebus in pane et aqua et herbis crudis.

2.1   Et omnis homo ad confessionem vadat et nudis pedibus ad ecclesiam et peccatis omnibus abrenuntiet emendando, cessando.

2.2   Et eat omnis presbyter cum populo suo ad processionem tribus diebus nudis pedibus. Et super hoc cantet omnis presbyter xxx missas et omnis diaconus et clericus xxx psalmos. Et apparetur iii diebus corredium uniuscuiusque sine carne; in cibo et potu, sicut idem comedere deberet, et dividatur hoc totum pauperibus.

7 Æthelred

Pr King Æthelred and his councilors decreed this at Bath:

1 First, that the one God is to be praised and honored above all, and that all should obey their king according to the best customs of their ancestors, and together with him defend his kingdom.

1.1 And they first agreed to call upon God's mercy and help by fasting, almsgiving, confession, and abstaining from sins and injustice.

1.2 Thus, a penny or the value of a penny is to be given from every plowland.

1.3 And everyone who has a household is to ensure that each of those under him gives one penny. If anyone does not have it, the lord is to give it for him; and every thane is to give one-tenth of all he has.

2 And we have decreed that every Christian who has reached adulthood is to fast for three days upon bread, water, and raw herbs.

2.1 And each person is to go to confession and, with bare feet, to church; and by repenting and abstaining, repudiate all his sins.

2.2 And for three days every priest is to go barefoot in the procession along with his people. And moreover, every priest is to sing thirty Masses, and every deacon and cleric thirty psalms. And for three days everyone is to be served meals without meat; and food and drink in the amount that would have been eaten is to be shared out among the poor.

2.3 Et sit omnis servus liber ab opere illis tribus diebus, quo melius ieiunare possit, et operetur sibimet quod vult. Hii sunt illi tres dies: dies Lunae, dies Martis, et dies Mercurii proximi ante festum sancti Michaelis.

2.4 Si quis ieiunium suum infringat, servus corio suo componat, liber pauper reddat xxx denarios et tainus regis cxx sol.; et dividatur hec pecunia pauperibus.

2.5 Et sciat omnis presbyter et tungravius et decimales homines, ut haec elemosina et ieiunium proveniat, sicut in sanctis iurare poterunt.

3 Et praecipimus, ut in omni congregatione cantetur cotidie communiter pro rege et omni populo suo una missa ad matutinalem missam, quae inscripta est *contra paganos.*

3.1 Et ad singulas horas decantet totus conventus extensis membris in terra psalmum illum: *Domine, quid multiplicati sunt* et collectam contra paganos; et hoc fiat, quamdiu necessitas ista nobis est in manibus.

3.2 Et in omni coenobio et conventu monachorum celebret omnis presbyter singulatim xxx missas pro rege et omni populo, et omnis monachus xxx psalteria.

4 Et praecipimus, ut omnis homo super dilectionem Dei et omnium sanctorum det cyricsceattum et rectam decimam suam, sicut in diebus antecessorum nostrorum stetit, quando melius stetit: hoc est sicut aratrum peragrabit per decimam acram.

4.1 Et omnis consuetudo reddatur super amicitiam Dei ad matrem ecclesiam, cui adiacet.

2.3   And all slaves are to be freed from work on those three days so that they will be able to fast better and make what they wish for themselves. These are the three days: the Monday, Tuesday, and Wednesday just before the Feast of Saint Michael.

2.4   If anyone breaks the fast: a slave is to be whipped, a poor freeman is to pay thirty pence and a king's thane one hundred twenty shillings; and this money is to be distributed to the poor.

2.5   And let every priest, town reeve, and tithingman oversee the almsgiving and fasting, so that they can swear to it on holy relics.

3   And we command that a Mass entitled *Against the Pagans* is to be sung daily at Matins in every religious foundation by the entire community for the king and his people.

3.1   And at each of the canonical hours, all members of the community, lying on the ground with limbs extended, are to chant the psalm, *Why, O Lord, are they multiplied,* and the Collect against the pagans; and this is to be done as long as we have the need.

3.2   And in every monastery or community of monks, every priest is to individually celebrate thirty Masses for the king and for all the people, and every monk to chant his psalter thirty times.

4   And we command that everyone, for the love of God and all the saints, is to render their Church dues and proper tithes, just as was done and done better in the days of our ancestors; that is, according to every tenth acre turned up by the plow.

4.1   And all dues are to be paid, for the love of God, to the appropriate mother church.

4.2 Et nemo auferat Deo quod ad eum pertinet et praede-
cessores nostri concesserunt ei.

5   Et prohibemus, ne aliquis extra vendatur. Si quis hoc
presumat, sit praeter benedictionem Dei et omnium sanctorum et praeter omnem Christianitatem, nisi paeniteat et
emendet, sicut episcopus suus edocebit.

6   Et prohibemus omnem robariam omni homini.

6.1 Et sit omnis homo dignus iure publico, pauper et dives.

6.2 Et reddatur omnis robaria, si quis aliquam fecerit et
emendet, sicut prius et postea stetit.

6.3 Et si quis praepositus eam fecerit, dupliciter emendet
quod alii iudicaretur.

7   Et reddatur pecunia elemosinae hinc ad festum sancti
Michaelis, si alicubi retro sit, per plenam witam.

7.1 Et omnibus annis deinceps reddantur Dei rectitudines
in omnibus rebus quae supradictae sunt per amiciciam Dei
et sanctorum omnium, ut Deus omnipotens misericordiam
nobis faciat et de hostibus triumphum nobis et pacem in-
dulgeat; quem sedulo deprecemur, ut misericordiam eius
consequamur et gratiam hic et in futuro requiem sine fine.
Amen.

4.2   And no one is to take from God that which belongs to him and which our forebears granted to him.

5   And we forbid anyone to be sold out of the country. If anyone presumes to do so, he is to be excluded from the blessing of God and all the saints, and from the entire Christian communion, unless he does penance and makes amends as his bishop shall instruct.

6   And we forbid to all people all forms of theft.

6.1   And all persons, poor or wealthy, are entitled to legal remedies.

6.2   And if anyone has committed theft, let him return all that has been stolen and make amends, as was the practice before and will be afterward.

6.3   And if a reeve has committed theft, he shall make amends at twice the rate imposed upon anyone else.

7   And if anyone is behind in his almsgiving, let it be paid between now and the Feast of Saint Michael, or the full penalty shall be assessed.

7.1   And every year henceforth God's dues are to be paid in every case as decreed above, for the friendship of God and all the saints, so that the omnipotent God will grant us mercy, and victory over our enemies, and peace. Let us earnestly beseech him to grant us mercy and grace here and rest without end in the future. Amen.

7a Æthelred

Đis man gerædde, ða se micele here com to lande:

Pr   Ealle we beþurfan þæt we geornlice earnian þæt we
Godes miltse and his mildheortnesse habban moton and
þæt we, þurh his fultum, magon feondum wiðstandan.

1   Nu wille we þæt eal folc to gemænelicre dædbote þrig
dagas be hlafe and wirtum and wætere, þæt is on Monandæg
and on Tiwesdæg and on Wodnesdæg ær Michaeles mæssan.

2   And cume manna gehwilc bærefot to circan, buton
golde and glæncgum, and ga man to scrifte.

2.1   And gan ealle ut mid halidome and clipian inweardre
heortan georne to Criste.

2.2   And sceote man æghwilce hide pænig oððe pæniges
weorð.

2.3   And bringe man þæt to cirican and siððan on þreo dæle
be scriftes and be tunes gerefan gewitnesse.

3   And gif hwa þis ne gelæste, ðonne gebete he þæt, swa
swa hit gelagod is: bunda mid xxx pænigum, þræl mid his
hide, þegn mid xxx scillingum.

4   And swa hwar swa þæt feoh up arise, dæle man on
Godes est æghwilcne pænig.

7a Æthelred

This was decreed when the great army came to this land:

Pr   We all must strive diligently so that we may receive God's mercy and compassion and, with his help, withstand our enemies.

1   Now we ordain that the whole realm consume only bread, herbs, and water in shared penance for three days, that is, the Monday, Tuesday, and Wednesday before the Feast of Saint Michael.

2   And everyone is to come to church barefoot, without gold or ornaments, and they are to go to confession.

2.1   And all shall process out with the holy relics and fervently call upon Christ with their innermost hearts.

2.2   And a penny or the equivalent of a penny is to be paid by every hide.

2.3   And it is to be brought to church and subsequently divided in three with the confessor and town reeve acting as witnesses.

3   And if anyone does not pay this, then he shall compensate for it in the manner that the law decrees: a householder with thirty pence, a slave with a beating, and a thane with thirty shillings.

4   And wherever that levy comes to be assessed, every penny is to be distributed for God's favor.

4.1 And ealswa þone mete þe gehwa brucan wolde gif him þæt fæsten swa geboden nære, dæle man on Godes est georne æfter þam fæstene eal þearfigendum mannum and bedridan and swa gebrocedum mannum, þe swa fæstan ne magon.

5 And hiredmanna gehwilc sille pænig to ælmessan, oððe his hlaford sille for hine buton he silf hæbbe, and heafodmen teoðian.

5.1 And þeowemen þa ðrig dagas beon weorces gefreode wið ciricsocne and wið ðam, þe hi þæt fæsten þe lustlicor gefæstan.

6 And on æghwilcan mynstre, singe eal geferræden ætgædere heora saltere þa ðry dagas.

6.1 And ælc mæssepreost mæssige for urne hlaford and for ealle his þeode.

6.2 And þartoeacan mæssige man æghwilce dæge on ælcan minstre ane mæssan sinderlice for ðare neode, þe us nu on handa stent, oð þæt hit betere wurðe.

6.3 And æt ælcan tidsange eal hired aþenedum limum ætforan Godes weofode singe þone sealm: *"Domine, quid multiplicati sunt,"* and *preces* and *col.*

7 And ealle gemænelice, gehadode and læwede, bugan to Gode georne and geearnian his mildse.

8 And æghwilce geare heonon forð gelæste man Godes gerihta huru rihtlice, wið ðam þe us God ælmihtig gemiltsige and us geunne, þæt we ure fynd ofercuman motan. God ure helpe. Amen.

4.1 Furthermore, all the food that would have been enjoyed had the fast not been decreed is to be diligently distributed for God's favor after the fast to the poor, the bedridden, and those so afflicted that they are not able to fast.

5 And every retainer is to give a penny as alms, or his lord is to give it for him if he does not have it himself, and those of high status shall pay tithes.

5.1 And slaves are to be released from work on these three days to attend church and keep the fast more readily.

6 And in every monastery, the whole community is to chant from their psalters on these three days.

6.1 And each priest is to celebrate Mass for our lord and all of his people.

6.2 Additionally, a special Mass is to be celebrated each day in every church because of the peril that confronts us until it is resolved.

6.3 And at each service, the whole community, prostrate with outstretched arms before God's altar, is to sing the psalm, "*Lord, how are they multiplied,*" and the prayers and Collect.

7 And all collectively, clerical and lay, are to submit to God wholeheartedly and deserve his mercy.

8 And every year henceforth, Church dues are to be paid with special conscientiousness, so that the almighty God will have mercy on us and enable us to overcome our enemies. May God help us. Amen.

8 Æthelred

Anno MXIIII *ab incarnatione Domini nostri Iesu Christi:*

Pr Þis is an ðara gerædnessa þe Engla cyningc gedihte mid his witena geþeahte.

1 Þæt is ærest, þæt he wile, þæt ealle Godes circan beon fulles griðes wurðe.

1.1 And gif æfre ænig man heonan forð Godes ciricgrið swa abrece, þæt he binnon ciricwagum mansleaga wurðe, þonne sy þæt botleas and ehte his ælc þara þe Godes freond sy, buton þæt gewurðe þæt he þanon ætberste and swa deope friðsocne gesece þæt se cyningc him þurh þæt feores geunne wið fulre bote ge wið God ge wið men.

2 And þæt is þonne ærest: þæt he his agenne wer gesille þam cyninge and Christe and mid þam hine silfne inlagige to bote.

2.1 Forðam Cristen cyning is Cristes gespelia on Cristenre þeode, and he sceal Cristes abilgðe wrecan swiðe georne.

3 And gif hit þonne to bote gega, and se cyngc þæt geþafige, þonne bete man þæt ciricgrið into ðare circan be þæs cyninges fullan mundbryce and þa mynsterclænsunge

8 Æthelred

In the 1014th year since the incarnation of our Lord Jesus Christ:

Pr   This is one of the decrees which the king of the English issued with the advice of his councilors.

1   First, he desires that all God's churches be entitled to offer full sanctuary.

1.1   And henceforth, if anyone ever violates the sanctuary of God's church by committing murder within its walls, then no compensation can be made and all of God's friends must track him down, unless it so happens that he escapes and obtains such powerful protection that the king therefore grants him his life in exchange for full penance to God and the community.

2   And the first component of this shall be that he is to pay his own wergild to the king and to Christ, and thereby restore for himself the right to offer compensation.

2.1   For a Christian king is Christ's representative among a Christian people, and he must avenge most zealously offenses against Christ.

3   And then if compensation becomes possible, and the king allows it, the fine for violating the church's sanctuary is to be paid to that church in an amount equal to the fine paid for a full violation of the king's protection, and the purification of the church is to begin, just as is appropriate, and

begite, swa þarto gebirige, and ægþer ge mægbote ge manbote fullice gebete, and wið God huru þingian georne.

4   And gif elles be cwicum mannum ciricgrið abrocen
beo, betan man georne be þam þe seo dæd sy, sy hit þurh
feohtlac, si hit þurh reaflac si hit þurh unrihthæmed, si þurh
þæt þæt hit sy.

4.1   Bete man æfre ærest þone griðbryce into ðare circan be
þam þe seo dæd sy and be þam þe þare circan mæð sy.

5   Ne syn ealle cyrcan na gelicre mæðe worldlice wirðe,
þeah hi godcundlice habban halgunge gelice.

5.1   Heafodmynstres griðbryce æt botwurðan þingan bete
man be cyninges munde, þæt is mid v pundum on Engla
lage; and medemran mynstres mid hundtwelftigan scillingum þæt is be cyninges wite; and þonne git læssan, þær
legerstow þeh sy, mid sixtigan scillingum; and æt feldcircan
mid xxx scillingum.

5.2   A sceal mid rihte dom æfter dæde and medmung be
mæþe.

6   And be teoðunge, se cyng and his witan habbað gecoren
and gecweden, ealswa hit riht is, þæt ðriddan dæl þare teoðunge, þe to circan gebyrge, ga to ciricbote, and oðer dæl
þam Godes þeowum, þridde Godes þearfum and earman
þeowetlingan.

7   And wite Cristenra manna gehwilc, þæt he his Drihtene his teoþunge—a swa seo sulh þone teoðan æcer gega—

compensation is to be fully paid to the victim's family and lord, and most importantly, God is to be appealed to zealously.

4   And if the church's sanctuary is violated yet the victim nonetheless remains alive, compensation must be readily made according to the nature of the crime, whether it be fighting or theft or sexual misconduct or anything else.

4.1   Compensation for the violation of a church's sanctuary must always be paid first to that church according to the nature of the crime and the status of the church.

5   Not all churches are to be considered alike in worldly status, although they all possess the same spiritual sanctity.

5.1   In the case of crimes for which restitution can be made, the compensation for violating the sanctuary of a cathedral shall be a fine equal to that paid for violation of the king's protection, that is, five pounds under English law; and for midlevel churches one hundred and twenty shillings, that is, the penalty for disobeying the king; and for those still smaller, though which possess a graveyard, sixty shillings; and for a country church thirty shillings.

5.2   In accordance with justice, judgment must always reflect the nature of the deed and punishment the seriousness of the crime.

6   And with reference to tithing, the king and his councilors have decided and decreed, just as is right, that a one-third portion of the tithes belonging to the Church are to go to the upkeep of the church, and another portion to God's servants, and one-third to God's poor and impoverished slaves.

7   And for the grace of God, every Christian must understand that he is to offer up his tithes properly to the Lord—

rihtlice gelæste be Godes miltse and be þam fullan wite þe Eadgar cyningc gelagode.

8   Ðæt is: gif hwa teoþunge rihtlice gelæstan nelle, þonne fare to þæs cyninges gerefa and þæs mynstres mæsse-preost—oððe þæs landrican and þæs biscopes gerefa—and niman unþances ðone teoðan dæl to ðam mynstre þe hit to gebirige, and tæcan him to ðam nigoðan dæle, and todæle man ða eahta dælas on twa and fo se landhlaford to healfum, to healfum se biscop, si hit cyninges man, sy hit þegnes.

9   And sy ælc geoguðe teoðung gelæst be Pentecosten be wite.

9.1   And eorðwestma be emnihte oððe huru be Ealra Hal-gena mæssan.

10   And Romfeoh gelæste man æghwilce geare be Petres mæssan.

10.1   And se þe þæt nelle gelæstan sille þartoeacan xxx pæniga and gilde þam cyninge cxx scillinga.

11   And ciricsceat gelæste man be Martinus mæssan.

11.1   And se þe ðæt ne gelæste forgilde hine mid twelffeal-dan, and þam cyninge CXX scillinga.

12   Sulhælmessan gebireð þæt man gelæste be wite æg-hwilce geare, þonne XV niht beoð agan ofer Eastertid.

12.1   And leohtgescot gelæste man to candelmæssan; do oftor se ðe wille.

13   And sawlsceat is rihtast, þæt man symle gelæste a æt openum græfe.

always to be a one-tenth yield of every acre traversed by the plow—or suffer the full penalty set forth by King Edgar.

8   That is: if anyone refuses to offer up his tithes properly, then the king's reeve and the priest of the church—or the reeves of the landlord and bishop—are to go and seize without consent a one-tenth portion for the church to which it belongs, and the next tenth is to be left for the recreant, and the remaining eight-tenths are to be divided in two and the landlord shall receive half and the bishop the other half, whether he is a king's man or a thane's.

9   And each tithe of the young animals is to be paid by Pentecost or there will be a penalty.

9.1   And the tithe of the fruits of the earth by the equinox, or at least by the Feast of All Saints.

10   And the dues to Rome are to be paid each year by the Feast of Saint Peter.

10.1 And anyone who refuses to pay them are to give an additional thirty pence and pay one hundred and twenty shillings to the king.

11   And Church dues are to be paid by the Feast of Saint Martin.

11.1 And anyone who does not pay them must render them twelvefold and pay one hundred and twenty shillings to the king.

12   It is appropriate that plow dues be paid each year fifteen nights after Easter or there will be a penalty.

12.1 And the dues for the lighting of the church are to be paid by Candlemas, but may be rendered more often if one wishes.

13   And it is most appropriate that dues for the souls of the dead always be paid while the grave is yet open.

14   And ealle Godes gerihta firðrige man georne, ealswa hit
þearf is.

15   And gif hwa þæt nelle, gewilde man hine to rihte mid
worldlicre steore; and þæt si gemæne Criste and cyninge,
ealswa hit iu wæs.

16   And freolsa and fæstena be wite healde man rihtlice.

17   And Sunnondaga cypinga forbeode man georne be fullan worldwite.

18   And weofodþena mæðe medemige man for Godes ege.

19   Gif man mæssepreost tihtlige, þe regollice libbe, andfealdre spræce, mæssige, gif he durre, and ladige hine on
ðam husle silf hine silfne.

19.1   And æt þrifealdre spræce ladige, gif he durre, eac on
ðam husle mid twam his gehadan.

20   Gif man diacon tihtlige, þe regollice libbe, andfealdre
spræce, nime twegen his gehadan and ladige hine mid þam.

20.1   And gif man hine tihtlige þryfealdre spræce, nime six
his gehadan and ladige mid þam and beo he silf seofoða.

21   Gif man folciscne mæssepreost mid tihtlan belecge þe
regollif næbbe, ladige hine swa swa diacon þe regollife libbe.

22   Gif man freondleasne weofodþen mid tihtlan belecge,
þe aðfultum næbbe, ga to corsnæde, and þar þonne æt gefare þæt þæt God wille, buton he on husle ladian mote.

14   And all God's dues are to be paid readily, just as is required.

15   And if anyone will not do so, he is to be brought to justice by means of a civil penalty; and this shall be shared between Christ and the king, just as it was of old.

16   And feasts and fasts are to be properly observed or there will be a penalty.

17   And Sunday markets are entirely prohibited, or suffer the full civil penalty.

18   And the rights of the clergy who serve at the altar are to be respected for fear of God.

19   If a simple accusation is brought against a priest who lives according to a rule, he shall celebrate the Mass if he dares, and exculpate himself on his own through the sacrament.

19.1 And if it is a threefold accusation, he shall, if he dares, exonerate himself through the sacrament and the oaths of two clerics of his rank.

20   If a simple accusation is brought against a deacon who lives according to a rule, he is to take two clerics of his rank and exculpate himself with them.

20.1 And if a threefold accusation is brought against him, he is to take six clerics of his rank and, himself being the seventh, exculpate himself with them.

21   If an accusation is brought against one of the secular clergy who does not live according to a rule, he may exonerate himself as does a deacon who lives according to a rule.

22   If an accusation is brought against a friendless cleric who serves at the altar, one who does not have supporters for his oath, he shall undergo the ordeal of consecrated bread, and there endure whatever God wills, unless he is permitted to exonerate himself by the sacrament.

23   And gif man gehadodne mid fæhðe belecge and secge, þæt he wære dædbana oððe rædbana, ladige mid his magan, þe fæhðe moton mid beran oððe fore betan.

24   And gif he sy mægleas, ladige mid geferan oððe fæste to corsnæde, and þaræt gefare þæt þæt God ræde.

25   And ne þearf ænig mynstermunuc ahwar mid rihte fæhðbote biddan ne fæhðbote betan; he gæð of his mæglage, þonne he gebihð to regollage.

26   Gif mæssepreost manslaga wurðe oððe elles manweorc to swiðe gewurce, þonne þolige he ægðres ge hades ge eardes, and wræcnige swa wide swa papa him scrife and dædbete georne.

27   Gif mæssepreost ahwar stande on leasre gewitnesse oððe on mænan aðe oððe þeofa gewita and geweorhta beo, þonne sy he aworpen of gehadodra gemanan and þolige ægðer ge geferscipes, ge freondscipes, ge æghwilces wurð-scipes, buton he wið God and wið men þe deoplicor gebete fullice swa biscop him tæce, and him borh finde, þæt he þanan forð æfre swilces geswice.

27.1   And gif he ladian wille, geladige be dæde mæðe swa mid þryfealdre lade, swa mid anfealdre, be þam þe seo dæd sy.

28   Gif weofodþen be boca tæcincge his agen lif rihtlice fa-dige, þonne sy he fulles þegnweres and weorðscipes wurðe, ge on life ge on legere.

23   And if charge of feud is brought against a member of the clergy, and he is accused of either murder or complicity in a murder, he shall exonerate himself with the help of his family, who must either share in the feud or make compensation for it.

24   And if he is without family, he shall exonerate himself with the help of other clergy, or fast to prepare for the ordeal of consecrated bread, and there endure whatever God decides.

25   And no monk anywhere who belongs to a monastery is permitted to either claim or pay compensation related to a feud; he renounces the rights of his kindred when he accepts the monastic rule.

26   If a priest commits murder or any other deeds of great wickedness, then he is to be deprived of his office and his home, and he is to go on a pilgrimage as far as the pope prescribes for him and he is to repent sincerely.

27   If a priest is anywhere guilty of bearing false witness or committing perjury or being the aide or accomplice to thieves, then he is to be expelled from holy orders and deprived of companionship, friendship, and all entitlements unless he repents most deeply to God and the community entirely as the bishop instructs, and finds surety that he thenceforth will cease all wrongdoing.

27.1 And if he wishes to clear himself, he shall do so in the manner appropriate for the offense, either the triple mode of proof or the single, whichever the deed calls for.

28   If a priest who serves at the altar conducts his life properly according to canon law, then he is to be deemed worthy of the full wergild and privileges of a thane, both in life and after death.

29   And gif he his lif misfadige, wanige his weorðscipe be
þam þe seo dæd sy.

30   Wite, gif he wille: ne gebirað him nan þingc ne to wife
ne to worldwige, gif he Gode wile rihtlice hyran and Godes
laga healdan, swa swa his hade gedafenað mid rihte.

31   Ac we lærað georne and luflice biddað þæt ælces hades
men þam life libban þe heom to gebirige.

31.1   And heonan forð we willað, þæt abbodas and munecas
regollicor libban, þonne hi nu ær ðisan on gewunan hæfdon.

32   And se cyngc beodeð eallum his gerefan on æghwilcere
stowe þæt ge þam abbodan æt eallum worldneodum beorgan swa ge betst magon, and be þam þe ge willan Godes
oððe minne freondscipe habban, filstan heora wicneran
æghwar to rihte, þæt heo sylfe magan þe oftor on mynstrum
fæste gewunian and regollice libban.

33   And gif man gehadodne oððe ælþeodigne man þurh
ænig þinc forræde æt feo oððe æt feore, oððe hine bænde
oððe hine beate oððe gebismrige on ænige wisan, þonne
sceal him cyngc beon for mæg and for mundboran, buton he
elles oðerne hæbbe.

34   And bete man ægðer ge him ge þam cynge, swa swa hit
gebirige, be þam þe seo dæd sy, oððe he ða dæde wrece swiðe
deope.

35   Cristenum mannan gebirað swiðe rihte þæt he Godes
abilgðe wrece swiðe georne.

36   And wise wæran worldwitan þe to godcundan rihtlagan
woroldlaga settan folce to steore, and Criste and cyninge

29   And if he conducts his life wrongly, then his privileges are to be diminished according to the severity of his transgression.

30   Let him understand, if he will do so, that it is not appropriate in any way for him to take a wife or to become involved in the warfare of this world, if he desires to obey God properly and heed his laws, as rightly befits his office.

31   But we fervently instruct and lovingly beseech those of every class to conduct their lives in the manner most fitting for them.

31.1   And we order abbots and monks to live henceforth more in accordance with their rule than they have been wont to do previously.

32   And the king commands all of his reeves in every community to assist the abbots in all their worldly needs as best you can, and if you seek to obtain God's friendship and mine, support their representatives everywhere in their legal interests, so that they themselves may, more often, remain secure in their monasteries and live by their rule.

33   And if anyone conspires against the property or life of a cleric or a stranger, or if he is bound or beaten or humiliated in any way, then the king shall be his kinsman and protector, if he does not have another.

34   And as is right, compensation suitable to the severity of the crime is to be paid both to him and the king, or the king will punish that crime most severely.

35   It is most justly appropriate that a Christian should avenge affronts to God with the greatest resolve.

36   And wise were the secular councilors who established worldly laws in support of divine justice, for the guidance of the people, and to allocate compensation to Christ and the

gerehtan þa bote, þar man swa scolde manega for neode
gewildan to rihte.

37 Ac on þam gemotan, þeah rædlice wurdan on nam-
cuðan stowan, æfter Eadgares lifdagum, Cristes lage
wanodan and cyninges laga litledon.

38 And þa man getwæmde þæt ær wæs gemæne Criste
and cynincge on worldlicre steore; and a hit wearð þe wirse
for Gode and for worlde. Cume nu to bote, gif hit God wille.

39 And git mæg ðeah bot cuman, wille hit man georne on
eornost aginnan.

40 And gif man eard wille rihtlice clænsian, þonne mot
man smeagan and geornlice spirian hwar ða manfullan
wununge habban, þe nellað geswican ne for Gode betan; ac
swa hwar swa hi man finde, gewilde hi to rihte þances oððe
unðances, oððe hi afirsige mid ealle of earde, buton hi gebugan and to rihte gewændan.

41 Gif munuc oððe mæssepreost wiðersaca wurðe mid
ealle, he sy amansumod æfre, buton he þe rædlicor gebuge
to his þearfe.

42 And se þe Godes utlagan ofer þone andagan, þe se
cyngc sette, hæbbe on gewealde, plihte to him sylfum and
ealre his are wið Cristes gespelian, þe Cristendom and cynedom healdað and wealdað þa hwile þe þæs God geann.

43 Ac uton don swa us þearf is: uton niman us to bisnan
þæt ærran worldwitan to ræde geræddon—Æþelstan and
Eadmund and Eadgar, þe nihst wæs—hu hi God weorðodon
and Godes lage heoldon and Godes gafel læstan, þa hwile þe
hi leofodon.

king so that out of necessity many must therefore submit to the law.

37   But in those assemblies that met after Edgar's lifetime, though wisely held in prominent places, Christ's laws have been ignored and the king's laws disparaged.

38   And then the proceeds from secular penalties that previously had been shared between Christ and the king were split, and ever since it has gotten worse in both divine and worldly matters. May things now get better, if God so wills!

39   And improvement may still come, assuming there is a sincere desire to act upon it in earnest.

40   And if the land is to be cleansed properly, one must investigate and diligently seek out the dwelling places of the wicked who refuse to renounce their sins and repent before God; and they are to be brought to justice, willingly or unwillingly, wherever they are found, or they will be wholly expelled from this land, unless they yield and submit to the law.

41   If a monk or a priest turns entirely to apostasy, he is to be excommunicated forever, unless he resumes his duty with greater prudence.

42   And the person who keeps an excommunicate under his protection beyond the period of time decreed by the king risks forfeiting his life and all his possessions to the representatives of Christ, who are to uphold and defend the Christian faith and royal authority for as long as God so permits.

43   But let us do what is required of us: let us take as our example that which was wisely ordained by the secular powers of old—Æthelstan and Edmund and Edgar, the most recent—how they worshipped God and obeyed his law and paid tribute to him as long as they lived.

43.1 And utan God lufian innewerdre heortan and Godes laga giman, swa wel swa we betst magon.

44 And uton rihtne Cristendom geornlice wurðian and ælcne hæðendom mid ealle oferhogian.

44.1 And uton ænne cynehlaford holdlice healdan and freonda gehwilc mid rihtan getriwðan oðerne lufige and healde mid rihte.

43.1 And let us love God with our innermost heart and heed his laws as best as we can.

44 And let us fervently exalt the true Christian faith, and wholly reject all heathen practices.

44.1 And let us faithfully support one royal lord, and let each of our friends love each other with true devotion and heed him properly.

9 Æthelred

Pr   Ðis is sio gerædnes þe Æþelred cyning and ealle his witan æt Wudustoce geræddan.

1   An ærest þæt þe ealle to Gode ælmihtigan georne gebugan and his bebodu healdan and unrihtes ealle geswican. . . .

Ex   And uton ænne God lufian and weorðian and ænne
Cristendom ealle healdan and ælcne hæþendom mid ealle
aweorpan. Uton ænne cynehlaford holdliche. . . .

9 Æthelred

Pr   This is the decree which King Æthelred and his whole council proclaimed at Woodstock.

1   First, that we all willingly submit to almighty God and observe his commandments and wholly reject injustice. . . .

Ex   And let us love and praise the one God and keep to the one Christian faith and wholly repudiate every heathen practice. Let us faithfully support one royal lord. . . .

10 Æthelred

Pr   An is ece Godd wealdend and wyrhta ealra gesceafta;
and on þæs naman weorðunge, ic, Æðelred cyning, ærest
smeade hu ic Cristendom æfre mihte and rihtne cynedom
fyrmest aræran, and hu ic mihte þearflicast me sylfum geræ-
dan for Gode and for worolde, and eallum minum leodscype
rihtlicast lagian þa þing to þearfe, þe we scylan healdan.

Pr.1 Me arn to gemynde oft and gelome þætte godcunde
lara and wislice woroldlaga Cristendom fyrðriað and cynedom micliað, folce gefremiað and weorðscypes wealdað, sib-
biað and sehtað and sace twæmað and þeode þeawas ealle
gebetað.

Pr.2 Nu wille ic georne æfter þam spyrian hu we lara and
laga betst magan healdan and æghwylce unlaga swyþost
aweorpan.

Pr.3 And þis is seo gerædnes þe we willað healdan, swa swa
we æt Eanham fæste gecwædon.

1   Ðæt is þonne ærest: þæt we ealle fram synnan georne
gecyrran and ure misdæda geornlice betan and ænne God
æfre lufian and weorðian and ænne Christendom georne
healdan and ælcne hæðendom mid ealle aweorpan.

2   And witena gerædnes is þæt man rihte laga upp arære
and ælce unlaga georne afylle, and þæt man læte beon æghwylcne man rihtes wyrðe,

2.1   and þæt man frið and freondscype rihtlice healde for
Gode and for worolde.

10 Æthelred

Pr   One is the eternal God, ruler and maker of all creation; and in praise of his name, I, King Æthelred, first contemplated how I might always best uphold the Christian faith and just kingship, and how I might govern in a manner most suitable for myself before God and the world, and legislate most justly for all my people concerning those necessities which we must heed.

Pr.1   It occurred to my mind often and frequently that divine teachings and wise secular laws advance the Christian faith and enhance the king's power, support the people and bring renown, make peace and lead to reconciliation and end dissension and wholly improve the habits of the people.

Pr.2   Now I fervently wish to discover how we might best adhere to the teachings and laws and totally reject all injustice.

Pr.3   And this is the decree that we wish to observe, just as we firmly established at Enham.

1   This is foremost: that we all zealously turn from sin and sincerely repent for our misdeeds and love and praise the one God forever and fully abide by the one Christian faith and entirely reject all heathen practices.

2   And the judgment of the council is that just laws be upheld and each injustice zealously eradicated, and that each person be afforded their legal rights,

2.1   and that peace and friendship be justly preserved before God and the world.

Cnut's Oxford Legislation of 1018

Pr   *In nomine Domini.* Ðis is seo gerædnes þe witan geræddon and be manegum godum bisnum asmeadon. And þæt
wæs geworden sona swa Cnut cyngc, mid his witena
geþeahte, frið and freondscipe betweox Denum and Englum
fullice gefæstnode and heora ærran saca ealle getwæmde.

1   Þonne is þæt ærest þæt witan geræddan: þæt hi ofer
ealle oðre þingc ænne God æfre wurðodon and ænne Cristendom anrædlice healdan and Cnut cyngc lufian mid rihtan
and mid trywðan and Eadgares lagan geornlice folgian.

1.1   And hig gecwædan þæt hi furðor on æmtan smeagan
woldan þeode þearfe, mid Godes filste, swa hi betst mihton.

1.2   Nu wille we swutelian hwæt us mæg to ræde for Gode
and for worlde, gime se þe wille.

1.3   Uton swiðe georne fram sinnan acirran and ure misdæda geornlice betan, and ænne God rihtlice lufian and
wurðian, and ænne Cristendom anrædlice healdan, and
ælcne hæðendom georne forbugan.

2   And uton Godes cirican griðian and friðian, and gelomlice secan us silfan to þearfe.

2.1   Ælc cirice is mid rihte on Cristes agenan griðe, and ælc
Cristen man ah micele þearfe þæt he on ðam griðe micele

Cnut's Oxford Legislation of 1018

Pr   *In the name of the Lord.* This is the decree which the council decided upon and deemed to be in accordance with many good practices. And that came about just as soon as King Cnut, on the advice of his council, fully established peace and friendship between the Danes and the English and resolved all their former strife.

1   And this is the first decree of the council: that above all other things, they would always honor the one God and steadfastly observe the one Christian faith and love King Cnut with virtue and loyalty and readily follow the laws of Edgar.

1.1   And they proclaimed that, with God's help, when time permitted they would reflect upon the needs of the realm as best they could.

1.2   Now it is our will to make known that which may be to our advantage before God and the world, take heed who will.

1.3   Let us turn very readily from sins and sincerely repent our misdeeds, praise and honor the one God, steadfastly observe the one Christian faith, and zealously reject each heathen practice.

2   And let us preserve and protect God's churches, and attend them frequently for our own benefit.

2.1   Every church is, by right, under Christ's own protection, and every Christian has the particular obligation to

mæðe wite: forðam Godes grið is ealra griða selost to geearnianne and geornost to healdenne, and þar nihst cynges.

2.2 Ðonne is swiðe rihtlic, þæt Godes ciricgrið binnon
wagum and Cristenes cynges handgrið stande efenunwæmme.

3 And witena gerædnes is þæt man rihte laga upp arære
and æghwilce unlaga georne afille, and þæt man aweodige
and awyrtwalige æghwilc unriht swa man geornost mæge of
þisan earde, and arære up Godes riht.

3.1 And heonan forð læte manna gehwilcne, ge earmne ge
eadigne, folcrihtes wurðe beon.

4 And witena gerædnes is þæt þeah hwa agilte and hine
silfne deope forwyrce, þonne medemige man þa steore swa
hit for Gode sy gebeorhlic and for worlde aberendlic.

4.1 And geþence swiðe georne se ðe domes geweald age,
hwæt he æt us sylf gyrne, þonne he þus cweðe: *Et dimitte
nobis debita nostra, sicut et nos dimittimus.*

5 And witena gerædnes is þæt man Cristene men for
ealles to litlum huru to deaðe ne forræde; ac elles geræde
man friðlice steora folce to ðearfe, and ne forspille for litlum
Godes handgeweorc and his agenne ceap, þe he deore gebohte.

6 And witena gerædnes is þæt man Cristene men ealles
to swiðe of earde ne sille, ne on hæðendom huru ne ge-
brynge; ac beorge man georne þæt man þa sawla ne forfare
þe Crist mid his agenum life gebohte.

show great respect for that protection; for of all forms of protection, the best to be sought and the most faithfully to be respected is the protection of God, and after that the king's.

2.2 Accordingly, it is most proper that the sanctuary within the walls of God's church and the protection received from a Christian king's hand remain equally inviolate.

3 And the council's decree is that just laws are to be upheld and all wrongdoing is to be zealously brought low, and all injustice is to be weeded out from this land and eradicate as zealously as possible, and the law of God is to be exalted.

3.1 And henceforth, all people, both poor and rich, shall be entitled to their legal rights.

4 And the council's decree is that even if someone sins and dishonors himself entirely, the penalty shall be assessed in such a way as shall be justifiable before God and acceptable to the community.

4.1 And the person who has the power to pass judgment shall reflect sincerely upon his own motivations when he recites thus: *And forgive us our debts as we also forgive our debtors.*

5 And the council's decree is that Christians are especially not to be sentenced to death for too little; instead, merciful penalties are to be established for the good of the people, and so that God's handiwork, which he paid for himself at a high cost, not be destroyed because of petty crimes.

6 And the council's decree is that Christians are not to be sold too frequently out of this land, and especially not be brought into heathen lands; but we must zealously ensure that the souls not be destroyed which Christ purchased with his own life.

7   And witena geræednes is þæt man eard georne clænsian onginne on æghwilcon ende and manfulra dæda æghwar geswice; and gif wiccan oððe wigleras, morðwirhtan oððe hórcwenan, ahwar on lande wurðan agitene, fise hi man georne ut of þisan earde, oððe on earde forfare hi mid ealle, buton hi geswican and þe deoppor gebetan.

8   And witena geræednes is þæt wiðersacan and utlagan Godes and manna of earde gewitan, buton hi gebugon and þe geornor gebetan.

8.1   And þeofan and þeodscaðan to timan forwurðan, buton hig geswican.

9   Manslagan and manswaran, hadbrican and æwbrican, gebugan and gebetan, oððe of cyððe mid synne gewitan.

10   Liceteras and leogeras, riperas and reaferas, Godes graman habban, buton hig geswican.

10.1   And se ðe eard wille rihtlice clænsian and unriht alecgan and rihtwisnesse lufian, þonne mot he georne þillices styran and þillic ascunian.

11   And witena geræednes is þæt hi willað þæt ælces hades men georne gebugan, ælc to ðam rihte þe him to gebyrige; and huruþinga Godes þeowas—biscopas and abbodas, munecas and minicena, canonicas and nunnan—to rihte gebugan and regollice libban, and dæges and nihtes oft and gelome clipian to Criste, and for eal Cristen folc þingian georne.

11.1   And ealle Godes þeowas we biddað and lærað, and huruþinga sacerdas, þæt hi Gode hiran and clænnesse lufian and beorgan him silfum wið Godes irre and wið ðone weallendan bryne, þe wealleð on helle.

11.2   Fulgeorne hi witan þæt hi nagan mid rihte þurh hæmedþingc wifes gemanan, and se ðe þæs geswican wille

7   And the council's decree is that the people are to undertake to purify the entire land and eradicate everywhere all sinful deeds; and if wizards or magicians, murderers or prostitutes be found anywhere in this land, they are to be zealously expelled from the realm or be entirely abolished from the earth, unless they cease and most sincerely repent.

8   And the council's decree is that apostates and those in defiance of the laws of God and the realm are to leave this land unless they submit and most sincerely repent.

8.1 And thieves and criminals will henceforth be destroyed, unless they cease their crimes.

9   Murderers and perjurers, those who violate holy orders and those who violate their marriage vows shall submit and do penance or leave their native land with their sins.

10   Hypocrites and liars, thieves and looters will suffer God's wrath unless they cease.

10.1 And anyone who desires to properly purify the realm and eradicate injustice and embrace righteousness must diligently stamp out and condemn such crimes.

11   And the council's decree is that that those of every rank shall faithfully submit to the duty most appropriate for them; and God's servants especially—bishops and abbots, male and female monastics, canons and nuns—are to submit to their duty and live according to their rule, and often and frequently call on Christ by day and night, and fervently intercede for all Christian people.

11.1 And we require and instruct that all servants of God, especially priests, obey God, embrace celibacy, and protect themselves against the burning fire that rages in hell.

11.2 They know full well that they may not rightfully engage in sexual relations with a woman, but he who will renounce

and clænnesse healdan, hæbbe he Godes miltse, and to worldwurðscipe sy he þegenlaga wyrðe.

11.3 And æghwilc Cristen man eac for his Drihtenes ege unrihthæmed georne forbuge and godcunde laga rihtlice healde.

12 And we lærað and we biddað and on Godes naman beodað þæt ænig Cristen man binnon six manna sibfæce on his agenum cynne æfre ne wifige, ne on his mæges lafe þe swa neahsib wære,

12.1 ne on ðæs wifes nydmagan þe he silf ær hæfde, ne on his gefæderan, ne on gehalgodre nunnan.

12.2 Ne on alætan ænig Cristen man ne wifige æfre.

12.3 Ne ænig forligeru ahwar ne begange.

12.4 Ne na ma wifa hæbbe þonne an, ac beo be þare anre, þa hwile þe heo libbe, se þe wille Godes laga giman mid rihte and wið hellebryne beorgan his sawle.

13 And gelæste man Godes gerihta georne rihtlice æghwilce geare.

13.1 Þæt is sulhælmessan huru xv niht ofer Eastron.

13.2 And geoguðe teoðunge be Pentecosten.

13.3 And eorðwæstma be Ealra Halgene mæssan.

13.4 And Romfeoh be Petres mæssan.

13.5 And leohtgescot þriwa on geare.

13.6 And sawlsceat is rihtast þæt man gelæste æt ðam openum græfe.

13.7 And gif man ænig lic of rihtre scriftscire elles hwar lecge, gelæste man þone sawlsceat swa ðeah into ðam mynstre þe hit to hyrde.

marriage and practice celibacy will have God's favor, and also, as a privilege in this world, he shall be deemed worthy of a thane's rights.

11.3 And for fear of the Lord, every Christian must diligently avoid unlawful intercourse and rightly uphold the divine law.

12 And we instruct, pray, and decree in God's name that no Christian man shall ever take a wife within six degrees of kinship in his own family, nor the widow of one so closely related,

12.1 nor a close relative of his first wife, his godmother, or a professed nun.

12.2 Nor may a Christian man ever marry a divorced woman.

12.3 Nor may he ever commit adultery anywhere.

12.4 Nor may he have more than one wife, but he who desires to obey the law of God rightly and guard his soul from hellfire must stay with one wife as long as she lives.

13 And God's dues are to be paid readily every year.

13.1 That is, plow dues fifteen nights after Easter.

13.2 And the tithe of the young animals by Pentecost.

13.3 And the tithe on the fruits of the earth by the Feast of All Saints.

13.4 And the dues to Rome are to be paid by the Feast of Saint Peter.

13.5 And the dues for the lighting of the church are to be paid three times a year.

13.6 And it is most appropriate that dues for the souls of the dead always be paid while the grave is yet open.

13.7 And if any person's body is buried other than in its proper parish, the dues should still be paid to the church to which he belonged.

14   And ealle Godes gerihta friðige man georne, ealswa hit
þearf is, and freolsa and fæstena healde man rihtlice.

14.1 Sunnandæges freols healde man georne swa þarto gebirige, and cipincga, and folcgemota, and huntaðfara, and
worldlicra weorca on ðam halgan dæge geswice man georne.

14.2 And sancta Marian freolstida wurðige man georne,
ærost mid fæstene and siððan mid freolse.

14.3 And to æghwilces apostoles heahtide fæste man
georne, buton Philippus and Iacobus freolse ne beode we
nan fæsten forðam Eastran dæges freolse.

14.4 Elles oðre freolsa and fæstena healde man georne, swa
swa þa heoldon þa ðe betst heoldon.

14.5 And ymbrenfæstena, swa swa sanctus Gregorius Angelcynne silf gedihte.

14.6 And sancte Eadwardes mæssedæg witan habbað ge-
coran þæt man freolsian sceal ofer eall Englaland on xv
kalendas Aprilis.

14.7 And fæste man ælce frigedæg, buton hit freols sy.

15   And ordol and aðas syndon tocwedene freolsdagum
and rihtymbrendagum and fram adventum Domini oð octabas Epiphania, and fram Septuagessima oð xv niht ofer
Eastron.

15.1 And beo þam halgan tidan, ealswa hit riht is, eallum
Cristenum mannum sibb and som gemæne, and ælc sacu
totwæmed.

15.2 And gif hwa oðrum scule borh oððe bote æt worldlican
þingan, gelæste hit him georne, ær oððe æfter.

16   And sy ælc wuduwe þe hy silfe mid rihte gehealde on
Godes griðe and on ðæs cynges.

14   And all God's dues are to be given willingly, just as is required, and feasts and fasts are to be properly observed.

14.1 And the Sunday holy day is to be diligently observed in the manner most appropriate for it, and markets, public meetings, hunts, and secular business are to be assiduously avoided on that holy day.

14.2 And the Feasts of Saint Mary are to be celebrated faithfully, first with fasting and then with a holiday.

14.3 And a fast is to be diligently observed on the feasts of each of the apostles, but we order no fast for the Feasts of Philip and James because of Easter.

14.4 Otherwise, feasts and fasts are to be kept assiduously, just as they were kept when they were kept best.

14.5 And the Ember Fasts are to be kept, just as Saint Gregory himself ordained for the English.

14.6 And the council has determined that the Feast of Saint Edward shall be celebrated throughout England on the fifteenth day before the kalends of April.

14.7 And there shall be a fast each Friday unless it is a feast.

15   And ordeals and oaths are always prohibited during feasts and authorized Ember Days and from Advent until the eighth day of Epiphany and from Septuagesima until the fifteenth night after Easter.

15.1 And at holy times, just as is proper, there is to be peace and friendship among all Christians, and each dispute is to be resolved.

15.2 And if anyone must pay a debt or compensation to another because of a worldly matter, he is to do so promptly before or after the feast.

16   And all widows who comport themselves properly shall be under the protection of God and the king.

16.1 And sitte ælc xii monað wereleas, and ceose siððan þæt heo silf wille.

17 And æghwilc Cristen man do swa him þearf is: gime his Cristendomes georne, and gewunige gelomlice to his scrifte, and unforwandodlice his synna gecyðe, and geornlice bete swa swa him man tæce.

17.1 And gearwige eac to huselgange huru þriwa on geare gehwa hine silfne þe his agene þearfe understandan cunne swa swa him þearf sy.

18 And word and weorc freonda gehwilc fadige mid riht, and að and wed wærlice healde.

19 And æghwilc unriht awurpe man georne of þisan earde þæs ðe man don mæge, and lufige man Godes riht heonan forð georne wordes and dæda. Þonne wurð us Godes miltse þe gearuwre.

20 Wytan eac ealle ymbe friðes bote and ymbe féos bote smeagan swiðe georne.

20.1 Swa ymbe fryðes bote swa beo þam bondan selost and þam þeofan sy laðost.

20.2 And swa ymbe feos bote þæt an mynet gange ofer ealle þas þeode, buton ælcon false.

21 And gemeta and gewihta rihte man georne, and ælces unrihtes heonan forð geswice.

22 And burhbota and bricbota aginne man georne,

23 and fyrdunga eac swa a þonne þearf sy, for gemænelicre neode.

24 And smeage man symle on ælce wisan hu man firmest mæg ræd aredian þeode to þearfe, and rihtne Cristendom

16.1 And each of them is to remain husbandless for twelve months, and then she may choose as she pleases.

17 And each Christian shall do what is required of him: attend diligently to his Christian faith, and go frequently to confession, and confess his sins without hesitation, and sincerely repent just as he is instructed.

17.1 And anyone who wishes to understand his own obligations must prepare himself to receive the sacrament at least three times during the year, just as is required of him.

18 And all of our friends must order their words and deeds properly, and carefully uphold their oath and pledge.

19 And all injustice is to be banished from this land as much as possible, but God's law is to be willingly embraced henceforth in word and deed. Then will God the more readily show mercy to this people.

20 Let us all also consider very carefully the enhancement of public safety and the improvement of the currency.

20.1 Public safety is to be improved so that it is best for the citizen and worst for the thief.

20.2 The currency is to be improved so that there is one standard coinage throughout the realm without any adulteration.

21 And weights and measures are to be assiduously made right, and all unlawful practices abolished henceforth.

22 And improvements to fortifications and bridges are to be undertaken zealously,

23 and also the provisioning of the army as the need arises, for the common good.

24 And consideration must always be given in every way to how first to establish policy to meet the needs of the people and to best uphold the true Christian faith and to most zeal-

swiðost aræran, and æghwilce unlaga geornost afillan. Forðam þurh þæt hit sceal on earde godian to ahte þæt man unriht alecge and rihtwisnesse lufige for Gode and for worlde.

25   And se ðe unlaga arære oððe undom deme heonan forð, for læððe oððe feohfange, beo se wið þone cyngc CXX scillinga scildig, buton he geladige þæt he na bet ne cuðe.

26   And se ðe rihte lage and rihtne dom forsace beo se scildig wið ðone þe hit age;

26.1 swa wið cyningc: CXX scillinga;

26.2 swa wið eorl: XL scillinga;

26.3 swa wið hundred: XXX scillinga;

26.4 swa wið ælc þara gif hit swa gewurðe on Engla lage.

27   And se ðe on Denelaga, rihte laga wirde gilde he lahslite.

28   And git we willað myngian freonda gehwilcne, ealswa us neod is gelome to donne, þæt gehwa hine silfne georne beþence; and þæt he fram sinnum georne gecirre, and oðrum mannum unrihtes stire; and þæt he ofer ealle oðre þingc lufige his drihten; and þæt he oft and gelome hæbbe on gemynde þæt mannum is mæst þearf oftost to gemunnenne, þæt is þæt hi rihtne geleafan habban on ðone soðan God þe is waldend and wirhta ealra gesceafta, and þæt hi rihtne Cristendom rihtlice healdan, and þæt hi godcundum lareowum geornlice hyran, and Godes larum and lagum rihtlice filigan.

29   And þæt hi Godes circan æghwar georne griðian and friðian, and mid leohte and lacum gelome hig gegretan, and hig silfe þar georne gebiddan.

ously eradicate all injustice. For it is in this way that improvement in this land can be achieved: by rejecting injustice and embracing righteousness before God and the world.

25 And anyone henceforth who promotes injustice or hands down unjust judgments, either because of bias or bribery, shall be liable to the king for one hundred twenty shillings, unless he can declare under oath that he did not know how to deliver a more just sentence.

26 And anyone who rejects just laws and judgments is to be liable to the proper authority;

26.1 thus to the king: one hundred twenty shillings;

26.2 thus to an earl: forty shillings;

26.3 thus to the hundred: thirty shillings;

26.4 thus to all of them if it is appropriate in areas under English law.

27 And in the Danelaw, anyone who rejects just law is to pay *lahslit*.

28 Moreover, we also earnestly desire to admonish each of our friends, just as there is often need for us to do, to sincerely give thought to themselves; and to readily turn from sin, and to curb the injustice caused by others; and to love God above all other things; and to bear in mind often and frequently that which there is the greatest need to remember, that is, to maintain proper faith in the true God, who is the Lord and maker of all creation, and to properly adhere to the true Christian faith, and to willingly heed their spiritual teachers, and sincerely follow God's laws and teachings.

29 And that they shall everywhere diligently preserve and protect God's churches, and visit them frequently with candles and offerings, and there themselves pray fervently to Christ.

30   And þæt hi Godes gerihta æghwilce geare mid rihte gelæstan, and freolsa and fæstena. rihtlice healdan.

31   And þæt hi Sunnandæges cypinga and folciscra gemota georne geswican.

32   And þæt hig Godes þeowas symle werian and wurðian.

33   And þæt hi Godes þearfan frefrian and fedan.

34   And þæt hi wuduwan and steopcild to oft ne ahwænan, ac georne hi gladian.

35   And þæt hi ælþeodige men and feorran cumene ne tyrian ne tynan.

36   And þæt hi oðrum mannum unriht ne beodan ealles to swiðe, ac manna gehwilc oðrum beode þæt riht sy, þæt he wille þæt man him beode, be þam þe hit mæð sy.

30   And that each year God's dues are to be paid promptly, and feasts and fasts properly kept.

31   And that on Sundays markets and public meetings are to be assiduously avoided.

32   And that God's servants are to be protected and honored.

33   And that God's poor are to be comforted and fed.

34   And that widows and orphans are not to be continually persecuted, but instead readily uplifted.

35   And that strangers and those who have come from afar are not to be harassed or mistreated.

36   And that they are not to offer injustice to others all too greatly, but that to the best of their ability, everyone is to show that justice to others that they desire to be shown to themselves.

Cnut's Proclamation of 1020

Cnut cyning gret his arcebiscopas and his leodbiscopas and Þurcyl eorl and ealle his eorlas and ealne his þeodscype, twelfhynde and twyhynde, gehadode and læwede, on Englalande freondlice. And ic cyðe eow þæt ic wylle beon hold hlaford and unswicende to Godes gerihtum and to rihtre woroldlage. Ic nam me to gemynde þa gewritu and þa word, þe se arcebiscop Lyfing me fram þam papan brohte of Rome: þæt ic scolde æghwær Godes lof upp aræran and unriht alecgan and full frið wyrcean be ðære mihte þe me God syllan wolde.

2   Nu ne wandode ic na minum sceattum þa hwile þe eow unfrið on handa stod; nu ic mid Godes fultume þæt totwæmde mid minum scattum. Þa cydde man me þæt us mara hearm to fundode, þonne us wel licode; and þa for ic me sylf, mid þam mannum þe me mid foron, into Denmearcon, þe eow mæst hearm of com; and þæt hæbbe ic mid Godes fultume forene forfangen, þæt eow næfre heonon forð þanon nan unfrið to ne cymð þa hwile þe ge me rihtlice healdað and min lif byð. Nu ðancige ic Gode ælmihtigum his fultumes and his mildheortnesse, þæt ic þa myclan hearmas þe us to fundedon, swa gelogod hæbbe þæt we ne þurfon þanon nenes hearmes us asittan, ac us to fullan fultume and to ahreddingge hycgan gyf us neod byð. Nu wylle ic þæt we ealle eadmodlice Gode ælmihtigum þancian þære mildheortnesse, þe he us to fultume gedon hæfð.

Cnut's Proclamation of 1020

King Cnut offers friendly greetings to his archbishops, his subordinate bishops, Earl Thurkil, all his earls, and all his people in England, those with a wergild of twelve hundred shillings and those with a wergild of two hundred shillings, clergy and laymen. And I proclaim to you that I will be a gracious lord, devoted to the rights of the church and to just secular law. I have taken to heart the letters and messages from the pope which Archbishop Lyfing brought to me from Rome: that I should everywhere uphold God's worship and cast down injustice and establish perfect peace through the power which God has chosen to give to me.

Now then, I did not withhold my money when a threat to 2 you was at hand; now with God's help, I have dispersed it with my wealth. At that time, it was made known to me that a danger approached us greater than we would have preferred; then I myself went, alongside those who traveled with me, to Denmark, from which the greatest danger threatened you; and with God's help I have forestalled it, so that from now on hostility from there will never threaten you as long as you obey me faithfully and my life continues. Now I thank almighty God for his help and benevolence, in that I have resolved the great threat which loomed over us so that we need not anticipate danger from there, but rather aid and relief if the need should arise. Now it is my will that we all humbly thank almighty God for his favor, which through his assistance he has granted to us.

3   Nu bidde ic mine arcebiscopas and ealle mine leodbiscopas þæt hy ealle neodfulle beon ymbe Godes gerihta, ælc on
his ende, þe him betæht is; and eac minum ealdormannum
ic beode þæt hy fylstan þam biscopum to Godes gerihtum
and to minum kynescype and to ealles folces þearfe.

4   Gif hwa swa dyrstig sy—gehadod oððe læwede, Denisc
oððe Englisc—þæt he ongean Godes lage ga and ongean
minne cynescype oððe ongean woroldriht, and nelle betan
and geswican æfter minra biscopa tæcinge, þonne bidde ic
Þurcyl eorl and eac beode þæt he ðæne unrihtwisan to rihte
gebige, gyf he mæge. Gyf he ne mæge, þonne wille ic, mid
uncer begra cræfte þæt he hine on earde adwæsce oððe ut of
earde adræfe, sy he betera sy he wyrsa.

5   And eac ic beode eallum minum gerefum, be minum
freondscype and be eallum þam þe hi agon and be heora
agenum life, þæt hy æghwær min folc rihtlice healdan and
rihte domas deman be ðæra scira biscopa gewitnesse and
swylce mildheortnesse þæron don, swylce þære scire biscope riht þince and þe man acuman mæge. And gyf hwa
þeof friðige oððe forena forlicge, sy he emscyldig wið me
þam ðe þeof scolde, buton he hine mid fulre lade wið me ge-
clænsian mæge.

6   And ic wylle, þæt eal þeodscype, gehadode and læwede,
fæstlice Eadgares lage healde, þe ealle men habbað gecoren
and to gesworen on Oxenaforda. Forðam þe ealle biscopas
secgað þæt hit swyþe deop is wið God to betanne þæt man
aðas oððe wedd tobrece. And eac hy us furðor lærað, þæt we

I now charge my archbishops and all my subordinate 3
bishops to be conscientious concerning the rights of the
Church, each in the region assigned to him; and I also command my ealdormen to support the bishops in advancing
the rights of the Church and my royal authority and the welfare of the whole people.

If anyone—either cleric or lay, Danish or English—is so 4
bold as to act in opposition to the law of God and in opposition to my royal authority or in opposition to secular law,
and he refuses to repent and refrain in keeping with the
teachings of my bishops, then I ask, and indeed command,
Earl Thurkil to bring the offender to justice, if he can. If he
cannot, then I desire him to wipe him from the earth or
drive him from the land with our combined strength,
whether he is of higher or lower status.

And further, I command all my reeves, for the sake of 5
my friendship and all that they possess and their very lives,
to govern my people with righteousness everywhere and to
hand down just rulings with the oversight of the bishops of
their shires, and to act with such mercy thereby that the
bishop deems it just and the subject can abide by it. Moreover, if anyone shelters a thief or intercedes on his behalf, he
will be as deserving of punishment before me as the thief,
unless he can be cleared by fully vindicating himself before
me.

And I command that the entire populace, clergy and laity, 6
shall faithfully obey the law of Edgar which all people have
accepted and to which they swore allegiance at Oxford, for
all the bishops decree that very great penance must be performed before God for the violation of oaths or pledges. In
addition, they further instruct us that we should sincerely

sceolon eallan magene and eallon myhton þone ecan mildan God inlice secan, lufian and weorðian, and ælc unriht ascunian, ðæt synd mægslagan and morðslagan and mansworan and wiccean and wælcyrian and æwbrecan and syblegeru. And eac we beodað on Godes ælmihtiges naman and on ealra his haligra, þæt nan man swa dyrstig ne sy þæt on gehadodre nunnan oððe on mynecenan gewifige. And gyf hit hwa gedon hæbbe, beo he utlah wið God and amansumod fram eallum Cristendome, and wið þone cyning scyldig ealles þæs þe he age, buton he ðe raðor geswice and þe deopplicor gebete wið God. And gyt we furðor maniað þæt man Sunnandæges freols mid eallum mægene healde and weorðige fram Sæternesdæges none oð Monandæges lyhtinge, and nan man swa dyrstig ne sy þæt he aðor oððe cypinge wyrce oððe ænig mot gesece on þam halgan dæge. And ealle men, earme and eadige, heora cyrcan secean and for heora synnum þingian and ælc beboden fæsten geornlice healdan and þa halgan georne weorðian, þe us mæssepreostas beodan sceolan. Þæt we magan and moton ealle samod þurh þæs ecean Godes mildheortnesse and his halgena þingrædene to heofena rices myrhðe becuman and mid him wunian, þe leofað and rihxað a butan ende. Amen.

seek, love, and honor the eternal merciful God with all our power and all our might, and reject all forms of wrongdoing, especially those of parricides, murderers and perjurers, witches, enchantresses, adulterers, and the incestuous. And we also command, in the name of almighty God and all of his saints, that no man be so bold as to wed a nun in orders or a woman under monastic vows. And if anyone has done so, he is to be an outlaw before God and excommunicated from the Christian faith, and he is to be liable to the king for all that he possesses, unless he swiftly renounces that union and greatly repents before God. And we yet further emphasize that the Sunday holy day is to be kept and honored with all effort from midafternoon Saturday until dawn on Monday, and no one is to be so bold as to either transact business or attend any meeting on that holy day. And all people, the poor and the wealthy, are to attend their churches and pray for their sins and readily observe every mandated fast, and sincerely honor the saints' days which the priests have set for us. Thus we all may and can reach the joy of the heavenly kingdom through the mercy of the eternal God and the intercession of his saints, and dwell with him who lives and rules forever without end. Amen.

1 Cnut

Pr   Ðis is seo gerædnys þe Cnut ciningc, ealles Englalandes
ciningc and Dena cining, mid his witena geþeahte gerædde,
Gode to lofe and him sylfum to cynescipe and to þearfe; and
þæt wæs on ðære halgan midewintres tide on Winceastre.

1   Ðæt is þonne ærest: þæt hi ofer ealle oþre þingc ænne
God æfre woldan lufian and wurðian, and ænne Cristendom
anrædlice healdan, and Cnut cingc lufian mid rihtan ge-
trywþan.

2   And uton Godes cyrican griðian and friðian, and gelomlice secean saulum to hæle and us sylfum to þearfe.

2.1   Ælc cyrice is, mid rihte, on Cristes agenan griðe, and
ælc Cristen man ah mycele þearfe þæt he on þam griðe mycele mæðe wite; forðam Godes grið is ealra griða selost to
geearnigenne and geornost to healdenne, and þær nehst
cininges.

2.2   Þonne is swiðe rihtlic þæt Godes ciricgrið binnon
wagum and Cristenes ciningces handgrið stande æfre unwemme; and se ðe aðor fulbrece þolige landes and lifes, butan him se ciningc gearian wylle.

2.3   And gyf æfre ænig mann heonon forð Godes cyricgrið
swa abrece, þæt he binnon ciricwagum mannslaga weorðe,

1 Cnut

Pr This is the decree which King Cnut, king of all England and king of the Danes, decided upon on the advice of his councilors, for the glory of God and his own sovereignty and the common welfare; and that was during the holy Christmas season at Winchester.

1 This is foremost, then: that they always love and honor the one God above all else, and single-mindedly uphold the one Christian faith, and love King Cnut with true faithfulness.

2 And let us respect the peace and sanctity of God's churches, and regularly attend them for the salvation of our souls and our own benefit.

2.1 Every church is, by right, under Christ's own protection, and every Christian has the particular obligation to show great respect for that protection; for of all forms of protection, the best to be sought and the most faithfully to be respected is the protection of God, and after that the king's.

2.2 Accordingly, it is most proper that the sanctuary within the walls of God's church and the protection received from the Christian king's hand remain always inviolate; and the person who defies either of them shall forfeit land and life unless the king is willing to pardon him.

2.3 And henceforth, if anyone ever violates the sanctuary of God's church by committing murder within its walls, that

þonne sig þæt botleas, and ehte his ælc þæra þe Godes freond sig, butan þæt geweorðe þæt he þanon ætberste and swa deope friðsocne gesece þæt se cyningc him þurh ðæt feores geunne, wiþ fulre bote ge wið God ge wið menn.

2.4 And þæt is þonne ærest: þæt he his agenne wer Criste and þam cyningce gesylle, and mid þam hine sylfne inlagie to bote.

2.5 And gif hit þonne to bote gega and se cyningc þæt geþafige, þonne bete man þæt cyricgrið into þære cyricean be ciningces fullan mundbryce, and þa mynsterclænsunge begyte, swa þærto gebyrige, and ægþer ge mægbote ge manbote fullice gebete, and wið God huru þingie georne.

3 And gyf elles be cwicum mannum ciricgrið abrocen sy, bete man georne be þam þe seo dæd sy, sy hit þurh feohtlac, si hit þurh reaflac, sig þurh þæt þe hit sy. Bete man ærest þone griðbryce into þære cyrican, be þam þe seo dæd sy and be þam þe ðære cyricean mæð sy.

3.1 Ne synd ealle cyricean na gelicre mæðe woruldlice wurðscipes wyrðe, þeah hig godcundlice habban halgunge gelice.

3.2 Heafodmynstres griðbryce is æt botwyrþum þingum be cingces munde, þæt is mid v pundum on Engla lage—and on

violation shall be deemed beyond compensation, and all those who are friends of God shall hunt him down, unless it so happens that he escapes from there and seeks out protection so powerful that the king therefore spares his life as long as he does full penance toward God and the community.

2.4 And this is first: that he pay his own wergild to Christ and the king, and thereby make himself eligible to pay compensation.

2.5 And if it then reaches the point at which compensation may be paid and the king allows it, payment of an amount equal to the full penalty for violating the king's protection shall be given to the particular church as penance for the violation of the church's sanctuary, and the cleansing of the church shall take place in the proper manner, and compensation to both the family and lord of the victim shall be fully paid, and most importantly, prayers are to be faithfully offered up to God.

3 And if the sanctuary of the church is violated in some other way without the loss of life, penance shall be readily carried out according to the nature of the deed, whether it is violence or robbery or whatever it may be. Penance for the violation of sanctuary is to be made first to the church according to the nature of the deed and likewise according to the status of the church.

3.1 Not all churches are considered alike in worldly status, although spiritually they all possess equal sanctity.

3.2 The penalty for a sanctuary violation at a cathedral, when the violation is deemed eligible for compensation, is to be equal to that paid for a violation of the king's protection, that is, five pounds under English law—and in Kent for

Centlande æt þam mundbryce v pund þam cingce and þreo
þam arcebiscope—and medemran mynstres mid cxx scillingum, þæt is be cingces wite, and þonne gyt læssan, þær
lytel þeowdom sig, and legerstow þeah sig, mid lx scillingum, and feldcyricean, þær legerstow ne sig, mid xxx scyllinga.

4 Eallum Cristenum mannum gebyrað swiðe rihte, þæt
hig haligdom and hadas and gehalgode Godes hus æfre
swiþe georne griðian and friðian, and þæt hi hada gehwylcne
weorðian be mæðe.

4.1 Forþam understande se ðe cunne: mycel is and mære
þæt sacerd ah to donne folce to þearfe, gif he his Drihtne
gecwemeð mid rihte.

4.2 Mycel is seo halsung and mære is seo halgung þe deofla
afyrsað and on fleame gebringeð, swa oft swa man fullað
oððe husel halgað; and halige englas þær abutan hwearfiað
and þa dæda beweardiað and þurh Godes mihta þam sacer-
don fylstað swa oft swa hig Criste ðeniað mid rihte.

4.3 And swa hi doð symle, swa oft swa hig geornlice inweardre heortan clypiað to Criste and for folces neode þingiað georne, and þi man sceal for Godes ege mæðe on hade
gecnawan mid gesceade.

5 And gyf hit geweorðe þæt man mid tyhtlan and mid
uncræftum sacerd belecge, þe regollice libbe, and he hine
sylfne wite þæs clænne, mæssige, gyf he durre, and ladige on
þam husle he ana hine sylfne, æt anfealdre spæce. And æt

a violation of protection, five pounds to the king and three to the archbishop—and at a midlevel church, one hundred twenty shillings, that is, equivalent to the penalty paid for an offense to the king; and at one yet smaller, where there is little divine service but there is a graveyard, sixty shillings; and at a country church where there is no graveyard, thirty shillings.

4   It very properly befits all Christians to always very zealously ensure the peace and sanctity of holy places, of those in orders, and of consecrated houses of God, and to respect all persons in orders according to their rank.

4.1   For let this be understood by those who can: great and wondrous are those things which a priest can do for the benefit of the people if he pleases his Lord rightly.

4.2   Great is the exorcising and wondrous is the sanctifying by which devils are cast out and brought to flight, just as often as he baptizes anyone or consecrates the Eucharist; and holy angels hover about that place and watch over those deeds, and through the power of God they assist the priests just as often as they serve Christ properly.

4.3   And thus the angels always do, just as long as the priests zealously call upon Christ from their innermost hearts and fervently intercede for the needs of the people, and so the different categories of holy orders must be recognized with discernment for fear of God.

5   And if it so happens that a priest who lives according to a rule is accused and charged with wrongdoing, and he knows himself to be innocent, he shall celebrate Mass if he dares, and exculpate himself on his own through the sacrament in the case of a simple accusation. And if it is a

þryfealdre spæce ladige he, gyf he durre, eac on þam husle mid twam his gehadan.

5.1 Gif man deacon tihtlige, þe regollice libbe, anfealdre spæce, nime twegen his gehadan and ladige hine mid þam. And gyf man hine tihtlige þryfealdre spæce, nime VI his gehadan and ladige hine mid ðam, and beo he sylf seofeþa.

5.2 Gif man folciscne mæssepreost mid tihtlan belecge, ðe regollif næbbe, ladige hine swa diacon þe regollife libbe. And gyf man freondleasne weofodþen mid tihtlan belecge, þe aðfultum næbbe, ga to corsnæde, and þær þonne æt gefare þæt þæt God wylle, buton he on husle geladian mote. And gyf man gehadodne mid fæhþe belecge and secge, þæt he wære dædbana oððe rædbana, ladige mid his magum, þe fæhðe moton mid beran oððe fore betan. And gyf he sig mægleas, ladige mid geferan oððe on fæsten fo, gif he þæt þurfe, and ga to corsnæde, and þær æt gefare swa swa God ræde. And na þearf ænig mynstermunuc ahwær mid rihte fæhðbote biddan ne fæhþbote betan; he gæð of his mægð-lage þonne he gebyhð to regollage.

5.3 And gyf mæssepreost æfre ahwær stande on leasre gewitnesse oððe on mænan aðe oððe þeofa gewita oððe gewyrhta beo, þonne sy he aworpen of gehadodra gemanan

threefold accusation, he shall, if he dares, exonerate himself through the sacrament and the oaths of two clerics of his rank.

5.1 If a simple accusation is brought against a deacon who lives according to a rule, he is to take two clerics of his rank and exculpate himself with them. And if a threefold accusation is brought against him, he is to take six clerics of his rank and, himself being the seventh, exculpate himself with them.

5.2 If an accusation is brought against one of the secular clergy who does not live according to a rule, he may exonerate himself as does a deacon who lives according to a rule. And if an accusation is brought against a friendless cleric who serves at the altar, one who does not have supporters for his oath, he shall undergo the ordeal of consecrated bread, and there endure whatever God wills, unless he is permitted to exonerate himself by the sacrament. And if charge of feud is brought against a member of the clergy, and he is accused of either murder or complicity in a murder, he shall exonerate himself with the help of his family, who must either share in the feud or make compensation for it. And if he is without family, he shall exonerate himself with the help of other clergy, or fast to prepare for the ordeal of consecrated bread, and there endure whatever God decides. And no monk anywhere who belongs to a monastery is permitted to either claim or pay compensation related to a feud; he renounces the rights of his kindred when he accepts the monastic rule.

5.3 If a priest is anywhere guilty of bearing false witness or committing perjury or being the aide or accomplice to thieves, then he is to be expelled from holy orders and

and þolige ægþer, ge geferscipes, ge freondscipes ge æghwylces weorðscipes, butan he wið God and wið menn þe deoplicor gebete, swa bisceop him tæce, and him borh finde þæt
he þanon forð æfre swylces geswice.

5.4   And gyf he ladian wylle, geladige þonne be dæde mæðe:
swa mid þryfealdre swa mid anfealdre lade, be ðam þe seo
dæd sy.

6   And we wyllað þæt ælces hades menn georne gebugan,
ælc to þam rihte þe him to gebyrige. And huruþinga Godes
þeowas—bisceopas and abbodas, munecas and mynecena,
canonicas and nunnan—to rihte gebugan and regollice libban, and dæges and nihtes oft and gelome clypian to Criste,
and for eall Cristen folc þingian georne.

6.1   And ealle Godes þeowas we biddað and lærað, and
huruþinga sacerdas, þæt hi Gode hyran and clænnesse lufian
and beorgan heom sylfum wið Godes yrre and wið ðone
weallendan bryne, þe weallað on helle.

6.2   Fullgeorne hig witan þæt hig nagon mid rihte þurh
hæmedþingc wifes gemanan. And se ðe þæs geswican wille
and clænnesse healdan hæbbe he Godes miltse, and to
woruldwurðscipe si he þegenlage wyrðe.

6.3   And æghwylc Cristen mann eac for his Drihtenes ege
unrihthæmed georne forbuge and godcunde lage rihtlice
healde.

7   And we lærað and biddað and on Godes naman beodað
þæt ænig Cristen mann binnon VI manna sibfæce on his
agenum cynne æfre ne gewifie, ne on his mæges lafe, þe swa
neahsib wære, ne on þæs wifes nedmagon þe he sylf ær
hæfde.

7.1   Ne on his gefæderan, ne on gehalgodre nunnan, ne on
ælætan ænig Cristen mann æfre ne gewifige.

deprived of companionship, friendship, and all entitlements unless he repents most deeply to God and the community entirely as the bishop instructs, and finds surety that he thenceforth will cease all wrongdoing.

5.4   And if he wishes to clear himself, he shall do so in the manner appropriate for the offense: either the triple mode of proof or the single, whichever the deed calls for.

6   And we desire that those of every rank shall faithfully submit to the duty most appropriate for them. And indeed, God's servants—bishops and abbots, male and female monastics, priests and nuns—are to submit to their duty and live according to their rule, and often and frequently call on Christ by day and night, and fervently intercede for all Christian people.

6.1   And we require and instruct that all servants of God, especially priests, obey God, embrace celibacy, and protect themselves against God's wrath and against the burning fire that rages in hell.

6.2   They know full well that they may not rightfully engage in sexual relations with a woman. But he who will renounce marriage and practice celibacy will have God's favor, and also, as a privilege in this world, he shall be deemed worthy of a thane's rights.

6.3   And for fear of God, every Christian must diligently avoid unlawful intercourse and rightly uphold the divine law.

7   And we instruct, pray, and decree in God's name that no Christian man shall ever take a wife within six degrees of kinship in his own family, nor the widow of one so closely related, nor a close relative of his first wife.

7.1   Nor may a Christian man ever marry his godmother, a professed nun, or a divorced woman.

7.2   Ne ænige forligru ahwar ne begange.

7.3   Ne na ma wifa þonne an hæbbe, and þæt beo his be-
weddode wif; and beo be þære anre þa hwile þe heo libbe se
ðe wyle Godes lage giman mid rihte and wið hellebryne
beorhgan his sawle.

8   And gelæste mann Godes gerihta æghwylce geare rihtlice georne.

8.1   Þæt is, sulhælmesse xv niht ofer Eastran and geoguþe
teoðunge be Pentecosten and eorðwæstma be Ealra Halgena
mæssan.

8.2   And gyf hwa þonne þa teoþunge gelæstan nelle swa we
gecweden habbað—þæt is se teoða æcer, ealswa seo sulh hit
gega—þonne fare þæs cingces gerefa to, and þæs bisceopes
and þæs landrican and þæs mynstres mæssepreost, and
niman unþances ðone teoðan dæl to þam mynstre þe hit to
gebyrige, and tæcan him to þam nigoðan dæle, and todæle
mann þa eahta dælas on twa, and fo se landhlaford to healfum, to healfum se bisceop, si hit ciningces mann se hit
þegnes.

9   And Romfeoh be Petres mæssan.

9.1   And se ðe ofer þæne dæg hit healde, agyfe þam bisceope
þæne penig and þærto xxx and þam cingce cxx scyllinga.

10   And cyricsceat to Martines mæssan.

10.1 And se ðe hine ofer þæne dæg healde, agyfe hine þam
bisceope and forgylde hine xi siðan and ðam cingce cxx
scyllinga.

7.2   Nor may he ever commit adultery anywhere.

7.3   Nor may he have more than one wife, and she shall be his lawfully wedded wife; but he who desires to obey the law of God rightly and guard his soul from hellfire must stay with one wife as long as she lives.

8   And God's dues are to be paid readily every year.

8.1   That is, plow dues fifteen nights after Easter, and the tithe of the young animals by Pentecost, and the tithe on the fruits of the earth by the Feast of All Saints.

8.2   And if anyone refuses to pay his tithes in the manner that we have decreed—that is, a one-tenth yield of every acre traversed by the plow—then the king's reeve and the reeves of the bishop and landlord and the priest of the church are to go and forfeit without consent a one-tenth portion for the church to which it belongs, and the next tenth is to be left for the recreant, and the remaining eight-tenths are to be divided in two and the landlord shall receive half and the bishop the other half, whether he is a king's man or a thane's.

9   And the dues to Rome are to be paid by the Feast of Saint Peter.

9.1   And anyone who withholds it beyond that day shall give the money and a further thirty pence to the bishop, and one hundred twenty shillings to the king.

10   And Church dues are to be paid by the Feast of Saint Martin.

10.1 And anyone who withholds it beyond that day shall give the money to the bishop, and do so again eleven times over, and one hundred twenty shillings to the king.

11 Gyf hwa þonne þegna sig þe on his boclande cyrican hæbbe, þe legerstow on sig, gesylle þone þriddan dæl his agenre teoþunge into his cyrican.

11.1 And gyf hwa cyricean hæbbe, þe legerstow on ne sig, do he of ðam nigon dælum his preoste þæt þæt he wylle.

11.2 And ga ælc cyricsceat into þam ealdan mynstre be ælcon frigan heorðe.

12 And leohtgesceot þriwa on geare: ærest on Easteræfen healfpenigwurð wexes æt ælcere hide and eft on Ealra Halgena mæssan eallswa mycel, and eft to þæm æfene Sanctan Marian clænsunge ealswa.

13 And sawlsceat is rihtast þæt man symle gelæste a æt openum græfe.

13.1 And gyf man ænig lic of rihtscriftscire elles hwær lecge, gelæste man þone sawlsceat swa þeah into þam mynstre þe hit to hyrde.

14 And ealle Godes gerihta fyrðrige man georne, ealswa hit þearf is.

14.1 And freolsa and fæstena healde mon rihtlice.

14.2 And healde man ælces Sunnandæges freolsunge fram Sæternesdæges none oð Monandæges lihtingce, and ælcne oðerne mæssedæg, swa he beboden beo.

15 And Sunnandaga cypingce we forbeodað eac eornostlice and ælc folcgemot, butan hit for micelre neodþearfe sig.

15.1 And huntaðfara and ealra woruldlicra weorca on þam halgan dæge geswicæ man georne.

16 And þæt man ælc beboden fæsten healde, si hit ymbrenfæsten, si hit lengctenfæsten, si hit elles oðer

11   Yet if there is a thane who has a church possessing a graveyard on land he holds by charter, he is to give one-third of his own tithes to his church.

11.1 If anyone has a church without a graveyard, then let him give what he chooses to his priest out of the next one-tenth share after that paid as tithe.

11.2 And all Church dues from every free household are to go to the old minster.

12   And the dues for the lighting of the church are to be paid three times a year: first, a halfpennyworth of wax from each hide on the eve of Easter, and just as much afterward on the Feast of All Saints, and an equal amount again at the Feast of the Purification of Saint Mary.

13   And it is most appropriate that dues for the souls of the dead always be paid while the grave is yet open.

13.1 And if any person's body is buried other than in its proper parish, the dues should still be paid to the church to which he belonged.

14   And all God's dues are to be given willingly, just as is required.

14.1 And feasts and fasts are to be properly observed.

14.2 And each Sunday holy day is to be observed from midafternoon on Saturday until dawn on Monday, and every other feast day just as is ordained for it.

15   And we also prohibit most strictly the transaction of business on Sundays and all public meetings, unless there is a great need for one.

15.1 And hunts and worldly business are to be assiduously avoided on that holy day.

16   And each ordained fast is to be observed with all assiduousness, whether it is the Ember Fast, the Lenten fast, or

fæstæn, mid ealre geornfulnesse. And to Sancta Marian mæssan ælcere and to ælces apostoles mæssan fæste man— butan to Philippi and Iacobi mæssan we ne beodað nan fæsten for þam Easterlican freolse—and ælces Frigedæges fæsten, butan hit freols sig.

16.1 And na þearf man na fæstan fram Eastran oð Pentecosten butan hwa gescrifen sig oððe he elles fæstan wylle; eallswa of middanwintra oð octabas Epiphanige, þæt is seofen niht ofer Twelftan mæssedæge.

17 And we forbeodað ordal and aðas freolsdagum and ymbrendagum and lengctendagum and rihtfæstendagum and fram Aduentum Domini oð se eahtaþa dæg agan sig ofer Twelftan mæssedæge and fram Septuagessima oð xv nihton ofer Eastron.

17.1 And Sancte Eadweardes mæssedæg witan habbað gecoren, þæt man freolsian sceal ofer eall Englaland, þæt is on þam xv dæge (on Martige xviii) kalendas Aprilis and Sancte Dunstanes mæssedæg on xiiii kalendas Iunii, þæt ys on þam þreotteoðan dæge þe byð on Mæge.

17.2 And beo þam halgum tidum, ealswa hit riht is, eallum Cristenum mannum sib and som gemæne, and ælc sacu totwæmed.

17.3 And gyf hwa oðrum sceole borh oððe bote æt woruldlicum þingum, gelæste hit him georne ær oððe æfter.

18 And we biddað for Godes lufan, þæt ælc Cristen mann understande georne his agene þearfe. Forþam ealle we sceolon ænne timan gebidan þonne us wære leofre þonne eall þæt on middanearde is, þæt we aworhtan, þa hwile þe we mihton, georne Godes willan. Ac þonne we sceolan habban

any other fast. And a fast is to be observed on all of the feasts of Saint Mary as well as on the feasts of each of the apostles—but we order no fast for the Feasts of Philip and James because of Easter—and a fast is to be held every Friday unless there is a feast.

16.1 And no one need fast between Easter and Pentecost unless it has been assigned as a penance or he otherwise wishes to fast; or from Christmas until the eighth day of Epiphany, that is, seven days after the Twelfth Night.

17 And we forbid ordeals and oaths on feasts and Ember Days, during Lent, on legally designated fast days, from Advent until the eighth day after Twelfth Night, and from Septuagesima until fifteen days after Easter.

17.1 And the council has determined that the Feast of Saint Edward shall be celebrated throughout England on the fifteenth day before the kalends of April (the nineteenth of March) and the Feast of Saint Dunstan on the fourteenth day before the kalends of June, that is, the thirteenth day of May.

17.2 And at holy times, just as is proper, there is to be peace and friendship among all Christians, and each dispute is to be resolved.

17.3 And if anyone must pay a debt or compensation to another because of a worldly matter, he is to do so promptly before or after the feast.

18 And for the love of God, we pray that every Christian fully understand what is expected of him. For we all will reach a point when we will wish more than anything in the world that we had readily carried out God's will as long as we could. But then we will receive a reward fitting for that

anfeald lean ðæs þe we on life ær geworhtan. Wa þam þonne þe ær geearnode hellewite!

18.1 Ac uton swiðe georne fram synnum gecyrran and ure ælc his misdæda urum scriftum geornlice andettan, and æfre geswican and geornlice betan.

18.2 And ure ælc oðrum beode þæt we willon þæt man us beode; þæt is rihtlic dom and Gode swiðe gecweme; and se byð swiðe gesælig þe þone dom gehylt.

18.3 Forþam God ælmihtig us ealle geworhte and eft deopum ceape gebohte, þæt is mid his agenum life, þe he for us eallum sealde.

19 Ac gehwylc Cristen man do swa him þearf is: gime his Cristendomes georne and gearwige hine eac to huselgange huru þriwa on geare gehwa hine sylfne þe his agene þearfe wylle understandan, swa swa him þearf sig.

19.1 And word and weorc freonda gehwylc fadige mid rihte, and að and wedd wærlice healde.

19.2 And æghwylc unriht aweorpe man georne of þysum earde, þæs þe man don mæge

19.3 And lufige Godes riht heonon forð georne wordes and dæde: ðonne wurð us eallum Godes milts þe gearuwre.

20 Uton don eac georne, swa we gyt læran wyllað: utan beon a urum hlaforde holde and getrywe and æfre eallum mihtum his wurðscipe ræran and his willan gewyrcan.

20.1 Forðam eal þæt we æfre for rihthlafordhelde doð, eall we hit doð us sylfum to mycelre þearfe; forþam byð witodlice God hold, þe byð his hlaforde rihtlice hold.

20.2 And eac ah hlaforda gehwylc þæs formycle þearfe þæt he his men rihtlice healde.

which we previously accomplished during our lifetime. Woe then to that person who has earned the pains of hell!

18.1 But let us most readily turn from sin, and each of us sincerely confess our misdeeds to our confessor, and ever after cease our wrongdoing and fervently repent.

18.2 And let each of us treat others as we wish to be treated; that is a just rule and most pleasing to God; and the person who adheres to that rule will be very happy.

18.3 For God almighty created us all and afterward paid a high cost for us, namely, his own life which he gave for us all.

19 But let each Christian do that which is required of him: attend diligently to his Christian faith and likewise prepare himself to receive the sacrament at least three times during the year if he wishes to understand his responsibilities, just as he should.

19.1 And all of our friends must order their words and deeds properly, and carefully uphold their oath and pledge.

19.2 And all injustice is to be banished from this land as much as possible.

19.3 And God's law is to be willingly embraced henceforth in word and deed; then will God show mercy the more readily to us all.

20 Let us also do just as we further intend to instruct: let us always be faithful and true to our lord and ever with all our might uphold his sovereignty and carry out his will.

20.1 For all that we ever do because of the loyalty justly owed to our lord, we do to our own great benefit; for certainly God will be true to the person who is justly true to his lord.

20.2 And likewise the principal obligation of every lord is to treat his people justly.

21   And ealle Cristene men we læra∂ swi∂e georne þæt hig
inweardre heortan æfre God lufian and rihtne Cristendom
geornlice healdan and godcundan lareowan geornlice hyran,
and Godes lara and laga smeagan oft and gelome him sylfum
to þearfe.

22   And we læra∂, þæt ælc Cristen man geleornige, þæt he
huru cunne rihtne geleafan and ariht understandan and Pater noster and Credan geleornian.

22.1 For∂am mid þam oþrum sceal ælc Cristen mann hine
to Gode gebiddan and mid þam o∂rum geswutelian rihtne
geleafan.

22.2 Crist sylf sang Pater noster ærest and þæt gebed his
leorningccnihtum tæhte.

22.3 And on þam godcundan gebede syn VII gebedu; mid
þam se ∂e hit inweardlice gesing∂, he geærnda∂ to Gode sylfum ymbe æfre ælce neode, þe man beþearf a∂or o∂∂e for
þysum life o∂∂e for ∂am toweardan.

22.4 Ac hu mæg þonne æfre ænig mann hine inweardlice to
Gode gebiddan butan he hæbbe inweardlice so∂e lufe and
rihtne geleafan to Gode?

22.5 Forþam he nah æfter for∂si∂e Cristenra manna gemanan ne on gehalgedan lictune to restene, ne he nah þæs
halgan husles to onfonne her on life.

22.6 Ne he ne by∂ wel Cristen þe þæt geleornian nele, ne he
nah mid rihte o∂res mannes to onfonne æt fulluhte, ne æt
bisceopes handa þe ma, ær he hit geleornige þæt he hit wel
cunne.

23   And we læra∂ þæt man wi∂ healice synna and wi∂
deoflice dæda scylde swyþe georne on æghwylcne timan;
and bete swyþe georne be his scriftes geþeahte, se ∂e þurh
deofles scyfe on synna befealle.

21   And we most sincerely instruct all Christians to always love God with their innermost hearts and fervently uphold the true Christian faith and readily heed their spiritual teachers, and often and frequently reflect upon God's precepts and laws for their own benefit.

22   We instruct every Christian to study so that he can, in particular, know and properly understand the true faith and learn the Paternoster and Creed.

22.1 For with the first of these, every Christian shall pray to God, and with the second testify to the true faith.

22.2 Christ himself first recited the Paternoster and taught that prayer to his disciples.

22.3 And in that holy prayer are seven entreaties; he who recites it in his soul pleads with God himself concerning all things which may be to a person's benefit, both in this life and in the life to come.

22.4 But how then can anyone ever pray to God in his soul unless he has true love for and faith in God in his soul?

22.5 For after his death he cannot lie in the company of Christians nor rest in hallowed ground, nor can he be eligible to receive the holy sacrament here in this life.

22.6 That person who refuses to learn it is not a good Christian, nor can he legitimately sponsor another at baptism, much less at confirmation, until he learns it so that he knows it well.

23   And we instruct that people are to guard themselves most zealously against mortal sins and devilish deeds at all times; and those who fall into sin by the temptation of the devil are to repent most sincerely according to the guidance of their confessor.

24   And we lærað þæt man wið fulne galscipe and wið unrihthæmed and wið æghwylcne æwbryce warnige symle.

25   And we lærað eac georne manna gehwylcne þæt he
Godes ege hæbbe symle on his gemynde, and dæges and
nihtes forhtige for synnum, Domdæg ondræde and for helle
agrise, and æfre him gehende endedæges wene.

26   Bisceopas syndan bydelas and Godes lage lareowas, and
hi sceolon bodian and bysnian georne godcunde þearfe,
gyme se ðe wylle.

26.1 Forþam wace byð se hyrde funden to heorde þe nele þa
heorde þe he healdan sceal, mid hreame bewerian, butan he
elles mæge gyf þær hwylc þeodsceaða sceaðian onginneð.

26.2 Nis nan swa yfel sceaða swa is deofol sylf; he byð a ymbe
þæt an, hu he on mannum saulum mæst gesceaðian mæge.

26.3 Þonne moton þa hyrdas beon swyðe wacore and geornlice clypigende, þe wið þone þeodsceaðan folce sceolon scyldan: þæt syndan bisceopas and mæssepreostas, þe godcunde
heorda bewarian and bewerian sceolon mid wislican laran,
þæt se wodfreca werewulf to swyðe ne slite, ne to fela ne
abite of godcundre heorde.

26.4 And se ðe oferhogie, þæt he Godes bodan hlyste,
hæbbe him gemæne þæt wið God sylfne. A sy Godes nama
ecelice gebletsod, and lof him and wuldor and wurðmynt
symble æfre to worulde. Amen.

24   And we instruct that foul lust, illicit intercourse, and all forms of adultery are to be zealously avoided.

25   And we likewise fervently instruct everyone to hold the fear of God constantly in their mind, and to live in fear of sin both day and night, and dread the Day of Judgment, and tremble at the prospect of hell, and always expect their last day to be near at hand.

26   Bishops are messengers and teachers of God's law, and they are to diligently proclaim and embody our spiritual duty, heed them who will.

26.1 For the shepherd will be found wanting who will not cry out in defense of the flock entrusted to his care, if he can do nothing else when a predator comes to prey upon it.

26.2 There is no predator so evil as the devil himself; he is always concerned with only one thing, how he can best prey upon people's souls.

26.3 Thus, the shepherds who must defend the people against this predator must be very watchful and zealously cry out: these are the bishops and the priests, who must oversee and provide for their spiritual flock with wise teachings, so that the madly voracious werewolf does not wound too greatly nor consume too many of their spiritual flock.

26.4 And the person who neglects to heed God's messengers will have to account for that to God himself. May the name of God be sanctified forever, and praise and honor and glory be to him eternally. Amen.

2 Cnut

Pr   Þis is seo woruldcunde gerædnes þe ic wylle, mid minan witenan ræde, þæt man healde ofer eall Englaland.

1   Ðæt is þonne ærest: þæt ic wylle þæt man rihte laga upp arære and æghwylc unlaga georne afylle, and þæt man aweodige and awyrtwalige æghwylc unriht, swa man geornost mæge, of þysum earde, and arære up Godes riht.

1.1   And heonon forð læte manna gehwylcne, ge earmne ge eadigne, folcrihtes weorðne and him man rihte domas deme.

2   And we lærað þæt þeah hwa agylte and hine sylfne deope forwyrce, þonne gefadige man ða steore swa hit for Gode sy gebeorhlic and for worulde aberendlic. And geþence swyþe georne se ðe domes geweald age hwæs he sylf gyrne þonne he þus cweðe: *Et dimitte nobis debita nostra, sicut et nos dimittimus;* þæt is on Englisc: "and forgyf us, Drihten, ure gyltas, swa we forgyfað þam ðe wið us agyltað."

2.1   And we forbeodað þæt man Cristene men for ealles to lytlum huru to deaþe ne forræde; ac elles geræde man friðlice steora folce to þearfe and ne forspille for lytlum Godes handgeweorc and his agenne ceap, þe he deore gebohte.

3   And we forbeodað þæt man Cristene men ealles to swiðe of earde ne sylle ne on hæðendome huru ne gebringe;

254

2 Cnut

Pr   This is the secular decree which, on the advice of my councilors, I desire to be observed throughout all England.

1   This is foremost, then: I desire just laws to be upheld and all wrongdoing to be entirely brought low, and all injustice to be weeded out from this land and eradicated as zealously as possible, and the law of God to be exalted.

1.1   And henceforth, all people, both rich and poor, shall be granted their legal rights and just rulings shall be issued for them.

2   And we instruct that even if someone sins and dishonors himself entirely, the penalty shall be assessed in such a way as shall be justifiable before God and acceptable to the community. And the person who has the power to pass judgment shall reflect sincerely upon his own motivations when he recites thus: *And forgive us our debts as we also forgive our debtors,* that is in English, "Forgive us, Lord, our trespasses as we forgive those who trespass against us."

2.1   And we forbid Christians to be sentenced to death for entirely too little; instead, merciful penalties are to be established for the good of the people, and so that God's handiwork, which he paid for himself at a high cost, not be destroyed because of petty crimes.

3   And we forbid the all-too-common practice of selling Christians out of this land, and especially bringing them

ac beorge man georne þæt man þa saule ne forfare, þe Crist mid his agenum life gebohte.

4   And we beodað þæt man eard georne clænsian aginne on æghwylcan ende and manfulra dæda æghwær geswice. And gif wiccean oððe wigleras, morðwyrhtan oððe horcwenan ahwær on lande wurðan agitene, fyse hig man georne ut of þysum earde, oððon on earde forfare hig mid ealle, butan hig geswican and þe deoppar gebetan.

4.1   And we beodað þæt wiðersacan and utlagan Godes and manna of eardæ gewitan butan hig gebugan and þe geornor gebetan.

4.2   And þeofas and þeodsceaðan to timan forweorðan butan hig geswican.

5   And we forbeodað eornostlice ælcne hæðenscipe.

5.1   Hæðenscipe byð þæt man deofolgyld weorðige, þæt is þæt man weorþige hæðene godas and sunnan oððe monan, fyr oððe flod, wæterwyllas oððe stanas oððe æniges cynnes wudutreowa, oððon wiccecræft lufige oððon morðweorc gefremme on ænige wisan, oððon on blote oððon fyrhte, oð-ðon swylcra gedwimera ænig þingc dreoge.

6   Manslagan and manswaran, hadbrecan and æwbrecan gebugan and gebetan, oððe of cyððe mid synnan gewitan.

7   Licceteras and leogeras, ryperas and reaferas Godes graman habban butan hig geswican and þe deoppar gebetan.

7.1   And se ðe eard wylle rihtlice clænsian and unriht alecgan and rihtwisnesse lufian, þonne mot he georne þyllices styran and þyllic ascunian.

into heathen lands; but we must zealously ensure that the souls not be destroyed which Christ purchased with his own life.

4   And we command that the people undertake to purify the entire land and eradicate everywhere all sinful deeds. And if wizards or magicians, murderers or prostitutes be found anywhere in this land, they are to be zealously expelled from the realm or they shall be entirely abolished from the earth, unless they cease and most sincerely repent.

4.1   And we command that apostates and those in defiance of the laws of God and the realm are to leave this land unless they submit and most sincerely repent.

4.2   And thieves and criminals will henceforth be destroyed unless they cease their crimes.

5   And we earnestly forbid all heathen practices.

5.1   Heathen practices are devil worship, that is, the worshipping of heathen gods, of the sun or the moon, of fire or water, or of springs or stones or any type of tree; the devotion to witchcraft or conspiring to bring about a person's death by any means, either through sacrifice or divination or by engaging in any other similar idiocies.

6   Murderers and perjurers, those who violate holy orders and those who violate their marriage vows shall submit and do penance or leave their native land with their sins.

7   Hypocrites and liars, thieves and looters will suffer God's wrath unless they cease and most sincerely repent.

7.1   And anyone who desires to properly purify the realm and eradicate injustice and embrace righteousness must diligently stamp out and condemn such crimes.

8   Uton eac ealle ymbe friðes bote and ymbe feos bote smeagan swyðe georne: swa embe friðes bote, swa ðam bondan si selost, and þam þeofan si laþast; and swa embe feos bote, þæt an mynet gange ofer ealle þas þeode butan ælcan false, and þæt nan man ne forsace.

8.1   And se ðe ofer þis fals wyrce þolige þæra handa þe he þæt fals mid worhte, and he hi mid nanon þingon ne gebicge, ne mid golde ne mid seolfre.

8.2   And gyf man þonne þæne gerefan teo, þæt he be his leafe þæt fals worhte, ladige hine mid þryfealdre lade; and gyf seo lad þonne berste, hæbbe þone ylcan dom þe se þe þæt fals worhte.

9   And gemeta and gewihta rihte man georne and ælces unrihtes heonon forð geswice.

10   And burhbota and bricbota and scipforðunga aginne man georne, and fyrdunga eac swa a þænne þearf si, for gemænelicre neode.

11   And smeage man symle on æghwylce wisan hu man fyrmest mæge ræd aredian þeode to þearfe and rihtne Cristendom swyðost aræran and æghwylce unlage geornost afyllan.

11.1   Forðam þurh þæt hit sceal on earde godian to ahte: þæt man unriht alecge and rihtwisnesse lufige for Gode and for worulde. Amen.

12   Ðis syndon þa gerihta þe se cingc ah ofer ealle men on Wessexan: þæt is mundbryce and hamsocne, forsteal and

8   Furthermore, let us all also consider very carefully the enhancement of public safety and the improvement of the currency; public safety is to be improved so that it is best for the citizen and worst for the thief; and the currency is to be improved so that there is one standard coinage throughout the realm without any adulteration, and no one will refuse it.

8.1 And henceforth, the person who produces counterfeit money shall forfeit the hands with which he made the false coinage, and he may not save it by any means, neither with gold nor with silver.

8.2 And if a reeve is charged with permitting the counterfeit to be made, he shall exonerate himself with the three-fold oath of exculpation; and if the oath fails, he shall suffer the same penalty as the counterfeiter.

9   And weights and measures are to be assiduously made right, and all unlawful practices abolished henceforth.

10   And improvements to fortifications and bridges are to be undertaken with care, and also the provisioning of the navy and army as the need arises, for the common good.

11   And consideration must always be given in every way to how first to establish policy to meet the needs of the people and to best uphold the true Christian faith and to most zealously eradicate all injustice.

11.1 For it is in this way that improvement in this land can be achieved: by rejecting injustice and embracing righteousness before God and the world. Amen.

12   These are the fines to which the king is entitled from all the people of Wessex: that is, fines for the violation of the

flymena fyrmðe and fyrdwite, butan he hwæne ðe furðor
gemæðrian wylle and he him ðæs weorðscipes geunne.

13   And se ðe utlages weorc gewyrce, wealde se cingc þæs
friþes.

13.1 And gyf he bocland hæbbe, þæt sy forworht þam cingce
to handa, si ðæs mannes man, þe he sig.

13.2 And lochwa þone flyman fede oððe feormie, gylde v
pund þam cingce, butan he hine geladige, þæt he hine fleame
nyste.

14   And on Myrcean he ah eallswa her beforan awriten is
ofer eall men.

15   And on Dæna lage he ah fihtewita and fyrdwita, gryðbryce and hamsocne, butan he hwæne ðe furður gemæðrian
wylle. And gyf hwa þæne friðleasan man healde oððe flyman
feormie, bete þæt, swa hit ær lagu wæs.

15.1 And se ðe unlage rære oððe undom gedeme heonon
forð, for læððe oððe for feohfange, beo se wið þone cingc
CXX scyllinga scyldig on Engla lage—butan he mid aðe cyðan
durre, þæt he hit na rihtor ne cuþe—and þolige aa his þegnscipes, butan he hine æt þam cingce eft gebicge, swa he him
geþafian wylle. And on Dena lage lahslites scyldig, butan he
geladige þæt he na bet ne cuðe.

15.2 And se ðe rihte lage and rihtne dom forsace, beo se
scyldig wið þone þe hit age: swa wið cyningc CXX scyllinga,

king's protection and for home invasion, for assault, harboring of fugitives, and shirking military service, unless he wishes to specially privilege someone by allocating these fines to him.

13   And the king has the power to grant clemency to those who engage in outlawry.

13.1   And if he holds land by charter, it shall be forfeited into the king's hand, no matter which lord he serves.

13.2   And anyone who feeds or shelters a fugitive must pay five pounds to the king, unless he can exonerate himself by proving that he did not know he was a fugitive.

14   And in Mercia the king is entitled to everything listed here from all the people.

15   And in the Danelaw the king is entitled to the fines for fighting and shirking military service, breaching the peace and home invasion, unless he wishes to specially privilege someone. And accordingly, if anyone protects or shelters an outlaw, he shall be penalized according to the law.

15.1   And anyone henceforth who promotes injustice or hands down unjust judgments, either because of bias or bribery, shall be liable to the king for one hundred twenty shillings in areas under English law—unless he can declare under oath that he did not know how to deliver a more just sentence—and he shall forfeit forever his rights as a thane, unless he redeems it from the king if he is willing to permit it. In the Danelaw, he shall be liable for his *lahslit,* unless he can exonerate himself by proving that he did not know any better.

15.2   And in areas under English law, anyone who rejects just laws and judgments is to be liable to the proper authority: either one hundred twenty shillings to the king, sixty

swa wið eorl LX scyllinga, swa wið hundred XXX scyllinga, swa wið ælc þæra, gyf hit swa geweorðeþ, on Engla lage.

15.3 And se ðe on Dena lage rihte lage wyrde, gylde he lahslit.

16 And se þe oþerne mid wo forsecgan wylle, þæt he aðer oððe feo oððe freme þe wyrse sig, gyf þonne se oðer þæt geunsoðian mæge, þæt him man on secgan wolde, sy he his tungan scyldig butan he hine mid his were forgylde.

17 And ne gesece nan man ðone cingc butan he ne mote beon nanes rihtes wyrðe innan his hundrede.

17.1 And sece man hundredes gemot be wite, eallswa hit is to secenne.

18 And hæbbe mann þriwa on geare burhgemot and tuwa scirgemot, butan hit oftor sig.

18.1 And þær beo on þære scire bisceop and se ealdorman, and þær ægþer tæcan ge Godes riht ge woruldriht.

19 And ne nime nan man nane næme, ne innan scire ne ut of scire, ær mann hæbbe þriwa on hundrede his rihtes gebeden.

19.1 Gif he æt þam þriddan cyrre nan riht næbbe, þonne fare he feorðan siðe to scirgemote, and seo scir him sette þone feorðan andagan.

19.2 Gyf se þonne berste, nime þonne leafe ægþer ge heonon ge þanan þæt he mote hentan æfter his agenan.

shillings to the earl, thirty shillings to the hundred, or to all of them if it is relevant.

15.3 And in the Danelaw, anyone who rejects just law is to pay *lahslit*.

16 And if anyone who seeks to bring a false charge against another so that he is the worse in either property or well-being, and if the accused can disprove the charge that has been brought against him, then the accuser shall lose his tongue unless he can redeem himself through the payment of his wergild.

17 And no one may petition the king unless he cannot obtain his rights within his hundred.

17.1 And everyone is to attend the hundred court whenever summoned or suffer a penalty.

18 And the borough court is to meet three times a year and the shire court twice unless the need arises more frequently.

18.1 And the bishop of the diocese and the ealdorman shall both be in attendance, and there administer the ecclesiastical and secular laws.

19 And no one shall execute a legal repossession of property, either within or outside the shire, until he has brought his claim to the hundred court three times.

19.1 If he does not receive what is rightfully owed him after the third petition, then he shall appeal on a fourth occasion to the shire court, and the shire court shall set a day for the fourth hearing.

19.2 And if this proves futile, he shall get permission either here or from the previous court to repossess his property.

20 And we wyllað þæt ælc freoman beo on hundrede and
on teoðunge gebroht, þe lade wyrðe beon wylle oððon weres
wyrðe gyf hine hwa teon wylle, ofer þæt he byð xii wintre;
oððon he ne beo syððan æniges freorihtes wyrðe. Si he
heorðfæst, si he folgere, þæt ælc si on hundrede and on
borge gebroht, and gehealde se borh hine and gelæde to
ælcan rihte.

20.1 Manig strec man wyle, gyf he mæg and mot, werian his
man, swa hwæðer swa him þingð, þæt he hine eað awerian
mæge, swa for frigne swa for þeowne; ac we nellað geðafian
þæt unriht.

21 Ac we wyllað þæt ælc man ofer xii wintre sylle þone að
þæt he nelle þeof beon ne þeofes gewita.

22 And sy ælc getrywa man þe tihtbysig nære and naðor ne
burste ne að ne ordal, innan hundrede anfealdre lade wyrðe.

22.1 And ungetrywan men ceose man anfealdne að on þrim
hundredum; and þryfealdne að, swa wide swa hit to ðære
byrig hyre; oððon ga to þam ordale. And ofga man anfealde
lade mid anfealdan foraðe and þryfealde lade mid þryfealdan
foraðe.

22.2 And gyf þegen hæbbe getrywne man to foraðe for hine,
þæt swa sig; gyf he næbbe, ofga sylf his spæce.

22.3 And ne beo æfre ænig forað forgyfen.

20 And we desire that every freeman over the age of twelve who wishes to be entitled to swear an oath of exculpation and to be eligible for wergild compensation if he is slain is to be enrolled in a hundred and in a tithing; otherwise, he will not be entitled to any of the rights of a freeman. Whether independent or in service, everyone is to be enrolled in a hundred and under a surety, and that surety shall maintain him and guide him in his legal obligations.

20.1 Many recalcitrant individuals, if they may and can, seek to maintain control over their underlings by whatever means that they think easiest, either by treating them as if they were free or as if they were slaves; but we will not allow this injustice.

21 But we desire that each person over the age of twelve give their oath that they will be neither a thief nor a thief's accomplice.

22 And every trustworthy man who had never been under suspicion and had not failed an oath or ordeal, shall be eligible to exonerate himself by the simple oath of exculpation.

22.1 And guarantors for the simple oath of the untrustworthy man shall be chosen from the three hundreds; and for the threefold oath, from throughout the jurisdiction of the borough court; otherwise he must undergo the ordeal. And a case requiring the simple oath of exculpation is to be initiated with a simple oath of accusation, and a case requiring the threefold oath of exculpation is to be initiated with a threefold oath of accusation.

22.2 And if a thane has a trustworthy man to make a claim on his behalf, he may use him; if he does not, then he must make the claim himself.

22.3 And an oath of accusation can never be waived.

23   And ne beo ænig man æniges teames wyrðe butan he getrywe witnesse hæbbe, hwanan him come þæt him man æt befehþ.

23.1 And gecyðe seo gewitnes, þæt on Godes helde and on hlafordes, þæt heo him on soðre gewitnesse sy, swa heo hit eagum oferseah and earum oferhyrde, þæt he hit mid rihte begeate.

24   And nan man nan þingc ne bigce ofer feower peniwurð, ne libbende ne licgende, butan man hæbbe getrywe gewitnesse feower manna, seo hit binnan byrig, sy hit upp on lande.

24.1 And gyf hit man þonne befo, and he þyllice gewitnesse næbbe, ne beo þær nan team, ac agyfe man þam agenfrigan his agen and þæt æftergild, and þæt wite þam þe hit age.

24.2 And gyf he gewitnesse hæbbe, swa we her beforan cwædon, þonne tyme hit man þriwa; æt þam feorðan cyrre, agnige hit oððe agyfe þam þe hit age.

24.3 And us ne þingð na riht þæt ænig man agnian sceole þær gewitnesse byð, and man gecnawan cann þæt þær bregde byð; þæt nan man hit nah to geahnianne raþost þinga ær syx monðum, æfter ðam þe hit forstolen wæs.

25   And se ðe tyhtbysig sig and folce ungetrywe and þas gemot forbuge þriwa, þonne sceawie man of þam feorðan gemote þa ðe him to ridan; and finde þonne gyt borh, gif he mæge. Gif he þonne ne mage, gewylde man hine swa hwæðer swa man mæge, swa cucne swa deadne, and niman eall þæt he ahte.

23 And no one shall be entitled to vouch to warranty unless he has reliable witnesses to the manner by which he came by the goods in his possession.

23.1 And the witnesses, if they wish to enjoy the protection of God and their lord, shall swear that, as truthful witnesses to his legal possession, they are testifying to just what they saw with their eyes and heard with their ears.

24 And no one shall buy anything worth more than four pence, either livestock or goods, unless he has four men as honest witnesses, whether he is in a town or in the country.

24.1 Yet if the purchased goods had previously been in someone's possession and the purchaser had no such witnesses, then there can be no vouching to warranty, but the goods must be returned to their owner along with a penalty payment and a fine to the proper authority.

24.2 And if he has witnesses, just as we have set forth here, then he is to vouch to warranty three times; on the fourth time, he shall prove his ownership or return it to its proper owner.

24.3 And it does not seem just to us that anyone should assert possession when there are witnesses and fraud can be proven; such being the case, no one should assert possession of anything less than six months at least from when it was stolen.

25 And anyone who is of ill repute and considered untrustworthy by the community and fails to attend the court three times, at the fourth meeting men shall be appointed to ride to him; and he may then still find a surety, if he can. If he cannot do so, they are to capture him however they can, either alive or dead, and seize all that he owns.

25.1 And gilde man þam teonde his ceapgild, and fo se hlaford elles to healfum, to healfum þæt hundred.

25.2 And gif aðor oððe mæg oððe fræmde þa rade forsace, gylde þam cingce cxx scyllinga.

26 And gesece se æbæra þeof þæt þæt he gesece, oððe se ðe on hlafordsearwe gemet sig, þæt hig næfre feorh ne ge-secean.

26.1 And se ðe ofer þis stalige, gesece þæt he gesece, þæt he næfre þæt feorh ne gesece æt openre þyfðe.

27 And se ðe on gemote mid wiðertihtlan hine sylfne oððon his mann werige, hæbbe þæt eall forspecen, and geandwerde ðam oþrum, swa hundrede riht þince.

28 And þæt nan man nænne man ne underfo na længc þonne þreo niht, butan hine se befæste, þe he ær folgade.

28.1 And nan man his men fram him ne tæce ær he clæne sy ælcere spræce þe he ær beclypod wæs.

29 And gyf hwa þeof gemete and hine his þances aweg læte butan hreame, gebete be þæs ðeofes were oððe hine mid ful-lan aðe geladige þæt he him nan facn mid nyste.

29.1 And gyf hwa hream gehyre and hine forsitte, gylde þæs cingces oferhyrnesse oððe hine be fullan geladige.

25.1 And they shall give to the accuser a single payment equivalent to the market value of his goods, and half of the remainder is to be taken by the landlord and half by the hundred.

25.2 And if anyone, either his relative or a stranger, refuses to participate in the ride, he is to pay the king one hundred twenty shillings.

26 And anyone convicted of theft or caught conspiring against his lord shall not be able to save his life, no matter where he hides.

26.1 And anyone who commits theft after this shall not be able to save his life no matter where he hides, if his guilt is proven.

27 And anyone who seeks to protect himself or his follower in court by bringing a countercharge shall have spoken wholly in vain, and he shall respond to his opponent's charge in whatever fashion the hundred court thinks best.

28 And no one shall detain a servant for more than three nights unless the latter has been entrusted to him by the person he previously followed.

28.1 And no one is to release one of his followers from service unless he has been shown to be innocent of any accusation that has been brought against him.

29 And if anyone encounters a thief and of his own accord permits him to escape without raising an alarm, he is to make amends by paying an amount equivalent to the thief's wergild or exonerate himself by swearing a full oath that he did not know that the fugitive was guilty of any wrongdoing.

29.1 And if anyone hears the alarm and ignores it, he is to pay the fine for disobedience to the king or exonerate himself with a full oath.

30   And gyf hwylc man si swa ungetrywe þam hundrede and swa tihtbysig, and hine þonne þreo men ætgædere teon, ðonne ne beo þær nan oðer butan þæt he gange to ðam þryfealdan ordale.

30.1 Gyf se hlaford þonne secge þæt him naðor ne að ne ordal ne burste syððan þæt gemot wæs on Winceastre, nime se hlaford him twegen getrywe men to innon þam hundrede, and swerian þæt him næfre að ne burste ne ordal, ne he þeofgyld ne gulde, butan he þone gerefan hæbbe, þe ðæs wyrðe sig, þe þæt don mæge.

30.2 Gyf se að þonne forðcume, ceose se man þe þær betihtled syg swæðer he wylle: swa anfeald ordal swa pundes weorðne að innan þam þrim hundredan ofer xxx peninga.

30.3 And gif heo þone að syllan ne durren, gange he to þam þryfealdan ordale. And ofga man þæt þryfealde ordal þus: nime fife and beo he sylf syxta. And gif he þonne ful weorðe, æt ðam forman cyrre bete ðam teonde twygylde and þam hlaforde his wer, þe his wites wyrðe sig, and sette getrywe borgas þæt he ælces yfeles eft geswice.

30.4 And æt þam oðrum cyrre, ne si þær nan oðer bot gif he ful wurðe butan þæt man ceorfe him ða handa oððe þa fet oððe ægþer, be þam ðe seo dæd sig.

30.5 And gif he þonne gyt mare wurc geworht hæbbe, þonne do man ut his eagan, and ceorfan of his nosu and his earan and þa uferan lippan oððon hine hættian, swa hwylc þyssa

30   And if anyone deemed especially untrustworthy by the hundred and especially frequently accused is charged by three men at once, then he shall have no other recourse except to undergo the threefold ordeal.

30.1 Yet if his lord declares that he has failed neither oath nor ordeal since the court was held at Winchester, then the lord shall appoint two men from within the hundred to swear that he has never failed an oath or ordeal, nor has he been convicted of theft, unless he has a reeve entitled to do this.

30.2 Then, if the oath taking will proceed, the person who is accused shall there select whichever he prefers: a simple ordeal or an oath valued at one pound supported by witnesses from within the three hundreds in disputes involving property valued at more than thirty pence.

30.3 And if the accused dare not take the oath, he is to undergo the threefold ordeal. And the threefold ordeal is to be undertaken thus: the accuser shall choose five witnesses, and he himself shall be the sixth. And then if the accused is proven guilty, the first time he shall pay twice the fine to his accuser and the value of his wergild to his lord, who is entitled to receive his fine, and he shall choose trustworthy sureties to guarantee that he will afterward cease from all wrongdoing.

30.4 And if he is proven guilty a second time, there shall be no other possible compensation except to have his hands or feet cut off or both, according to the seriousness of the crime.

30.5 And if he has committed an even greater crime, then his eyes shall be put out and his nose, ears, and upper lip cut off or his scalp taken off, whichever of these is decreed by

swa man þonne geræde, ða þe ðærto rædan sceolon; swa man mæg styran and eac þære sawle beorgan.

30.6 Gif he þonne ut hleape and þæt ordal forbuge, gilde se borh ðam teonde his ceapgyld and þam cingce his wer oððe þam þe his wites wurðe sig.

30.7 And gif man þone hlaford teo, þæt he be his ræde ut hleope and ær unriht worhte, nime him v getrywe to and beo him sylf syxta and ladige hine þæs.

30.8 Gyf seo lad forðcume, beo he þæs weres wyrðe.

30.9 And gif heo forð ne cume, fo se cingc to þam were and beo se þeof utlah wið eal folc.

31 And hæbbe ælc hlaford his hiredmen on his agenum borge. And gif hine man æniges þingces teo, andswarie innan þam hundrede, þær he on beclypod beo, swa hit rihtlagu sig.

31.1 And gyf he betihtlod weorðe and he ut oðhleape, gilde se hlaford þæs mannes were ðam cingce. And gyf man þone hlaford teo, þæt he be his ræde ut hleope, ladige hine mid V þegnum, and beo him sylf syxta.

31.2 Gyf him seo lad berste, gylde þam cingce his were; and si se man utlah.

32 And gyf þeowman æt þam ordale ful weorðe, mearcie man hine æt þam forman cyrre.

32.1 And æt þam oðran cyrre ne si þær nan oðer bot butan þæt heafod.

the person with the authority to pass judgment; thus may a person be punished yet his soul be saved.

30.6 Yet if he escapes and shuns the ordeal, his surety is to give the market value of his goods to the accuser and the value of his wergild to the king or to whoever is entitled to receive that fine.

30.7 And if the lord is accused of providing advice to the person who had previously committed a crime so that he escapes, he must name five trustworthy witnesses and himself make a sixth, and exonerate himself of this.

30.8 If the exoneration is successful, he will be entitled to the wergild.

30.9 And if it does not succeed, the king shall take his wergild and the thief shall be adjudged an outlaw by the entire realm.

31 And every lord shall himself serve as surety for his followers. And if an accusation is brought against any of them, he is to answer it in the appropriate hundred, just as the law decrees.

31.1 And if he comes to be accused and escapes, the lord is to pay the fugitive's wergild to the king. And if the lord is accused of advising him to escape, he must exonerate himself with the support of five thanes, and himself will make the sixth.

31.2 If the exoneration fails, he is to pay a fine equal to his wergild to the king, and the fugitive is to be declared an outlaw.

32 And if a slave is proven guilty by ordeal, the first time he is to be branded.

32.1 And on the next occasion he shall not be able to make compensation except with his head.

33 And gif hwylc man si, þe eallum folce ungetrywe si, fare þæs cingces gerefa to, and gebringan hine under borge, þæt hine man to rihte læde þam ðe him on spræcan.

33.1 Gif he þone borh næbbe, slea hine man and on fulan lecge. And gif hine hwa forene forstande, beon hi begen anes rihtes wyrðe.

33.2 And se ðe þis forsitte and hit geforþian nelle, swa ure ealra cwyde is, sylle þam cingce CXX scillinga.

34 And stande betux burgum an lagu æt ladunge.

35 And gyf freondleas man oððe feorrancuman swa geswenced weorðe þurh freondleaste, þæt he borh næbbe, æt frymtyhtlan þonne gebuge he hengenne and þær gebide oð ðæt he ga to Godes ordale, and gefare ðær þæt he mæge.

35.1 Witodlice, se ðe freondleasan and feorrancumenan wyrsan dom demeð þonne his geferan, he dereð him sylfum.

36 And gyf hwa mæne að on haligdome swerige, and he oferstæled weorðe, þolige þæra handa oððe healfes weres, and þæt sy gemæne hlaforde and bisceope.

36.1 And na beo he þanon forð aðes wyrðe, butan he for Gode þe deoppar gebete and him borh finde þæt he æfre eft swylces geswice.

37 And gyf hwa on leasre gewitnesse openlice stande and he oferstæled weorðe, ne stande his gewitnes syððan for naht, ac gylde þam cingce oððe landrican þe his socne ahe be healsfange.

33   And if there is anyone judged untrustworthy by the community, the king's reeve shall go and place him under surety so that he may be brought to justice before those who have accused him.

33.1 If he has no surety, he is to be executed and buried in unconsecrated ground. And if anyone intervenes on his behalf, they shall both suffer the same justice.

33.2 And anyone who ignores this and refuses to uphold what we have all pronounced shall give to the king one hundred twenty shillings.

34   And within the boroughs there shall be one law establishing the means of exoneration.

35   If a person who is friendless or come from afar is so bereft of friends as to lack a surety, on the first accusation he is to be suspended in chains and there abide until he undergoes God's ordeal, and there suffer what he may.

35.1 Truly, whoever hands down a more severe sentence on the friendless or those come from afar than upon his own companions does injury to himself.

36   And if anyone swears a false oath over the relics and is convicted, he shall either lose his hand or half his wergild, which is to be shared between king and bishop.

36.1 And thenceforth, he shall not be considered worthy to swear an oath, unless he repents most sincerely before God and appoints a surety to guarantee that he will afterward cease from such perjury.

37   And if anyone publicly bears false witness and is proven guilty, his testimony thenceforth shall count for nothing, and he shall pay to the king or to the lord who holds jurisdiction a fine equivalent to his *healsfang*.

38   Nis on ænigne timan unriht alyfed; and þeah man sceal freolstidan and fæstentidan and on freolsstowan geornlicost beorgan.

38.1 And a swa man byð mihtigra oððe maran hades, swa scæl he deoppor for Gode and for worulde unriht gebetan.

38.2 And godcunde bote sece mann symle georne be boctæcinge, and woruldcunde bote sece man be woruldlage.

39   Gyf hwa weofodþen afylle, sy he utlah wið God and wið men, butan he þurh wræcsið þe deoppor gebete, and eac wið ða mægðe; oððe geladige hine mid werlade.

39.1 And binnon xxx nihton aginne bote ægþer ge wið God ge wið menn be eallum þam þe he age.

40   Gyf man gehadodne oððe ælþeodigne þurh ænig þingc forræde æt feo oððe æt feore, þonne sceal him cingc beon for mæg and for mundboran butan he elles oðerne hlaford hæbbe.

40.1 And bete man þam cingce, swa hit gebyrige, oððe he ða dæde wrece swiþe deope.

40.2 Cristenan kyningce gebyrað swyðe rihte þæt he Godes æbylgðe wrece swyðe deope, be ðam þe seo dæd si.

41   Gyf weofedþen manslaga weorðe oððon elles to swyðe manweorc gewyrce, þonne þolige he ægþer ge hades ge eðles, and wræcnige swa wide swa papa him scrife, and dædbete georne.

41.1 And gyf he ladian wylle, ladige mid þryfealdan.

38 Wrongdoing shall not be tolerated at any time; yet during holy seasons and at holy places it must be suppressed with the greatest diligence.

38.1 And always, the mightier a person is or the higher his rank, so must he do penance for his crimes all the more sincerely before God and the world.

38.2 And spiritual penance shall always be assessed according to canon law, and secular penalties according to the civil law.

39 If anyone kills a minister of the altar, he shall be excommunicated and outlawed, unless he repents all the more sincerely by making pilgrimage and also by paying compensation to his victim's family; or he may exonerate himself by an oath equal to the value of his wergild.

39.1 And he must start to make amends within thirty days to both God and the community or forfeit all that he owns.

40 If anyone conspires against the property or life of a cleric or a stranger in any way, then the king shall be his kinsman and protector if he does not have another guardian.

40.1 And appropriate compensation shall be paid to the king, or he shall avenge that deed most severely.

40.2 It is most justly appropriate that a Christian king should avenge affronts to God with the greatest resolve, according to the nature of the offense.

41 If a minister at the altar commits murder or any other serious crime, then he shall forfeit both his office and his native land, and he must go on a pilgrimage as far as the pope prescribes for him, and fervently do penance.

41.1 And if he desires to exonerate himself, he must do so by the threefold oath.

41.2 And butan he binnan xxx nihton bote aginne wið God and wið men, þonne si he utlah.

42 Gyf hwa gehadodne man bende oððon beate oððon swyðe gebysmrige, bete wið hine, swa swa hit riht sy, and bisceope weofodbote be hades mæðe and hlaforde oððe cyningce be fullan mundbryce; oððe geladige hine mid fulre lade.

43 Gyf gehadod man hine forwyrce mid deaðscylde, gewylde hine man and healde to bisceopes dome, be þam þe seo dæd si.

44 Gif deaðscyldig man scriftspæce gyrne, ne wyrne him man æfre.

44.1 And gif him hwa wyrne, gebete þæt wið þone cing mid cxx scyllingum; oððe geladige hine: nime v and beo sylf syxta.

45 Gyf man wealdan mæge, ne dyde man æfre on Sunnandæges freolse ænigne forwyrhtne man, butan he fleo oððe feohte; ac wylde and healde, þæt se freolsdæg agan sy.

45.1 Gyf freoman freolsdæge wyrce, þonne gebete þæt mid his halsfange, and huru wið God bete hit georne, swa swa man him tæce.

45.2 Þeowman gif wyrce, þolige his hyde oððon hydgyldes, be þam seo dæd sy.

45.3 Gyf hlaford his þeowan freolsdæge nyde to weorce, þolige þæs þeowan, and beo he syððan folcfrig; and gylde lahslit se hlaford mid Denum, wite mid Englum, be ðam þe seo dæd sig, oððe hine geladige.

41.2 And unless he starts to make amends within thirty days to both God and the community, he will become an outlaw.

42 If anyone binds or beats or greatly shames someone in holy orders, he shall make amends to him according to the law, and pay to the bishop the fine for assaulting an ecclesiastic according to the victim's status, and to his lord or the king the full penalty for the violation of his protection; or he shall exonerate himself by the full oath of exculpation.

43 If a person in orders compromises himself with a capital crime, he is to be arrested and held for the bishop's judgment, according to the nature of the offense.

44 If someone sentenced to death desires confession, it shall never be denied to him.

44.1 And if anyone denies him confession, he shall atone for that with a payment to the king of one hundred and twenty shillings; or he may exonerate himself: he may select five witnesses and himself be the sixth.

45 If it can be managed, no one sentenced to death should ever be executed on a Sunday holy day, unless he flees or fights; but he is to be arrested and held until the holy day has ended.

45.1 If a freeman works on a feast day, he shall atone for that with the payment of his *healsfang*, and he shall most zealously repent before God in the manner assigned to him.

45.2 If a slave works, he shall suffer the lash or pay a fine in its stead, according to the nature of the deed.

45.3 If a lord compels his slave to work on a holy day, he shall lose the slave, who will be free thenceforth; and he must pay *lahslit* within the Danelaw and a penalty among the English according to the nature of the deed; or he must exonerate himself.

46 Gif frigman rihtfæsten abrece, gilde lahslit mid Denum, wite mid Englum, be þam þe seo dæd sy.

46.1 Yfel byð, þæt man rihtfæstentide ær mæle ete, and gyt
wyrse þæt man mid flæscmete hine sylfne afyle.

46.2 Gif hit þeowman gedo, þolige his hyde oððe hydgyldes,
be þam þe seo dæd sy.

47 Gif hwa openlice lengctenbryce gewyrce þurh feohtlac
oððe þurh wiflac oððe þurh reaflac oððe þurh ænige healice
misdæda, sy þæt twybete, swa on heahfreolse, be ðam þe seo
dæd si.

47.1 And gif man ætsace, ladige mid þryfealdre lade.

48 Gif hwa mid wige godcundra gerihta forwyrne, gilde
lahslit mid Denum, fullwite mid Englum; oððe geladige
hine: nime xi and beo sylf twelfta.

48.1 Gif he man gewundige, gebete þæt and gylde fulwite
þam hlaforde, and æt bisceope þa handa alyse oððe hig
alæte.

48.2 Gif he mann afylle, beo he utlah and his hente mid
hearme ælc þæra þe riht wylle.

48.3 Gyf he gewyrce, þæt man hine afylle, þurh þæt þe he
ongean riht geondbyrde, gif man þæt gesoðige, licge ægilde.

46   If a freeman breaks a legally mandated fast, he must pay *lahslit* within the Danelaw and a penalty among the English, according to the nature of the deed.

46.1 During a legally mandated fast, it is sinful for anyone to eat before the appropriate time, and still worse for anyone to befoul himself with flesh.

46.2 If a slave does so, he shall suffer the lash or pay a fine in its stead, according to the nature of the deed.

47   If anyone openly violates the Lenten fast by fighting or engaging in illicit intercourse or by robbery or any serious crime, he shall pay a double penalty according to the seriousness of the offense, as is appropriate during a religious feast.

47.1 And if anyone denies the accusation, he must exonerate himself with the threefold oath.

48   If anyone resists the payment of their ecclesiastical dues with violence, he must pay *lahslit* within the Danelaw and the full penalty among the English; or he must exonerate himself: he must select eleven supporters and himself make the twelfth.

48.1 If he wounds anyone, he must pay compensation for that and pay the full penalty to the lord, and ransom his hands from the bishop or lose them.

48.2 If he kills someone, he shall be outlawed and hunted without regard for his safety by those who desire to uphold the law.

48.3 If he acts in such a way as to cause his own death through opposition to the law, he shall die without compensation, if this can be proved.

49   Gif hwa hadbryce gewyrce, gebete þæt be hades mæðe, swa be were swa be wite swa be lahslite swa be ealre are.

50   Gif hwa æwbryce gewyrce, gebete þæt be þam þe seo dæd sy.

50.1 Yfel æwbryce byð þæt eawfæst man mid æmtige forlicge, and mycele wyrse wið oðres æwe oððe wið gehadode.

51   Gif hwa sibleger gewyrce, gebete þæt be sibbe mæðe, swa be were swa be wite swa be ealre æhte.

51.1 Ne byð na gelic, þæt man wið swustor gehæme and hit wære feorr sibb.

52   Gif hwa wudewan nydnæme, gebete þæt be were.

52.1 Gif hwa mæden nydnæme, gebete þæt be were.

53   Gif be cwicum ceorle wif hi be oðrum were forlicge and hit open weorðe, geweorðe heo to woruldsceame syððan hyre sylfre, and hæbbe se rihtwer eall þæt heo ahte; and heo þolige nasa and earena.

53.1 And gif hit tihtle sig and lad forberste, bisceop þonne wealde and stiðlice deme.

54   Gif wiffæst wer hine forligce be his agenre wylne, þolige þære and bete for hine sylfne wið God and wið men.

54.1 And se ðe hæbbe rihtwif and eac cifese, ne do him nan preost nan þæra gerihta þe man Cristenum men don sceal,

49   If anyone injures a member of the clergy, compensation must be paid according to the victim's rank, either by the payment of wergild, a fine, *lahslit,* or by the confiscation of all of the offender's property.

50   If anyone violates the marriage vows, compensation must be paid according to the seriousness of the deed.

50.1 It is a terrible transgression for a married man to have intercourse with an unmarried woman, and much worse with another's wife or with a woman in orders.

51   If anyone commits incest, the penalty shall be assessed according to the degree of kinship, either by the payment of wergild, a fine, or by the confiscation of all of the offender's property.

51.1 Fornication with one's sister shall not be considered comparable to fornication with a distant relation.

52   If anyone rapes a widow, compensation shall be made through the payment of the offender's wergild.

52.1 If anyone rapes a maiden, compensation shall be made through the payment of the offender's wergild.

53   If a woman has intercourse with another man while her husband is still alive and it comes to be discovered, she shall bring worldly shame upon herself, and her legal husband shall have all that she possesses; and she shall lose her nose and ears.

53.1 And if there is an accusation and the oath of exculpation fails, the bishop shall judge and he is to judge harshly.

54   If a married man engages in intercourse with his own slave, she shall be confiscated and he must do penance for himself before God and the community.

54.1 And if anyone has a legal wife as well as a mistress, no priest shall perform for him any of the sacraments to which

ær þam he geswice and swa deope gebete swa bisceop him tæce, and æfre swylces geswice.

55 Ælþeodige men, gif hig heora hæmed rihtan nellan, driue hi man of lande mid heora æhtum and synnan gewitan.

56 Gif open morð weorðe þæt man sy amyrðred, agyfe man þam magum þone banan.

56.1 And gif hit tihtle sig and æt lade mistide, deme se bisceop.

57 Gif hwa ymb ciningc oððe hlaford syrwe, si he his feores scyldig and ealles þæs ðe he age, butan he ga to þry-fealdan ordale.

58 Gif hwa ciningces borh abrece, gebete þæt mid v pun-dan.

58.1 Gif hwa arcebisceopes borh oððe æþelingces abrece, gebete þæt mid þrim pundan.

58.2 Gif hwa leodbisceopes oððe ealdormannes borh ab-rece, gebete þæt mid II pundan.

59 Gif hwa on ciningces hirede gefeohte, þolige þæs lifes butan se cincg him gearian wylle.

60 Gif man æt unlagum man bewæpnige, forgilde hine be halsfange; and gif hine man gebinde, forgilde be healfan were.

61 Gif hwa on fyrde gryðbryce fulwyrce, ðolige lifes oððe weregildes.

61.1 Gif he samwyrce, bete, be þam þe seo dæd sy, hine.

62 Gif hwa hamsocne gewyrce, gebete þæt mid v pundan þam cingce on Engla lage; and on Cent æt hamsocne, v þam

a Christian is entitled until he ceases and repents as profoundly as the bishop instructs, and afterward entirely abstains from such sins.

55 If foreigners will not make their marriages conform to the law, they shall be expelled from the realm with their possessions and leave with their sins.

56 If it comes to be shown that someone who has died violently has been murdered, the murderer shall be surrendered to the family of the victim.

56.1 And if there is an accusation and the oath of exculpation fails, the bishop shall judge the case.

57 If anyone conspires against the king or his own lord, his life and all that he owns shall be forfeit, unless he undergoes the threefold ordeal.

58 If anyone violates the king's protection, he shall be penalized five pounds.

58.1 If anyone violates the protection of the archbishop or a nobleman, he shall be penalized three pounds.

58.2 If anyone violates the protection of a diocesan bishop or an ealdorman, he shall be penalized two pounds.

59 If anyone fights within the king's household, he shall lose his life unless the king is willing to show mercy to him.

60 If anyone illegally seizes a man's weapons, he is to pay him compensation equivalent to his *healsfang;* and if he binds him, he must compensate him with half his wergild.

61 If anyone commits a capital crime while serving in the army, he shall lose either his life or his wergild.

61.1 If anyone commits a lesser crime, he is to compensate the victim according to the seriousness of the offense.

62 If someone is guilty of home invasion, he is to pay five pounds to the king in areas under English law; and in Kent

cingce and þreo þam arcebisceope; and on Dena lage, swa
hit ær stod.

62.1 And gif hine mon þær afylle, licge ægilde.

63 Gif hwa reaflac gewyrce, agyfe and forgylde, and beo
his weres scyldig wið þone cingc oððe wið þone þe his socne
age.

64 Husbryce and bærnet and open þyfð and æbære morð
and hlafordswyce æfter woruldlage is botleas.

65 Gif hwa burhbote oððe brycgbote oððe fyrdfare forsitte, gebete mid CXX scyllingum þam cingce on Engla lage,
and on Dena lage swa hit ær stod, oððe geladige hine: namie
man him XIIII, and begyte XI.

65.1 To cyricbote sceal eall folc fylstan mid rihte.

66 Gif hwa Godes flyman hæbbe on unriht, agyfe hine to
rihte and forgilde þam þe hit gebyrige, and gylde þam cingce
be his weregylde.

66.1 Gif hwa amansodne man oððe utlahne hæbbe and
healde, plihte him sylfum and ealre his are.

67 And gif hwa wylle georne fram unrihte gecirran eft to
rihte, miltsige man for Godes ege, swa man betst mæge,
þam swyþe georne.

for home invasion, five pounds to the king and three to the archbishop; and in the Danelaw, as it was previously decreed.

62.1 And if he is killed in the course of his crime, he shall die without compensation.

63 If anyone commits a robbery, he must make restoration and compensation, and his wergild is to be forfeit to the king or to the authority that holds jurisdiction.

64 According to secular law, no compensation can be paid for housebreaking, arson, a theft which is openly proved, a murder which has been publicly discovered, or conspiracy against one's lord.

65 If anyone neglects the upkeep of fortifications, the repair of bridges, or required military service, he is to pay one hundred twenty shillings to the king in areas under English law, and under the Danelaw as it was previously decreed, unless he exonerates himself: fourteen potential witnesses shall be identified for him, of which he must obtain the support of eleven.

65.1 As is just, the whole realm shall contribute to the upkeep of churches.

66 If anyone illegally shelters an excommunicated person, he shall surrender him to the lawful authorities and pay compensation to whom it belongs, and pay his wergild to the king.

66.1 If anyone shelters and supports an excommunicated person or an outlaw, it shall be at the risk of his life and all his property.

67 And if anyone sincerely desires to turn from lawlessness to justice, as much mercy as possible must be shown to him with very great eagerness, for fear of God.

68 And utan don, swa us þearf is: helpan aa þam raþost þe helpes betst behofað; þonne nime we þæs lean, þær us leofast byð.

68.1 Forðam a man sceal þam unstrangan men for Godes lufe and ege liþelicor deman and scrifon þonne þam strangan. Forþam ðe ne mæg se unmaga þam magan, we witon full georne, gelice byrðene ahebban, ne se unhala þam halan gelice. And þy we sceolon medmian and gesceadlice todælan ylde and geogoþe, welan and wædle, freot and þeowet, hæle and unhæle. And ægþer man sceal ge on godcundan scriftan ge on woruldcundan doman þas þingc tosceadan.

68.2 Eac on mænigre dæde, þonne man byð nydwyrhta, þonne byð se gebeorges þe bet wyrðe, þe he for neode dyde þæt þæt he dyde.

68.3 And gyf hwa hwæt ungewealdes gedeð, ne byð þæt eallunga na gelic þe hit gewealdes gedeð.

69 Þis is þonne seo lihtingc þe ic wylle eallon folce gebeorgan, þe hig ær þyson mid gedrehte wæran ealles to swyðe.

69.1 Þæt is þonne ærest: þæt ic bebeode eallum minan gerefan þæt hi on minan agenan me rihtlice tilian and me mid þam feormian, and þæt him nan man ne þearf to feormfultume na þingc syllan butan he sylf wylle.

69.2 And gif hwa æfter ðam wite crafige, beo he his weres scyldig wið þone cingc.

70 And gif hwa cwydeleas of þysum life gewite, si hit þurh his gymeleaste, si hit þurh færlicne deað, þonne ne teo se hlaford na mare on his æhta butan his rihtan heregeata.

68 And let us do what is required of us: always aid as soon as possible those who most need our help; then we will receive the reward for that when it will be of greatest value to us.

68.1 For out of love and fear of God, one must always show greater mercy in passing judgment and imposing penance upon the weak than upon the strong. For we truly know that the weak cannot bear the same burden as the strong, nor the sick the same as the well. And thus we must acknowledge and carefully distinguish between the old and the young, the rich and the poor, the free and the unfree, the well and the sick. And these considerations must be weighed when assigning spiritual penance and secular judgment.

68.2 Moreover, in many cases, when the criminal has acted out of compulsion, then he is more deserving of leniency because he did what he did out of necessity.

68.3 And if anyone does something unintentionally, then it is not to be treated in any way as if the act were carried out with intent.

69 Accordingly, this is the mitigation by which I mean to protect the people in cases where they previously were all too greatly oppressed.

69.1 This is foremost, then: I command all my reeves to provide for me in a lawful fashion from my own property and thus support me, and that no one be required to give them additional provisions unless he so desires.

69.2 And if any of my reeves solicits a bribe, his wergild shall be forfeit to the king.

70 If anyone passes away without having made a will, either because of negligence or sudden death, the lord shall take no more from his estate than his legal tribute.

70.1 Ac beo be his dihte, seo æht gescyft swyðe rihte wife and cildum and nehmagum, ælcum be þære mæðe, þe him to gebyrige.

71 And beon þa heregeata swa fundene, swa hit mæðlic si. Eorles swa ðærto gebyrige, þæt syndon VIII hors, IIII gesadelode and IIII unsadelode, and IIII helmas and IIII byrnan and VIII spera and eallswa fela scylda and IIII swurd and twa hund mances goldes.

71.1 And syððan cingces þegnas þe him nyhste syndan, IIII hors, II gesadelode and II unsadelode, and II swurd and IIII spera and swa feala scylda and helm and byrnan and L mances goldes.

71.2 And medemra þegna: hors and his geræda and his wæpn oððe his healsfang on Wessexan; and on Myrcan II pund; and on Eastenglan II pund.

71.3 And cingces þegnes heregeata inne mid Denum, þe his socne hæbbe: IIII pund.

71.4 And gif he to þam cingce furðor cyððe hæbbe: II hors, I gesadelod and oðer unsadelod, and swurd and II spera and II scyldas and L mances goldes.

71.5 And se ðe læsse maga si: II pund.

72 And þær se bonda sæt uncwydd his deig and unbecrafod, sitte þæt wif and þa cild on þam ylcan unbesacen.

72.1 And gif se bonda, ær he dead wære, beclypod wære þonne andwyrdan þa yrfenuman swa he sylf sceolde, þeah he lif hæfde.

73 And sitte ælc wuduwe werleas xii monað, ceose syððan þæt heo sylf wylle. And gif heo binnan geares fæce wer

70.1 But under his direction, the estate shall be divided most fairly among his wife, children, and close relatives, each receiving the share appropriate for them.

71 And a person's tribute shall be assessed according to his status. The tribute to be paid by an earl, as is proper, shall be eight horses, four saddled and four unsaddled, and four helmets, four mail shirts, eight spears, just as many shields, four swords, and two hundred mancuses of gold.

71.1 And moreover, the tribute to be paid by the thanes closest to the king shall be four horses, two saddled and two unsaddled, and two swords and four spears, and just as many shields, helmets, and mail shirts, and fifty mancuses of gold.

71.2 And by the common thane: in Wessex, a horse and its trappings, and his weapons or his *healsfang;* and in Mercia, two pounds; and in East Anglia, two pounds.

71.3 And the tribute paid in the Danelaw by a king's thane who possesses jurisdictional rights over his property shall be four pounds.

71.4 And if he has a closer relationship with the king: two horses, one saddled and the other unsaddled, and a sword, two spears, two shields, and fifty mancuses of gold.

71.5 And for those lower in rank: two pounds.

72 And if a householder has remained free of claims and accusations during his lifetime, his wife and children may afterward hold that same property uncontested.

72.1 And if a claim had been made against the householder before he died, then his heirs shall respond to the claim as he himself would have had he lived.

73 And every widow shall remain without a husband for twelve months, and afterward she shall choose as she herself desires. Yet if she then chooses a husband within a year, she

geceose, þonne þolige heo þære morgengyfe and ealra þæra æhta þe heo þurh ærran wer hæfde; and fon þa nehstan frynd to ðam landan and to þan æhtan þe heo ær hæfde.

73.1 And si he his weres scyldig wið þone cingc oððe wið þone þe he his socne geunnen hæbbe.

73.2 And þeah heo nydnumen weorðe, þolige þæra æhta butan heo from þam ceorle wylle eft ham ongean and næfre heo eft his ne weorðe.

73.3 And na hadige man æfre wudewan to hrædlice.

73.4 And gelæste ælc wuduwe þa heregeatu binnan XII monðum, butan hyre ær to onhagige, witeleas.

74 And na nyde man naðer ne wif ne mæden to þam þe hyre sylfre mislicie, ne wið sceatte ne sylle butan he hwæt agenes ðances gyfan wylle.

75 And ic læte riht, þeah hwa his spere sette to oðres mannes huses dura, and he þiderinn ærende hæbbe, oððon gif mon oðer wæpne gedreohlice lecgce, þær hig stille mihtan beon, gif hi moston, and hwylc man ðonne þæt wæpn gelæcce and hwylcne hearm þærmid gewyrce, þonne is þæt riht þæt se ðe þone hearm geworhte, þæt se þone hearm eac gebete.

75.1 And se ðe þæt wæpn age, hine geladige, gif he durre, þæt hit næfre næs naðer ne his gewill ne his geweald ne his ræd ne his gewitnes; þonne is þæt Godes riht þæt he beo clæne.

75.2 And wite se oðer, þe þæt weorc geworhte, þæt he hit bete swa swa lagan tæcean.

shall forfeit her morning gift and all the property she inherited from her previous husband; and his closest relatives shall take the land and possessions that she had hitherto held.

73.1 And her new husband shall forfeit his wergild to the king or to the lord entitled to receive it.

73.2 And even if she has been married against her will, she must forfeit her possessions unless she is willing to leave the man and return home and never again be his.

73.3 And a widow is not to be consecrated as a nun too quickly.

73.4 And each widow is to pay the tributes owed by her deceased husband within twelve months without incurring a penalty, if it has not been possible for her to pay earlier.

74 And no woman or maiden shall ever be compelled to take a husband whom she dislikes, nor is money ever to be paid for her unless the suitor wishes to give something of his own free will.

75 And I believe it to be just that if anyone leaves his spear at the door of another's house while carrying out his business inside, or if anyone carefully sets down any other weapons where they might remain safely if left to do so, and if someone then takes the weapon and does harm with it, then the law shall be that the person who committed the crime is thus to pay the penalty for that crime.

75.1 And the weapon's owner shall, if he dares, swear an oath of exculpation that he had neither intention nor authority nor complicity nor awareness concerning the crime; then by God's law he shall be considered innocent.

75.2 And the other who committed the crime shall be sure to make amends for it just as the law decrees.

76   And gyf hwylc man forstolen þingc ham to his cotan bringe and he arasod wurðe, riht is þæt he hæbbe þæt he æftereode.

76.1 And butan hit under þæs wifes cæglocan gebroht wære, si heo clæne. Ac þære cægean heo sceal weardian: þæt is hyre hordern and hyre cyste and hyre tege; gif hit under þyssa ænigum gebroht byð, þonne byð heo scyldig. And ne mæg nan wif hyre bondan forbeodan, þæt he ne mote into his coton gelogian þæt þæt he wylle.

76.2 Hit wæs ær þyson, þæt þæt cild þe læg on cradele, þeah hit næfre metes ne abite, þæt þa gitseras letan efen scyldig and hit gewittig wære.

76.3 Ac ic hit forbeode heonon forð eornostlice, and swylce manege þe Gode syndon swyðe laþe.

77   And se man þe ætfleo fram his hlaforde oððe fram his geferan for his yrhþe, si hit on scipfyrde, si hit on landfyrde, þolige ealles þæs þe he age and his agenes feores; and fo se hlaford to þam æhtan and to his lande þe he him ær sealde.

77.1 And gyf he bocland hæbbe, ga þæt þam cincge to handa.

78   And se man, þe on þam fyrdunge ætforan his hlaforde fealle, si hit innan lande, si hit of lande, beon ða heregeata forgyfene; and fon þa erfenuman to lande and to æhtan and scyftan hit swyðe rihte.

79   And se ðe land gewerod hæbbe on scire gewitnesse and se nolde oððe ne mihte, þe hit ær ahte, hæbbe unbesacen on dæge and æfter dæge to syllenne and to gyfenne þam þe him leofost si.

76   And if anyone brings stolen goods back to his home and is discovered, the law is that the finder shall have that which he has found.

76.1 And unless the goods had been placed under the wife's lock and key, she shall be considered innocent. And these are the keys for which she shall be responsible: her storeroom, her chest, and her cupboard; if the goods have been placed in any of these, she shall be considered guilty. Yet no wife can prevent her husband from storing anything he wishes in his home.

76.2 It so happened before this that avaricious persons would treat a child in the cradle, even though it had never eaten solid food, as if it were guilty and complicit.

76.3 But I firmly prohibit such practices henceforth, and also many things that are most hateful to God.

77   And the man who abandons his lord or his comrades on a campaign out of cowardice, whether on sea or land, shall forfeit all that he possesses and his own life, and his lord shall confiscate all the property and land that he had previously given to him.

77.1 And if he holds land by charter, it shall pass into the hands of the king.

78   And the tributes of a man who falls before his lord during a campaign, whether at home or abroad, shall be returned; and his heirs shall receive his land and possessions and share them most fairly.

79   And the person who, with the knowledge of the shire, has overseen an estate, and the previous owner would not or could not, shall hold it uncontested during his lifetime and afterward be entitled to give or grant it to whomever he prefers.

80   And ic wylle þæt ælc man si his huntnoðes wyrðe on wuda and on felda on his agenan.

80.1 And forga ælc man minne huntnoð, locehwær ic hit gefriðod wylle habban, be fullan wite.

81   And drincelean and hlafordes rihtgifu stande æfre unawend.

82   And ic wylle þæt ælc man si griðes wyrðe to gemote and fram gemote, butan he si æbære þeof.

83   And se ðe þas laga wyrde, ðe se cingc hæfð nu ða eallon mannon forgyfen, si he Denisc oððe Englisc, beo he his weres scyldig wið þone cingc.

83.1 And gif he hit eft wyrde, gylde tuwa his were.

83.2 And gyf he þonne swa dyrstig sig, þæt he hit þriddan syðe wyrde, þolige ealles þæs þe he age.

84   Nu bidde ic georne and on Godes naman beode manna gehwylcne, þæt he inweardre heortan gebuge to his drihtne and oft and gelome smeage swyðe georne hwæt him sig to donne and hwæt to forganne.

84.1 Eallum us is mycel þearf þæt we God lufian and Godes lage fylgean and godcundan lareowan geornlice hyran. Forðam hi sceolon us lædan forð æt þam dome þonne God demð manna gehwylcum be ærran gewyrhtan.

84.2 And gesælig byð se hyrde þe þonne ða heorde into Godes rice and to heofonlicre myrhþe bliðe mot lædan for ærran gewyrhtan. And wel þære heorde, ðe gefolgað þam hyrde þe hig deoflum ætweneð and Gode hig gestryneð.

80   And it is my desire that each person be entitled to hunt in his own woods and fields.

80.1 And let each person abstain from my hunting grounds, which I wish to be preserved, or incur the full penalty.

81   And let the negotiated contract and the lord's legal gift always remain unaltered.

82   And it is my will that everyone shall be entitled to protection on the way to and from assemblies unless he is a known thief.

83   And anyone, Danish or English, who violates the law which the king has granted to all of his people shall forfeit his wergild to the king.

83.1 And if he violates it again, he shall pay twice his wergild.

83.2 And if he is brazen enough to violate it a third time, he shall forfeit all that he possesses.

84   Now in God's name, I sincerely charge and command all the people to submit to their Lord in their innermost hearts and often and frequently reflect carefully upon what they should do and what they should forgo.

84.1 There is a great need for all of us to praise God and follow God's law and zealously heed our spiritual teachers. For they must lead us forth to that judgment when God will judge each person by the deeds he has done.

84.2 And blessed is the shepherd who may then happily lead his flock into the kingdom of God and into heavenly bliss for the deeds they have done. And it shall go well for the flock which follows the shepherd who delivers them from devils and redeems them for God.

84.3 Utan þonne ealle anmodre heortan georne urum Drihtne cweman mid rihte and heononforð symle scyldan us georne wið þone hatan bryne, þe wealleð on helle.

84.4 And don nu eac lareowas and godcunde bydelas, swa swa hit riht is and ealra manna þearf is: bodian gelome god-cunde þearfe. And ælc þe gescead wite hlyste him georne and godcunde lare gehwa on geþance healde swyðe fæste, him sylfum to þearfe. And a manna gehwylc to weorðunge his Drihtne do to gode þæt he mæge wordes and dæde glædlice æfre; þonne byð us eallum Godes milts þe gearwur.

84.5 A sy Godes nama ecelice gebletsod, and lof him and wuldor and wyrðmynt symle æfre to worulde.

84.6 God ælmihtig us eallum gemiltsige, swa his milda willa sig and gehealde us æfre on ecnesse. Si hit swa. Amen.

84.3 Therefore, let us all, with a humble heart, zealously strive to please our Lord rightly, and henceforth always virtuously guard ourselves assiduously from the blazing fire that rages in hell.

84.4 And likewise, let teachers and spiritual ministers do what is right and necessary for all people: frequently preach their spiritual obligations. And everyone capable of reason shall sincerely listen to them and hold their spiritual teachings firmly in mind for their own good. And to honor the Lord, each person must always gladly do all that he can to promote righteousness by word and by deed; then will God's mercy be the more certain for us all.

84.5 May God's name be eternally blessed, and may there always be praise and glory and honor to him forever throughout the world.

84.6 May God almighty have mercy upon us all, just as his merciful will may be, and preserve us forever in eternity. May it be so. Amen

APPENDIX 1
Questionable Attributions

The Northumbrian Priests' Law

Norðhymbra preosta lagu

1 Gyf hwa ænigum preoste ænig woh beode, beon ealle geferan—mid biscopes filste—georne ymbe þa bote and beon to ælcan rihte, swa swa hit awriten is, *quasi cor unum et anima una.*

2 And Godes forbode, we forbeodað þæt ænig preost oðres cirican naðer ne gebicgæ ne geþicgæ, buton hine hwa mid heafodgilte forwyrce þæt he weofodþenunge þanon forð wyrðe ne sy.

2.1 And gif hit ænig preost elles gedo, þolige his wurð-scipes and geferena freondscipes, and he nahwar ne mæssige ær hig hæbbe se þe hi mid rihte age.

2.2 And gilde se þe woh dide xx or þam biscope, xii or þam preoste þe he of his circan asette, xii or eallum geferan, and þolige þæs feos eac gif he on unriht ænig for oðres preostes circan sealde.

2.3 And ælc preost finde him xii festermen, þæt he preost-lage wille healdan mid rihte.

3 And gif hwilc preost agilte and he ofer biscopes gebod mæssige, gilde for ðam gebode xx or, and þartoeacan þone gilt gebete ðe hit ær geworhte.

The Northumbrian Priests' Law

The Northumbrian Priests' Law

1   If anyone inflicts harm on any priest, all of his fellows—
with the bishop's help—are to be persistent about the compensation, and in every legal matter they are to be, just as it
is written, as *one heart and one soul.*

2   And because of God's prohibition, we forbid that any
priest either buy or accept another's church, unless the
other ruins himself with a capital crime so that afterward he
is unworthy to serve at the altar.

2.1   Yet if any priest does so for any other reason, he is to
forfeit his status and the fellowship of his colleagues, and he
is not to hold Mass anywhere until he who properly possesses that church recovers it.

2.2   And he who committed that offense is to pay twenty
oras to the bishop, twelve oras to the priest whom he dis-
placed from his church, and twelve oras to all of his colleagues, and he is also to forfeit the payment if he paid anything wrongfully for another priest's church.

2.3   And every priest is to find for himself twelve bondsmen, to ensure that he will properly abide by the priests' law.

3   And if any priest sins and he holds Mass in spite of the
bishop's command, he is to pay twenty oras for neglecting
that command, and also do penance for the wrong which he
committed previously.

4   Gif preost biscopes agen geban forbuge, gilde xx or.

5   Gif preost dom to læwedum sceote, þe he to gehadedum scolde, gilde xx or.

6   Gif preost arcediacones geban forbuge, gilde xii or.

7   Gif preost scildig sy and he ofer arcediacones gebod
mæssige, gilde xii or.

8   Gif preost fulluhtes oððe scriftes forwyrne, gebete þæt
mid xii or and huru wið God þingige georne.

9   Gif preost to rihtes timan crisman ne fecce, gilde xii or.

10   Æghwilc cild sy, we lærað, gefullod binnon nigon
nihton, be wite vi or.

10.1 And gif hæþen cild binnon ix nihton þurh gimeliste
forfaren sy, betan for Gode buton worldwite; and gif hit ofer
nigan niht gewurðe, betan for Gode and gilde xii or for ðare
heorde, þe he wæs hæþen swa lange.

11   Gif preost folce miswissige æt freolse oððe fæstene,
bete wið God and gilde xii or.

12   Gif preost on unriht ut of scire had begite, gilde xii or,
and diacon vi or; and þolie his hades, buton scirebiscop him
hades geunne.

13   Gif preost on unhalgodon huse mæssige, gilde xii or.

14   Gif preost buton gehalgedon weofode mæssige, gilde
xii or.

4   If a priest disregards a bishop's own decree, he is to pay twenty oras.

5   If a priest turns judgment in a dispute over to a layman, when he should refer it to an ecclesiastic, he is to pay twenty oras.

6   If a priest disregards an archdeacon's decree, he is to pay twelve oras.

7   If a priest is guilty of wrongdoing and he holds Mass in spite of the archdeacon's command, he is to pay twelve oras.

8   If a priest refuses to perform baptism or confession, he is to compensate for that with twelve oras and most especially plead fervently with God.

9   If a priest does not fetch the chrism at the right time, he is to pay twelve oras.

10   We instruct that every child is to be baptized within nine nights, or there will be a fine of six oras.

10.1   And if a child dies a heathen within nine nights out of neglect, penance is to be done before God without a secular penalty; and if it occurs after nine nights, penance is to be done before God and twelve oras are to be paid for that neglect, because the child remained a heathen for so long.

11   If a priest misleads the people concerning a holy day or a fast, he is to do penance before God and pay twelve oras.

12   If a priest wrongfully receives ordination outside of his diocese, he is to pay twelve oras and a deacon six oras; and he is to forfeit his ordination unless the bishop of the diocese permits him to retain it.

13   If a priest holds Mass in an unconsecrated building, he is to pay twelve oras.

14   If a priest holds Mass without a consecrated altar, he is to pay twelve oras.

15 Gif preost on treowenan calice husl gehalgige, XII or.

16 Gif preost buton wine mæssige, gilde XII or.

17 Gif preost husl forgime, gilde XII or.

18 Gif preost anes dæges mæssige oftor þonne ðriwa, gilde XII or.

19 Gif man ciricgrið abrece, bete be circan mæðe and be þam þe hire mund sy.

20 Gif man mid cirican mangie, bete be lahslite.

21 Gif man cirican nydþeowige, gebete þæt be lahslihte.

22 Gif man preost of circan on unriht utige, bete þæt be lahslite.

23 Gif man preost gewundige, gebete man þa wyndlan, and biscope to weofodbote for his hade sille XII or; æt diacone VI or to weofodbote.

24 Gif man preost ofslea, forgilde man hine be fullan were, and biscope feower and XX or to weofodbote; æt diacone XII or to weofodbote.

25 Gif preost circan miswurðige, þe eal his wurðscipe of sceal arisan, gebete þæt.

26 Gif preost on circan ungedafenlice þingc gelogige, gebete þæt.

27 Gif preost ciricþingc utige, gebete þæt.

15   If a priest consecrates the host in a wooden chalice, twelve oras.

16   If a priest holds Mass without wine, he is to pay twelve oras.

17   If a priest neglects the host, he is to pay twelve oras.

18   If a priest holds Mass more often than three times in one day, he is to pay twelve oras.

19   If anyone violates Church sanctuary, compensation is to be paid according to the status of the church and according to its degree of protection.

20   If anyone uses a church as currency, he is to compensate for that with *lahslit*.

21   If anyone compels service from a church, he is to compensate for that with *lahslit*.

22   If anyone wrongfully expels a priest from his church, he is to compensate for that with *lahslit*.

23   If anyone injures a priest, compensation is to be made for the injuries and, because of his order, twelve oras are to be given to the bishop as compensation to the Church; for a deacon, six oras as compensation to the Church.

24   If anyone kills a priest, he is to compensate for him with his full wergild and twenty-four oras to the bishop as compensation to the Church; for a deacon, twelve oras as compensation to the Church.

25   If a priest dishonors the Church, from which all his honor must come, he is to atone for that.

26   If a priest puts inappropriate things in a church, he is to atone for that.

27   If a priest removes the possessions of the church, he is to atone for that.

28   Gif preost silfwilles þa circan forlæte ðe he to gehadod wæs, gebete þæt.

29   Gif preost oðerne forseo oððe gebismrige mid worde oððe mid weorce, gebete þæt.

30   Gif preost wið oðerne gefeohte, bete him and biscope.

31   Gif preost oðrum on unriht on fultume beo, gebete þæt.

32   Gif preost oðrum rihtes fultumes forwyrne, gebete þæt.

33   Gif preost oðerne unwarnode læte þæs, þe he wite þæt him hearmian wille, gebete þæt.

34   Gif preost sceare misgime beardes oððe feaxes, gebete þæt.

35   Gif preost cwenan forlæte and oðre nime, *anathema sit!*

36   Gif preost on gesetne timan tida ne ringe oððe tida ne singe, gebete þæt.

37   Gif preost mid wæpnum innan circan cume, gebete þæt.

38   Gif preost misendebirde ciriclice gearþenunga, dæges oððe nihtes, gebete þæt.

39   Gif preost ordol misfadige, gebete þæt.

40   Gif preost searwað bewinde, gebete þæt.

41   Gif preost oferdruncen lufige oððe gliman oððe ealascop wurðe, gebete þæt.

42   Gif preost forhele hwæt on his scriftscire betweox mannum to unrihte rixige, gebete þæt.

28   If a priest of his own volition abandons the church to which he was consecrated, he is to atone for that.

29   If a priest disrespects or shames another with words or deeds, he is to atone for that.

30   If a priest fights with another, he is to make amends to him and to the bishop.

31   If a priest abets another in wrongdoing, he is to atone for that.

32   If a priest denies rightful assistance to another, he is to atone for that.

33   If a priest allows another to be unaware of what he knows will do him harm, he is to atone for that.

34   If a priest neglects to cut his beard or hair, he is to atone for that.

35   If a priest abandons one woman and takes another, *let him be accursed!*

36   If a priest does not ring or sing the canonical hours at the set time, he is to atone for that.

37   If a priest enters the church with weapons, he is to atone for that.

38   If a priest performs the annual services of the church in the wrong sequence, by day or night, he is to atone for that.

39   If a priest errs while carrying out an ordeal, he is to atone for that.

40   If a priest conceals fraud while conducting an ordeal, he is to atone for that.

41   If a priest embraces drunkenness, or becomes an entertainer or a singer among drinkers, he is to atone for that.

42   If a priest conceals what injustice reigns among the people of his parish, he is to atone for that.

43 Gif preost geargerihta unmynegode læte, gebete þæt.

44 Gif preost sinoð forbuge, gebete þæt.

45 Gif preost to rihte gebugan nelle, ac ongean biscopes gerædnesse wiðerige, gebete þæt oððe beo he asyndred of gehadodra gemanan and þolige ægðer ge geferscipes ge æghwilces wurðscipes, buton he gebuge and ðe deoppor gebete.

46 Gif hwa Godes lage oððe folclage wirde, gebete hit georne.

47 Ealle we sculon ænne God wurðian and lufian and ænne Cristendom georne healdan and ælcne hæþendom mid ealle awurpan.

48 Gif þonne æni man agiten wurðe þæt ænigne hæðenscipe heonan forð dreoge oððe on blot oððe on firhte oððe on ænig wiccecræft lufige oððe idola wurðinge, gif he sy cynges þegn, gilde x healfmarc: healf Criste, healf þam cynge.

49 Gif hit sy elles landagende man, gilde vi healfmarc, healf Criste and healf landrican.

50 Gif hit si færbena, gilde xii or.

51 Gif cyninges þegn ætsace, þonne nemne man him xii, and nime his maga xii and xii wallerwente; and gif his að berste, þonne gilde he lahsliht: x healfmarc.

52 Gif landagende man ætsace, þonne nemne man him his gelican ealswa micel wente swa cyninges þegne; gif him þæt berste, gilde lahsliht: vi healfmarc.

53 Gif cyrlisc man ætsæce, þonne nemne man him his gelicena ealswa micel wente swa ðam oðrum; gif him þæt berste, þonne gilde he lahsliht: xii or.

43   If a priest permits the yearly dues to go uncollected, he is to atone for that.

44   If a priest fails to attend a synod, he is to atone for that.

45   If a priest refuses to submit to what is right, but rebels against the bishop's decree, he must atone for it, or he is to be cut off from those in orders and lose both companionship and every dignity unless he submits and atones for it very deeply.

46   If anyone violates the law of God or the law of the people, he is to atone sincerely for that.

47   We must all revere and love one God and fervently adhere to one Christian faith and wholly reject every heathen practice.

48   Accordingly, if anyone comes to be discovered who henceforth practices any heathen rituals, either through sacrifice or through divination or through any form of witchcraft or the worship of idols, if he is the king's thane, he is to pay ten half-marks: half to Christ, half to the king.

49   If he is a landholder of another kind, he is to pay six half-marks: half to Christ, half to the local lord.

50   If he is a commoner, he is to pay twelve oras.

51   If a king's thane denies the charge, then twelve are to be chosen for him, and he is to select twelve kinsmen and twelve neutral witnesses; and if his oath fails then he is to pay *lahslit:* ten half-marks.

52   If a landholder denies the charge, then just as many witnesses of his same status are to be chosen for him as for a king's thane; if that fails, he is to pay *lahslit:* six half-marks.

53   If a commoner denies the charge, then just as many witnesses of his same status are to be chosen for him as for the others; if that fails, then he is to pay *lahslit:* twelve oras.

54   Gif friðgeard sy on hwæs lande abuton stan oððe treow
oððe wille oððe swilces ænigge fleard, þonne gilde se ðe hit
worhte lahsliht: healf Criste healf landrican.

54.1 And gif se landrica nelle to steore filstan, þonne habbe
Crist and cyningc þa bote.

55   Sunnandæges cypingc we forbeodað æghwar and ælc
folcgemot and ælc weorc and ælce lade, ægðer ge on wæne,
ge on horse, ge on byrdene.

56   Se þe ænig þissa do, gilde wite: friman xii or, ðeowman
ða hyde; buton wegferende, þa moton for neode mete fe-
rian; and for unfriðe man mot freolsæfenan nide fulfaran
betweonan Eferwic and six mila gemete.

57   Se þe freols oððe rihtfæsten brece, gilde wite xii or.

57.1 And we willað, þæt ælc Rompæni beo gelæst be Petres
mæssan to ðam bisceopstole.

57.2 And we willað, þæt man namige on ælcon wæpengetace
ii triwe þegnas and ænne mæssepreost, þæt hi hit gegade-
rian and eft agifan, swa hi durran to swerian.

58   Gif cyninges þegn oððe ænig landrica hit forhæbbe,
gilde x healfmarc: healf Criste, healf cynge.

59   Gif hwilc tunes man ænigne pænig forhele oððe forhæbbe, gilde se landrica þone pænig and nime ænne oxan æt
ðam men; and gif landrica þæt forgime, þonne fo Crist and
cyningc to fulre bote: xii or.

60   Gif hwa teoðinge forhealde and he sy cyninges þegn,
gilde x healfmarc, landagende vi healfmarc, ceorl xii or.

61   And we forbeodað on Godes forbode, þæt nan man na

54 If there is a hallowed space on anyone's property near a stone or a tree or a well or any silliness of this sort, then the one who made it is to pay *lahslit:* half to Christ, half to the local lord.

54.1 And if the local lord will not aid in the enforcement, then Christ and the king are to receive the compensation.

55 We everywhere forbid trade on a Sunday and every public meeting and every type of labor and every type of transport, either by wagon or by horse or by carried load.

56 One who does any of these is to pay a penalty: a free-man twelve oras, a slave with a beating; except for travelers, who may carry food out of necessity. And in times of conflict one may, out of necessity, journey a distance of up to six miles from York on the eve of a holy day.

57 One who violates a holy day or a legally mandated fast is to pay a penalty of twelve oras.

57.1 And we ordain that all dues to Rome are to be paid to the episcopal see by Saint Peter's Day.

57.2 And we ordain that two trustworthy thanes and one priest in each wapentake be chosen to collect it and deliver it again, as they dare to swear to it.

58 If a king's thane or any local lord holds it back, he is to pay ten half-marks: half to Christ, half to the king.

59 If any townsman hides or holds back any penny, the local lord is to pay the penny and seize one ox from that man; and if the landlord fails in this, then Christ and the king are to confiscate the full penalty: twelve oras.

60 If anyone holds back his tithes and he is a king's thane, he is to pay ten half-marks, a landholder six half-marks, a peasant twelve oras.

61 And on account of God's prohibition, we forbid any

ma wifa næbbe buton 1; and seo beo mid rihte beweddod and forgifen.

61.1 And þæt nan man ne wifige on neahsibban men þonne wiðutan þam IIII cneowe; ne nan man on his godsibbe ne wifige.

61.2 And gif hit hwa gedo, nabbe he Godes mildse, buton he geswice and bete swa biscop getæce.

62 Gif he þonne on ðam unrihte geendige, þolige he clænes legeres and Godes mildse.

63 Gif hwa wið nunnan forlicge, sy ægðer his weres scildig, ge he ge heo.

63.1 And gif hi on ðam geendigan buton geswicennesse, þolian clænes legeres and Godes mildse.

64 Gif hwa his rihtæwe lifigende forlæte and on oðran wife on unriht gewifige, næbbe he Godes myldse buton he hit gebete.

65 Ac healde gehwa mid rihte his æwe þa hwile þe heo libbe; buton þæt gewurðe, þæt hi buta geceosan be biscopes geþeahte, þæt hi getwæman and þanon forð willan clænnesse healdan.

66 Gif ænig man heonan forð rihte laga wyrde, gebete hit georne.

67 Ealle we sculon ænne God lufian and wurðian and ænne Cristendom georne healdan and ælcne hæðendom mid ealle awurpan.

67.1 And we willað þæt landceap and lahceap and witword and getrywe gewitnes and riht dom and fulloc and frumtalu fæste stande, and dryncelean and hlafordes rihtgifu, and huru an Cristendom and an cynedom æfre on ðeode.

Sit nomen Domini benedictum ex hoc nunc et usque in seculum.

man to have more than one wife, and she is to be properly promised and wedded.

61.1 And that no man shall marry anyone more closely related than the fourth degree; nor is any man to marry one spiritually related to him.

61.2 And if anyone does so, let him not have God's mercy, unless he desists and repents as the bishop instructs.

62 Yet if he dies in that sin, he is to be deprived of Christian burial and God's mercy.

63 If anyone fornicates with a nun, they both—he and she—are liable for their wergild.

63.1 And if they die without putting an end to that, let them be deprived of Christian burial and God's mercy.

64 If anyone deserts his living lawful wife and wrongfully weds another woman, let him not receive God's mercy unless he does penance for it.

65 But everyone is to keep his lawful wife as is right while she lives, unless it so happens with the bishop's guidance that they both decide to separate and remain celibate henceforth.

66 Henceforth, if anyone violates just laws, he is to atone for it sincerely.

67 We must all love and revere one God and fervently adhere to one Christian faith and wholly reject every heathen practice.

67.1 And we ordain that land transactions, legal fines, sworn statements, honest testimony, just judgments, final settlements, and initial claims are to remain binding, likewise negotiated settlements, the lord's lawful gift, and most of all one Christian faith and one kingdom in the realm forever.

Blessed be the name of the Lord, from henceforth now and forever.

The Obligations of Individuals *and* On Reeves

Rectitudines singularum personarum

Đegenes lagu

1   Đegenlagu is þæt he sy his bocrihtes wyrðe, and þæt he ðreo ðinc of his lande do: fyrdfæreld and burhbote and bryc-geweorc.

1.1   Eac of manegum landum mare landriht arist to cyniges gebanne, swilce is deorhege to cyniges hame and scorp to friðscipe and sæweard and heafodweard and fyrdweard, ælmesfeoh and cyricsceat and mænige oðere mistlice ðingc.

Geneates riht

2   Geneatriht is mistlic be ðam ðe on lande stænt. On summon, he sceal landgafol syllan and gærsswyn on geare and ridan and averian and lade lædan, wyrcan and hlaford feormian, ripan and mawan, deorhege heawan and sæte haldan, bytlian and burh hegegian, nigefaran to tune feccan, cyricsceat syllan and ælmesfeoh, heafodwearde healdan and

The Obligations of Individuals *and* On Reeves

The Obligations of Individuals

The Duty of the Thane

1   The thane's duty is to fulfill the obligations of his charter, and do three things with his estate: raise a militia, oversee the upkeep of the buildings and walls, and repair the
bridges.

1.1   Furthermore, on many estates additional property obligations arise out of the king's command, such as maintain-
ing the animal hedge for the royal estate, provisioning a ship
for defense, service in the coastguard, the royal guard, and
the military watch, and the rendering of alms, Church dues,
and many other various things.

The Duty of the Tenant

2   The tenant's duty varies according to what is practiced
on the estate. On some, he must pay rent on the land, and
give a pig for the use of the pasture each year, and ride and
act as his lord's messenger, and carry loads, work, and supply
food for his lord, reap and mow, trim the animal hedge, assist in ensnaring game, build and erect a fence around
the homestead, guide newcomers to the community, pay
Church dues and alms, serve as a guard to the lord and to the

horswearde, ærendian fyr swa nyr, swa hwyder swa him mon to tæcð.

Kotsetlan riht

3   Kotesetlan riht be ðam ðe on lande stent. On sumon, he sceal ælce Mondæge ofer geares fyrst his laforde wyrcan, oðð III dagas ælcre wucan on hærfest.

3.1   *Apud quosdam operatur per totum Augustum omni die et unam acram avene metit pro diurnali opere (et de ulla annona dimidiam acram); et habeat garbam suam, quam praepositus vel minister domini dabit ei.*

3.2   Ne ðearf he landgafol syllan.

3.3   Him gebyriað v æceres to habbanne, mare gyf hit on lande ðeaw sy; and to lytel hit bið beo hit a læsse, forðan his weorc sceal beon oftræde.

3.4   Sylle his heorðpænig on Halgan Ðunresdæg, ealswa ælcan frigean men gebyreð, and werige his hlafordes inland, gif him man beode, æt sæwearde and æt cyniges deorhege and æt swilcan ðingan swilc his mæð sy, and sylle his cyricsceat to Martinus mæssan.

Gebures gerihte

4   Geburgerihta syn mislice: gehwar hy syn hefige; gehwar eac medeme. On sumen lande is þæt he sceal wyrcan to wicweorce II dagas swilc weorc swilc him man tæcð, ofer geares fyrst ælcre wucan, and on hærfest III dagas to wicweorce and of Candelmæsse oð Eastran III; gif he aferað, ne ðearf he wyrcan ða hwile ðe his hors ute bið.

horses, carry out errands both far and near or to wherever he is instructed to go.

The Duty of the Cottager

3   The cottager's duty follows that which is practiced on the estate. On some, he must work for his lord each Monday throughout the year, or for three days per week during the harvest.

3.1   *On some, he works every day during all of August and harvests one acre of oats and a half acre of other grains as his daily labor; and he is to have his sheaf, which the reeve or servant of the lord will give to him.*

3.2   He does not need to pay rent on the land.

3.3   It is appropriate for him to have five acres, more if it is the practice on the estate; yet it is too little if it be less, for his work must be frequent.

3.4   He shall give his hearth penny on Holy Thursday, just as is proper for each free man, and defend his lord's land if commanded and keep watch over the sea, and over the king's animal hedge, and over such things as befit his status, and he is to render his Church dues the Feast of Saint Martin.

The Duty of the Tenant Farmer

4   The tenant farmer's duties vary: in some places they are heavy; likewise, in others they are moderate. On some estates, he is to labor two days each week doing such work as he is directed, and over the harvest he is to work three days a week, and three days a week from Candlemas to Easter; if he is acting as a messenger, he does not need to work while his horse is out in the fields.

4.1   He sceal syllan on Michaeles mæssedæig x gafolpæniga, and on Martinus mæssedæg xxiii systra beres and ii henfugelas, on Eastran an geong sceap oððe ii pæniga. And he sceal licgan of Martinus mæssan oð Eastran æt hlafordes falde, swa oft swa him to begæð. And of ðam timan ðe man ærest ereð oð Martinus mæssan, he sceal ælcre wucan erian i æcer and ræcan sylf þæt sæd on hlafordes berne. Toeacan ðam iii æceras to bene and ii to gærsyrðe; gyf he maran gærses beðyrfe, ðonne earnige ðæs, swa him man ðafige.

4.2   His gauolyrðe iii æceras erige and sawe of his aganum berne. And sylle his heorðpænig. Twegen and twegen fedan ænne headorhund. And ælc gebur sylle vi hlafas ðam inswane, ðonne he his heorde to mæstene drife.

4.3   On ðam sylfum lande ðe ðeos ræden on stænt, gebure gebyreð þæt him man to landsetene sylle ii oxan and i cu and vi sceap and vii æceras gesawene on his gyrde landes. Forðige ofer þæt gear ealle gerihtu, ðe him to gebyrigean. And sylle him man tol to his weorce and andlaman to his huse. Ðonne him forðsið gebyrige, gyme his hlaford ðæs he læfe.

4.4   Ðeos landlagu stænt on suman lande. Gehwar hit is, swa ic ær cwæð, hefigre, gehwar eac leohtre, forðam ealle landsida ne syn gelice.

4.5   On sumen landa gebur sceal syllan huniggafol, on suman metegafol, on suman ealugafol.

4.1   On Feast of Saint Michael, he must pay rent of ten pennies, and twenty-three sesters of barley and two hens on the Feast of Saint Martin, and a young sheep or two pennies at Easter. And from the Feast of Saint Martin to Easter, he must watch over his lord's sheepfold as often as his turn comes to him. And from the first plowing until the Feast of Saint Martin, he must plow one acre each week and get the seed himself from his lord's barn. In addition to that, he must plow three acres as mandatory labor and two for pasturage. If he requires more pasture, then let him earn it in an appropriate manner.

4.2   As plow dues, he is to plow three acres and sow it from his own barn. And he should pay his hearth penny. And he should share with another the cost of feeding one hunting hound. And each tenant farmer is to give six loaves to the lord's swineherd when he drives his herd to pasture.

4.3   On the same estate on which this custom is observed, it is appropriate that the tenant farmer be given for the cultivation of the land two oxen, one cow, six sheep, and seven acres already sown on his allotment of land. Let him perform all the duties assigned to him over the course of the year. And let him be given the tools for his labor and the utensils for his house. When he dies, his lord should oversee whatever he leaves behind.

4.4   This rule for estate management applies on certain properties. In some places, as I said before, it is heavier, in others even lighter, for all local customs are not alike.

4.5   On some estates, the tenant farmer must pay honey dues, on some meat dues, on some ale dues.

4.6 Hede se ðe scire healde þæt he wite a hwæt ealdland ræden sy and hwæt ðeode ðeaw.

Be ðam ðe beon bewitað

5 Beoceorle gebyreð, gif he gafolheorde healt, þæt he sylle þæt on lande geræd beo.

5.1 Mid us is geræd þæt he sylle v sustras huniges to gafole; on suman landum gebyreð mare gafolræden.

5.2 Eac he sceal hwiltidum geara beon on manegum weorcum to hlafordes willan, toeacan benyrðe and bedripe and mædmæwette.

5.3 And gyf he wel gelend bið, he sceal beon gehorsad þæt he mæge to hlafordes seame þæt syllan oððe sylf lædan, swæðer him man tæce.

5.4 And fela ðinga swa gerad man sceal don; eal ic nu atellan ne mæig.

5.5 Ðonne him forðsið gebyrige, hede se hlaford ðæs he læfe, bute hwet friges sy.

Gafolswane

6 Gafolswane gebyreð þæt he sylle his slyht, be ðam ðe on lande stent.

4.6 The person who would oversee a shire should always take care to know what the previous estate agreements were and what the local customs are.

Regarding Those Who Keep Bees

5   It is appropriate that the beekeeper, if he possesses a swarm subject to taxation, pay whatever is assessed on that estate.

5.1 Among us it is agreed that he is to pay five sesters of honey as dues; on some estates, it is the practice to assess a greater amount.

5.2 Additionally, he must sometimes be prepared to take on many tasks at his lord's desire, as well as required plowing, mandatory reaping, and mowing the meadows.

5.3 And if he is well provided with land, he shall be supplied with a horse that he may lend out or lead himself for the purpose of carrying his lord's loads, whichever is commanded him.

5.4 A person thus bonded must do many things, all of which I cannot now list.

5.5 When he dies, it his appropriate that his lord should oversee whatever he leaves behind, except that which might be free of his lord's control.

Tenant Swineherd

6   It is appropriate that the tenant swineherd give his animals for slaughter, according to the practices observed on the estate.

6.1   On manegum landum stent þæt he sylle ælce geare xv swyn to sticunge, x ealde and v gynge, hæbbe sylf þæt he ofer þæt arære. On manegum landum gebyreð deopre swanriht.

6.2   Gyme eac swan, þæt he æfter sticunge his slyhtswyn wel behweorfe and sæncge: ðonne bið he ful wel gewyrces wyrðe.

6.3   Eac he sceal beon swa ic ær be beocere cwæð, oftræde to gehwilcon weorce and gehorsad to hlafordes neode.

6.4   Ðeow swan and ðeow beocere æfter forðsiðe be anre lage wyrðe.

Be æhteswane

7   Æhteswane ðe inheorde healt gebyreð stifearh and his gewirce, ðonne he spic behworfen hæfð, and elles ða gerihtu ðe ðeowan men to gebyriað.

Be manna metsunge

8   Anan esne gebyreð to metsunge xii pund godes cornes and ii scipæteras and i god metecu, wuduræden be landside.

Be wifmonna metsunge

9   Ðeowan wifmen: viii pund cornes to mete, i sceap oððe iii pæniga to wintersufle, i syster beana to længten-sufle, hwæig on sumera oððe i pænig.

6.1   On many estates, it is the practice that every year he gives fifteen swine for slaughter, ten mature and five young, and that he keep for himself whatever he should raise over that. On many estates, greater obligations are expected from the swineherd.

6.2   Furthermore, the swineherd should take care that each swine after it is slaughtered be well prepared and smoked; then will he be fully worthy of his privileges.

6.3   Also, as I said before concerning the beekeeper, he must always be ready to take on any task, and equipped with a horse for his lord's needs.

6.4   After their death, the peasant swineherd and the peasant beekeeper are subject to the same law.

Enslaved Swineherd

7   To the enslaved swineherd who oversees the estate's herd is due a young pig, and his privileges when he has prepared the bacon, as well as all the other rights which pertain to an enslaved person.

Regarding the Feeding of the Men

8   For his food, each laborer is due twelve pounds of good grain, two sheep carcasses, one cow for meat, and an arrangement for gathering wood according to the local custom.

Regarding the Feeding of the Women

9   Female servants are due eight pounds of grain as food, one sheep or three pennies as supplies for winter, one sester of beans as supplies for spring, and whey in the summer or one penny.

9.1 Eallum æhtemannum gebyreð Midwintres feorm and Eastorfeorm, sulhæcer and hærfesthandful toeacan heora nydrihte.

Be folgeran

10 Folgere gebyreð, þæt he on twelf monðum 11 æceras geearnige, oðerne gesawene and oðerne unsawene—sædige sylf ðæne—and his mete and scoung and glofung him gebyreð.
10.1 Gyf he mare geearnian mæig, him bið sylfum fremu.

Be sædere

11 Sædere gebyreð þæt he hæbbe ælces sædcynnes ænne leap fulne ðonne he ælc sæd wel gesawen hæbbe ofer geares fyrst.

Be oxanhyrde

12 Oxanhyrde mot læswian 11 oxan oððe ma mid hlafordes heorde on gemænre læse be his ealdormannes gewitnesse; earnian mid ðam scos and glofa him sylfum.
12.1 And his metecu mot gan mid hlafordes oxan.

Be kuhyrde

13 Cuhyrde gebyreð, þæt he hæbbe ealdre cu meolc VII niht syððan heo nige cealfod hæfð and frymetlinge bystinge XIIII niht.
13.1 And ga his metecu mid hlafordes cu.

9.1   All enslaved people are due meals for Christmas and Easter, an allotment of land for farming, a portion of the harvest, as well as their necessities.

Regarding the Plowman

10   For the plowman, it is appropriate that he earn two acres per year, one sown and the other unsown—he must sow it himself—and his food and his shoes and gloves are due to him.

10.1 If he can earn more for himself, it will be for his own benefit.

Regarding the Sower

11   For the sower, it is appropriate that he have one full bucket of each variety of seed after he has sown all his seed satisfactorily over the course of the year.

Regarding the Oxherd

12   The oxherd may graze two oxen or more with the lord's herd in the common pasture with his overseer's knowledge; he may earn shoes and gloves for himself with them.

12.1 And the cow he intends for food may go with the lord's oxen.

Regarding the Cowherd

13   For the cowherd, it is appropriate that he have the milk of a mature cow for seven nights after she bears a new calf and the colostrum of a young cow for fourteen nights.

13.1 And the cow he intends for food may go with the lord's cows.

Be sceaphyrdan

14   Sceaphyrdes riht is þæt he hæbbe twelf nihta dingan to middanwintra, and 1 lamb of geares geogeðe, and 1 belflys, and his heorde meolc VII niht æfter emnihtes dæge, and blede fulle hweges oððe syringe ealne sumor.

Be gathyrde

15   Gathyrde gebyreð his heorde meolc ofer Martinus mæssedæig, and ær ðam his dæl hwæges, and 1 ticcen of geares geogoðe, gif he his heorde wel begymeð.

Be cyswyrhte

16   Cyswyrhtan gebyreð hundred cyse, and þæt heo of wringhwæge buteran macige to hlafordes beode; and hæbbe hire ða syringe, ealle butan ðæs hyrdes dæle.

Be berebrytte

17   Berebryttan gebyreð corngebrot on hærfeste æt bernes dure, gif him his ealdorman ann and he hit mid getrywðan geearnoð.

Be bydele

18   Bydele gebyrað þæt he for his wycan sy weorces frigra ðonne oðer man, forðan he sceal beon oftræde.
18.1 Eac him gebyreð sum landsticce for his geswince.

Regarding the Shepherd

14 It is the right of the shepherd to have twelve nights' worth of dung at midwinter, and one lamb from the year's young, and the fleece of one bellwether, and the flock's milk for seven nights after the autumn equinox, and a bowlful of whey or buttermilk for the entire summer.

Regarding the Goatherd

15 To the goatherd is due the milk of his herd after the Feast of Saint Martin, and before that his share of whey, and one kid from the year's young if he looks after his herd well.

Regarding the Cheesemaker

16 To the cheesemaker is due one hundred cheeses, and she is to make butter from the strained whey for the lord's table; and she should keep the buttermilk for herself, all save the shepherd's share.

Regarding the Barley Keeper

17 To the barley keeper is due the grain dropped at the barn door at harvest, if his overseer grants it to him and he has earned it by his diligence.

Regarding the Beadle

18 Because of his duties, it is appropriate that the beadle be freer of work than other men, for he must always be available.

18.1 In addition, a plot of land is due to him for his labor.

Be wudewarde

19   Wuduwearde gebyreð ælc windfylled treow.

20   Hæigwerde gebyreð þæt man his geswinces lean gecnawe on ðam endum ðe to etenlæse licgan, forðam he mæig wenan, gyf he þæt ær forgymð, þæt him man *dampnum segetis imputabitur.*

20.1 Hwilces landsticces geann, þæt sceal beon mid folc-rihte nyhst etenlæse forðam gyf he for slæwðe his hlafordes forgymð, ne bið his agnum wel geborgen gif hit bið ðus funden.

20.2 Gyf he ðonne eal wel gefriðað he healdan sceal, ðonne bið he godes leanes ful wel wyrðe.

21   Landlaga syn mistlice, swa ic ær beforan sæde.

21.1 Ne sette we na ðas gerihtu ofer ealle ðeoda, ðe we ær beforan ymbe spræcon; ac we cyðað, hwæt ðeaw is ðær ðær us cuð is.

21.2 Gyf we selre geleorniað, þæt we willað georne lufian and healdon be ðære ðeode ðeawe ðe we ðænne onwuniað.

21.3 Forðam laga sceal on leode luflice leornian, lof se ðe on lande sylf nele leosan.

21.4 Feola syndon folcgerihtu: on sumre ðeode gebyreð winterfeorm, Easterfeorm, bendform for ripe, gytfeorm for yrðe, mæðmed, hreacmete, æt wudulade wæntreow, æt cornlade hreaccopp and fela ðinga, ðe ic getellan ne mæig.

21.5 Ðis is ðeah myngung manna biwiste and eal þæt ic ær beforan ymberehte.

Regarding the Forester

19   To the forester is due every tree felled by the wind.

20   For the person appointed to oversee the hedges and fields, it is appropriate that the reward for his efforts be understood to lie at the ends of the field alongside the common pasture, because if he first neglects that, he can expect *to be held responsible for any damage to the land.*

20.1 Whichever plot of land is allotted to him should be, according to the common law, closest to the common pasture, for if he neglects his lord's land out of laziness, his own will not be well protected if thus located.

20.2 Yet if he guards well all that he must protect, then he will be entirely worthy of a good reward.

21   The rules for estate management are diverse, as I said before.

21.1 Nor do we impose the obligations that we have previously discussed on the entire realm, but we are describing what the practice is here, where it is known to us.

21.2 If we learn of better ones, we will readily praise and observe them according to the practices of the community in which we then dwell.

21.3 For the law must be willingly learned from the people if one does not wish to lose esteem in the community.

21.4 The people's rights are many: in some communities they are due a meal at Christmas, a meal at Easter, a feast at harvest, a feast for the plowing, a hayrick feast for the cutting of the grass, a log in return for the carting of wood, the topmost grain on the cart for the transportation of the crop, and many other things that I cannot list.

21.5 Yet this is an admonition concerning the provisioning of the people, and all that I have previously described.

Gerefa

Be gesceadwisan gerefan

1 Se scadwis gerefa sceal ægðær witan ge hlafordes
landriht ge folces gerihtu be ðam ðe hit of ealddagum witan
geræddan, and ælcre tilðan timan ðe to tune belimpð.

1.1 Forðam on manegum landum tilð bið redre ðonne on
oðrum: ge yrðe tima hrædra, ge mæda rædran, ge winterdun
eac swa, ge gehwilc oðer tilð.

2 Hede se ðe scire healde þæt he friðige and forðige ælce
be ðam ðe hit selest sy, and be ðam he eac mot ðe hine weder
wisað.

2.1 He sceal snotorlice smeagean and georne ðurhsmugan
ealle ða ðing ðe hlaforde magan to ræde.

3 Gyf he wel aginnan wile, ne mæig he sleac beon ne to
oferhydig, ac he mot ægðer witan ge læsse ge mare, ge betere
ge mætre ðæs ðe to tune belimpð, ge on tune ge on dune, ge
on wuda ge on wætere, ge on felda ge on falde, ge inne ge
ute.

3.1 Forðam to soðe ic secge: oferhogie he oððe forgyme ða
ðing to beganne and to bewitanne, ðe to scipene oððe to
odene belimpað, sona hit wyrð on berne þæt to ðam belimpað.

4 Ac ic lære þæt he do swa ic ær cwæð: gyme ægðer ge
ðæs selran ge þæs sæmran þæt naðor ne misfare gyf he

On Reeves

Concerning the Prudent Reeve

1   The prudent reeve must know both his lord's property rights and the rights of the people as determined by the councilors in days of old, as well as the proper time for each task on the estate.

1.1   Certain tasks for the land must come before others: earlier plowing times, earlier mowing and winter pasturage also, as well as each other chore.

2   The person who wishes to oversee a shire must take care to observe and carry out each of these as is most needed, and also to be guided by the weather.

2.1   He is to wisely consider and assiduously reflect upon all those things that might be of help to his lord.

3   If he desires to do well, he must be neither slack nor overcautious, but he must know both the lesser things and the greater, the better things and the worse, of all that belongs to the estate, both on the homestead and in the hills, both in the woods and in the waters, both in the fields and in the folds, both indoors and out.

3.1   For it is true what I say: if he is disdainful or he overlooks those duties which must be carried out and overseen, then that which belongs in the cow stalls or on the threshing floor will soon turn up in the barn.

4   But I instruct him to do as I said earlier: care for both the better and the worse so that nothing will go astray if he

wealdan mæge, ne corn ne sceaf, ne flæsc ne flotsmeru, ne cyse ne cyslyb, ne nan ðera ðinga ðe æfra to note mæge.

5   Swa sceal god scyrman his hlafordes healdan, do ymbe his agen, swa swa he wylle.

5.1   A swa he gecneordra swa bið he weorðra, gyf he wið witan hafoð his wisan gemæne.

6   Symle he sceal his hyrmen scyrpan mid manunge to hlafordes neode, and him eac leanian be ðam ðe hy earnian.

7   Ne læte he næfre his hyrmen hyne oferwealdan, ac wille he ælcne mid hlafordes creafte and mid folcrihte: selre him is æfre of folgoðe ðonne on, gyf hine magan wyldan ða ðe he scolde wealdan. Ne bið hit hlaforde ræd, þæt he þæt ðafige.

8   Æfre he mæig findan, on ðam he mæig nyt beon, and ða nytte don ðe him fylstan scylan. Huru is mæst neod þæt he asece hu he yrde mæge fyrme geforðian ðonne ðæs tima sy.

9   He mæig in Maio and Iunio and Iulio on sumera fealgian, myxendincgan ut dragan, lochyrdla tilian, sceap scyran, bytlian, boteatan, tynan, tymbrian, wudian, weodian, faldian, fiscwer and mylne macian.

10   On hærfeste ripan, in Agusto and Septembri and Octobri mawan, wad spittan, fela tilða ham gæderian, ðacian, ðecgan and fald weoxian, scipena behweorfan and hlosan eac swa, ær to tune to stið winter cume, and eac yrðe georne forðian.

can prevent it, neither grain nor sheaf, neither meat nor scrap of fat, neither cheese nor rennet, nor any of those things which might ever be of use.

5   A good shire reeve must oversee his lord's property thus, no matter what he does about his own.

5.1   If he is ever the more diligent, so shall he be the more deserving, if he takes his guidance from a wise man.

6   He must constantly encourage his subordinates with advice for his lord's benefit, and reward each of them as they deserve.

7   Nor must he ever permit his subordinates to manipulate him, but he should govern each of them according to his lord's rule and the laws of the people; it would always be better for him to be out of service than in if he would be governed by those whom he should govern. The lord is not wise who tolerates this.

8   He must always seek out that in which he might be helpful, and take advantage of anything he shall find useful. In particular, it is most necessary that he learn how to cultivate the earth when it is time.

9   In May, June, and July over the summer, one must plow the fields, spread the manure from the dung pile, prepare fences for the sheepfolds, shear the sheep, build, repair, enclose, construct, chop wood, weed, erect the sheepfolds, and make fish weirs and mills.

10   During the harvest season, reap in August, September, and October, mow, plant woad, collect many crops for the home, thatch the roof, clean the fold, attend to the cowshed and also the pigsty before excessive winter harshness comes to the estate, and prepare the ground diligently.

11   On wintra erian and in miclum gefyrstum timber cleofan, orceard ræran and mænige inweorc wyrcean, ðerhsan,
wudu cleofan, hryðeran styllan, swyn stician, on odene cylne
macian, ofn and aste and fela ðinga sceal to tune, ge eac
henna hrost.

12   On længtene eregian and impian, beana sawan, win-
geard settan, dician, deorhege heawan and raðe æfter ðam,
gif hit mot gewiderian, mederan settan, linsed sawan, wad-
sæd eac swa, wyrtun plantian and fela ðinga; ic eal geteallan
ne mæig, þæt god scirman bigan sceal.

13   A he mæig findan hwæt he mæig on byrig betan, ne
ðearf he na unnyt beon ðonne he ðær binnan bið: oððe hus
godian, rihtan and weoxian and grep hegian, dicsceard
betan, hegas godian, weod wyrtwalian, betweox husan bric-
gian, beoddian, bencian, horsan styllan, flor feormian, oððe
swilces cynnes sum ðing ðe to nyte mæge.

14   He sceal fela tola to tune tilian and fela andlomena to
husan habban:

15   æcse, adsan, bil, byrse, scafan, sage, cimbiren, tigehoc,
næfebor, mattuc, ippingiren, scear, culter and eac gadiren,
siðe, sicol, weodhoc, spade, scofle, wadspitel, bærwan,
besman, bytel, race, geafle, hlædre, horscamb and sceara,
fyrtange, wæipundern.

15.1   And fela towtola: flexlinan, spinle, reol, gearnwindan,
stodlan, lorgas, presse, pihten, timplean, wifte, wefle,

11 During the winter, one is to plow, fell trees during the great frost, tend to the orchard, carry out indoor tasks, thresh, chop wood, put cattle in stalls, put pigs in their sty, construct a kiln on the threshing floor and an oven and an oast, and do many other things on the estate such as building chicken roosts.

12 During the spring, one is to plow and graft, sow beans, prepare the vineyard, construct dykes, trim the animal hedge, and soon thereafter, if the weather happens to be fair, to plant madder, sow linseed and woad, and also plant the garden and many other things; I cannot list all that a good shire reeve must carry out.

13 He must always seek out anything he can improve out in the community, nor need he be without occupation when he is inside: he may repair the house, put things right and clean, clear the drainage ditches, fix breaks in the dikes, fix the hedges, pull weeds, lay pavement between buildings, do joiner's work, build benches, put the horses in their stalls, wash the floors, or do anything else that might need to be done.

14 He must obtain many tools for the estate and have many utensils for the house:

15 ax, adze, billhook, chisel, plane, saw, clamp, pull hook, auger, mattock, crowbar, plowshare, coulter, and likewise a goad, scythe, sickle, hoe, spade, shovel, woad dibble, barrow, broom, mallet, rake, fork, ladder, horse comb and shears, fire tongs, scale.

15.1 Also many spinning tools: a line for hanging flax, spindle, reel, yarn winders, loom uprights, heddle rods, a cloth press, comb beater, temples, weft thread, warp thread, wool

wulcamb, cip, amb, crancstæf, sceaðele, seamsticcan, scearra, nædle, slic.

16 And gif he smeawyrhtan hæfð, ðam he sceal to tolan fylstan—mylewerde, sutere, leodgotan and oðran wyrhtan. Ælc weorc sylf wisað, hwæt him to gebyreð; nis ænig man, þæt atellan mæge ða tol ealle, ðe man habban sceal.

17 Man sceal habban wængewædu, sulhgesidu, egeð-getigu, and fela ðinga ðe ic nu genæmnian ne can ge eac mete: awel and to odene fligel and andlamena fela; hwer, lead, cytel, hlædel, pannan, crocca, brandiren, dixas, stel-melas, cyfa, cyflas, cyrne, cysfæt, ceodan, wilian, windlas, systras, syfa, sædleap, hriddel, hersyfe, tæmespilan, fanna, trogas, æscena, hyfa hunigbinna, beorbydene, bæðfæt, beo-das, butas, bleda, melas, cuppan, seohhan, candelstafas, sealtfæt, sticfodder, piperhorn, cyste, mydercan, bearm-teage, hlydan, sceamelas, stolas, læflas, leohtfæt, blacern, cyllan, sapbox, camb, yrsebinne, fodderhec, fyrgebeorh, meluhudern, ælhyde, ofnrace, mexscofle.

18 Hit is earfoðe eall to gesecganne þæt se beðencan sceal ðe scire healt.

18.1 Ne sceolde he nan ðing forgyman ðe æfre to note mehte: ne forða musfellan ne, þæt git læsse is, to hæpsan pinn.

18.2 Fela sceal to holdan hames gerefan and to gemetfæstan manna hyrde.

19 Ic gecende be ðam ðe ic cuðe; se ðe bet cunne, gecyðe his mare.

comb, yoke beam, beater, crank, sheath, seam picks, fabric shears, needle, wooden mallet.

16   And if he has skilled workmen, then he must provide them with tools—miller, shoemaker, plumber, and other laborers. Each type of work demonstrates the tools most appropriate for it; there is no one who can list all the tools that a worker must have.

17   One must have a wagon cover, the equipment for a plow, the equipment for a harrow, and many things which I cannot name now; also a measuring stick, awl, flail for the threshing floor, many loom weights, pot, cauldron, kettle, ladle, pans, crockery, firedog, dishes, pots with handles, tubs, buckets, churn, cheese vat, bags, rolled baskets, baskets, pitchers, sieves, seed bucket, coarse sieve, hair sieve, sieve frame, winnowing fans, troughs, ash-wood buckets, bucket to collect honey from the hive, beer barrel, bathtub, dishes, vessels, goblets, bowls, cups, sieve, candlesticks, saltcellar, spoon case, pepper horn, chest, money chest, yeast box, seats, benches, stools, basins, lantern, lamp, leather bottle, soapbox, comb, manger, fodder rack, fire screen, meal storehouse, eel-skin bag, oven rake, dung shovel.

18   It is difficult to recount all that that must be remembered by the person who oversees a shire.

18.1 He must not neglect anything that might ever be of importance: not even a mousetrap, nor even something as insignificant as a fastening pin.

18.2 Many things are required of the trusty reeve of a homestead and of a responsible manager of people.

19   I have revealed what I know; let anyone who knows better make known more.

APPENDIX 2

Revisions and Reworkings

1 Æthelstan

Æðelstanes gerædnes

Pr   Ic Æðelstan cyng, mid geþehte Wulfhelmes arcebiscopes and eac minra oþerra biscopa, cyðe þam gerefan to
gehwylcere byrig and eow bidde on Godes naman and on
ealra his haligra, and eac be minum freondscipe beode, þæt
ge ærest of minum agenum gode agyfan þa teoþunga, ægþer
ge on cwicum ceape ge on þæs geares eorðwæstmum, swa
man rihtast mæge oððe gemetan oððe getellan oððe awe-
gan. And þa biscopas þonne þæt ylce don on heora agenum
gode, and mine ealdormen and mine gerefan þæt sylfe.

1   And ic wille þæt biscopas and þa gerefan hit beodan
eallum þam þe him hyran scylan, and þæt hit to þam rihtan
andagan gelæst sy.

2   Utan geþencan, hu Iacob cwæð se heahfæder: *decimas et
hostias pacificas offeram tibi;* and hu Moyses cwæð on Godes
lage: *decimas et primitias non tardabis offerre Domino.*

3   Us is to geðencanne hu ondryslic hit on bocum gecweden is: "Gif we þa teoþunga Gode gelæstan nellað, þæt
he us benimeð þara nigon dæla, þonne we læst wenað, and
eac we habbað þa synne toeacan."

4   And ic wille eac þæt mine gerefan gedon þæt man agyfe
þa cyricsceattas and þa sawlsceattas to ðam stowum þe hit
mid rihte to gebyrige and sulhhælmessan on geare, on ða

I Æthelstan

Pr   I, King Æthelstan, with the advice of Archbishop Wulfhelm and also my other bishops, proclaim to the reeves in
every community and command you in the name of God
and all of his saints, and charge you likewise by my friendship, that you first pay the tithes from my own holdings,
both from the livestock and from the year's produce, seeing
that they are measured, counted, and weighed to the best of
your ability. And let the bishops do likewise with their holdings, and my ealdormen and my reeves with theirs.

1   And I direct the bishops and reeves to convey this
command to those who must obey them, and that the tithes
are to be rendered on the lawfully appointed day.

2   Let us recall how the patriarch Jacob said, *tithes and sacrifices I offer to you;* and how Moses proclaimed in God's law,
do not hesitate to offer tithes and first fruits unto the Lord.

3   It is incumbent upon us to bear in mind how dreadful is
the judgment which is preserved in books: "If we refuse to
pay our tithes to God, he will take from us the other nine
portions when we least expect it, and moreover we will have
sinned."

4   And I likewise command my reeves to act so that
Church dues and dues for the souls of the dead are paid at
the legally designated places, and plow dues each year, on

gerad þæt þa his brucan æt ðam haligan stowan, þe heora
cyrcan began willað and to Gode and to me geearnian willað.
Se ðe þonne nelle, þolige þære are oððe eft to rihte gecyrre.

5   Nu ge gehyrað, cwæð se cyng, hwæs ic Gode ann and
hwæt ge gelæstan sceolan be minre oferhyrnysse. And gedoð eac, þæt ge me unnon mines agenes, þe ge me mid rihte
gestrynan magan. Nelle ic, þæt ge me mid unrihte ahwar oht
gestrynan, ac ic wille eowres agenes geunnan eow rihtlice,
on þa gerad þe ge me unnan mines. And beorgað ægðer ge
eow ge þam þe ge myngian scylan wið Godes yrre and wið
mine oferhirnesse.

the understanding that they will be used at the holy places by those by those willing to care for their church and who wish to be deserving before God and me. Whoever refuses to do this shall either forfeit his office or resume his proper duties.

5   Now you shall hear, the king said, what I grant to God and what you must do, lest you show disobedience to me. And you shall likewise act so that you give to me that which is my own, and which you can rightfully obtain for me. I do not desire that you should obtain anything anywhere unlawfully, but I will grant you justly that which is yours, just as long as you grant me what is mine. And you are to guard yourselves and those whom you must admonish against the wrath of God and disobedience to me.

1 Edmund

Her onginneð Eadmundes gerædnes:

Pr   Eadmund cyngc gesamnode micelne sinoð to Lunden-
birig on ða halgan Easterlican tid ægðer ge godcundra hada
ge worldcundra. Ðar wæs Oda arcebiscop and Wulfstan
arcebiscop and manega oðre biscopas smeagende ymbon
heora sawla ræd and þara þe him underþeodde wæron.

1   Ðæt is ærest þæt hi budon: þæt þa halgan hadas þe
Godes folc læron sculon lifes bisne, ðæt hi heora clænnesse
healdan be heora hade, swa werhades swa wifhades, swa
hwaðer swa hit sy. And gif hi swa ne don, þonne syn hi þæs
wyrðe þe on ðam canone cweð, and þæt hi þolian worldæhta
and gehalgodre legerstowe buton hi gebetan.

2   Teoðunge we bebeodað ælcum Cristene men be his
Cristendome and ciricsceat and Romfeoh and sulhælmessan. And gif hit hwa don nelle, si he amansumod.

3   Gif hwa Cristenes mannes blod ageote, ne cume he na
on ðæs cyninges neawiste ær he on dædbote ga, swa him
biscop tæce and his scrift him wisige.

1 Edmund

Here begins Edmund's decree:

Pr   King Edmund convened a great assembly of both the spiritual and secular orders at London during the holy Easter season. Archbishop Oda and Archbishop Wulfstan and many other bishops were there to consider what would be of benefit to their souls and those of the people subject to them.

1   This was the first of their decrees: that those in holy orders who must teach God's people using their own life as an example are to embrace celibacy in the manner appropriate to their order, whether it is for men or women. And if they do not do so, let them suffer that which is decreed in the canon, and let them forfeit all their worldly property and burial in consecrated ground unless they repent.

2   We direct every Christian to pay tithes and Church dues and dues to Rome and plow dues in accordance with Christian doctrine. And if anyone refuses to do so, let him be excommunicated.

3   And if anyone sheds Christian blood, he may not come into the proximity of the king until he undertakes penance as the bishop instructs him and his confessor directs him.

4   Se þe wið nunnan hæme, gehalgodre legerstowe ne sy
he wyrðe—buton he gebete—þe ma þe manslaga. Þæt ilce
we cwædon be æwbrice.

5   Eac we gecwædon þæt ælc biscop bete Godes hus on
his agenum, and eac þone cyningc minegige þæt ealle Godes
circan syn wel behworfene, swa us micel þearf is.

6   Ða ðe mansweriað and liblac wyrcað beon hi a fram
ælcum Godes dæle aworpene buton hi to rihtre dædbote
gecirran þe geornor.

4   Anyone who has intercourse with a nun cannot—without repentance—be buried in consecrated ground any more than can a murderer. We have decreed the same concerning adultery.

5   Furthermore, we command each bishop to restore the houses of God in his own see, and also to admonish the king that all God's churches are to be attended to properly, as is greatly required of us.

6   Those who commit perjury and work magic are to be expelled forever from the communion of God unless they embark upon the proper penance all the more zealously.

2 Edgar *and* 3 Edgar

2 Edgar

Pr   Ðis is seo gerædnys þe Eadgar cyng mid his witena geðeahte gerædde, Gode to lofe and him sylfum to cynescipe and eallum his leodscipe to þearfe.

1   Þæt syndon þonne ærest: þæt Godes cyrican syn rihtes wyrðe.

1.1   And man agife ælce teoðunge to þam ealdan mynstre þe seo hernes tohyrð; and þæt sy þonne swa gelæst, ægðer ge of þegnes inlande ge of geneatlande, swa swa hit seo sulh gega.

2   Gyf hwa þonne ðegna sy ðe on his boclande cyrican habbe, þe legerstow on sy, gesylle he þane þriddan dæl his agenre teoðunge into his cyrican.

2.1   Gyf hwa cyrican habbe þe legerstow on ne sie, ðonne do he of þam nigan dælum his preoste þæt þæt he wille.

2.2   And ga ælc cyricsceat into þam ealdan mynstre be ælcum frigan eorðe.

2.3   And gelæste man sulhælmessan, þonne xv niht beon onufan Eastran.

3   And sie ælcre geoguðe teoðung gelæst be Pentecosten and þara eorðwæstma be emnihte, and ælc cyricsceat sy

2 Edgar *and* 3 Edgar

2 Edgar

Pr   This is the decree which King Edgar has issued with the advice of his councilors for the glory of God and his own sovereignty and for the benefit of all his people.

1   Accordingly, this is foremost: that the churches of God be guaranteed of their rights.

1.1   And each tithe is to be rendered to the old minster to which obedience is due; and that the render must come both from the thane's personal land and the land let out for rent, whatever is under the plow.

2   Yet if there is a thane who has a church possessing a graveyard on land he holds by charter, he is to give one-third of his own tithes to his church.

2.1   If anyone has a church without a graveyard, then let him give what he chooses to his priest out of the remaining nine shares after that paid as tithe.

2.2   And all Church dues from every free household are to go to the old minster.

2.3   Plow dues are to be paid on the fifteenth night after Easter.

3   And the tithe of all the young animals is to be paid by Pentecost, and that of the fruits of the earth by the equinox,

gelæst be Martinus mæssan, be þam fullon wite, þe seo domboc tæcð.

3.1   And gyf hwa þonne ða teoðunge gelæstan nelle, swa
we gecwedan habbað, fare þæs cynges gerefa to and þæs
biscopes and þæs mynstres mæssepreost, and niman unþances þæne teoðan dæl to þam mynstre, þe hit togebyrige,
and tæcan him to ðam nigeðan dæle. And todæle man þa
eahta dælas on twa, and fo se landhlaford to healfan, to healfan se biscop, sy hit cynges man, sy hit þegnes.

4   And sy ælc heorðpæning agyfen be Petres mæssedæg.

4.1   And se ðe þonne to ðam andagan gelæst næbbe, læde
hine to Rome and þærtoeacan xxx pænega, and bringe
þonne þanon swytolinga þæt he þær swa micel betæht
hæbbe; and þonne he ham cume, gylde þam cynge hundtwelftig scillinga.

4.2   And gyf he hine eft syllan nylle, læde hine eft to Rome
and oðre swylce bote; and þonne he ham cume, gylde þam
cynge twahund scillinga.

4.3   Æt þam þriddan cyrre gyf he þonne git nelle, þolie
ealles þæs ðe he age.

5   And healde man ælces Sunnandæges freols fram non-
tide þæs Sæternesdæges oð ðæs Monandæges lihtinge, be
þam wite, þe domboc tæcð, and ælcne oðerne mæssedæg,
swa he bebodan beo.

5.1   And man beboden fæsten healde mid ælcre geornfulnesse, and ælces Frigedæges fæsten, buton hit freols sy.

and all Church dues are to be paid by the Feast of Saint Martin, or suffer the full penalty decreed by the written law.

3.1   And if someone refuses to pay the tithes, just as we have commanded, then the king's reeve, the bishop's reeve, and the priest of the church are to go to him and, without his consent, seize the tenth part for the church to which it is owed, and the ninth share shall be reserved for him. Let the other eight parts be divided in two, and his lord take half and the bishop half, whether he be a king's man or a thane's.

4   And every hearth penny is to be paid by the Feast of Saint Peter.

4.1   And anyone who has not paid his dues at the proper time is to take the payment to Rome along with thirty pence added thereto, and then bring back evidence that he paid there the full amount; and when he has returned, he is to pay one hundred twenty shillings to the king.

4.2   And if he refuses to pay a second time, he is to take the payment again to Rome along with the same amount as a penalty; and when he has returned, he is to pay two hundred shillings to the king.

4.3   And if he still refuses to pay for a third time, he is to suffer the forfeiture of all that he owns.

5   And each Sunday holy day is to be observed as the written law instructs from midafternoon on Saturday until dawn on Monday, lest a penalty be incurred, and every other feast day just as is ordained for it.

5.1   And ordained fasts are to be observed with utter zealousness, and each Friday fast unless it is a feast.

5.2   And læste man saulsceat æt ælcan Cristenan men to þam mynstre þe hit togebyrige.

5.3   And stande ælc cyricgrið swa swa hit betst stod.

3 Edgar

1   Ðis is þonne seo woruldcunde gerædnes þe ic wille þæt man healde.

1.1   Þæt is þonne ærest: þæt ic wille ðæt ælc man sy folc-rihtes wyrðe, ge earm ge eadig, and him man rihte domas deme.

1.2   And sy on þære bote swylc forgifnes, swylce hit for Gode gebeorglic sy and for worulde aberendlic.

2   And ne gesece nan man þone cyng for nanre spræce bu-tan he æt ham rihtes wyrðe beon ne mote oððe riht abiddan ne mæge.

2.1   Gyf þæt riht to hefig sy, sece siþþan ða lihtinge to þam cynge.

2.2   And æt nanum botwyrðum gylte ne forwyrce man mare þane his wer.

3   And se dema, se ðe oðrum on woh gedeme, gesylle þam cynge hundtwelfti scillinga to bote—butan he mid aðe ge-cyðan durre þæt he hit na rihtor ne cuðe—and þolige a his þegnscipes, butan he hine eft æt þam cynge gebigge, swa he

5.2   And dues for the souls of the dead are to be paid on be-half of every Christian to the church to which they are owed.

5.3   And the right of holy sanctuary is to be upheld just as it was when it was most respected.

3 Edgar

1   This is the secular decree that I command my subjects to obey.

1.1   This is foremost: I command that every person, rich or poor, be granted their rights under civil law and granted just judgments.

1.2   And that penalties are to be assessed with such leni-ency as would be fitting before God and acceptable in the eyes of the world.

2   And no one may petition the king concerning a lawsuit unless he cannot obtain his rights at home and cannot ap-peal to another court.

2.1   If the law is too harsh, let him petition the king for mit-igation.

2.2   And no one is to be fined more than his wergild for any offense for which compensation can be paid.

3   And a judge who rules unjustly against another must give one hundred twenty shillings to the king as compensa-tion—unless he is confident enough to declare on oath that he did not know how to rule more justly—and forfeit for-ever his status as thane, unless he redeems it from the king in such a manner as the latter will permit him; and the

him geðafian wille; and amanige þære scyre biscop þa bote to ðæs cynges handa.

4   And se þe oðerne mid woge forseggan wille þæt he aþor oððe feo oððe feore þe wyrsa sy, gyf þonne se oðer geunsoðian mæge, þæt him man onsecgan wolde, si he his tungan scyldig butan he hine mid his were forgylde.

5   And sece man hundredgemot, swa hit ær geset wæs.

5.1   And habbe man þriwa on geare burhgemot and tuwa scirgemot.

5.2   And þær beo on ðære scire biscop and se ealdorman, and þær ægðer tæcan ge Godes riht ge woruldriht.

6   And finde him ælc man, þæt he borh hæbbe, and se borh hine þonne to ælcum rihte gelæde and gehealde.

6.1   And gyf hwa þonne woh wyrce and ut oðberste, abere se borh þæt he aberan scolde.

6.2   Gyf hit þeof beo, and gyf he hine binnan twelf monðum gelangian mæge, agyfe hine to rihte, and him man agyfe þæt he ær sealde.

7   And se ðe tyhtbysig sy and folce ungetriwe and þas gemot forbuge þriwa, þonne sceawie man of ðam gemote þa þe him to ridan. And finde him þonne gyt borh, gyf he mæge.

bishop of the diocese shall exact the fine on the king's behalf.

4   And if anyone who seeks to bring a false charge against another so that he is the worse in either property or well-being, and if the accused can disprove the charge that has been brought against him, then the accuser shall lose his tongue unless he can redeem himself through the payment of his wergild.

5   And the hundred court is to be attended, just as has been previously established.

5.1   And the borough court is to meet three times a year and the shire court twice.

5.2   And the bishop and the ealdorman shall both be in attendance, and there administer the ecclesiastical and secular laws.

6   And each person is to find a surety for himself, and this surety shall lead and hold him to each of his legal obligations.

6.1   And if anyone commits a crime and escapes, his surety shall suffer what he would have suffered.

6.2   If the fugitive is a thief, and if the surety can capture him within twelve months, let him be surrendered to the law and let the fine which the surety had previously paid be returned to him.

7   And if anyone who is disreputable or deemed untrustworthy by the community fails to attend public meetings three times, then let three men of that meeting be chosen to ride to him. And he may still find a surety, if he can.

7.1   Gyf he þonne ne mæge, gewylde man hine swaðor man mæge, swa cwicne swa deadne, and nime man eal þæt he age and gylde man þam teonde his ceapgyld angeldes, and fo se landhlaford to healfan, to healfan þæt hundred.

7.2   And gyf aðor oððe mæg oþþe fremde þa rade forsace, gylde þam cynge hundtwelftig scillinga.

7.3   And gesece se æbæra ðeof ðæt þæt he gesece, oþþe se ðe on hlafordsearwe gemet sie, þæt hi næfre feorh ne gesecen.

8   And ga an mynet ofer ealne þæs cynges anweald, and þane nan man ne forsace.

8.1   And gange an gemet and an gewihte swylce man on Lundenbyrig and on Wintanceastre healde.

8.2   And ga seo wæg wulle to healfan punde, and hie nan man na undeoror ne sylle.

8.3   And gyf hwa hi þonne undeoror sylle, oððe eawunga oððe dearnunga, gylde ægþer þam cynge LX scyllinga ge se þe hy sylle ge se þe hy bicge.

7.1   If he cannot do so, they are to capture him however they can, either alive or dead, and seize all that he owns, and give to the accuser a single payment equivalent to the market value of his goods, and half of the remainder is to be taken by the landlord and half by the hundred.

7.2   And if anyone, either his relative or a stranger, refuses to participate in the ride, he is to pay the king one hundred twenty shillings.

7.3   And anyone convicted of theft or caught conspiring against his lord shall not be able to save his life, no matter where he hides.

8   And there is to be one coinage throughout the king's whole realm and no one may refuse it.

8.1   And there is to be one standard of weights and one standard of measures, just as is used in London and Winchester.

8.2   And a wey of wool is to be valued at half a pound, and no one may sell it for a lower price.

8.3   And if anyone does sell it at a lower price, either publicly or in secret, both the seller and the buyer are to pay the king sixty shillings.

Note on the Texts

The texts in this volume are revised, in some cases significantly, and corrected versions of those found in the most widely used scholarly editions. With the exception of the three damaged texts (*Northumbrian Church Sanctuary, 9 Æthelred,* and *10 Æthelred*), they have also been checked against the base manuscripts used for each edition in this volume. These manuscripts have been identified in italics in the textual notes. The printed sources used for each edition are:

Liebermann, *Die Gesetze der Angelsachsen,* for *The Laws of Edward and Guthrum, The Compilation on Status, On Sanctuary, Northumbrian Church Sanctuary, On Episcopal Duties, 5–10 Æthelred, Cnut's Proclamation of 1020, 1–2 Cnut, The Northumbrian Priests' Law, The Obligations of Individuals* and *On Reeves, 1 Æthelstan, 1 Edmund,* and *2–3 Edgar.*

Jost, *Die "Institutes of Polity, Civil and Ecclesiastical,"* for *1–2 Polity, Instructions for Bishops, An Admonition to Bishops.*

Fowler, *The Canons of Edgar,* for *The Canons of Edgar.*

Clayton, "The Old English *Promissio regis,*" for *The Oath of the King.*

Kennedy, "Cnut's Law Code of 1018," for *Cnut's Oxford Legislation of 1018.*

Fehr, *Die Hirtenbriefe Ælfrics,* for *On the Remedy of Souls.*

All manuscript abbreviations have been silently expanded, and the capitalization and punctuation have been regularized. The complex transmission of many of Wulfstan's texts has occasionally made it necessary to supply passages from other manuscripts. These have been identified in the textual notes, as have all emendations. Because many of Wulfstan's works survive in widely differing versions, I have listed major variants in the textual notes, though I have not attempted to make the notes comprehensive. In particular, I have omitted minor differences of spelling and syntax. In some instances, manuscripts were not available for consultation (such as manuscripts Hk and M of 7 *Æthelred*). In such cases, I have relied on Liebermann's *Gesetze* for the collation.

Manuscript rubrics and scriptural passages are indicated in italics in the text. Both the numbering of clauses and the paragraph divisions are editorial. The former follows the traditional numbering scheme set forth by Schmid and Liebermann. Although there is good reason to reconsider both the numbering and the division of clauses in many of these texts, this edition was not thought to be a good venue for such a dramatic departure from previous editorial practice.

Some of the translations here are revised and corrected versions of those found in my book *The Political Writings of Archbishop Wulfstan of York* (Manchester, 2015). Readers are encouraged to consult that volume for its more detailed introduction, annotations, and manuscript appendices. The remaining translations are original to this volume. In general, the notes have been kept to a minimum, with an emphasis on clarifying confusing passages, explaining relevant points of law, and elaborating on the historical context. A more complete discussion and identification of Wulfstan's sources can be found in *Political Writings*.

Notes to the Texts

The list of collated manuscripts can be found above the set of notes for each text. The base manuscript for each edition is listed in italics.

The Laws of Edward and Guthrum

B = Cambridge, Corpus Christi College MS 383, fols. 13r–14v; *H* = *Strood, Medway Archive and Local Studies Centre MS DRc/R1 (Textus Roffensis), fols. 41r–v.*

	Þis . . .gecuron: Eft his and Guðrumes and Eadwardes *B*
Pr.1	Ðæt is: Ðis *H*
Pr.2	hy sceolden: hy sceolde *H*; he sceolde *B*
	gesetton: settan *B*
2	dæd: dæde *H*
3	þam þe seo: þam seo *B*
3.1	healfmarc: healmare *H*
4	dæd: dæde *H*
4.1	Gif: And *B*
	oððe: oððon *B*
	genydmagas: genyhe magas *H*
4.2	Gif: And *B*
5	ne wyrne: *omitted B*
5.1	gerihto forðige: gerihte fyrðrie *B*
6	Gif: And *B*
6.7	he ongean: hine man gean *H*
7.1	wite oððe lahslite: wite lahslite *BH*
7.2	se hlaford: *omitted H*

8   hyde: *omitted B*

9   Denum, wite: Denum and wite *B*

10   limlæwed: limlæweo *H*; limlæþeo *B*

12   dæd: dæde *H*

THE COMPILATION ON STATUS

O = Cambridge, Corpus Christi College MS 190, pp. 418–20; *D* = Cambridge, Corpus Christi College MS 201, pp. 101–3; *H* = Strood, *Medway Archive and Local Studies Centre MS DRc/R1 (Textus Roffensis), fols. 7r–v, 39v, 93r–v, 93v–94r.*

On the Ranks of People and Law

      Be . . . lage: Be wergildum and be geðinðum *D*

1   Hit . . . lagum: Hwilum wæs *D*

      leodwitan: þeodwitan *D*

      eorl . . . þeoden: ge eorl ge ceorl, ge þegen ge þeoden *D*

2   cirican and kycenan: *omitted D*

      bellhus: bellan *D*

3   gif: se *D*

      utware: *omitted D*

      æt mistlicon neodan: *omitted D*

      sceolde: þorfte *D*

5   And . . . weorðe: *omitted D*

6   And . . . weorðe: *omitted D*

7   geþeh: wære, þe *D*

      ðærto: ðonne þam hade *D*

      buton . . . moste: mid rihte, gif he hine heolde, swa swa he scolde *D*

8   hit . . . þæt: *omitted D*

On Wergild

      Be wergylde: Norðleoda laga *D*

1   Cynges: Norðleoda cynges *D*

	inne . . . folcriht: *omitted D*
	weres: wergildes *D*
	þam magum: þam *omitted D*
2	Æþelinges: Arcebiscopes and æþelinges *D*
7	CCXX: CXX *D*
7.1	wergild: wer *D*
11	þrymsa: *omitted D*

On the Law of the Mercians

	Be Mircna laga: *omitted H, text supplied from D*
2	wergyld: wer *OD*
3	folces . . . laga: *omitted H, text supplied from D*

On the Mercian Oath

On the order of clauses and the division between *On the Mercian Oath* and *On Priests' Oaths*, see the notes to the translation.

| | Be Miriscan aðe: *omitted H, text supplied from D* |

On Priests' Oaths

	Be gehadodra manna aðe: *omitted H, text supplied from D*
1	mæssepreost: preost *OD*
	he . . . wyrþe: *omitted OD*
	gastes: *omitted O*
	sceolon God herian: sculon hergan *D*
1.1	griþian: nerion/nerian *OD*
1.2	oððe mid weorce: oððe weorce *D*
	and be . . . sy: *omitted D*
2	ane: *omitted OD*
5	pund to: to . . . scrifte: *omitted H, text supplied from D*
6	toeacan þam rihtwere: *omitted D*
9	sambryce: se brice *O*
9.1	And . . . gefærscipe: *this clause occurs as 10.1 in H*

þridde þam gefærscipe: þridde geferscipe *OD*

10   medemung: myltsung *O*

11   And . . . griðedon: *omitted H, text supplied from D*

ON SANCTUARY

G = London, British Library, Cotton MS Nero A.i, fol. 92v–95v.

3   beðorfton: *final three letters concealed by binding. This reading follows Liebermann.*

31.1   Cristes: Cristenes *G*

NORTHUMBRIAN CHURCH SANCTUARY

G = London, British Library, Cotton MS Nero A.i, fol. 96v.
Due to an ill-advised attempt by Liebermann to restore a difficult passage in the manuscript using a solution of sulfuric acid, much of the page on which this text appears is now unreadable. Accordingly, editions must now rely heavily on Liebermann's initial transcription and subsequent reconstruction of illegible words.

1   cyricfrið: *reconstructed by Liebermann*
    Iohannes: *reconstructed by Liebermann*
    hundred: *reconstructed by Liebermann*
    botleas: *reconstructed by Liebermann*

2   mærþe: *reconstructed by Liebermann*

3   And preoste: *reconstructed by Liebermann*
    forbodene wifum: *Liebermann supplies* mid *after* forbodene

4   dyre æghwar: *Liebermann supplies* man *after* dyre

THE OATH OF THE KING

C = London, British Library, Cotton MS Cleopatra B.xiii, fols. 56r–57v.

2   ge eac: ge ac *C*

THE INSTITUTES OF POLITY (1)

D = Cambridge, Corpus Christi College MS 201, pp. 86–93; G = London, British Library, Cotton Nero A.i, fols. 70r–76v, 97v–98v.

1   swiðe rihte: on Cristenre þeode *G*
     on fæder . . . þeode: ealswa hit riht is *G*
     and on . . . geteald is: folces frofer and rihtwis hyrde ofer Cris-
        tene heorde *G*
     eac: *omitted G*
     his afole: mægene *G*
     lufige: rære *G*
     and hæðendom ascunige: *omitted G*
     weorðige and werige: fyrðrie and friðrie *G*
     geornost mæge: *G adds* and þurh ælc þing rihtwisnesse lufie for
        Gode and for weorolde
     geþeon Gode: ge þeon and his þeodscype eac swa *G*
     and unriht ascunige: for Gode and for worolde *G*

2   And: Forþam *G*
     sceal: *G adds* sylf firmest
     And him . . . geearnian wylle: *The remainder of this chapter is omit-
        ted from D. Text supplied from G.*

3   veritas: *Latin glosses added above the line in the same hand D*
     modþwærnes: modignes *D*
     bonos: bonas *D*
     pascere: pasce *D*
     be: beo *D*
     similem: simile *D*
     iusto: isto *D*

4   wæpnum: pæpnum *D*
     mid rihte: *G adds* on Cristenre þeode *above the line in Wulfstan's
        handwriting*
     þearf: þeaf *D*

5   De episcopis: Item de episcopis *G*
     and on weorcum: and weorcum *G*
     swiðlæte: *erasure of one letter, possibly an* e, *between the* ð *and the* l *D*;
        swyðe læte *G*
     ac swa: ac swa swa *G*
     Forðam: *omitted G*
     higeleas: iuncglic *G*
     heom: heo *D*

6   wulf: *approximately four letters erased before* wulf *D*; werewolf *G*

367

7   Alibi . . . benedixeritis: *omitted G, but added in the margin in a later hand, preceded by* Et item, Quorum remiseritis peccata, remit-tuntur eis et cetera

terribiliter: *a later hand added* de malignis *above the line in* G

Qui: Quid *D*

ab eo: *G adds* Swilc is to beþæncenne and wið Godes yrre to war-nianne symle. Nu lære we eac georne manna gehwyl[c]ne, þæt he Godes larum and his lagum fylg[i]e, þonne geearna[ð] he him ece myrhðe. Amen

8   bedæled: belæded *G*

10   Nis nanum . . . forboden: Riht is þæt preost him lufie clænlic wimman to gebeddan *G*

10   wyrcað: wyrcð *D*

11   ne prita: *omitted G*

12   a to . . . clypian: Godes lof lufian and georne God heregan *G*

15   þam læwedum: læwede *G*

hwile: hwile þe *G*

getimige: gebyrige *G*

16   þæs þe: þæt þe *D*

17   cirican: cirice *D*

cirican: cirice *D*

18   and side: *omitted D*

ælcera: ælcere *D*

wel gehwar: gewel hwær *with two erased letters between the words* G

qui: que *G*

healdan: *three letters erased before the* h *G*

awurpan: *G adds* And utan ænne cynehlaford holdlice healdan, and freonda gehwylc oðerne helade mid rihtan getrywðan

19   þe ða: þa ða *D*

THE INSTITUTES OF POLITY (2)

D = Cambridge, Corpus Christi College MS 201, pp. 40–43, 57–61; *G* = London, British Library, Cotton MS Nero A.i, fols. 102r–9v, 120r; *N* = London, British Library, Cotton MS Tiberius A.iii, fols. 93r–v; *Uc* = Cambridge, University Library Additional MS 3206 (fragment); *X* = *Oxford,*

Bodleian Library, MS Junius 121, fols. 9–13v, 15r–v, 17r–19v, 20v–23v, 32v–34r, 57v–59r.

I   Be heofonlicum cyninge: *this chapter occurs in X and G*
Be: *preceded by the roman numeral* I *in X*
In . . . domini: *omitted G*
ece cyning: ece God *G*
He is: Se is *G*
Amen: *omitted G*

2   Be eorðlicum cyninge: *this chapter occurs in X and G*
Be: *preceded by the roman numeral* II *in X*
gebyreð . . . rihtre lage: *in Wulfstan's handwriting G*
on Cristenre þeode: swyðe rihte, þæt he Cristen folc rihtlice
   healed *G*
and ðurh . . . for worulde: *struck through in G*
steore: *end of chapter in G*
styrnlice: styrlice *X*

5   Be cynedome: *this chapter occurs in X*
Be: *preceded by the roman numeral* III *in X*
Persuasibilitas: Persuabilitas *X*
gedafeniað: gedafenað *X*

6   Be cynestole: *this chapter occurs in X*
Be: *preceded by the roman numeral* IV *in X*

7   Be ðeodwitan: *this chapter occurs in X and G*
Be: *preceded by the roman numeral* V *in X*
sculan riht: riht *omitted XG*
Gif þu þam: þam *omitted G*

8   He . . . forhogað: *this sentence omitted by the scribe and added in
   Wulfstan's handwriting; some letters lost by trimming of the margin G*
forhogað: forhicgeð *G*

9   beseo: *a letter has been erased between the* be *and the* seo *X*
þara . . . þeode: *in Wulfstan's handwriting G*

10   Item de episcopis: *this chapter occurs in X*
Item: *preceded by the roman numeral* VI *in X*

11   Qui noluit: ui noluit *with space for the initial X*
Swylc: wylc *with space for the initial X*

12	Item: *this chapter occurs in X*
13	Item: *this chapter occurs in X*
	cunnen: cunne *X*
14	Be eorlum: *this chapter occurs in X*
	Be: *preceded by the roman numeral* ix *in X*
15	Be gerefan: *this chapter occurs in X and G*
	Be: *preceded by the roman numeral* x *in X*
	swyðe: wide *G*
	swa . . . wolde: *added in Wulfstan's handwriting G*
	ryperas: *added in Wulfstan's handwriting G*
16	Be sacerdum: To mæsseprostum *N*; Be sacerdan *in Wulfstan's handwriting G*; *this chapter occurs in X, G, and N, and portions of it also occur in D and Uc*
	Be: *preceded by the roman numeral* xvii *in X*
	Sacerdas . . . scriftscirum: Sacerd sceal on his scriftscire *GN*
	Ægðer: And ægðer *G*
	And gyf . . . lare: *omitted GN*
	folce gescyldan: folce *omitted X*
	ne mæg wandian: na mæig na wandian *N*
	sylfum gebeorgan sceall: riht deþ *N*
	ne for lufe ne for ege: ne for heanum ne for ricum *N*
	rihtteste: rihtlicost *N*
	Ne mæg . . . for ricum: *omitted N*
	ne deþ: na þet *N*
	eargie . . . spreconne: forsceamehe þæt riht to secgenne, and forsugie he hit, biterlice scel hit him wyrþan forgolden on þam toweardan life. *N*
	Earme . . . forð mid: *omitted N*
	And hwæt: And *omitted GN*
	hwæt: wæt *with space for the initial X*
	cunnon gehealdon: gehealdon *omitted GN*
	heorde: heorde healdan *N*
	þe Crist . . . hi cuðan: þe hig heoldan sceoldan Criste to handa *N*
	Ac naþor: Ac hy naþor *G*
	Ac naþor . . . rihtlice: Ah hi na cunnan naþor þurh larleaste ne lædan, ne læran, ne leacnian. *N*

hi hi þonne: *N adds* læt we nu, þæt hi healdon sceoldan

hi gehealdon: *N adds* þa godcunde heorde

La: *omitted N*

lædan: *N adds* oððe

dema: þema *G*; mann *N*

witodlice: *omitted N*

wyrs: wyrst git *N*

and nele: *N adds a chapter break here with the heading* To mæsse-preostum

17   Eala, eala: Eala *N*

swa hit ð . . . gylpe and: mæssepreosthades *N*

cwæð: spæc *G*; spræc *N*

witega: *N adds* swiþe egeslice

et reliqua: þæt is on Englisc *N*

and forswelgað: *omitted N*

ðe nellað . . . folc: þæ na cunnan folce *N*

ac gyrnað . . . cyricgerihtum: and nimaþ heora sceattas to teoþin-gan and eac on manegum oþrum þingum *N*

bysnungum: bodengum *N*

lædað: lærað *N*

bodungum: bisnuncgum *N*

lærað: tæcaþ *N*

fore ne þingiað: forgeþingiaþ *N*

þingiað: þingia *X*

Ac læccað . . . heora þing syllað: *omitted N*

hernumenra: hernumera *X*

Godes: godest *G*

Þonne is mycel . . . georne gebete: *N replaces this sentence with* Ah hit is swiþe micel þearf [þæt] se, þe ær þysum misdyde, þæt he hit heonanforþ hit georne gebete and rihtlæce hine sylfne be þam, þe he wille beon wiþ God geborgen, oþþe he sceal-mid ealle forwyrþan on þam toweardan life. Bitere scel hit him wyrþan forgolden, þæt he for deadum mann[um] nimþ, butan he hit mid mæssan and mid sealmsange and mid ælmessan in-lice forgilde. Hali Drihten gemiltsige us eallan! Amen. *End of N*

georne gebete: *end of this chapter in G*

18   mycel is . . . mid sceade: *this section (with the heading* Be sacerdan*)*
         occurs as the opening to a homily in D
      to þearfe: *D adds* understande, se ðe cunne
      deofla afyrsað: deofla afirhteð *D*
      Godes mihta: *start of chapter in fragmented version in* Uc

19   us is: is *omitted* Uc
      egeslic, þe: egeslic, þæt *Uc*
      sceal habban þæs: sceal þæs *Uc*

20   Be gehadedum mannum: *this chapter occurs in* X *and* D
      Be: *preceded by the roman numeral* XXII *in* X
      sylfum geornost: geornost *omitted* D
      abræcan: laðlice abræcan *D*
      beode: beodað *D*
      ælc wif: *D adds* þurh Godes lage
      unriht and: *D adds* gehadodan
      morðes: unrihtes *D*
      heononforð georne: georne *omitted* D
      and nah . . . mid rihte: *omitted* X, *text supplied from* D

21   Constantinus: Hit gewearð þæt Constantinus *D*
      sinoð: *D adds* swa we ær sædon
      Nicea: þe is Nicea genamod *D*
      Hy cwædon: And hi cwædon *D*
      oððe diacon: *omitted* D
      æfre: ðananforð æfre *D*
      Se forma wæs: *D adds* swa we sædon
      CC biscopa: *omitted* D
       ætgædere: *D adds* swiðe wide gesamnode
      wiflac: wifunge *D*

22   habban sculon: *D adds* buton hi geswican
      fylðe: unriht *D*
      Weofodþenas: Ac weofodþegnas *D*
      ælcere fylðe: ælcere unclænnesse *D*
      betst magon: *D adds* and healdan heora clænnesse
      Nis: *D adds* ful galnes
      on feonda hand . . . mid ealle: wyrs þonne he be beþorfte *D*
      And eac se: And witod se *D*

edlean: *D adds* on Heofona rice

Amen: Sit nomen Domini benedictum ex hoc nunc et usque in saeculum et reliqua *D*

23   Be abbodum: *this chapter occurs in X and G*

Be: *preceded by the roman numeral* XI *in X*

24   Be munecum: *this chapter occurs in X and G*

Be: *preceded by the roman numeral* XII *in X*

libban: *omitted G*

25   Þæt is: *added in Wulfstan's handwriting G*

ealdras hit: hit *added in Wulfstan's handwriting G*

26   Be mynecenan: *this chapter occurs in X*

Be: *preceded by the roman numeral* XIII *in X*

27   Be preostan and be nunnan: *this chapter occurs in X*

Be: *preceded by the roman numeral* XIV *in X*

28   Be læwedum mannum: *this chapter occurs in X and D*; To gehadedum and læwedum *D*

Be: *preceded by the roman numeral* XXI *in X*

Riht is . . . healdan: Gehadedum mannum gebiraỡ eac, þæt hi læwede men wisian, hu hig heora rihtæwe healdan sculon. *D*

gebyrige: getimige *D*

wydewa: wydewe *X*

canones: canonbec *D*

geset: gescrifen *D*

þæt he: þæt hi *X*

oftor: *D adds* And þæt biỡ micel syn, þæt gehwa his rihtæwe lifigende alæte and him on unriht oỡre geceose.

timan: *D adds* Sit nomen Domini benedictum et reliqua

29   Be wudewan: *this chapter occurs in X*

Be: *preceded by the roman numeral* XV *in X*

30   Be cyrican: *this chapter occurs in X; an alternate version occurs in D and has been edited separately*

Be: *preceded by the roman numeral* XXXV *in X*

and þa we sculon: þa *omitted X*

gelomlice and geornlice: and *omitted X*

31   butan he hi mid: hi *omitted X*

mæỡe: inæỡe *X*

32   Be eallum Cristenum mannum: *this chapter occurs in X and D; ru-*
         bric omitted D
      Be: *preceded by the roman numeral* XXXVI *in X*
      þe ða wisian: þa ða scriftas *D*
      oðþon þa þe: oððe þe þe *D*
      ealles: ealle *with the* s *erased X; emendation follows D*
      And soð is, þæt ic secge: *omitted D*
      beweardiað: beweriað *D*

ON EPISCOPAL DUTIES

X = Oxford, Bodleian Library, MS Junius 121, fols. 13v–15r.

      Item: *preceded by* VII. *in manuscript*
6   gewiht: gewihte *X*
      þæt be: þæt he *X*
10   furðum: forðan *X*
12   beon: *omitted X*
15   Þy: y *with a preceding space for a rubricated initial X*

ON THE REMEDY OF SOULS

G = London, British Library, Cotton MS Nero A.i, fols. 164v–65v.

1   pre: per *G*
      de cura eclesiarum et: *added above the line in Wulfstan's handwriting*
      penitentibus: *corrected from* peniten *in Wulfstan's handwriting*
      leges: legis *G*
      penitentibus: petentibus *G*
      instruant: instuant *G*
2   eclesiasticis: eclesiastices *G*
      sapiens: sapien *G*
      extendebat: extedebat *G*
      quam: *G uses the abbreviation for* quoniam
      sacerdotis: sacedotis *G*
      regnum: rgnum *G*
3   sublime: sublme *G*
      eclesiasticis causis: eclesiasticis casis *G*
      dispensent: dispesent *G*

4 inportune: *added above the line in Wulfstan's handwriting*
  sed habeant: sed habean *G*
  causas: casas *G*
  resistendum: resistendam *G*
  Et quoniam: E quoniam *G*
  saecularis: saeculares *G*
  scriptum: sciptum *G*
  psalmista: spalmista *G*
  de maligno: *added above the line*
  Qui noluit: Qu noluit *G*
5 suimet: sumet *G*
  exibeant: eibeant *G*
  lege: leg *G*
  predicantes: precantes *G*

Instructions for Bishops

G = London, British Library, Cotton MS Nero A.i, fols. 99r–100r; *X* =
Oxford, Bodleian Library, MS Junius 121, fols. 15v–17r.

1 intende: *omitted G*
  ter: ter et tunc *G*
  eleison: *omitted G*
  inducas: *omitted G*
  Benedicamus Domino: Bened et reliqua *with omission of the rest*
   of clause 1 and all of clause 2 G
  Benedictio: Bened *X*
2 Quod: uod *with space for capital X*
3 hæþendom: æþendom *with* h *added later in space left for capital X*
5 Bisceopum: isceopum *with* h *added later in space left for capital X*
  gebyreð: gebyrað *X*
6 þæt hi: and hi *G*
10 gebyreð: gebyrað *X*
  heom: *omitted G*
  na hy sylfe: na *added above the line in Wulfstan's handwriting G*
11 gebyreð: gebyrað *X*
  ne betan: gebetan *G*
12 gebyreþ: gebyrað *X*

þonne ænig: hwilc þonne *G*

13   gebyreð: gebyrað *X*

14   gebyreð: gebyrað *X*

An Admonition to Bishops

G = London, British Library, Cotton MS Nero A.i, fols. 102v–r.

1   Biscpas . . . adumbiað: *in Wulfstan's handwriting*

      unnyt and soþes: unnyt soþes *G*

      þæt we geornost: þæt hy geornost *G*

      drencan: *corrected from* drecan *in a different hand*

2   olæcað georne: olæcað geone *G*

3   þe we læst: þæt læst *G*

4   to wencle . . . gebæran: *in Wulfstan's handwriting*

The Canons of Edgar

D = Cambridge, Corpus Christi College MS 201, pp. 97–101; *Uc* = Cambridge, University Library Additional MS 3206 *(mutilated fragment missing parts of individual words and all clauses after 8); X = Oxford, Bodleian Library, MS Junius 121, fols. 25v–31v.*

      Item Sinodalia decreta: *omitted Uc; preceded by roman numeral* xx *in X*; Her gebirað nu to Eadgares geræriss be gehadodra manna liffadunge *D*

1   Riht is: *here and following, D reads* We lærað

      Riht . . . beon: *in capitals X*

      preostas: Godes þeowas *D*

2   hyran: *glossed* obedient *X*

      getæce: *glossed* docet *X*

3–4   *clauses omitted from X, text supplied from D*

5   swa se bisceop: swa biscop *D*

6   wite: *glossed* sciat *X*

      Gode: *glossed* deo *X*

      oferhyre: *glossed* inobedientes

      heafodleahtrum: *the scribe has added three dots above* -leahtrum *to indicate a gloss, but the gloss is omitted X*; heafordleahtrum, *with the first three letters missing Uc*

7	some: *glossed* congregatione X
	sceoton: *the scribe has added three dots above the line to indicate a gloss, but the gloss is omitted* X
8	ænig: *end of* Uc *after the* æ-
	forlæte: *glossed* deferat X
	rihtæwe: *glossed* uxore X; *glossator adds* þa hwile þe his lif sig *in margin* X
12	samlæredan: *glossed* semidoctum X
13	anra gebyrda: *glossed* Natalie unius X
14	mangeara: man geara X
	massere: *glossed* Mercator X
15	tyðige: *glossed* concedat X
	beode: *glossed* iubeat X
	VII: XXXVII D
16	lære: aræreD
	wyllweorðunga: *glossed* fontis uenerationem X
	hwata: *glossed* omen X
	and treowwurðunga . . . tihð: and manweorðunga D
	on geares niht: *omitted* D
	ellenum: *incorrectly glossed* eluene X; D *adds* and eac on oðrum mistlicum treowum and on stanum
	gedwimerum: *glossed* fantasiis X
	dreogað: *glossed* þolieð X
18	freolsdagum: æt cyrcan *added above the line* X
	gamena: *incorrectly glossed* custodian *and crossed out* X
19	cypincge: D *adds* and folcgemota
20	wæda: ræda D
	efesunge: *glossator adds* oððe unefesunge X
21	*clause omitted from* X, *text supplied from* D
23	mannum: D *adds* ealles to swiðe
26	gedryh: þa *added above, perhaps by glossator* X
	cyrictune: *glossed* cimiterio X
	ne hors: *omitted* D
	The scribe has written andreas *in the margin* X.
27	logie: *glossed* ponat X
	ungedafenlic: *glossed* indecens X
28	sy: *glossator adds* beo *above the line* X

29   Gode: *glossed* deo *X*

    læte: *glossed* iudicet *X*

30   butan . . . oferseocnesse: *crossed out with a single line X*

31   preost: *D adds* huru

32   butan: *glossed* sine *X*

    þæ . . . misse: þu lest he misse *added in margin X*

    læs þe: læste *X*

34   gode: *glossed* bonos *X*

35   næbbe: hæbbe *X*

36   abyrige: *glossed* gustet *X*

37   *A small cross has been added before this section X.*

    þriwa: *altered to* twiga *by glossator X*

    mæstra: mæst þara *D*

38   warnige: *glossed* caueat *X*

    brucan: *glossed* frui *X*

    under: unde *D*

    forgyme: *altered to* forgeme *by glossator X*

39   preost æfre ne: næfre preost *D*

    geþristlæce *glossed* presumat *X*

    þæt is clæne: þæt his clæne *X*

    Wa: *glossed* ve *X*

    ful: *glossed* fetidum *X*

    forðam he deð: *omitted D*

    forðam: þe *added afterward above the line X*

    eced: *glossed* eisil *by glossator X*

40   *A small cross has been added before this section X.*

41   beo: *glossator adds in the margin* Gylden oððe seolfren tinen

    ænig: glossator *adds above the line* Gif he nylle beon amansumad,
        intended as an addition to clause 40 X

    ne nænne . . . æne: *omitted D; may have been intended to follow*
        clause 40 instead of 41 X

42   fules: *omitted D*

    byrnende: *altered to* bernende *X*

43   forgyme: *altered to* forgeme *X*

    ne gehalgode . . . oflete: *omitted D*

    oflete: oft *X*; *incorrectly glossed* fruit *X*

	Ac ... gebringe: *omitted D*
46	mæssapreosta: *D adds* oððe mysterpreosta
	butan: *glossed* sine X
48	anræde: *glossed* constantes X
49	est: *glossed* deuotione X
50	an: *glossed* unum X
	ofer geares: on geares D
	fæc: *glossed* spacium X
51	geogoðe: *glossed* iuuenes X
53	ænig: nan D
	þycge: *glossed* gustet X
54	Gode: *glossed* deo X
	And riht ... gegaderod: *omitted D*
	oðre: *glossed* iterum X
	sulhælmessan: sulh- *glossed as* suluh- *by glossator X*
	and leohtgesceotu ... æfen: *omitted D*
56	*clause omitted D*
58	beorgen: *glosse* caueantur X
	belean: *glossed* forbeoden *by glossator X*
59	gliwige: *glossed* ludat X
60	wið: *glossed* contra X
62	gewita: *glossed* testis X
65	plege: *glossed* ludat X
	se canon ... VII: *omitted D*
66–67	*clauses omitted from D*
66	rædlice: *glossed* scienter X
68a	*occurs as clause 61 in D*
	rihtæwe: *glossed* legem coniugem *by glossator X*
68b–i	*omitted D*
68b	fadige: *glossed* lede *by glossator X*
	misfadige: *glossed* let X
	woruldwige: *glossed* prelio X
	hyran: *glossed* pavere X
68e	tihtlan: *glossed* ortationibus suggestionibus X
	belecge: *glossed* mentitur X
	þe *glossed* qui X

68i   magum: *glossed* meies *n glossator*

69   a gearu: eac geara *D*

5 ÆTHELRED

D = Cambridge, Corpus Christi College MS 201, pp. 48–51; *G1* = *London, British Library, Cotton MS Nero A.i, fols. 89v–92r; G2* = London, British Library, Cotton MS Nero A.i, fols. 116v–19r.

	In . . . MVIII: Be Angolwitena gerednesse *G2*; *In nomine domini D*
Pr	cyng . . . gehadode: cyningc ægðer gehadode *D*
1	Ðæt is: Þis *D*
	we ealle: *G2 adds* fram synnan georne gecyrran and ure misdæde geornlice betan and
	and þæt we . . . willað: *omitted G2*
1.1	ures . . . his: *omitted G2*
1.2	þæt: *omitted D*
	innan . . . worolde: *omitted D*
2	ures . . . his: *omitted G2*
	leode: þeode *D*
3	ures . . . his: *omitted G2*
	fordeme: fordemde *D*
3.1	steora: stepra *G2*
4	ures . . . his: *omitted G2*
4.1	þingian georne: geornlice þingian *D*
5	ures . . . his: *omitted G2*
	þe he Gode: þæt he Gode *G2*
6	cume to scirebiscope: cume scirebiscope *G1*; cume him to scirebiscope *D*
	þæt he huru: and he huru *G1*
10.2	cyricmangunge: cyricmagunge *G1G2*
11	georne: *omitted G2*
11.1	sulhælmessan: *G2 adds* huru
12	gelæste æt: gelæste a æt *G2*
12.2	gerihta fyrðrige: gerihta friðige *D*
14	weorðie: wurðian *D*
14.1	man and: man georne and *G2*

18	and fram: and ab *D*
	octabas Epiphanie: XIIII niht ofer middewintres tid *D* xv: XIIII *D*
25	æwbrican: *G2 adds* and on freolsbrycan, on fæstenbrycan
26.1	burhbota: bricbota *G2*; *D adds* and ymbe bricbote æghwar on earde
27	mæge: *G2 adds* gif man þæt geræde *in Wulfstan's handwriting*
28	and ealre his are: oððe wergylde *G2D*
28.1	*omitted D*
	elles: *G2 adds* ham
29	plihte he him: plihte he to him *D*
	and eallan: oððe to *D*
30	cyninges: cynine *D*
	and gif . . . lage: buton he hine ladige be þam deopestan, þe witan gerædan *D*
	cynges: cynge *G2*
31.1	þæt hine man: and hine man þonne þurh þæt *D*
32	alicgan: alecgan *D*
	ær . . . wide: ure hlaford oft and gelome silf het alecgan *D*
32.1–5	*These clauses are found only in D.*
33	*omitted D*
33.1	þe man: þæt man *D*
	worolde: *G2 adds* Amen
34	weorðian: *G2 and D add* and ænne cristendom georne healdan
35	biddan: *G2 adds* sit nomen domini benedictum et reliqua; *D adds* sit nomen domini benedictum

6 ÆTHELRED

K = London, Cotton MS Claudius A.iii, fols. 35v–37r.

7	clænsige: clæsig *K*
15	þeowige: þowige *K*
25	heahfreolsdagum: heah- *added in Wulfstan's handwriting K*
25.1	riht: *added in Wulfstan's handwriting K*
35	sylf on: *added in Wulfstan's handwriting K*
41	eac: *added in Wulfstan's handwriting K*

42   gyt: *added in Wulfstan's handwriting K*
          georne: *added in Wulfstan's handwriting K*

7 ÆTHELRED

Br = Johannis Brompton Chronicon (Cambridge, Corpus Christi College
MS 96, and London, British Library, Cotton MS Tiberius C.xiii); *Hk* =
Holkham 228 (privately held), fols. 82r–83v; *M* = Macro (privately held); *T*
= *London, British Library, Cotton MS Titus A.xxvii, fol. 145r.*

Pr   rex: *omitted Br*
          Badam: habam *BrHkM*
1.1   et abstinentia . . . iniustitia: et malefactis et iniustitia absti-
               nere *Br*
1.2   Hoc est ut: et ut *Br*; hoc ut *Hk*
1.3   Qui si: Quod si *Br*
2   herbis crudis: bis crudis *Br M*; erudis *Hk*; *Br adds* ante festum
               sancti Michaelis
2.5   haec elemosina: hae elemosinae *Br*
          proueniat: perueniat *HkBr*
3.1   illum: *omitted BrHkM*
3.2   monacus: *Br adds* dicat
4   nostrorum stetit: nostrorum fecit *Br*
          melius stetit: melius fecit *Br*
          per: *omitted BrHkM*
4.1   matrem: *Br adds* nostram
4.2   eum: Deum *BrHkM*
          ei: *omitted Br*
5   aliquis: quis *BrHkM*
          extra uendatur: extra patriam *Br*
6.2   stetit: fecit *Br*
7   hinc: hic *Br*
          retro: rectus *T*
7.1   et gratiam *omitted Br*
          futuro: futuram *T*
          Amen: *omitted Br*

7A ÆTHELRED

D = *Cambridge, Corpus Christi College MS 201, p. 30.*

8 ÆTHELRED

D = *Cambridge, Corpus Christi College MS 201, pp. 93–96;* G = London, British Library, Cotton MS Nero A.i, fol. 95v.

	Anno . . . Christi: Be cyricgriðe. In nomine Domini *G*
2.1	gespelia: gespelia geteald *G*
3	be þæs cyninges: be cyninges *G*
	and ægþer . . . gebete: *omitted D; text supplied from G*
4	elles: *omitted G*
	betan: bete *G*
	si hit . . . unrihthæmed: *omitted G*
4.1	æfre: *omitted G*
5.1	þær . . . sy: *omitted D; text supplied from G*
5.2	mæþe: *end of G*
22	aðfultum: adfultum *D*
27.1	swa mid anfealdre: *omitted D; text supplied from I Cnut 5.4*
35	mannan: mannum *D*
36	gerehtan: gerihtan *D*
37	wurðan : wurdan *D*
43	þearf: þeaf *D*

9 ÆTHELRED

MS = London, British Library, Cotton MS Otho A.x.
Since the manuscript was almost completely destroyed in the Ashburnham House fire of 1731, this edition relies on the text of Liebermann, *Gesetze*, vol. 1, p. 269.

Ex	And: An *MS*
	healdan: healed *MS*
	holdliche: *Liebermann recommends emending to* holdlice, *though* holdliche *is a legitimate late form of the word*

10 ÆTHELRED

MS = Vatican, Codex Reginensis Latina MS 946, fol. 75v.

The text, found on one of a small collection of leaves bound into a fourteenth-century French miscellany, has been damaged by damp and tearing on the folio's margins. This edition relies on the text of Liebermann, *Gesetze*, vol. 1, pp. 269–70.

Pr.1   þætte: þe *MS*

CNUT'S OXFORD LEGISLATION OF 1018

D = Cambridge, Corpus Christi College MS 201, pp. 126–30.

7	gebetan: gebeten *D*
11.1	þæt hi: and hi *D*
12	lafe: leafe *D*
15.1	tidan: *omitted D*
19	man georne: man geore *D*
26.3	hundred: unræd *D*
27	on: *omitted D*
28	þæt gehwa: and þæt gehwa *D*
	þæt he: he þæt *D*

CNUT'S PROCLAMATION OF 1020

Υ = York, York Minster, Additional MS 1, fols. 160r–v.

2	hæbbe ic mid: hæbbe mid *Υ*
	hycgan: *omitted Υ; supplied following Liebermann*
3	him: heom *Υ*
4	þæt he ongean: þæt ongean *Υ*
5	þe man: se man *Υ*
6	deop is: is *omitted Υ*
	gesece: gesæce *Υ*
	on þam halgan: on *omitted Υ*
	fæsten: fæstan *Υ*

I Cnut

A = London, British Library, Harley MS 55, fols. 5r–7v; *B* = Cambridge, Corpus Christi College MS 383, pp. 43–47; *G = London, British Library, Cotton MS Nero A.i, fols. 3r–16r.*

Pr   Ðis: *A precedes this with* Ðis is seo gerednes, þe Cnut cyning, ealles Englalandes cyningc and Dena cyningc and Norþrigena cyningc, gerædde, and his witan, Gode to lofe and him sylfum to cynescipe and to þearfe, rade swa hwæðer swa man wille.

        ealles . . . cining: *omitted A*

        ðære: ðam *A*

2   uton: *omitted G;* witan *A*

        saulum . . . and: *omitted A*

2.2   him: *omitted G; supplied from A*

2.3   sig: is *A*

2.5   þa mynsterclænsunge begyte: þas mynstres clansunge *A*

        mynsterclænsunge: mynsterclænsunge *G*

3.1   wurðscipes: *omitted A*

        halgunge: halsunge *G*

3.2   and on . . . arcebiscope: *omitted A*

4.1   se ðe: *A adds* wylle oðð

4.2   þe deofla: þe he deofla *A*

        swa man: swa he man *A*

        halige: *omitted A*

        abutan: *omitted A*

5   ladige he: *A omits* he

5.1   tihtlige: thtlige *A*

        mid: *omitted A*

5.2   sig: is *A*

        ladige mid: ladige hine mid *A*

5.4   he ladian: he hine ladian *A*

        swa mid anfealdre: *omitted A*

7   þæs: his *A*

7.3   Ne . . . wif; and: Ac *A*

        libbe: *G adds, probably in error,* þus scyldon æfre ge

8.2   gega: gegað *A*

9.1   xxx: ðrittig þenega *A*

        cxx scyllinga: twa hundred and twentig scillinga *A*

10.1   cxx scyllinga: twa hundred and twentig scillinga *A*

11.1   And: *omitted A*

12   eft on: eft to *A*

        and eft to þæm æfene sanctan Marian clænsunge ealswa: *omitted*
           G (likely by scribal error), but added in a sixteenth-century hand

14   fyrðrige: friðige *A*

14.1   rihtlice: *omitted A*

14.2   And healde man: *omitted A*

        mæssedæg: *start of B*

16   *B adds rubric* Be fæstene

        And: *omitted B*

16.1   eallswa: and *AB*

        þæt . . . mæssedæge: *omitted AB*

17   And: *omitted B*

        and rihtfæstendagum: *omitted B*

        Twelftan mæssedæge: Twelftadæg *AB*

17.1   þæt is . . . Aprilis: *omitted AB*

        xviiii: xviii *G*

        þæt ys . . . Mæge: *omitted AB*

18   biddað: willað *B*

        þonne us: þæt us *B*

        þæt we: þær we *GB*

        awohtonaworhtan: a worhton *G*

18.1   *B adds rubric* Be scrifte

18.2   þæt is: þis *A*

18.3   life: blode *B*

        sealde: ageat *B*

19   Ac: *omitted B*

        þe: ðe þe *B*

20   georne: *omitted A*

20.1   byð: ðam byð *AB*

        witodlice: *omitted A*

        rihtlice: *omitted A*

21	smeagan: *B and A add* and spyrian, *which has been added here in a sixteenth-century hand*
22	geleafan and ariht: geleafan ariht *A*
22.1	sceal . . . oðrum: *omitted B, where a later hand has added* we sculan us gebiddan and mid þam credan
22.4	butan . . . Gode: buton he on God hæbbe inwardlice rihtne geleafan *AB*
22.5	Cristenra manna: Cristene *B*
	gemanan . . . life: gemanan on gehalgodon restan oððe her on life husles beon wyrðe *AB*
23	*B adds rubric* Godlar
24	warnige symle: warnian georne *B*
26	lage lareowas: larðeowas *B*
26.1	elles: helles *B*
26.2	mannum: manna *G*
26.4	A . . . Amen: *added in margin in a later hand in G; omitted A*

2 Cnut

A = London, British Library, Harley MS 55, fols. 7v–13v; *B* = Cambridge, Corpus Christi College MS 383, pp. 47–72; *G = London, British Library, Cotton MS Nero A.i, fols. 16r–41r.*

Pr	is seo: is ðonne seo *AB*
2	ða: *omitted G*
	þæt is . . . agyltað: *omitted AB*
2.1	forbeodað: beodað *AG*
	forspille: forspille man *B*
	deore: deope *A*
3	forbeodað: beodað *AG*
	huru . . . georne: *omitted A*
4	*B adds rubric* Wiccean
	forfare: forfaran *G*
5	*B adds rubric* Be hæðenscipe
	And: *omitted B*
	we: *omitted G*
5.1	Hæðenscipe . . . weorþige: Þæt bið þæt man idol weorðige *B*

	deofolgyld: idola *A*
	blote: hlotæ *A*
8	*B adds rubric* Feos bote
	and ymbe feos: and feos *G*
	georne: geore *G*
9	heonon forð: *omitted B*
10	bricbota: *B adds* heonan forð
11	symle: georne *B*
11.1	Amen: *omitted A*
12	and flymena fyrmðe: *omitted AB*
	and he . . . geunne: *omitted AB*
13	*B adds rubric* Utlaga
15	ðe: *omitted AB*
	flyman: *omitted AB*
	þæt: *omitted B*
	ær: *omitted B*
15.1	eft: *omitted AB*
	he geladige: he hine geladige *AB*
15.2	xxx: xx *B*
16	freme: feorme *A*; freoma *B*
	hine: him *B*
17	And . . . ðone: *written in a sixteenth-century hand over an erasure in G*
17.1	And . . . hundredes: Sece man his hundred *B*
	hit is: hit riht is *AB*
18	on geare: *omitted B*
	tuwa: twa *AB*
	scirgemot: *B adds* be wite ealswa hit riht is
	oftor: *B adds* neod *in a sixteeenth-century hand*
19	*B adds rubric* Be name
	nane: *omitted A*
	þriwa . . . his: *omitted B*
19.1	he feorðan: he æt þam feorðam *A*
20	*B adds rubric* Þæt ælc man beo on teoðunge
	And: *omitted B*
	teon: afylle *B*
	wylle: fylle *A*

þæt he byð: *omitted AB*

20.1   eað: *omitted A*

21   *B adds rubric* Be ðeofan

Ac: *omitted B*; And *A*

22   innan: innan his *A*

22.1   to þam ordale: to ordale *B*

mid . . . lade: *omitted A*

22.3   æfre: *omitted B*

23   getrywe: *omitted B*

23.1   gewitnes: *B adds* hwanon him come

on hlafordes: on his hlafordes *B*

24.2   we: *omitted A*

her beforan: ær *B*

cwædon: cwædon is *A*

24.3   æfter ðam: *omitted B*

25   sceawie: sceþie *B*

ahte: ah *B*; age *A*

25.2   fræmde þa: fræmde man þa *B*

cxx: hundtwelfti *B*

26   þæt þæt: þæt *B*

gesecean: *omitted A*

26.1   And . . . ne: *omitted A*

28   ne: *omitted B*

butan: butan he *A*

30   *B adds rubric* Swyðe getreowe

hine þonne: hine *B*

30.1   ne he: *added in a sixteenth-century hand over an erasure in G*

30.3   *B adds rubric* Be ordale

beo he: beo him *B*; beo *A*

his wites: þæs *A*

eft: *omitted B*

30.4   gif he: buton gif he *B*

30.5   gif he: gif hit *B*

swa hwylc: hwylc *B*

man þonne: man wyle oððe þone *B*

mæg: sceal *B*

30.6   wites: weres *B*

30.7   getrywe to: getreowe men to *B*

30.8   forðcume . . . wyrðe: *omitted B*

30.9   And gif heo: *omitted B*

31   *B adds rubric* Be hiredmannum

        rihtlagu: lagu *B*

31.1   oðhleape: ætleape *B*; leape *A*

        man: hi *B*

31.2   Gyf . . . and: *omitted B*

        si: beo *B*

        utlah: *B adds* wið ðone cyng

32   þeowman: ðeofman *AB*

        man: *omitted B*

        hine: hine þonne *B*

32.1   oðer: *omitted B*

33   *B adds rubric* Be ungetreowum mannum

        ungetrywe si: si *omitted in G*

33.1   forene: *omitted B*; fora *A*

33.2   ealra: *omitted B*

35   *B adds rubric* Be freondleasan

        þonne: þone *G*

        And: *omitted B*

        gyf: *omitted G*

36   *B adds rubric* Be mænan aðe

        And: *omitted B*

37   *B adds rubric* Be leasre gewitnesse

        naht: aht *G*

        þe . . . ahe: *omitted AB*

38   and fæstentidan: *omitted AB*

        beorgan: bebyrgan *B*

38.2   symle georne: georne and symble *B*

        boctæcinge: boctale *AB*

        and woruldcunde: and for woruldcunde *A*; and woruldbote *B*

        bote: *omitted B*

39   *B adds rubric* Gif hwa preost ofslea

        geladige hine: ladige *B*

39.1	bote: þa bote *B*
40	gehadodne: gehadodne man *B*
	ælþeodigne: ælþeodigne man *B*
	him cingc: him se kingc *B*
	hlaford: *omitted B*
40.1	bete man: beton *B*
41	*B adds rubric* Be gehadedum mannum
	swa papa: swa se papa *B*
41.1	ladige mid: ladie hine mid *B*
42	*B adds rubric* Ðæt man gehadodne man [ne] bende ne beate
	swa swa hit: swa hi *B*
	be hades: be ðæs hades *B*
	and hlaforde: and ðam laforde *B*
	oððe cyningce: oððe ðam kyningce *B*
	hine mid: hine sylfne mid *B*
43	healde to: *B adds* ðæs
44	him man æfre: him nan man næfre *B*
44.1	hwa: man *B*
	þone: *omitted A*
	hine: *omitted G*
	V and: V men and *B*
	sylf: him sylf *B*
45	æfre: næfre *B*
	wylde: *B adds* man hine
45.1	*B adds rubric* Be haligdæiges freolse
	gebete: gebete he *B*
45.2	gif wyrce: gyf he wyrce *B*
46	*Be adds rubric* Be festene
46.1	Yfel byð: Yfel bið hit *B*
	rihtfæstentide: riht- *omitted AB*
	gyt: gyt hit bið *B*
46.2	oððe hydgyldes: *omitted A*
47	oððe þurh reaflac: *in a sixteenth-century hand over an erasure in G*
	swa on: swa eac on *B*
47.1	ladige mid: ladige hine mid *B*
48	*B adds rubric* Gif hwa forwyrne godcunde gerihte

	hine: -N- *G*
	XI and: XI men and *B*
48.1	æt: æt ðam *B*
	alæte: forlete *B*
48.3	gesoðige: gesoðian mæge
	licge: licge he *B*
49	be hades: be ðæs hades *B*
50	*B adds rubric* Be æwbryce
50.1	Yfel: fel *with space for the initial in G*
	man: men *B*
51	*B adds rubric* Be siblegere
51.1	and hit: and þes þe hit *B*
52	*B adds rubric* Be wydewan
	be were: be his were *B*
52.1	*B adds rubric* Mæden
	be were: be his were *B*
53	*B adds rubric* Ðæt nan wif heo ne forlicgge
	ahte: age *B*
	and heo . . . earena: and heo ðonne ðolie ægðer ge nosu ge ða earan *B*
53.1	bisceop: se bisceop *B*
54	God and: God *B*
54.1	bisceop him: him se bisceop *B*
55	driue hi man of: *omitted GA, added in B in a sixteenth-century hand*
	and synnan: and on synnan *B*
56	*B adds rubric* Open morð
	amyrðred: amyrred *G*
	þone banan: *omitted GA, added in B in a sixteenth-century hand*
57	*B adds rubric* Lafordes syrwunge
	oððe hlaford syrwe: syrwe oððe ymbe his hlaford *B*
	ordale: *B adds* and þær clæne wyrð *in a sixteenth-century hand*
58	*B adds rubric* Be borhbryce
58.1	Gif: if *with space for the initial in G*
58.2	borh: burg *A*
	þæt: *omitted B*
59	*B adds rubric* Be ðam þe on cynincges hirde feohteð

60	*B adds rubric* Be ðam þæt man oðerne bewepnað
	forgilde: forgildon hine
61	*B adds rubric* Griðbryce
	Gif: if *with space for the initial in* G
61.1	hine: -N- G
62	*B adds rubric* Hamsocne
	and on . . . arcebisceope: *omitted* AB
	and on Dena: and Dene G
62.1	afylle: alecge A
63	*B adds rubric* Reaflac
	oððe . . . age: *omitted* AB
64	*B adds rubric* Husbryce
65	*B adds rubric* Burhbote
	cxx: hundtweftigum A
	namie: and namige B
66	*B adds rubric* Be Godes flyman
	hine to: hine mid B
	his: *omitted* AB
67	eft to rihte: *omitted* B
	man for: man him for B
	betst: best G
	mæge: *B adds, then crosses out,* ðam men
68	aa: æfre B
	betst: *omitted* B
	þonne . . . byð: *omitted* B
68.1	*B adds rubric* Be unstrangan
	and ege: and for his ege B
	Forþamðe . . . georne, gelice: Forðamðe we magon witan ful-
	georne, þæt se unmaga and se mage ne mæg gelice B; Forþamþe
	ne mæg, we witan fulgeorne, se unmaga þam magan gelice A
	gelice byrðene: gelice mycele byrðene B
	byrðene . . . gelice: *omitted* A
	ahebban: aberan B
	freot: frige B
	þeowet: þeowe B
68.2	mænigre: gemeanre B

þonne byð . . . wyrðe: ðonne bið se man ðe bet wyrðe *B*

68.3   hwæt: *omitted A*

na: *omitted B*

gedeð: gewurþe *G*; deð *B*

69.1   me rihtlice: rihtlice *B*

69.2   ðam: *omitted A*

70   *B adds rubric* Be hergeate

And . . . gewite: Gyf of ðysum life man gewite *B*

71   swa fundene: *omitted A*

B adds rubric Eorles

eallswa: swa *B*

71.1   *B adds rubric* Kyncges ðeines

þegnas: *B adds* heregeata

swa: ealswa *B*

71.2   *B adds rubric* Oðres ðeines

71.5   maga: mage *G*

72   his deig: *omitted GA, added in B in a sixteenth-century hand*

on þam ylcan: *omitted B*

72.1   beclypod wære: beclypod *G*

73   *B adds rubric* Be wydewan þæt heo sitte xii monðas ceorlæs

monað: monað and *B*

ceose: ceose heo *B*

binnan: ðonne binnan ðæs *B*

73.1   his socne: hit *AB*

73.3   æfre: næfre *B*

74   nyde: nime *A*

man: man næfre *B*

75   *B adds rubric* Be ðam þæt man his spere to oðres mannes dure sette

ic læte riht: wille *A*; ic nelle *with* læte riht *added above the line B*

þeah: þe *B*

his spere: his agen spere *B*

and hwylcne: and he hwylcne *B*

hearm: hearm eac *AB*

eac: *omitted G*

75.2   lagan tæcean: *later revised to* laga tæcean *G*; lagu tæce *AB*

76   *B adds rubric* Be forstolene æhta

hwylc: hwa *B*

arasod: arefned *B*

76.1   hordern: heddernes cæge *B*

cyste: cyste cæge *B*

þonne: þone *B*

gelogian: gelaðyan *A*

76.2   on cradele: on ðam cradele *B*

letan efen scyldig: lætan ealswa scyldigne *B*

76.3   swylce: eac swyðe *B*

manege: manega ðincg *B*

77   *B adds rubric* Be ðam þe flihð fram his laforde

ealles: he ealles *B*

77.1   *omitted B*

78   *B adds rubric* Be ðam ðe toforan his laforde fealleð

þam: *omitted B*

hit of: hit ut of *B*

79   hæbbe on: *B adds* scypfyrde and on landfyrde be

and se ... ahte: *omitted AB*

80   *B adds rubric* Be huntnaðe

80.1   wylle habban: *B adds* on minon agenan *in a sixteenth-century hand*

83   ða: *omitted A*

83.2   hit: hi *B*; *omitted A*

wyrde: abrece *B*

84   swyðe georne: *omitted B*

84.1   geornlice: and georlice *B*

hyran: *A adds* and Godes lage fylgean

84.2   for ærran: for his ærran *B*

84.3   heononforð: *B adds* mid rihte

84.4   a: *omitted B*

þæt: þæs þe *A*

wordes: *B adds* and weorces

dæde: *B adds* and

Godes milts: God *B*

84.5	symle: *omitted B*
	worulde: *B adds* Amen
84.6	and . . . swa: *omitted AB*

THE NORTHUMBRIAN PRIESTS' LAW

D = Cambridge, Corpus Christi College MS 201, pp. 43–46.

2	forbode: forboda *D*
	oðres: oðre *D*
	gebicgæ ne geþicgæ: gebicgæn ne geþicgæn *with the final* n *in each* gebicgæn *marked out D*
3	hit: he *D*
12	þolie: þolian *D*
	him: heom *D*
23	biscope: þæt *D*
30	and biscope: *added later D*
41	oððe ealascop: vel ealascop *D*
48	oððe idola: vel idola *D*
49	VI: VI^te *Y*
51	að: *omitted D*
56	mete: meteneade *D*

THE OBLIGATIONS OF INDIVIDUALS *AND* ON REEVES

The Obligations of Individuals

B = Cambridge, Corpus Christi College MS 383, fols. 63v–66v.

3	ofer: ofeh *B*
3.3	ðeaw: ðeað *B*
4.1	ræcan: ræpan *B*
4.2	inswane: inswa *B*
4.3	forðsið: forðsit *B*
4.4	eac: ea *B*
4.6	hwæt . . . sy: *repeated B*
5	þæt on: þonne *B*
5.2	mædmæwette: mædmæwecte *B*

6.2	and: *omitted B*
7	inheorde: inherode *B*
9.1	hærfesthandful: hærfesthandsul *B*
14	dingan: ðingan *B*
17	getrywðan: getrywdan *B*
20	dampnum. . .imputabitur: *text omitted from B, supplied from* Quadripartitus
21.2	ðeode: ðede *B*

On Reeves

B = Cambridge, Corpus Christi College MS 383, fols. 63v–69r.

1.1	mæda: *emended to* mæde *B*
3.1	*omitted B; text supplied from* Quadripartitus
4	flotsmeru: slotsmeru *B*
7	is: his *B*
9	He: Me *B11*
	stician: stygian *B*
12	bigan: bycgan *B*
13	swilces cynnes: synnes *B*

I ÆTHELSTAN

D = Cambridge, Corpus Christi College MS 201, p. 53; G = London, British Library, Cotton MS Nero A.i, fols. 86v–87v.

	Æðelstanes gerædnes: Æðelstanes cinyncges gerædnes *D*
Pr	beode: *omitted D*
1	and þæt: þæt *D*
5	agenes: *omitted D*
	oferhirnesse: oferynesse *G*

I EDMUND

B = Cambridge, Corpus Christi College MS 383, fols. 54v–55r; D = Cambridge, Corpus Christi College MS 201, pp. 96–97; G = London, British Li-

brary, Cotton MS Nero A.i, fol. 87v; *H* = Strood, Medway Archive and Local Studies Centre MS DRc/R1 *(Textus Roffensis)*, fols. 44r–45r.

	Her . . . gerædnes: Eadmundes cyninges asetnysse *H*; Ead- mundes gerædnes *G; omitted B*
Pr	ymbon: georne ymbe *G*
	ræd: *end of G*
1	and þæt: ðæt is ðæt *HB*
2	Romfeoh: almesfeoh *HB*
	and sulhælmessan: *omitted HB*
	And gif: Gif *HB*
3	neawiste: ansyne *H; B adds* gyf he cyninges man sy
6	beon: syn *HB*
	gecirran þe geornor: *omitted HB*

2 EDGAR *AND* 3 EDGAR

A = London, British Library, Harley MS 55, fols. 3v–4v; *D* = Cambridge,
Corpus Christi College MS 201, pp. 46–48; *G1* = *London, British Library,
Cotton MS Nero A.i, fols. 42r–44v; G2* = London, British Library, Cotton
MS Nero A.i, fols. 88r–89r *(3 Edgar only)*.

2 Edgar

Pr	*D adds rubric* Her is Eadgares cynincges gerædnes
	his leodscipe: *omitted D*
1	rihtes: ælces rihtes *AD*
1.1	swa swa hit seo: swa his *G1*
	gega: gegange *AD*
2	gesylle: gesylle ðone *AD*
2.1	ne: *omitted D*
	nigan dælum: nigoðan dæle *D*
2.3	*omitted G1, text supplied from A*
	And: *omitted D*
3	sy gelæst be: to *AD*
3.1	fare: þonne fare *D*

healfan: *here and subsequently in* G1, ealfan *has been corrected to* healfan *in a later (possibly Wulfstan's?) hand*

4.1 þonne to: hine to *AD*

4.3 cyrre: syðe *A*; siðe *D*

5 freols: freolsunga *AD*

Sæternesdæges: *omitted A*

domboc: seo domboc *AD*

beo: sy *D*

5.1 and ælces . . . sy: *omitted D*

5.1–3 and ælces . . . betst stod: *omitted* G1; *text taken from A*

3 Edgar

1 *D adds rubric* Eadgares cynincges gerædnes

healde: ealde *G1*

1.1 ærest: *omitted G1*

1.2 swylce: swilce swilce *A*

3 se ðe oðrum on woh gedeme: ðe oðrum wo deme *AD*

-twelfti: *start of* G2

eft: *omitted AD*

swa he: swa swa he *A*

scyre: scyr *G1*

4 forseggan: forseccan *D*

feore: freme *DG2*; *A adds* uel freme

se oðer: *AD adds* þæt

5 hundredgemot: hundredes gemot *DG2*

6 gehealde: geealde *G1, corrected in a sixteenth-century hand*

6.2 hit: hit þonne *D*

þeof: þyfð *G1*

sealde: geald *ADG2*

7 þriwa: *omitted G1*

sceawie: selfte *D*

7.1 swaðor: swa hwaðer swa *D*

landhlaford: hlaford ells *ADG2*

7.3 gesecen: *D adds* buton se cyninge him feorhgeneres unne

8 ga: gange *ADG2*

8.1   *G1 reads* And gemet, swylce man on Wintancestre healde.
8.2   healfan: ealfan *G1*
        punde: *omitted D*
        undeoror: deoror *G1*
8.3   *omitted G1; text from A*

Notes to the Translations

The Laws of Edward and Guthrum

Pr   *And this also*: The prologue's opening phrase appears to connect this text with the one immediately preceding it in the manuscript, the so-called *Treaty of Alfred and Guthrum*, composed sometime after King Alfred of Wessex (849–899) defeated the Viking king Guthrum (d. 890) at the battle of *Ethandun* (identified as Edington in Wiltshire) in May 878. It seems likely that Wulfstan composed *The Laws of Edward and Guthrum* as a companion piece to the *Treaty*—possibly as a way of extending the provisions of the earlier treaty to encompass northern England as well as southern—and intended the two to circulate together.

1   *sanctuary*: The right of a church to protect an individual within its walls or other forms of boundary marker from secular prosecution. Sometimes also referred to by Wulfstan as "church sanctuary."

2   *lahslit*: Having no adequate modern English equivalent, *lahslit* is a term of Old Norse derivation used by Wulfstan to denote the Danish analogue to English "wergild" (literally, "man-price": an amount of money determined by rank paid by the responsible party as compensation for the injury or death of another). A partial sense of the values attached to *lahslit* can be gleaned from the prescriptions in *The Northumbrian Priests' Law* 51–54.

3.2   *proper day*: That is, on Maundy Thursday (the Thursday before Easter).

        twelve oras: The ora was a unit of coinage equal to sixteen pence or one-fifteenth of a pound.

4   *king shall have . . . lower*: The phrasing here is ambiguous: it may mean that the male offender was punished by the king and the female by the bishop, though were this the case, one would expect a feminine article before "the lower" (*þa nyþeran* rather than *ðone nyþeran*). A second possibility may be that the division between upper and lower refers to social class, and the distinction between the two represents a division of jurisdiction between king and bishop (with thanks to Robert Fulk for this suggestion).

6.1   *dues to Rome*: "Peter's Pence," a penny tax paid each Feast of Saint Peter to support the Holy See in Rome.

6.2   *dues for the lighting of a church*: A tax paid between one and three times a year to fund the lighting of the local church or minster.

6.3   *plow dues*: A tax levied based on the number of plows owned by a householder; typically one penny per plow.

9   *Ordeals and oaths*: Two methods used by early English to ascertain guilt or confirm a court's finding. The former was a ritual involving a physical test, the result of which was understood to be divine sanction of the court's verdict (the common belief that ordeals were used simply to determine guilt is largely inaccurate). Oathtaking permitted the participants in either a criminal or a civil dispute to enlist witnesses (the number required was based on social status) to swear to their innocence or honesty.

The Compilation on Status

The text here is based on that in *Textus Roffensis,* though Wulfstan's original order has been preserved. Significant variants from Cambridge, Corpus Christi College MSS 190 and 201 have been identified in the notes.

On the Ranks of People and Law

1   *people and law were ordered by status*: The word *geþincðu* lacks a direct modern English equivalent, and it previously has been translated as "rank," "status," "dignity," and "honor."

thane: A landowner lower in status than a lord, with military obligations to his superior.

2   *five hides*: One hide is equivalent to the amount of land a single plowman could till in one day. During the Old English period, depending on region, one hide could equate to an area ranging from 60 to 180 acres, though it was standardized following the Conquest to roughly 120 acres. The five-hide unit seems to have been a common standard of measurement in Old English law and may have indicated the threshold above which a landowner owed military obligations to the king.

On Wergild

title   *On Wergild*: The earlier version of the *Compilation* titles this text *The Law of the Northern People*. A major component of Wulfstan's revision was to diminish the regional specificity of the individual texts, though this should not be taken as a sign that the wergild values listed here necessarily applied south of the Humber.

1   *a king's wergild*: Cambridge, Corpus Christi College MS 201 reads, "The wergild of a king of the northern people."

thrymsas: The term "thrymsa" was used both as a general term for coins and more specifically as the equivalent of one-third of a shilling, about four pennies. It is the latter meaning which most likely applies here.

3   *ealdorman*: A royal appointee charged with overseeing portions of the kingdom. Within the political hierarchy of early eleventh-century England, ealdormen were considered of higher rank than a reeve but below that of members of the royal family. The ealdorman's responsibilities included presiding over courts, levying taxes, and supplying soldiers at the king's request.

4   *reeve*: The agent of either the king or the local landlord responsible for overseeing his master's property.

6   This is the final clause of the text's "original" section, which likely dates from the ninth century but may have been com-

posed as early as the mid-seventh century. The clauses that follow (nos. 7–12) are all composed by Archbishop Wulfstan.

9   *two thousand thrymsas*: The wergild here equates to that of a thane in clause 5, thus bringing the clauses on social promotion in this text in line with those in *On the Ranks of People and Law* above, especially clause 2.

11   *gesith*: A rank roughly equivalent to a thane found in Northumbrian legal texts.

On the Law of the Mercians

title   *On the Law of the Mercians*: The title is omitted from *Textus Roffensis* (MS *H*).

On the Mercian Oath

title   *On the Mercian Oath*: The title is omitted from *Textus Roffensis*. This text and the one following it in the *Compilation*, *On Priests' Oaths*, were significantly reworked by the *Textus* scribe: the single clause of *On the Mercian Oath* and the first sentence of *On Priests' Oaths* were extracted from their context in the *Compilation*, inverted, and appended as the twelfth and thirteenth clauses of the Old English oath compilation *Swerian*. The treatment of these texts in *Textus Roffensis* led Thorpe to treat this text simply as part of *Swerian*, and its subsequent editors, Schmid and Liebermann, to combine *On the Mercian Oath* and the first sentence of *On Priests' Oaths* (Liebermann's *Hadbot*) into a single, biclausal text, an editorial creation known as *Að (Oath)*. However, the fact that Cambridge, Corpus Christi College MSS 190 and 201, as well as the twelfth-century compilers of *Quadripartitus* and the *Instituta Cnuti,* construe the texts in the manner that they are treated above—the first clause of Liebermann's *Að* as an individual text entitled *On the Mercian Oath,* and the second clause as the first sentence of a longer text entitled *On Priests' Oaths*—indicates that the arrangement in *Textus Roffensis* should be understood simply as a scribal variation.

On Priests' Oaths

title   *On Priests' Oaths*: Title omitted from *Textus Roffensis*.

1   *Sevenfold are the gifts of the Holy Spirit*: Isaiah 11:2–3 lists the seven
gifts of the Holy Spirit as wisdom *(sapientia)*, understanding
(intellectus), counsel *(consilium)*, fortitude *(fortitudo)*, knowledge
(scientia), godliness *(pietas)*, and fear of the Lord *(timor Domini)*.

    seven are the steps of ecclesiastical ranks: The seven grades in the ec-
clesiastical hierarchy are doorkeeper *(ostiarius)*, reader *(lector)*,
exorcist *(exorcista)*, acolyte *(acolitus)*, subdeacon *(subdiaconus)*,
deacon *(diaconus)*, and priest *(presbyter)*.

4   *full breach of the peace*: Equivalent to the "loss of life" specified in
the previous clause.

5   *and by doing spiritual penance*: The end of this clause is omitted
from *Textus Roffensis*, likely inadvertently, but present in Cambridge, Corpus Christi College MSS 190 and 201.

9   *a partial violation*: That is, if the victim is only injured but not
killed.

11   *Textus Roffensis* inverts clauses 9.1 and 10 and omits clause 11 entirely. This is in keeping with the scribe's treatment of *The
Compilation on Status* generally, which he disarticulates and re-
edits in order to reformulate the component texts for a twelfth-
century readership and fit them into the manuscript's organi-
zational program. The preterite verb tenses of this clause recall
those of *On the Ranks of People and Law*, thus providing a neat
bookend to the *Compilation*.

ON SANCTUARY

1   *the sanctuary of God*: *Godes grið* is a favorite phrase of Wulfstan's
and survives almost exclusively in his writings.

    the king's: The extent of the king's sanctuary is defined in the
short tenth-century legal tract *Pax,* which reads in its entirety,
"Thus far shall be the king's sanctuary from the city gate,
where he is sitting, in four directions, that is, three miles and
three furlongs and three lineal acres and nine feet and nine
handspans and nine barleycorns" *(Đus feor sceal beon þæs cinges*

405

grið fram his burhgeate, þær he is sittende, on feower healfe his, ðæt is III mila and III furlang and III æcera bræde and IX fota and IX scæftamunda and IX berecorna). The mention of the king sitting at the city gate refers to the practice of holding court at a town's gate. For an early reference to this practice, see Deuteronomy 21:18–21.

3–5   The nostalgic tone of clauses 3 through 5 recalls the similar evocation of an idealized past in the opening clauses of the first item in *The Compilation on Status, On the Ranks of People and Law,* a text likely composed at approximately the same time as this one. It also highlights the present-day deterioration in ecclesiastical status, which made necessary the injunctions that follow.

7   This is the only surviving clause in Old English law to echo the first clause of Æthelbert's legislation, the earliest royal law code, though it is significant that Wulfstan assigns compensation to the archbishop, rather than to a bishop, as in the earlier text. Moreover, Æthelbert's laws do not mention the king, implying that one purpose of this clause may be to promote the church at the expense of the secular aristocracy.

13.1   This is the only instance of the loss of a hand serving as a penalty for assault.

16   *seeks sanctuary*: This clause employs *friðstol* as a general term for "sanctuary," although the word originated as the name for a specific "peace seat" for sanctuary seekers to use when claiming refuge. Such seats were present in the churches at York, Southwell, Hexham, and Beverly, the latter two of which still survive. Notably, York and Beverly are two of the three foundations whose privileges are set forth in the first clause of *Northumbrian Church Sanctuary.*

     punishment by hanging in bonds: The term used here, *hengenwitnung,* is a *hapax legomenon* often translated as "imprisonment"; however, the component parts (*hengen,* "hanging," and *witnung,* "torture" or "punishment") suggest a more severe sentence.

18   This clause mitigates the more severe punishment of execution decreed in *6 Æthelstan* 12.2 for those guilty of second offenses.

19   *security and ecclesiastical privileges*: Both *hælnesgrið* and *hadgrið* are
      hapax legomena.

23   *Who is as our Lord . . . of his people*: Psalms 112:5, 7–8.

23.1 *fear of God and heed wisdom*: See Proverbs 1:7.

29   *And it is also a great necessity . . . given to him*: A modified version of
      Matthew 7:12.

Northumbrian Church Sanctuary

Due to damage to the manuscript, this text is based on that found in Liebermann, *Die Gesetze der Angelsachsen*. Words that have been restored
based on Liebermann's notes are indicated below.

1   *Saint Peter's, Saint Wilfrid's, and within the walls of Saint John's*: The
      three churches specified are those at York, Ripon, and Beverly.
      Saint John's . . . compensated: "John's," "hundred," and "cannot be
      compensated" are all reconstructed.

2   "In scale" is reconstructed.

3   "And a priest" is reconstructed.

The Oath of the King

1   *which Archbishop Dunstan presented to our lord at Kingston*: Over
      the course of his archiepiscopate (959–978), Dunstan presided
      at four coronations — those of Edgar (an initial crowning in 960
      and a more elaborate ritual in 973), Edward (975), and Æthelred
      (978). As Edgar's 973 coronation took place at Bath, the cer-
      emony referred to must have been one of the others, all of
      which took place at Kingston-on-Thames, the traditional site
      of royal coronations since the reign of Æthelstan. The text does
      not indicate which ceremony it refers to, yet the reference to
      "our lord" rather than a named predecessor makes Æthelred's
      coronation the most likely.
      placed upon Christ's altar: The placing of official documents on
      the church altar was a common means of signifying the sacred-
      ness or official nature of their contents.
      In the name of the Holy Trinity: The king's threefold promise

closely follows that found in contemporary Latin texts concerning the ceremony for the coronation of a king, such as the *Benedictional of Robert*, Byrhtferth's *Vita Oswaldi,* and the so-called *First English Ordo.*

3   *condemn no one unjustly*: Old English *fordeme* means only "condemn," yet the modifier "unjustly" must be added for the injunction to make sense in context.

THE INSTITUTES OF POLITY (1)

2   *And it is fitting . . . God's favor*: This passage appears only in London, British Library, Cotton Nero A.i.

3   *There are eight columns . . . friend and stranger*: The eight columns are drawn from the tenth chapter of Sedulius Scottus's *Book on Christian Rulers*. The seven qualities appropriate for a righteous king are taken from the *Collectio canonum Hibernensis* 25.15.

4   *Each throne that stands . . . Amen*: This passage, the most famous in *Polity*, draws on a venerable, if only erratically attested, trope in early English political thought. The earliest extant division of society into three orders occurs in the Old English translation of Boethius's *Consolation of Philosophy*, attributed to King Alfred. The threefold division next appears in the work of Ælfric, although variations in his terminology suggest that he (and perhaps Alfred also) was drawing on a now-lost Latin source. Ælfric incorporates variations on the three-orders trope into a codicil to his commentary on *Maccabees*, a Latin letter to Wulfstan composed sometime between 1003 and 1005, and his *Book on the Old and New Testament* (*Libellus de Veteri Testamento et Novo*, also known as the *Letter to Sigeweard*). Wulfstan's discussion of the three orders in *Polity* most likely draws upon the last of these, the relevant text of which reads, "The throne stands on these three pillars: *those who labor, those who fight, those who pray*" (*Se cinestol stynt on þisum þrim stelum: laboratores, bellatores, oratores*). It is noteworthy, though, that Wulfstan alters the order of the three estates as listed by Ælfric, giving priority to "those who pray" rather than "those who labor."

5   *Paul...blameless*: 1 Timothy 3:2.

6   *by calling out*: Compare Isaiah 58:1.

7   *He that heareth*: See Luke 10:16.

         Whatsoever thou shalt bind: Matthew 16:19.

         Whatever you have blessed: An abbreviation of Numbers 24:9. See also *On the Remedy of Souls* 4.

         He would not ... from him: See Psalms 108:18.

13   *Women Monastics*: Old English *mynecenan,* a specific category of female monastics that emerged as part of the tenth-century Monastic Reform.

15   *remains chaste*: Literally, "retains his boyhood."

         By the Apostle's consent: See 1 Corinthians 7:8–9.

16   *example of Anna*: Wulfstan here refers to Anna the Prophetess (not to be confused with Anne, mother of Mary), a widow at the temple in Jerusalem granted a vision of Christ. See Luke 2:36–37.

18   *For anyone becomes ... goods of the Church*: Taken from Atto of Vercelli, *De pressuris ecclesiasticis* 138.14.

         Whoever plunders ... all said: Amen: This is presumably a quotation from the writings of Pope Gregory I (pope from 590 to 604), but the source for the quotation is unknown. The hortatory *Uton* ("Let us...") suggests oral presentation in the form of a homily.

THE INSTITUTES OF POLITY (2)

The text here is based on Oxford, Bodleian Library Junius 121. The Junius scribe has altered the chapter order slightly; this edition follows Jost, *Die "Institutes of Polity, Civil and Ecclesiastical,"* in restoring the order found in the earlier manuscripts. For notes on passages also found in *1 Polity*, see above.

1   *Concerning the Heavenly King*: Wulfstan adds this new introductory chapter to *2 Polity* in keeping with the emphasis in his later works on the subordination of royal power to divine authority. The addition of this chapter may have been inspired by

Æthelred's failures in the final years of his reign or as a way to symbolically limit the authority of the new king, Cnut.

7   *that silence*: Compare Isaiah 58:1.

     Thus sayeth the Lord . . . thy hand: An adaptation of Ezekiel 3:18.

8   *He that heareth . . . despiseth me*: Luke 10:16.

9   *Whatsoever they shall say . . . ye not*: Matthew 23:3.

10   *Likewise, Concerning Bishops*: This section and the one following are based on the short Latin text *De medicamento animarum (On the Remedy of Souls)*, edited and translated elsewhere in this volume.

11   *He that heareth*: Luke 10:16.

     Whatsoever thou shalt bind: Matthew 16:19.

     Whose sins. . .them, etc.: John 20:23.

     he would not . . . far from him: Psalms 108:18.

12   *Furthermore*: In the manuscript, this chapter is preceded by the text *On Episcopal Duties*, edited and translated elsewhere in this volume.

13   *praiseworthy ways*: See 1 Timothy 3:2.

14   *Concerning Nobles*: In the manuscript, this chapter is preceded by the text *Instructions for Bishops*, edited and translated elsewhere in this volume.

15   *Edgar died*: The sudden death of King Edgar (r. 959–975) and the subsequent conflict over the succession initiated a crisis in ecclesiastical authority that still resonated with Wulfstan more than twenty-five years later. The years between 975 and 978 witnessed a series of legal challenges to ecclesiastical power and violent attacks on monastic institutions against which the underage King Edward (later referred to as "the Martyr" following his assassination, possibly at the instigation of his stepmother, Queen Ælfthryth) could offer no protection. For Wulfstan and his contemporaries, Edgar's death signaled the end of the golden age of Monastic Reform and the beginning of a new age of national and ecclesiastical instability.

16   *which they must protect if they can*: Compare Ezekiel 34:10.

     how can a blind man lead another: Compare Matthew 15:14 and Luke 6:39.

17   *who eat the sins of the people*: Compare Hosea 4:8 and Ezekiel 44:29.

           gluttonous ravens: Compare Matthew 24:28.

19   *Cry, cease not . . . trumpet*: Isaiah 58.1.

           Yet if you do not do that . . . that they required: Compare Ezekiel 33:8.

           If you proclaim righteousness . . . soul nonetheless: Compare Ezekiel 33:9.

20   *and by right . . . status*: The text in Junius 121 is incomplete here. The passage in Cambridge, Corpus Christi College MS 201 is here substituted.

21   *Constantine*: Emperor of Rome from 306 to 337 CE.

           synod in the city of Nicea: The First Council of Nicea took place in 325 CE and resulted in the promulgation of the Nicene Creed.

           the second was later . . . many bishops together: Wulfstan here lists the three Church synods that followed Nicea: Constantinople (381 CE), Ephesus (431 CE), and Chalcedon (451 CE).

28   *Concerning the Laity*: In the manuscript, this chapter is preceded by *The Canons of Edgar* (titled in this manuscript *Synodal Decrees*), edited and translated elsewhere in this volume.

On Episcopal Duties

title   *Furthermore*: This is the only title given to the text in the manuscript, where it follows the sixth chapter of *2 Polity* ("Likewise, Concerning Bishops"). The title *Episcopus (On Episcopal Duties)* was given to it by Liebermann.

4   *resolve disputes*: The bishop's role in secular dispute resolution had been established in English law at least as early as *2–3 Edgar*.

7   *sow too much of his falseness*: See Matthew 13:39.

8   *God who despises all injustice*: See Deuteronomy 25:16.

9   *bishops must pronounce*: This clause marks one of the most significant points of conflict between Wulfstan and Ælfric, who strongly opposed cooperation between ecclesiastics and secular judges.

13   *slaves*: Old English *nidþeowum,* literally "slaves by compulsion,"

that is, those who have entered slavery because of poverty or starvation.

On the Remedy of Souls

1   *to the care of churches and*: This interlinear insertion was made to the manuscript in Wulfstan's handwriting.

2   *Isidore*: Bishop Isidore of Seville (ca. 560–636), author of the *Etymologiae* and the *Sententiae*. Wulfstan's source for this quotation was likely not the work of Isidore himself but of an Irish collection of passages from continental canon law tracts, the *Collectio canonum Hibernensis*. The passage in question occurs at 21.26.

    Uzza: The story of Uzza occurs in 1 Chronicles 13:7–14.

    Saul: The account of Saul performing a sacrifice in place of a properly designated priest occurs in 1 Samuel 13:9–14.

    But thy kingdom shall not continue: 1 Samuel 13:14.

    Ozias: The story of King Ozias's leprosy occurs in 2 Chronicles 26:16–21.

3   *Charge the rich . . . high-minded*: 1 Timothy 6:17.

    Alexander: Bishop Alexander of Jerusalem (d. 251). Wulfstan takes this passage from the *Collectio canonum Hibernensis* (21.28), where Alexander's interlocutor is identified as "Demetrius, king of the Greeks."

4   *No man . . . businesses*: 2 Timothy 2:4.

    He that heareth you . . . despiseth me: Luke 10:16.

    Whatsoever thou shalt bind upon earth: Matthew 16:19.

    he that blesseth thee shall also be blessed: An adaptation of Numbers 24:9.

    would not have blessing . . . from him: See Psalms 108:18.

Instructions for Bishops

1   The opening clause presents an order of prayer similar to that appointed for the first day of an episcopal synod in the tenth-century *Pontificale Romano-Germanicum*.

2   Like the order of prayer in the first clause, the benediction also occurs elsewhere—most notably in London, British Library,

Cotton MS Claudius A.iii, a pontifical likely used by Wulfstan early in his career—suggesting that it was part of an established ritual for episcopal synods.

5   *one heart and one soul*: Acts 4:32.

An Admonition to Bishops

1   *silent about what is right*: The text up to this point is written in Wulfstan's own handwriting.

mumble . . . diminishes: A favorite phrase of Wulfstan's, probably influenced by Isaiah 58:1.

too accommodating and too eager for praise: Wulfstan's criticism of those who are "too accommodating and too eager for praise" *(to liðie and to lofgeorne)* recalls the final line of *Beowulf*, in which the hero is described—perhaps ambivalently?—as "most beloved by men and most eager for glory" *(leodum liðost ond lofgeornost*, line 3182). Wulfstan's use of the first-person plural here is in keeping with his practice elsewhere of directing his admonitions at himself as well as his colleagues, as he does at the end of *Institutes of Polity (2)* section 9.

intoxicate with wisdom: Possibly an allusion to *Psalms* 22:5: "and my chalice which inebriateth me, how goodly is it!" *(et calix meus inebrians quam praeclarus est)*.

4   *like a child . . . behavior*: The final eight words (in the Old English, the last six) are in Wulfstan's handwriting.

The Canons of Edgar

title   *Synodal Decrees*: The title text of the version in Cambridge, Corpus Christi College MS 201 reads, "Here now are the practices fitting for those in orders according to the decrees of Edgar," hence the text's attribution to King Edgar by its nineteenth-century editors. It is unclear whether Wulfstan intended *Canons* to be an exercise in historical re-creation along the lines of *The Laws of Edward and Guthrum*, but it may be significant that the reference to Edgar disappears in what is likely the text's later versions.

1   *faithful and true*: Wulfstan's phrasing here also recalls the pledge

of loyalty preserved as the first item in the Old English oath compilation, *Swerian*: "By the Lord, before whom this relic is holy, I will be faithful and true to N, and love all that he loves and despise all that he despises, according to the law of God and the custom of the world" *(On ðone Drihten, þe ðes haligdom is fore halig, ic wille beon N hold and getriwe and eal lufian ðæt he lufað and eal ascunian ðæt he ascunað, æfter Godes rihte and æfter worold-gerysnum)*.

3–4 These clauses are supplied from Cambridge, Corpus Christi College MS 201.

6 *parish*: Old English *scriftscire*, a term particular to Wulfstan, is translated here as "parish," but it might be more literally rendered as "confessional district," indicating the administrative function of penance in late Anglo-Saxon pastoral practice.

8 *lawful wife*: A marginal note adds "as long as his life lasts."

16 *drawn through the earth*: The practice referred to here seems to be one whereby a sick child is drawn through a pit, hole, or trench in order to transfer his or her illness to the earth.

21 This clause is supplied from Cambridge, Corpus Christi College MS 201.

33 The alb and the amice are both vestments worn by the priest during the Mass, while the corporal is the small cloth upon which the chalice and the host rest on the altar.

37 *three times*: The limit of three Masses likely stems from the Council of Trebur, which barred priests from celebrating Mass more than three times per day on a single altar. In contrast, Wulfstan's contemporary Ælfric restricts priests to celebrating Mass only once per day.

39 *just as the Jews did*: The allusion is to the drink supposedly offered to Jesus on the cross when he complained of thirst in Matthew 27:34.

41 *cast of metal*: A marginal note in the manuscript specifies gold, silver, or tin.

54 *Rogation*: The three days prior to the Feast of the Ascension, also referred to as *gangdagas* (walking days) in Old English because of the penitential procession that formed part of the days' rituals.

midsummer: Feast of Saint John the Baptist, June 24.

plow dues: A tax levied based on the number of plows owned by a householder; typically one penny per plow.

tithe of the young animals: The offering to the Church of one out of every ten animals born over the previous year.

Pentecost: The seventh Sunday after Easter.

dues owed to Rome: "Peter's Pence," a penny tax paid each Feast of Saint Peter to support the Holy See in Rome.

Feast of Saint Peter: June 29.

tithe on the fruits of the earth: Not technically a tithe, but the offering of the first fruits of the season to one's church to be eaten by its clergy.

Feast of Saint Martin: November 11.

dues for the lighting of a church: A tax paid between one and three times a year to fund the lighting of the local church or minster.

Candlemas: February 2, also referred to as the Feast of the Purification of the Virgin.

All Saints: November 1.

60   There appears to have been some reordering of clauses here. The clause that follows this one in Cambridge, Corpus Christi College MS 201 (numbered 61 by modern editors) here occurs instead as canon 68a.

64   *initial oath*: The meaning of this canon is unclear, though it may be ruling that priests cannot be compelled to mount a defense against an accusation brought by a thane in a secular court unless that accusation has been leveled through a formal oath-taking ceremony.

65   *The canon says*: This penance also occurs in the *Old English Penitential* (also known as the *Penitential of Pseudo-Ecgbert*) at 4.27.

68b–i   These clauses, which appear in Oxford, Bodleian Junius 121 but not in Cambridge, Corpus Christi College MS 201, are typically identified with a number-letter designation in order to preserve the correspondence between clauses of each text. They are repeated almost exactly at *1 Cnut* 5–5.2.

68c   *Dunstan*: Dunstan served as archbishop of Canterbury from 960 to 978.

68h   *ordeal of the consecrated bread*: This ritual requires the proband to swallow a portion of the Eucharist without choking. This form of ordeal seems to have been reserved for priests and may have been designed to substitute for more physically painful ordeals, such as those of the hot iron or boiling water.

69   Cambridge, Corpus Christi College MS 201 adds one more clause after this one, reading, "And we instruct that every priest is to remember to announce, when he fetches the chrism, what he has done in his prayers for the king and the bishop" *(And we lærað þæt ælc preost wite to cyðanne, þonne he crisman fecce, hwæt he on gebedum for cyngc and biscop gedon hæbbe)*. Given the benedictional language of the previous clause, however, it is most likely misplaced.

5 Æthelred

4.1   *female monastics*: Old English *mynecena,* a special category of female monastic established during the Monastic Reform of the tenth century.

11.1   *plow dues*: On the dues listed in this clause, see the notes to *The Laws of Edward and Guthrum* 6.1–6.3 and *Canons* 54.

12   *dues for the souls of the dead*: A tax to the Church to be paid following an individual's death but before burial.

14.1   *Feasts of Philip and James*: The former is May 3, the latter April 30, though now more frequently celebrated on July 25.

16   *Feast of Saint Edward*: October 13.

           kalends: The first day of the month. In this case, "fifteen days before the kalends of April" refers to March 18.

18   *Ember Days:* Periods of fasting and prayer that take place during four weeks of the year (once during Lent and during the weeks of Pentecost, the Festival of the Exaltation of the Cross, and Saint Lucy's Day) and consisting of the Wednesday, Friday, and Saturday.

           Septuagesima: The ninth Sunday before Easter.

28   *all his property*: Cambridge, Corpus Christi College MS 201 replaces this phrase with "or his wergild."

30   *threefold ordeal*: That is, carrying a three-pound ball of hot iron

for a prescribed distance (often nine feet) rather than the typical one-pound ball. Cambridge, Corpus Christi College MS 201 requires the conspirator to exonerate himself only by "the most serious oath decreed by the council."

32.1   *in the west*: It is unknown what Wulfstan is referring to here and in his reference to "the north" in 32.4.

32.4   *on the same day*: That is, on the day of the crime.

6 ÆTHELRED

11   *his fourth cousin or closer*: This phrase has sometimes been translated as "within the fourth knee," but given the similar Indo-European roots for "kinship" and "knee" (*genə- and *genu-ᶦ, respectively), they may be more accurately translated as "within the fourth degree of kinship" (with thanks to Robert Fulk for pointing this out). In other words, the text rules that a man may not marry anyone to whom he is related as a fourth cousin or closer.

16   *God's dues*: On the dues discussed in this text, see the notes to *The Laws of Edward and Guthrum* 6.1–6.3, *Canons* 54, and 5 *Æthelred* 12.

18   *Feast of Saint Peter*: June 29.

18.1   *Saint Martin*: November 11.

22.3   *Feasts of Philip and James*: The former is May 3, the latter April 30, though now more frequently celebrated on July 25. Compare the similar clause at 5 *Æthelred* 14.1.

23   *Ember Fasts*: See note to 5 *Æthelred* 18.

25   *Epiphany*: Although Epiphany now occupies only one day, January 6, prior to 1955 it was an eight-day festival beginning on January 19.

51   *healsfang*: Literally, "neck seizing," though generally interpreted as a "neck fine," that is, a penalty paid in lieu of execution.

7 ÆTHELRED

1.3   *those under him:* The Old English term here is *hyremann*, which literally translates to "one who hears" or "one who obeys." Interestingly, the (presumably) Norman translator of *7 Æthelred* into Latin keeps this word and, below, *witam* ("penalty," clause 7) in Old English, though with Latin declensions.

2.1   *with bare feet*: Processions of this sort were particularly associated with Rogation days, called *gangdagas* (walking days) in Old English.

2.2   This clause has no equivalent in *7a Æthelred*.

2.3   *Feast of Saint Michael*: September 29.

2.4   *one hundred twenty shillings*: This amount is likely an error, as analogous passages elsewhere set the penalty for breaking the fast at only thirty shillings.

2.5   *tithingman*: The head of a tithing, an administrative unit consisting of one tenth of a hundred.

3.1   *Lord, how they are multiplied*: Psalms 3:2.

    Collect: A prayer, often used at the beginning of a service, to call the congregants together.

7A ÆTHELRED

title   *This was decreed . . . land*: The title likely refers to the invasion of the Viking "great army" under the leadership of Thurkil the Tall in 1009, the year in which the Latin version of *7 Æthelred* was composed.

1   *Feast of Saint Michael*: September 29.

3   *thirty shillings*: See the note to *7 Æthelred* 2.4 above.

6.3   *Lord, how they are multiplied*: Psalms 3:2.

8 ÆTHELRED

5.1   *five pounds under English law:* The valuation of the Anglo-Saxon pound was different than the twenty shillings it would later become. In this context, a pound is equivalent to the value of one pound weight of silver.

7   *King Edgar*: See the penalties established in *2 Edgar* 3.1. These are also reiterated with slight modifications in the following clause.

9–13   On the dues listed in these clauses, see the notes to *The Laws of Edward and Guthrum* 6.1–6.3, *Canons* 54, and *5 Æthelred* 12.

17   *suffer the full civil penalty*: Wulfstan does not specify who would suffer in this instance, the market organizer or those participating in it.

19   *simple accusation*: That is, an accusation against which the accused requires only the oath of a single supporting witness.
     on his own through the sacrament: In effect, the celebration of the Mass here substitutes for the oath of exculpatory witness.

19.1   *threefold accusation*: That is, an accusation against which the accused requires the oaths of three supporting witnesses.

22   *ordeal of consecrated bread*: An ordeal in which the accused was required to swallow a portion of bread, which if it caught in his throat was taken as a sign of guilt.

37   *after Edgar's lifetime*: Wulfstan here alludes to the so-called Anti-Monastic Reaction, a period following the sudden death of King Edgar in 975 when the succession dispute between his sons Edward and Æthelred resulted in weakened protections for the Church and the withdrawal of many of the privileges religious foundations had accrued over the previous half century.

43   *Æthelstan and Edmund and Edgar, the most recent*: Wulfstan here lists the three kings most associated with the tenth-century Reform movement: Æthelstan (r. 924–939), Edmund (r. 939–946), and Edgar (r. 959–975). Wulfstan has limited his list only to those kings in Æthelred's direct patrilineal line (Edgar was his father, and Edmund his grandfather). Notably omitted from this list are Eadred (r. 946–955), Eadwig (r. 955–959), and Edward the Martyr (r. 975–978), none of whose reigns were characterized by the same degree of support for Church prerogatives.

9 ÆTHELRED

Due to damage to the manuscript, this text is based on that found in Liebermann, *Die Gesetze der Angelsachsen*.

Pr   *Woodstock*: Woodstock, Oxfordshire, had been the site of an earlier meeting of the royal council in approximately 997, at which
the legislation *1 Æthelred* was issued. The meeting at which this
text was compiled likely took place between 1008 and 1016.

10 ÆTHELRED

Due to damage to the manuscript, this text is based on that found in Liebermann, *Die Gesetze der Angelsachsen*.

Pr.3   *Enham*: The site of the 1008 meeting at which *5 Æthelred* and *6
Æthelred* were promulgated.

CNUT'S OXFORD LEGISLATION OF 1018

Pr   *the council*: The opening clauses of this text (Pr to 1.3) place a
greater emphasis on the rights, privileges, and prerogatives of
the royal council than does the other legislation associated
with Wulfstan. It is unclear whether this reflects the priorities
of the Oxford meeting or whether it is instead indicative of the
archbishop's own interests.

13   *God's dues*: On the dues listed in here, see the notes to *The Laws
of Edward and Guthrum* 6.1–6.3, *Canons* 54, and *5 Æthelred* 12.

14.3   *Feasts of Philip and James*: The former is May 3, the latter April 30,
though now more frequently celebrated on July 25.

14.5   *Ember Fasts*: See note to *5 Æthelred* 18.

14.6   *Feast of Saint Edward*: October 13.

15   *Epiphany*: Although Epiphany now occupies only one day, January 6, prior to 1955 it was an eight-day festival beginning on
January 19.

26.3   *the hundred*: An administrative unit that served a function similar to that of the modern county.

CNUT'S PROCLAMATION OF 1020

1   *subordinate bishops*: Old English *leodbiscopas,* a blanket term for all
the categories of episcopal rank lower than an archbishop.
Earl Thurkil: Leader of a band of Jómsvíkings, Thurkil the Tall

(d. after 1023) was among Cnut's foremost supporters, though his wavering loyalty and the violence of his followers (who, among other depredations, murdered Archbishop Ælfheah of Canterbury in 1012) made him an inconstant ally at best.

Lyfing: Archbishop of Canterbury from 1018 until his death on June 12, 1020. The letters referred to, addressed to Cnut by Pope Benedict VIII and carried back from Rome by Archbishop Lyfing in 1018, have not survived.

2   *a threat to you*: It is unclear what the proclamation refers to here.

to Denmark: Cnut's trip to Denmark is recorded in the 1019 and 1020 entries in the *Anglo-Saxon Chronicle*.

6   *Oxford*: This ceremony is recorded in the entry for 1018 in the *Anglo-Saxon Chronicle*.

enchantresses: The word used here is *wælcyrian*, the Old English term for Valkyries. It is a feature of Wulfstan's prose that he would choose a word with pagan associations (especially for those living in the northern Danelaw) and repurpose it as the more general "enchantress" or "sorceress."

I CNUT

Pr   *the holy Christmas season*: Although meetings of the royal council often occurred at Christmas, the particular assembly at which this code was issued has not been identified.

1   *love King Cnut*: The naming of Cnut here contrasts with the more general phrasing of the loyalty clauses found in Wulfstan's earlier legislation for Æthelred.

3.2   *five pounds*: The higher amount granted to the king in this clause contrasts with the equivalent clause in *On Sanctuary,* which specifies that "in the laws of the Kentish people, the king and archbishop are owed an equal and likewise costly penalty for the violation of their protection" (clause 6).

8   *God's dues*: On the dues listed in the following clauses, see the notes to *The Laws of Edward and Guthrum* 6.1–6.3, *Canons* 54, and *5 Æthelred* 12.

9   *Feast of Saint Peter*: June 29.

NOTES TO THE TRANSLATIONS

10	*Feast of Martin*: November 11.
11.2	*old minster*: That is, the principal church in a region to which the smaller (and newer) parish churches are subordinate.
12	*Feast of the Purification of Saint Mary*: February 2. The feast is sometimes also referred to as Candlemas; compare *Canons* 54.
16	*Ember Fast*: See note to 5 *Æthelred* 18.
	Feasts of Philip and James: May 3 and April 30 (now more frequently celebrated on July 25), respectively.
16.1	*Epiphany*: An eight-day festival beginning on January 19.
17.1	*Feast of Saint Edward*: October 13.
	nineteenth day of March: The scribe errs here, writing the eighteenth of March rather than the nineteenth.
22.6	*at confirmation*: Literally, "at the bishop's hand."

2 Cnut

2	*Forgive us our debts . . . debtors*: Matthew 6:12.
8.1	*the hands*: The Old English *þæra handa* is ambiguous as to number. Analogous Old English texts use the plural, though Latin versions sometimes use singular and others plural.
8.2	*threefold oath of exculpation*: That is, a sworn declaration of innocence supported by the oaths of thirty-six witnesses, as a single oath of exculpation required the support of twelve witnesses.
20	*surety*: In other words, each free person is to have someone to guarantee that they will fulfill their obligations to the court and the community.
23	*vouch to warranty*: That is, swearing to the legal possession of goods.
23.1	*saw with their eyes and heard with their ears*: As he did in *The Canons of Edgar* 1, Wulfstan here again echoes the phrasing of the Old English oath formulary *Swerian*: "In the name of almighty God, so I stand here for N as a true witness, unbidden and unbought, to what I saw with my eyes and heard with my ears, which I testify on his behalf" (*On ælmightiges Godes naman, swa ic her N on soðre gewitnesse stande, unabeden and ungeboht, to swa ic*

mid minum egum oferseah and minum earum oferhyrde ðaet ðaet ic him mid sæcge).

30.1   *Winchester*: An earlier version of this clause appears in *1 Æthel-red* 1.2, with Bromdun cited as the relevant assembly rather than Winchester. The meeting referred to here is presumably the one at which *1 Cnut* and *2 Cnut* were issued. See *1 Cnut* Pr.

35   *suspended in chains*: The Old English word *hengen* was taken by Ælfric to refer to imprisonment, but as used elsewhere it refers to the subject hanging in bonds or chains.

37   *healsfang*: See the note to *6 Æthelred* 51.

71   *tribute*: The heriot, that is, the military obligations, material, or financial support owed to the king.

    mancuses: A mancus is a gold coin worth roughly the equivalent of thirty pence.

73   *morning gift*: A gift, often in the form of money or land, from a newly married husband to his wife, supposedly given the morning after their first night together. The gift was considered the woman's property and, in theory at least, was kept separate from the other aspects of the couple's finances overseen by the husband.

73.3   *And a widow is not to be consecrated as a nun too quickly*: The implication here seems to be that a widow's family may not compel her to take vows in order to prevent a second marriage.

79   In London, British Library, Harley MS 55, and Cambridge, Corpus Christi College MS 383, this clause reads, "And the person who, with the knowledge of the shire, has acted in defense of the land, either in the navy or army, shall hold his property uncontested during his lifetime and afterwards be entitled to give or grant it to whomever he prefers" (*And se ðe land gewerod hæbbe on scypfyrde and on landfyrde, habbe he unbesaken on dæge and æfter dæge to syllanne and to gyfane ðam ðe him leofost sy*).

81   *negotiated contract*: Old English *drincelean* literally refers to the drink that seals a negotiation, signaling the agreement of all parties and the legitimacy of the transaction.

The Northumbrian Priests' Law

1   *one heart and one soul*: Acts 4:32.

2.2   *oras*: The ora was a unit of coinage equal to sixteen pence or one-fifteenth of a pound.

2.3   *twelve bondsmen*: This passage provides the only surviving attestation of the Old Norse–derived word *festermen* in Old English legislation. The use of such bondsmen is attested by a record in the York Gospels of the *festermen* who testified on behalf of an otherwise unidentified priest named Ælfric.

24   The penalties prescribed here are considerably less than those found in texts more closely associated with Wulfstan.

35   This clause's condemnation of a priest abandoning his wife marks a significant departure from Wulfstan's thought. For Wulfstan, all clerical marriage was anathema, regardless of circumstance.

40   *conceals fraud while conducting an ordeal*: Literally, "If a priest deceives while binding," presumably a reference to the bandaging of a proband's burn or wound (so that the healing process may be inspected several days later) in the course of an ordeal.

50   *commoner*: The term used here is *færbena,* a word of uncertain meaning. The similar penalty for wrongdoing indicates that the *færbena* is equal in status to the *cyrlisc man* (commoner) and *ceorl* (peasant) of clauses 53 and 60 and the *tunes man* (townsman) of clause 59; however, the precise nature of his obligations to his lord remains unclear.

57.1   *dues to Rome*: Compare *The Laws of Edward and Guthrum* 6.1 and *Canons* 54. Saint Peter's Day is June 29.

57.2   *wapentake*: A division of land used in northern England that roughly equates to the hundreds of southern England.

61.1   *spiritually related to him*: Old English *godsibbe,* that is, his godparent or godchild.

67.1   *legal fines*: Literally, "law business," a compound referring to the payment of a fine by an outlaw to regain his legal status.

        negotiated contracts: See note to *2 Cnut* 81 above.

        Blessed . . . and forever: Psalms 112:2.

THE OBLIGATIONS OF INDIVIDUALS *AND* ON REEVES

The Obligations of Individuals

2 *ride and act as his lord's messenger*: Literally, "provide carrying service." There is disagreement over the meaning of this term, with some scholars arguing that it refers to the tenant's duty to provide horses for plowing. However, the likelihood that Old English *averian* is to be derived from Latin *averagium* (service by horse to one's lord) as well as its possible relationship to Old English *aferian* (to move or take), makes the translation used here more plausible.

3 *cottager's duty*: That is, a tenant of peasant status whose rental consisted of a house but no farmland.

3.1 This clause does not appear in the Old English. The text is supplied from the version in *Quadripartitus*.

3.4 *hearth penny*: A tax levied according to the number of hearths per household.

  Feast of Saint Martin: November 11.

4 *tenant farmer's duties*: That is, a tenant of peasant status whose rental included both homestead and farmland.

  Candlemas: February 2, also referred to as the Feast of the Purification of the Virgin.

4.1 *Feast of Saint Michael*: September 29.

  sesters: A sester is a dry measure of grain equivalent to approximately twelve bushels, or a liquid measure of honey or wine of between twenty-four and thirty-two ounces.

4.2 *plow dues*: A tax levied based on the number of plows owned by a householder; typically one penny per plow.

10 *plowman*: Literally, "follower of the plow."

20 *held responsible . . . land*: Though necessary grammatically, these words are omitted from the Old English. The text has been supplied from the post-Conquest Latin compilation *Quadripartitus*.

21.1 *practice is here*: The estate for which this text was drawn up has not been identified.

On Reeves

1   *reeve*: The agent of either the king or the local landlord responsible for overseeing his master's property.

2   *shire*: A term for a county or other administrative subunits of land.

3.1   *that which belongs in the cow stalls*: That is, grains meant for one purpose will be inadvertently used for another. In a broader sense, without proper care, the resources of the estate will be wasted.

4   *rennet*: Literally, "cheese medicine," the enzymes used to curdle milk into cheese.

11   *a kiln on the threshing floor and an oven and an oast*: The kiln and the oven were used to dry the harvest for preservation. An oast was a kiln specially designed for drying hops.

15.1   *spinning tools*: The implements listed here have occasioned considerable critical head-scratching. Though some are recognizable tools still in use, others remain obscure. The confusion is exacerbated by the fact that many of the terms in this list occur nowhere else in Old English.

1 ÆTHELSTAN

Pr   *Archbishop Wulfhelm*: Wulfhelm served as archbishop of Canterbury from approximately 926 until his death in 941. His prominent role as one of Æthelstan's advisors and the likelihood that he composed the laws issued in the latter's name make him perhaps Wulfstan's most explicit precursor.

2   *tithes and sacrifices I offer to you*: A reworking of Genesis 28:22.

        do not hesitate to offer tithes and first fruits unto the Lord: A reworking of Exodus 22:29 and Leviticus 27:30. The Latin version of the text quotes Matthew 25:29. The fact that this particular rephrasing of Exodus occurs several times in the collection of canon law excerpts compiled by Wulfstan, as well as the archbishop's tendency to cite Exodus's prescriptions on tithes, makes it likely that he was responsible for the substitution.

4   *dues for the souls of the dead . . . plow dues*: See notes to *The Laws of Edward and Guthrum* 6.3 and *5 Æthelred* 12. These prescriptions do not occur in the Latin versions of *1 Æthelstan*. Both the phrasing and the frequency with which such prescriptions occur in texts associated with Wulfstan make it likely that this passage is a later interpolation by him.

       Whoever refuses to do this . . . proper duties: Likely a Wulfstanian interpolation.

1 Edmund

Pr   *Archbishop Oda and Archbishop Wulfstan*: Oda served as archbishop of Canterbury from 941 to 958. Wulfstan (not to be confused with the subject of this volume) served as archbishop of York from 931 to 956.

       consider what would be of benefit: The version of the text in Cotton Nero A.i adds the adverb *georne* (zealously) following *smeagende* (considering), a stylistic feature common to Wulfstan's writing.

2   *dues to Rome and plow dues*: See notes to *The Laws of Edward and Guthrum* 6.1 and 6.3. These two forms of ecclesiastical dues are omitted from the versions of *1 Edmund* preserved in Cambridge, Corpus Christi College MS 383, *Textus Roffensis,* and *Quadripartitus.* As with similar passages in *1 Æthelstan,* it is likely these are an interpolation by Wulfstan.

4   *hearth penny*: See note to *The Obligations of Individuals* 3.4.

6   *embark . . . all the more zealously*: Omitted from Cambridge, Corpus Christi College MS 383, *Textus Roffensis,* and *Quadripartitus.* Likely an interpolation by Wulfstan.

2 Edgar *AND* 3 Edgar

2 Edgar

1.1   *old minster*: That is, the traditional mother church at the center of a community rather than the newer parish or satellite churches founded afterward.

2.3   *Plow dues . . . Easter*: This clause was likely added by Wulfstan. For the dues in this and the following clauses, see the notes to *The Laws of Edward and Guthrum* 6.3, *Canons* 54, *5 Æthelred* 12, and *The Obligations of Individuals* 3.4.

4   *Feast of Saint Peter*: June 29.

4.1   *payment to Rome*: This is the earliest mention in English law of what would later come to be known as "Peter's Pence," that is, a tax specifically designated for the Holy See in Rome. However, the similarity of this clause to the treatment of the dues owed to Rome in Wulfstan's writings raises the possibility that this might be an eleventh-century interpolation rather than a tenth-century decree.

5.1–3 These clauses were likely added by Wulfstan.

3 Edgar

1   *This is the secular decree*: Although it is editorial convention to divide these texts into two separate pieces of legislation, no such division is indicated in the manuscripts, where *2 Edgar* continues on to *3 Edgar* without a break.

7.3   *no matter where he hides*: Cambridge, Corpus Christi College MS 201 adds, "unless the king allows him to be spared" *(buton se cyninge him feorhgeneres unne)*.

8–8.3 Likely an addition by Wulfstan.

8.2   *wey*: A unit of weight for dry goods that varied over time, though a wool wey was typically the equivalent of approximately two hundred pounds.
       half a pound: One hundred twenty shillings.

Bibliography

EDITIONS AND TRANSLATIONS

Attenborough, F. L., ed. and trans. *The Laws of the Earliest English Kings.* Cambridge, 1922.

Bethurum, Dorothy. *The Homilies of Wulfstan.* Oxford, 1957.

Clayton, Mary. "The Old English *Promissio regis.*" *Anglo-Saxon England* 37 (2008): 91–150.

Cross, J. E., and Andrew Hamer, eds. *Wulfstan's Canon Law Collection.* Anglo-Saxon Texts 1. Woodbridge, 1999.

Fehr, Bernard. *Die Hirtenbriefe Ælfrics.* Bibliothek der angelsächsischen Prosa 9. Hamburg, 1914.

Fowler, Roger, ed. *Wulfstan's Canons of Edgar.* Early English Text Society o.s. 266. Oxford, 1972.

Franzen, Christine. *Worcester Manuscripts.* Anglo-Saxon Manuscripts in Microfiche Facsimile 6. Tempe, 1998.

Jost, Karl, ed. *Die "Institutes of Polity, Civil and Ecclesiastical."* Schweizer anglistische Arbeiten 47. Bern, 1959.

Kennedy, A. G. "Cnut's Law Code of 1018." *Anglo-Saxon England* 11 (1983): 57–81.

Liebermann, Felix, ed. *Die Gesetze der Angelsachsen.* 3 vols. Halle, 1903–1916.

Loyn, H. R., ed. *A Wulfstan Manuscript Containing Institutes, Laws and Homilies: British Museum Cotton Nero A.i.* Early English Manuscripts in Facsimile 17. Copenhagen, 1971.

Rabin, Andrew, ed. and trans. *The Political Writings of Archbishop Wulfstan of York.* Manchester, 2015.

Robertson, A. J., ed. and trans. *The Laws of the Kings of England from Edmund to Henry I.* Cambridge, 1925.

Sawyer, P. H., ed. *Textus Roffensis: Rochester Cathedral Library Manuscript A. 3. 5.* Vol 1. Early English Manuscripts in Facsimile 7. Copenhagen, 1957.

Schmid, Reinhold, ed. *Die Gesetze der Angelsachsen.* 2nd ed. Leipzig, 1858.

Tenhaken, Hans P., ed. *Das nordhumbrische Priestergesetz.* Dusseldorf, 1979.

Thorpe, Benjamin, ed. and trans. *Ancient Laws and Institutes of England.* London, 1840.

Whitelock, Dorothy, ed. *English Historical Documents, c. 500–1042.* English Historical Documents, edited by David Charles Douglas. 2nd ed. London, 1979.

Whitelock, Dorothy, Martin Brett, and C. N. L. Brooke, eds. *Councils and Synods with Other Documents Relating to the English Church: 871–1066.* Vol. 1, part 1. Oxford, 1981.

FURTHER READING

Jurasinski, Stefan. *The Old English Penitentials and Anglo-Saxon Law.* Cambridge, 2015.

Ker, Neil. "The Handwriting of Archbishop Wulfstan." In *England Before the Conquest: Studies in Primary Sources Presented to Dorothy Whitelock,* edited by Peter Clemoes and Kathleen Hughes, 315–31. Cambridge, 1971.

Keynes, Simon. "An Abbot, an Archbishop, and the Viking Raids of 1006–7 and 1009–12." *Anglo-Saxon England* 36 (2007): 151–220.

Lawson, M. K. "Archbishop Wulfstan and the Homiletic Element in the Laws of Æthelred II and Cnut." *The English Historical Review* 107, no. 424 (1992): 565–86.

Loomis, Dorothy Bethurum. "*Regnum* and *Sacerdotium* in the Early Eleventh Century." In *England Before the Conquest: Studies in Primary Sources Presented to Dorothy Whitelock,* edited by Peter Clemoes and Kathleen Hughes, 129–45. Cambridge, 1971.

Marafioti, Nicole. "Secular and Ecclesiastical Justice in Late Anglo-Saxon England." *Speculum* 94, no. 3 (2019): 1–32.

Pons-Sanz, Sara M. *Norse-Derived Vocabulary in Late Old English Texts: Wulfstan's Works, A Case Study.* Odense, 2007.

Rabin, Andrew. "Archbishop Wulfstan's 'Compilation on Status' in the Textus Roffensis." In *Textus Roffensis: Law, Language, and Libraries in Me-*

dieval England, edited by Barbara Bombi and Bruce O'Brien, 175–92. Turnhout, 2015.

——. "The Reception of Kentish Law in the Eleventh Century: Archbishop Wulfstan as Legal Historian." In *Languages of the Law in Early Medieval England: Essays in Memory of Lisi Oliver,* edited by Stefan Jurasinski and Andrew Rabin, Mediaevalia Groningana, 225–39. Louvain, 2019.

Richards, Mary P. "I–II Cnut: Wulfstan's Summa?" In *English Law Before Magna Carta: Felix Liebermann and "Die Gesetze der Angelsachsen,"* edited by Stefan Jurasinski, Lisi Oliver, and Andrew Rabin, 137–56. Leiden, 2010.

Townend, Matthew. *Archbishop Wulfstan of York: The Proceedings of the Second Alcuin Conference.* Turnhout, 2004.

Whitelock, Dorothy. "Archbishop Wulfstan, Homilist and Statesman." *Transactions of the Royal Historical Society,* 4th ser., 24 (1942): 25–46.

Wormald, Patrick. "Æthelred the Lawmaker." In *Ethelred the Unready: Papers from the Millenary Conference,* edited by David Hill, B. A. R. British Series, 47–80. Oxford, 1978.

——. "Archbishop Wulfstan and the Holiness of Society." In *Legal Culture in the Early Medieval West: Law as Text, Image, and Experience,* 225–52. London, 1999.

——. *The Making of English Law: King Alfred to the Twelfth Century.* Malden, 1999.

Index

433